Fundamentals of Early Childhood Education

Second Edition

George S. Morrison

University of North Texas

MERRILL
an imprint of Prentice Hall
Upper Saddle River, New Jersey
Columbus, Ohio

Library of Congress Cataloging-in-Publication Data
Morrison, George S.
    Fundamentals of early childhood education /
George S. Morrison.—2nd ed.
        p.   cm.
    Includes bibliographical references and index.
    ISBN 0-13-012095-2
    1. Early childhood education—United States.
I. Title.
LB1139.25.M67   2000
372.21—dc21   99-32554
                                              CIP

Cover photo: © Image Bank
Editor: Ann Castel Davis
Editorial Assistant: Pat Grogg
Production Editor: Linda Hillis Bayma
Production and Editorial Supervision: Carlisle
    Publishers Services
Photo Coordinator: Sherry Mitchell
Design Coordinator: Diane C. Lorenzo
Cover Designer: Ceri Fitzgerald
Production Manager: Laura Messerly
Director of Marketing: Kevin Flanagan
Marketing Manager: Meghan Shepherd
Marketing Coordinator: Krista Groshong

This book was set in Korinna BT by Carlisle Communications, Ltd. and was printed and bound by R.R.
Donnelley & Sons Company. The cover was printed
by Phoenix Color Corp.

Photo Credits: Children's Hospital, p. 18; Arlene
Collins/Monkmeyer Press Photo Service, p. 56; Cor-
bis-Bettman, p. 70; Scott Cunningham/Merrill,
pp. 141, 167, 203, 223, 257; Custom Medical Stock
Photo Inc., p. 196; Anthony Magnacca/Merrill, pp. 3,
113, 150, 176, 201, 202, 371; Tina Manley, p. 39;
PH/Merrill, p. 27; Photo Edit, p. 210; Tom
Pollak/Monkmeyer Press Photo Service, p. 353; Barbara Schwartz/Merrill, pp. 30, 103, 159, 281, 294,
297, 307, 334; Anne Vega/Merrill, pp. 1, 40, 77, 78,
81, 96, 98, 121, 133, 163, 184, 190, 205, 213, 217,
230, 241, 253, 266, 268, 283, 312, 317, 332, 356,
360; Todd Yarrington/Merrill, pp. 33, 340.

Printed in the United States of America

10 9 8 7 6 5 4 3

ISBN: 0-13-012095-2

Prentice-Hall International (UK) Limited, *London*
Prentice-Hall of Australia Pty. Limited, *Sydney*
Prentice-Hall of Canada, Inc., *Toronto*
Prentice-Hall Hispanoamericana, S. A., *Mexico*
Prentice-Hall of India Private Limited, *New Delhi*
Prentice-Hall of Japan, Inc., *Tokyo*
Prentice-Hall (Singapore) Pte. Ltd., *Singapore*
Editora Prentice-Hall do Brasil, Ltda., *Rio de Janeiro*

For Betty Jane—as always

ABOUT THE AUTHOR

George S. Morrison, Ed.D., is professor of early childhood education and holder of the Velma E. Schmidt Endowed Chair in early childhood education at the University of North Texas. Professor Morrison's accomplishments include a Distinguished Academic Service Award from the Pennsylvania Department of Education, an Outstanding Alumni Award from the University of Pittsburgh School of Education, and Outstanding Service and Teaching Awards from Florida International University.

Dr. Morrison is the author of many books on early childhood education, child development, curriculum, and teacher education, including *Early Childhood Education Today,* 7th edition and *Teaching in America,* 2nd edition.

Dr. Morrison's professional interests include the application of neuroscience and developmental research to early childhood programs. Dr. Morrison has developed **Success For Life,** a research-based program for children from birth to six years of age. The vision of **Success For Life** is to help children achieve a positive outlook on life through success in school and daily life. To achieve this mission, parents, teachers, and communities must be the driving forces in setting the standard for quality care and education. The curriculum is an interdisciplinary approach in applying theory and research to practice for the education and optimum development of children and families.

Currently, 38 Texas school districts, childcare, and early childhood education sites involving 1,100 children are collaborating in the implementation of **Success For Life.** By September, 2000, **Success For Life** will begin to be implemented in various sites across the country.

PREFACE

The new millennium will be a challenging but rewarding time for you and the field of early childhood education. As an early childhood professional you must be prepared to assist young children and their families to have productive lives in the twenty-first century. I believe this second edition of *Fundamentals of Early Childhood Education* will help prepare you and other professionals to rightfully, knowledgeably, confidently, and appropriately assume your roles of educating children, parents, and families. You touch the future through the lives of others.

GOALS AND COVERAGE

Fundamentals of Early Childhood Education, Second Edition, provides a thorough introduction to the field of early childhood education. It is written in a straightforward and engaging style. It analyzes current issues and ideas and applies practical, developmentally appropriate strategies and models to early childhood programs. This second edition has been extensively revised to reflect changes in society and the field of early childhood education. *Fundamentals of Early Childhood Education,* Second Edition, is comprehensive in its overview of early childhood practices.

CONTEMPORARY THEMES

Fundamentals of Early Childhood Education, Second Edition, incorporates many essential contemporary themes and outlines their implications for professional practice. Particularly significant themes include multiculturalism and multiculturally appropriate practice; technology and its application to early childhood programs; equity and diversity issues, including gender and culture; observation and assessment of young children; and developmentally appropriate practice applied across all program areas. Emphasis is also placed on the changing field of early childhood education and the changing role of early childhood professionals.

In addition to the reorganization of the text and an updating of the content, users of the second edition will find a new feature—video segments.

VIDEO VIEWPOINT

Integrated video segments of current issues, titled "Video Viewpoints," help connect theory and practice. Available to adopters of the text, these segments bring to life important topics relating to young children and families and ask readers to respond to reflective questions that promote reflective discussions. To receive a set of these video segments, please contact your local sales representative.

ACKNOWLEDGMENTS

In the course of my teaching, service, and consulting, I meet and talk with many professionals who are deeply committed to doing their best for young children and their families. I am always touched, heartened, and encouraged by the openness, honesty, and unselfish sharing of ideas that characterize these professional colleagues. I take this opportunity to thank them publicly for helping me make *Fundamentals of Early Childhood Education* a useful textbook.

I would also like to thank the following reviewers for their helpful comments: Audrey W. Beard, Albany State University; Ginny Buckner, Cuyahoga Community College; Sima Lesser, Miami Dade Community College; Patricia K. Lowry, Jacksonville State University; Helane S. Rosenberg, Rutgers University; and Elizabeth Walker-Knauer, Cuyahoga Community College.

I am thankful to Ann C. Davis, senior editor, for having the vision to know what faculty and students want in a basic introduction to early childhood education textbook. Ann is astute and savvy. I enjoy working with her. Pat Grogg, editorial assistant, is persistent, cheerful, and supportive. I appreciate all her help.

Ray Harder, Rhea Kulikova, Shawn McClintock, and Matt Woodward are cheerful co-workers and tireless research assistants. Their editing and research were essential to ensure that this book is up-to-date and meets the needs of early childhood professionals. Without their help, I would not have been able to do all of the things that I have to do as a professor and author. Special thanks to my wife, Betty Jane Morrison, who, as always, provides the loving support that makes living worthwhile.

Discover the Companion Website
Accompanying This Book

THE PRENTICE HALL COMPANION WEBSITE:
A VIRTUAL LEARNING ENVIRONMENT

Technology is a constantly growing and changing aspect of our field that is creating a need for content and resources. To address this emerging need, Prentice Hall has developed an online learning environment for students and professors alike—Companion Websites—to support our textbooks.

In creating a Companion Website, our goal is to build on and enhance what the textbook already offers. For this reason, the content for each user-friendly website is organized by chapter and provides the professor and student with a variety of meaningful resources. Common features of a Companion Website include:

FOR THE PROFESSOR—

Every Companion Website integrates **Syllabus Manager**™, an online syllabus creation and management utility.

- **Syllabus Manager**™ provides you, the instructor, with an easy, step-by-step process to create and revise syllabi, with direct links into Companion Website and other online content without having to learn HTML.

- Students may logon to your syllabus during any study session. All they need to know is the web address for the Companion Website and the password you've assigned to your syllabus.

- After you have created a syllabus using **Syllabus Manager**™, students may enter the syllabus for their course section from any point in the Companion Website.
- Class dates are highlighted in white and assignment due dates appear in blue. Clicking on a date, the student is shown the list of activities for the assignment. The activities for each assignment are linked directly to actual content, saving time for students.
- Adding assignments consists of clicking on the desired due date, then filling in the details of the assignment—name of the assignment, instructions, and whether or not it is a one-time or repeating assignment.
- In addition, links to other activities can be created easily. If the activity is online, a URL can be entered in the space provided, and it will be linked automatically in the final syllabus.
- Your completed syllabus is hosted on our servers, allowing convenient updates from any computer on the Internet. Changes you make to your syllabus are immediately available to your students at their next logon.

FOR THE STUDENT—

- **Chapter Objectives**—outline key concepts from the text
- **Interactive Self-quizzes**—complete with hints and automatic grading that provide immediate feedback for students

  After students submit their answers for the interactive self-quizzes, the Companion Website **Results Reporter** computes a percentage grade, provides a graphic representation of how many questions were answered correctly and incorrectly, and gives a question by question analysis of the quiz. Students are given the option to send their quiz to up to four email addresses (professor, teaching assistant, study partner, etc.).

- **Message Board**—serves as a virtual bulletin board to post—or respond to—questions or comments to/from a national audience.
- **Net Searches**—offer links by key terms from each chapter to related Internet content
- **Web Destinations**—links to www sites that relate to chapter content

To take advantage of these and other resources, please visit the Companion Website for *Fundamentals of Early Childhood Education,* Second Edition, at www.prenhall.com/morrison.

CONTENTS

Chapter 11

Preparation for Lifelong
Success   294

Chapter 12

Providing Appropriate
Education for All   317

Chapter 13

Cooperation and Collaboration 353

Appendix A

The National Association for
the Education of Young Children
Code of Ethical Conduct   379

Appendix B

CDA Competency Goals and
Functional Areas   387

CHAPTER

1

You and Early Childhood Education: What Does It Mean to Be a Professional?

FOCUS QUESTIONS

1. Who is an early childhood professional?
2. What is the knowledge base of the profession?
3. What qualities of early childhood professionals are worthy of emulation?
4. What is the terminology used by early childhood professionals?
5. What is the relationship among early childhood professionals' attitudes, their character, and children's development?
6. What important themes and concepts contribute to becoming a good professional?
7. What are the essential attitudes, skills, and behaviors that will enable you to have a joyful, productive, and professional career?
8. How can developing a philosophy of early childhood education help you become a professional?

> Children are not rugged individualists. They depend on the adults they know and on thousands more who make decisions every day that affect their well-being. All of us, whether we acknowledge it or not, are responsible for deciding whether our children are raised in a nation that doesn't just espouse family values but values families and children.
>
> Hillary Rodham Clinton

For all early childhood professionals, the beginning of the twenty-first century promises to be an exciting and challenging time. The public continues to be enthusiastic regarding the importance of children's early years in learning and development. Early childhood education's popularity is a strength that we must embrace and utilize to help us serve all children. As one millennium ends and another begins, early childhood professionals must continue to be leaders in providing quality programs. The issues and opportunities of the next decade will be exciting and challenging for all who work with young children and their families.

WHO IS AN EARLY CHILDHOOD PROFESSIONAL?

How would you explain *professional* to someone who asked you, "Who is an early childhood professional?" What does professional mean?

Figure 1–1 outlines professional categories as identified by the National Association for the Education of Young Children (NAEYC). These categories reflect the association's efforts to continually enhance the concept of professionalism in early childhood education. As you identify the differences in these professional areas, reflect about their meaning for you and how you can start now to develop the necessary knowledge and skills for success at whatever level you select.

Teaching is and should be a joyful experience for those who dedicate themselves to it. The profession demands and young children deserve the best from all who work with young children and their families. In what ways is teaching a joyful experience?

The Knowledge Base of the Profession

What knowledge do early childhood professionals need to possess? The National Association for the Education of Young Children identifies specific knowledge and abilities as content of the profession. To work effectively with all young children—infants and toddlers, preschoolers, and primary school-age children (including those with special needs)—early childhood professionals must be able to do the following:

• Demonstrate a basic understanding of the early childhood profession and make a commitment to professionalism.

• Demonstrate a basic understanding of child development and apply this knowledge in practice.

• Observe and assess children's behavior for use in planning and individualizing teaching practices and curriculum.

FIGURE 1–1

Definition of Early Childhood Professional Categories

- **Early Childhood Professional Level VI**

Successful completion of a Ph.D. or Ed.D. in a program conforming to NAEYC guidelines; OR Successful demonstration of the knowledge, performance, and dispositions expected as outcomes of a doctoral degree program conforming to NAEYC guidelines.

- **Early Childhood Professional Level V**

Successful completion of a master's degree in a program that conforms to NAEYC guidelines; OR Successful demonstration of the knowledge, performance, and dispositions expected as outcomes of a master's degree program conforming to NAEYC guidelines.

- **Early Childhood Professional Level IV**

Successful completion of a baccalaureate degree from a program conforming to NAEYC guidelines; OR

State certificate meeting NAEYC/ATE certification guidelines; OR

Successful completion of a baccalaureate degree in another field with more than 30 professional units in early childhood development/education including 300 hours of supervised teaching experience, including 150 hours each for two of the following three age groups: infants and toddlers, 3- to 5- year olds, or the primary grades; OR

Successful demonstration of the knowledge, performance, and dispositions expected as outcomes of a baccalaureate degree program conforming to NAEYC guidelines.

- **Early Childhood Professional Level III**

Successful completion of an associate degree from a program conforming to NAEYC guidelines; OR Successful completion of an associate degree in a related field, plus 30 units of professional studies in early childhood development/education including 300 hours of supervised teaching experience in an early childhood program; OR

Successful demonstration of the knowledge, performance, and dispositions expected as outcomes of an associate degree program conforming to NAEYC guidelines.

- **Early Childhood Professional Level II**

Successful completion of a one-year early childhood certificate program.

Successful completion of the CDA Professional Preparation Program OR

Completion of a systematic, comprehensive training program that prepares an individual to successfully acquire the CDA Credential through direct assessment.

- **Early Childhood Professional Level I**

Individuals who are employed in an early childhood professional role working under supervision or with support (e.g., linkages with provider association or network or enrollment in supervised practicum) and participating in training designed to lead to the assessment of individual competencies or acquisition of a degree.

Source: "NAEYC Position Statement: A Conceptual Framework for Early Childhood Professional Development, 1998." *Young Children,* 49(3), p. 74. Copyright © 1998 by the National Association for the Education of Young Children. Reprinted by permission.

- Establish and maintain an environment that ensures children's safety and their healthy development.
- Plan and implement a developmentally appropriate program that advances all areas of children's learning and development, including social, emotional, intellectual, and physical competence.
- Establish supportive relationships with children and implement developmentally appropriate techniques of guidance and group management.
- Establish positive and productive relationships with families.
- Support the uniqueness of each child, recognizing that children are best understood in the context of family, culture, and society.[1]

These items represent the core knowledge of the profession. Figure 1–2 shows how acquiring this core knowledge integrates with the ongoing process of becoming a professional. In this sense, the professional, at the moment of entry into the field, *at whatever level,* undertakes the responsibility to engage in increasing levels of preparation and knowledge acquisition.

While the above items represent core knowledge of the profession as outlined by NAEYC, the other early childhood professional organizations also specify what they believe is essential core knowledge. For example, the New York State Early Childhood Career Development Initiative developed the following core body of knowledge:

Knowledge of patterns of child growth and development shape decisions about the provision of experiences in group settings and the nature of adult/child interactions that support growth and development. A safe and healthy learning environment is dependent upon an understanding of each child's stage of development, and the ability to protect, support, and guide children as they mature and learn physically, socially, emotionally, and cognitively.[2]

THE PROCESS OF BECOMING A PROFESSIONAL

The professional undertakes the responsibility to engage in increasing levels of preparation and knowledge acquisition of the core knowledge of the profession.

Acquiring essential knowledge throughout one's professional life is part of the process of continuous professional development. The professional is never a "finished" product; one is always studying, learning, changing, and becoming more professional. The teachers of the year that you will read about in this chapter (see Box 1–1) would not think of themselves as "completed" professionals. All would say that they have more to learn and more to do. Figure 1–3 shows this process of continuous professional development.

Becoming a professional means you will participate in training and education beyond the minimum needed for your present position. You will also

FIGURE 1–2
Core Knowledge in
the Early Childhood
Profession

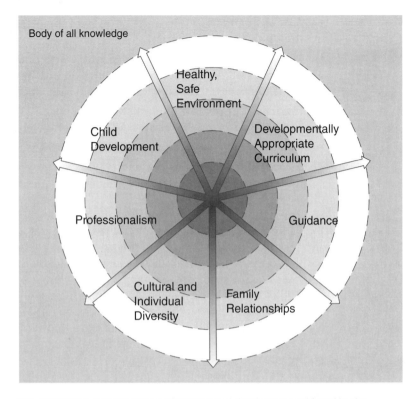

The dotted lines indicate stages of professional development achieved by the acquisition of recognized credentials that are based on professional standards of preparation. Moving from the innermost circle—the precredential level—individuals demonstrate knowledge required for the Child Development Associate (CDA) Credential and associate, baccalaureate, and advanced degrees. The arrows denote the continuum that extends from knowledge necessary for implementing effective practice to knowledge necessary for the generation and translation of knowledge; core knowledge is embedded within the larger body of all knowledge.

Source: From "Of Ladders and Lattices, Cores and Cones: Conceptualizing an Early Childhood Professional System," by Sue Bredekamp and Barbara Willer, 1992, *Young Children* 47(3), p. 49. Copyright © 1992 by the National Association for the Education of Young Children. Reprinted by permission.

want to consider your career objectives and the qualifications you might need for positions of increasing responsibility. NAEYC has established the National Institute for Early Childhood Professional Development, which promotes a professional development system that helps make the early childhood profession even more professional. Another organization, the National Academy of Early Childhood Programs, identifies staff qualifications and training appropriate for positions in early childhood programs.

FIGURE 1–3
A Continuum of Becoming a Professional

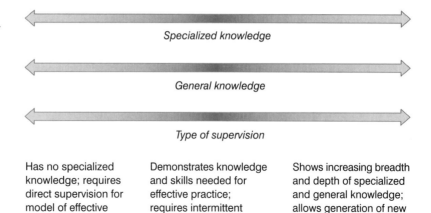

Specialized knowledge

General knowledge

Type of supervision

Has no specialized knowledge; requires direct supervision for model of effective practice.	Demonstrates knowledge and skills needed for effective practice; requires intermittent supervision and may supervise others.	Shows increasing breadth and depth of specialized and general knowledge; allows generation of new knowledge and skills; supervises others.

Source: From "A 'New' Paradigm of Early Childhood Professional Development," by Barbara Willer and Sue Bredekamp, 1993, *Young Children* 48(4), p. 65. Copyright © 1993 by the National Association for the Education of Young Children. Reprinted by permission.

Qualities of Early Childhood Professionals

Currently, there is a great deal of discussion about quality in early childhood programs, which is directly related to the quality of the professionals in these programs. As you will discover throughout this book, merely discussing quality is not sufficient—professionals must involve themselves in activities that will promote quality in their lives and the lives of the children they teach and care for.

Almost everyone who has contemplated teaching has probably asked, "Am I a person suited for a career in early childhood education?" This question is difficult to honestly answer. In general, early childhood professionals should demonstrate the following qualities: love and respect for children, knowledge of children and their families, caring, compassion, courtesy, dedication, empathy, enthusiasm, friendliness, helpfulness, honesty, intelligence, kindness, motivation, patience, sensitivity, trust, understanding, and warmth. Home and early school experiences are critical for developing these qualities. So if we want these qualities in our future professionals, we need to promote them now, in our teaching of young children. Toward that end, professionals might well concentrate on nurturing in themselves what is probably the most important of these characteristics: caring.

Figure 1–4 indicates the training involved in your ongoing development as a professional. You will want to continually strive to engage in professional development activities and organized courses and college programs that will lead you to a higher level of skills and qualifications.

FIGURE 1–4
Staff Qualifications and Development

Staff role	Relevant Master's	Relevant Bachelor's	Relevant Associate's	CDA Credential	Some training	No training
DIRECTOR	←	Degree and 3 years experience				
MASTER TEACHER	←	Degree and 3 years experience				
TEACHER	←		**ANT**			
ASSISTANT TEACHER		←				
TEACHING ASSIST			←			

This figure does not include specialty roles such as educational coordinator, social services director, or other providers of special services. Individuals fulfilling these roles should possess the knowledge and qualifications required to fulfill their responsibilities effectively.

Source: National Academy of Early Childhood Programs, *Accreditation Criteria and Procedures of the National Academy of Early Childhood Programs,* rev. ed. (Washington, D.C.: National Association for the Education of Young Children, 1991), p. 31. Reprinted by permission.

As a professional, you will work in classrooms, programs, and other settings in which things do not always go smoothly, in which children do not always learn ably and well, in which children are not always clean and free from illness and hunger, in which children's and parents' backgrounds and ways of life are different from yours. If you truly care, being an early childhood professional is not easy. Caring means you will lose sleep trying to find a way to help a child learn to read, that you will spend your own money to buy supplies, that you will spend long hours planning and gathering materials. Caring also means you will not leave your intelligence, enthusiasm, or talents at home but will bring them into the center, classroom, administration office, boards of directors' meeting, or wherever you can make a difference in the lives of children and their families. As Joe Farley, a 1997 Texas Teacher of the Year, says, "I am a teacher who cares. I am the product of teachers who cared."

WHAT IS THE TERMINOLOGY OF EARLY CHILDHOOD EDUCATION?

Knowing the appropriate terminology is a necessity when discussing early childhood education. As an early childhood professional, you will want to have a command of the terminology used by NAEYC and by early childhood professionals (see Table 1–1).

The term *professional* refers to all who work with, care for, and teach children. This designation is used for several reasons. First, it avoids the obvious confusion between the use of such terms as *caregiver* and *teacher.* Distinguishing between someone who promotes care for and someone who teaches children is no longer easy or desirable. For example, the caregiving and educating roles are now blended so that caring for and educating infants go hand in hand. However, the term *teacher* is and will continue to be used to designate professionals who educate and care for children. Second, the early childhood profession is trying to upgrade the image and role of all those who work with young children. Referring to everyone as a professional helps achieve this goal.

Early childhood refers to the child from birth through age eight, which is a standard and accepted definition used by the NAEYC.[3] The term frequently refers to children who have not yet reached school age, and the public often uses it to refer to children in any type of preschool. However, at the same time, professionals recognize that prenatal development is also important. The prenatal environment plays a tremendous role in development. Consequently, professionals also have a responsibility to encourage and support good maternal health.

Early childhood programs provide "services for children from birth through age eight in part-day and full-day group programs in centers, homes, and institutions; kindergartens and primary schools; and recreational programs."[4]

Early childhood education consists of the services provided in early childhood settings. The terms *early childhood* and *early childhood education* are often used synonymously.

Other terms frequently used when discussing the education of young children are *nursery school* and *preschool. Nursery school* is a program for the education of two-, three-, and four-year-old children. Many nursery schools are half-day programs, usually designed for children of mothers who do not work outside the home, although many children who have two working parents do attend. The purpose of the nursery school is to provide a child-centered program in an informal play setting.

TABLE 1–1
Types of Early Childhood Programs

Program	Purpose	Age
Early childhood program	Multipurpose	Birth to grade 3
Child care	Play/socialization; baby-sitting; physical care; provides parents opportunities to work; cognitive development; full-quality care	Birth to 6 years
High school child care programs	Provide child care for children of high school students, especially unwed parents; serve as an incentive for student/parents to finish high school and as a training program in child care and parenting skills	6 weeks to 5 years
Drop-off child care centers	Provide care for short periods of time while parents shop, exercise, or have appointments	Infancy through the primary grades
After-school care	Provides care for children after school hours	Children of school age; generally K to 6
Family day care	Provides care for a group of children in a home setting; generally custodial in nature	Variable
Corporate employer child care	Different settings for meeting child care	Variable; usually as early as 6 weeks to the beginning of school
Proprietary care	Provides care and/or education to children; designed to make a profit	6 weeks to entrance into first grade
Nursery school (public or private)	Play/socialization; cognitive development	2 to 4 years
Preschool (public or private)	Play/socialization; cognitive development	2 1/2 to 5 years
Parent cooperative preschool	Play/socialization; preparation for kindergarten and first grade; baby-sitting; cognitive development	2 to 5 years
Baby-sitting cooperatives (co-op)	Provide parents with reliable baby-sitting; parents sit for others' children in return for reciprocal services	All ages
Prekindergarten	Play/socialization; cognitive development; preparation for kindergarten	3 1/2 to 5 years
Junior kindergarten	Prekindergarten program	Primarily 4-year-olds
Senior kindergarten	Basically the same as regular kindergarten	Same as kindergarten

Program	Purpose	Age
Kindergarten	Preparation for first grade; developmentally appropriate activities for 4½- to 6-year-olds; increasingly viewed as the grade before first grade and as a regular part of the public school program	4 to 6 years
Pre-first grade	Preparation for first grade; often for students who "failed" or did not do well in kindergarten	5 to 6 years
Interim first grade	Provides children with an additional year of kindergarten and readiness activities prior to and as preparation for first grade	5 to 6 years
Transitional or transition classes	Classes specifically designed to provide for children of the same developmental age	Variable
Developmental kindergarten	Same as regular kindergarten; often enrolls children who have completed one or more years in an early childhood special education program	5 to 6 years
Transitional kindergarten	Extended learning of kindergarten; preparation for first grade	Variable
Preprimary	Preparation for first grade	5 to 6 years
Toy lending libraries	Provide parents and children with games, toys, and other materials that can be used for learning purposes; housed in libraries, vans, or early childhood centers	Birth through primary years
Lekotek	Resource center for families who have children with special needs; sometimes referred to as a *toy* or *play* library (*lekotek* is a Scandinavian word that means "play library")	Birth through primary years
Infant stimulation program (also called parent/infant stimulation and Mommy and Me programs)	Programs for enhancing sensory and cognitive development of infants and young toddlers through exercise and play; activities include general sensory stimulation for children and educational information and advice for parents	3 months to 2 years
Multiage grades or groups	Groups or classes of children of various ages; generally spanning 2 to 3 years per group	Variable

TABLE 1–1, *continued*

Program	Purpose	Age
Dual-age classroom	An organizational plan in which children from two grade levels are grouped together	Variable
Learning families	Another name for multiage grouping. However, the emphasis is on practices that create a family atmosphere and encourage living and learning as a family. The term was commonly used in open education programs. Its revival signifies the reemergence of progressive and child-centered approaches.	Variable
Junior first grade	Preparation for first grade	5 to 6 years
Split class	Teaches basic academic and social skills of grades involved	Variable, but usually primary
Head Start	Play/socialization; academic learning; comprehensive social and health services; prepares children for kindergarten and first grade	2 to 6 years
Early Head Start	Promotes healthy family functioning and self-sufficiency in low-income families; provides a smooth transition to Head Start	0 to 3 years
Even Start	Literacy program for low-income children and adults	Children ages 0–7 and their parents and family members
Follow Through	Extended Head Start services to grades 1, 2, and 3	6 to 8 years
Private schools	Provide care and/or education	Usually preschool through high school
Department of Children, Youth, and Families	A multipurpose agency of many state and county governments; usually provides such services as administration of state and federal monies, child care licensing, and protective services	All
Health and Human Services	Same as Department of Children, Youth, and Families	All
Health and Social Services	Same as Department of Children, Youth, and Families	All
Home Start	Provides Head Start service in the home setting	Birth to 6 or 7 years

Program	Purpose	Age
Laboratory school	Provides demonstration programs for preservice teachers; conducts research	Variable; birth through senior high
Child and Family Resource Program	Delivers Head Start services to families	Birth to 8 years
Montessori school (preschool and grade school)	Provides programs that use the philosophy, procedures, and materials developed by Maria Montessori (see Chapter 3)	1 to 8 years
Open education	Child-centered learning in an environment characterized by freedom and learning through activities based on children's interests	2 to 8 years
British primary school	Implements the practices and procedures of open education	2 to 8 years
Magnet school	Specializes in subjects and curriculum designed to attract students; usually has a theme (e.g., performing arts); designed to give parents choices and to integrate schools	5 to 18 years

Preschool generally means any educational program for children before their entrance into kindergarten. Preschool programs for three- and four-year-old children are rapidly becoming a part of the public school system, particularly those designed to serve low-income children and their families. For example, the public schools of Dade County, Florida, had an enrollment of nearly 9,200 students in pre-K programs in the 1997–98 school year.

Kindergarten is a program for five- and six-year-old children, and is now almost universal for five-year-old children (see Chapter 10). Kindergarten is now considered part of the elementary grades, so it can no longer be thought of as "preschool."

Prekindergarten (pre-K) refers to a wide range of programs providing care and education for three-, four-, and five-year-old children before they enter kindergarten. With the federal government and many states pushing for early education programs, prekindergarten programs will become more prevalent and popular.

Transitional kindergarten designates a program for children who are not ready for kindergarten and who can benefit from another year of the program. The term *transitional* also refers to grade school programs that provide additional opportunities for children to master skills associated with a particular grade. Transitional programs do not usually extend beyond the second and third grades.

Junior first grade or *pre-first grade* is a transitional program between kindergarten and first grade designed to help five-year-olds get ready to enter first grade. Not all children are equally "ready" to benefit from typical first grade. Because of the wide range of mental ages and experiential backgrounds, children frequently benefit from such special programs. However, the goal of many early childhood professionals is to have all children learning at levels appropriate for them.

A *parent cooperative* preschool is organized and operated by parents for their children. Programs of this type are generally operated democratically. Parents hire the staff, and some of the parents may be hired to direct or staff the program. Being part of a cooperative means parents have some responsibility for assisting in the program.

Child care encompasses many programs and services for preschool children. *Day care* is a term used for child care, but most people engaged in the care of young children recognize this as outmoded. *Child care* is more accurate and descriptive because it focuses on children themselves. The primary purpose of child care programs is to care for young children who are not in school and school-age children before and after school hours. Child care programs may have a total-quality orientation or an educational orientation, and some may offer primarily baby-sitting or custodial care. Quality child care programs are increasingly characterized by their comprehensive services that address children's total needs—physical, social, emotional, creative, and intellectual. Today, parents, the public, and the profession understand that *child care* means providing care and education for all children.

Family day care programs provide child care services in the homes of the caregivers. This alternative to center-based programs usually accommodates a maximum of four or five children in a *family day care home*. While many home care programs were custodial in nature, a growing trend is for these programs to provide a full range of services.

Church-related or *church-sponsored* preschool and elementary programs are quite common and are becoming more popular. These programs usually have a cognitive, basic-skills emphasis within a context of religious doctrine and discipline. The reason for the popularity of these church-sponsored programs, which often charge tuition, is their emphasis on basic skills and their no-nonsense approach to learning and teaching.

One popular service provided by some churches is designed to provide parents—usually mothers—with a few hours a week away from their children. These programs are referred to as *Parent's Day Out* or *Mother's Day Out,* and are a support service to parents through which churches provide quality child care and preschool programs in an environment of play and socialization. Churches also see programs as a means of inviting families into the total church program.

Head Start is a federally sponsored program for children from low-income families. Established by the Economic Opportunity Act in 1964, Head Start is intended to help children and their families overcome the effects of poverty.

Follow Through extends the Head Start program to children in grades 1 through 3 and works with school personnel rather than apart from the schools.

Early Head Start is a program for low-income families with infants and toddlers and pregnant women, and was created in 1994. Early Head Start programs seek to enhance very young children's development and promote healthy family functioning and self-sufficiency. Early Head Start seeks also to provide children from birth to three years with a seamless transition to regular Head Start programs.

The *Even Start Literacy Program* is a federally funded program designed to improve the educational opportunities of low-income children and adults. Even Start serves children ages from birth to seven years, parents, and other family members. Even Start supports the philosophy that the educational attainment of children and their parents is interrelated, and that improving the literacy skills of parents results in a positive effect on the educational experiences of their children.

Public and private agencies, including colleges, universities, hospitals, and corporations, operate many kinds of *demonstration programs*. Some have *laboratory schools* used primarily for research in teaching methods, demonstration of exemplary programs and activities, and teacher training. Many of these schools also develop materials and programs for children with disabilities.

A *toy library* makes toys and other learning materials available to children, parents, child care providers, and teachers. Toy libraries may be housed in libraries, shopping malls, churches, preschools, and mobile vans. Many toy libraries are supported by user fees and parent and community volunteers.

In addition to knowing names of programs, you will need to be familiar with titles for professionals who care for and educate young children. Table 1–2 describes the responsibilities and duties of such professionals.

WHAT CAN YOU DO TO PREPARE FOR A PROFESSIONAL CAREER?

A career as an early childhood professional can be greatly rewarding. Here are some things you can do to make your career happy and productive for yourself, children, and families.

- *Start now to develop a philosophy of education and teaching.* Base your philosophy on what you believe about children and the learning process, how you think children should be taught, and what your present values are. This process will be discussed in greater detail below.

- *Go where the opportunities are.* Sometimes people lock themselves into a particular geographic area or age range of children. Some locations may have an oversupply of professionals, while other areas, especially urban, have a chronic shortage of professionals. Cities usually offer challenging and rewarding opportunities. A job will always be available if you are willing to go where the jobs are.

TABLE 1–2
Titles for Professionals Who Care For and Educate Young Children

Title	Description
Early childhood professional	This is the preferred title for anyone who works with young children in any capacity. This designation reflects the growing belief of the early childhood profession that people who work with children at any level are professionals and as such are worthy of the respect, remuneration, and responsibilities that go with being a professional.
Early childhood educator	Works with young children and has committed to self-development by participating in specialized training and programs to extend professional knowledge and competence
Early childhood teacher	Responsible for planning and conducting a developmentally and educationally appropriate program for a group or classroom of children; supervises an assistant teacher or aide; usually has a bachelor's degree in early childhood, elementary education, or child development
Early childhood assistant teacher	Assists the teacher in conducting a developmentally and educationally appropriate program for a group or classroom; frequently acts as a coteacher but may lack education or training to be classified as a teacher (many people who have teacher qualifications serve as an assistant teacher because they enjoy the program or because the position of teacher is not available); usually has a high school diploma or associate degree and is involved in professional development
Early childhood associate teacher	Plans and implements activities with children; has an associate degree and/or the CDA* credential; may also be responsible for care and education of a group of children
Aide	Assists the teacher and teacher assistant when requested; usually considered an entry-level position
Director	Develops and implements a center or school program; supervises all staff; may teach a group of children
Home visitor	Conducts a home-based child development/education program; works with children, families, and staff members
Child development associate	Has completed a CDA assessment and received the CDA credential
Caregiver	Provides care, education, and protection for the very young in or outside the home; includes parents, relatives, child care workers, and early childhood teachers
Parent	Provides the child with basic care, direction, support, protection, and guidance
Volunteer	Contributes time, services, and talents to support staff. Usually are parents, retired persons, grandparents, and university/college/high school students

*CDA National Credentialing Program, *Child Development Associate Assessment System and Competency Standard* (Washington, DC: CDA National Credentialing Program, 1985), p. 551.

- *Seek every opportunity for experiences with all kinds of children in all kinds of settings.* Individuals often limit themselves to experiences in one setting (e.g., the public schools) and ignore church schools, child care programs, private and nonprofit agencies (e.g., March of Dimes, Easter Seal Society, etc.), baby-sitting, and children's clothing stores as places to broaden and expand their knowledge of children. These experiences can often be work related and doubly rewarding. Also be willing to volunteer your services, because volunteer positions have a way of leading to jobs. Many career possibilities and opportunities can become available this way.

Before committing yourself to training for one teacher specialty, volunteer in at least three different areas of education to find out exactly what age and field of education most interests you. Do other volunteer work with children in activities such as recreation, social events, or scouting. It is important for you to teach the age group of children for whom you are best suited. I heard a preschool teacher exclaim, "Why can't these preschoolers do what kindergartners are able to do?" This teacher would probably be better off teaching kindergarten children, and the children would be better off as well.

- *Honestly analyze your attitudes and feelings toward children.* Do you really want to work with young children, or would you be happier in another field? If you decide that working with children is not for you because of how you feel about them, then by all means do not teach.

- *Honestly believe that all children are capable of learning.* Some parents say that those who work with young children act as though their children cannot learn because of their culture or socioeconomic background. All children have the right to be taught by a professional who believes all children are capable of learning to their fullest capacity. When I asked a preschool director how I, as a university professor, could help her most, she replied, "Send me teachers who will help all children learn."

- *Explore the possibilities for educational service in fields other than the public school.* Do not limit your career choices and alternatives because of your limited conception of the teacher's role. Other opportunities for service are available in religious organizations; federal, state, and local agencies; private educational enterprises; hospitals; libraries; and social work. Do not make up your mind too quickly about teaching a certain grade level or age range. Many professionals find out, much to their surprise, that the grade or age level they *thought* was best for them was not.

- *Seize every educational opportunity to enhance your training program and career.* Through careful planning you can strengthen weaknesses and explore new alternatives. For example, if your program of studies requires a certain number of social science credits, use them to explore areas such as sociology and anthropology, which have fascinating relationships to education. Electives that teachers sometimes wish they had taken in college are computers, behavior modification/management, special education, creative writing, and art and music. Of course, a professional can never have a strong enough background in child development.

Volunteer activities provide an excellent opportunity to expand your vision of working with young children and to learn new skills. You should not hesitate to seek out appropriate volunteer activities as a way to enhance your personal and professional growth.

• *Examine your willingness to dedicate yourself to teaching.* Acquaint yourself thoroughly with what teaching involves. Visit many different schools and programs. Is the school atmosphere one in which you want to spend the rest of your life? Talk with several teachers to learn what is involved in teaching. Ask yourself, "Am I willing to work hard? Am I willing to give more time to teaching than a teaching contract may specify? Are teachers the kind of people with whom I want to work? Do I have the physical energy for teaching? Do I have the enthusiasm necessary for good teaching?"

As you enter the teaching profession, you will find other ways to make your career more productive and rewarding. Some of these are:

• *Adjust to the ever-emerging new careers of teaching and society.* All careers are molded by the needs of society and available resources. Many teachers and schools waste potential and miss opportunities because of their unwillingness to adjust to changing circumstances and conditions. A good professional is a flexible professional.

• *Improve your skills and increase your knowledge.* Many professionals choose to do this by returning to school, which is usually encouraged by state certification or licensing requirements. Some teachers fulfill education requirements through a master's degree. A trend in teacher certification is to allow accumulation of a specified number of "units," gained through college credits, in-service programs, attendance at professional meetings and conferences, and other professional involvements. These units can count toward certification and take the place of college courses.

- *Lifelong learning.* Learning is a lifelong process. All early childhood professionals are expected to engage in a process of continuous learning, growth, and development across their life span.

- *Be willing to try new things.* Don't get in a rut. There are new ideas and methods available for you to use and consider.

- *Be enthusiastic for teaching and in your teaching.* Time and again, enthusiasm is the one attribute that seems to separate the good teacher from the mediocre. Being enthusiastic will help a great deal on your professional journey.

- *Maintain an open-door policy in teaching.* Welcome into your classroom parents, colleagues, college students, and all who want to know what schools and centers are doing. Today collaboration, cooperation, and partnerships with parents and the community are hallmarks of professionalism.

Developing a Philosophy of Education

A philosophy of education is a set of beliefs about how one should teach and how children develop and learn. Your philosophy of education is based on your philosophy of life. What you believe about yourself, about others, and about life infuses and determines your philosophy of education. Knowing what others believe is important and useful and helps you clarify what you believe; but when it is all said and done, *you* have to decide what you believe. What you believe moment by moment, day by day, influences how you will teach young children.

A personal philosophy is based on core values and beliefs. Core values of life relate to your beliefs about the nature of life, the purpose of life, your role and calling in life, and your relationship and responsibilities to others. Core beliefs and values about education and teaching include what you believe about the nature of children, the purpose of education, the way people learn, the role of teachers, and what is worth knowing.

Your philosophy of education will guide and direct your daily teaching. Your beliefs about how children learn determine whether you individualize instruction or try to teach the same thing in the same way to everyone. Your philosophy determines whether you help children do things for themselves or whether you do things for them.

The following pointers describe ways to go about developing your philosophy.

Read widely in the professional literature to get ideas and points of view. A word of caution: When people refer to philosophies of education, they often think just of historic influences. This is only part of the information available for writing a philosophy. Make sure you explore contemporary ideas as well, for these will also have a strong influence on you as a professional.

Some professional journals and popular magazines are *Young Children, Childhood Education, Developmental Psychology, Child Development, Early Childhood Research Quarterly, Educational Leadership, Kappan, American Educational Research Journal, Parent, Child,* and *Scholastic.*

Begin now to reflect on your developing philosophy of education. The following headings will help you get started:

- I believe the purposes of education are . . .
- I believe children learn best when . . .
- The curriculum of any classroom should include certain "basics" that contribute to children's social, emotional, intellectual, and physical development. These basics are . . .
- Children learn best in an environment that promotes learning. Features of a good learning environment are . . .
- All children have certain needs that must be met if they are to grow and learn at their best. Some of these basic needs are . . .
- I would meet these needs by . . .
- All teachers should have certain qualities. Qualities I think important for teaching are . . .

Once you have written your philosophy of education, have others read it. This process helps clarify your ideas and redefine your thoughts, because your philosophy should be understandable to others (although they do not necessarily have to agree with you).

Talk with successful teachers and other educators. The accounts of the Teachers of the Year (Box 1–1) and Voices from the Field throughout the book are evidence that a philosophy can help you become an above-average teacher. Talking with others exposes you to their points of view and stimulates your thinking.

Finally, evaluate your philosophy against this checklist:

- Does my philosophy accurately reflect my beliefs about teaching? Have I been honest with myself?
- Is it understandable to me and others?
- Does it provide practical guidance for teaching?
- Are my ideas consistent with each other?
- Does what I believe make good sense?
- Have I been comprehensive, stating my beliefs about (1) how children learn, (2) what children should be taught, (3) how children should be taught, (4) under what conditions children learn best, and (5) what the qualities of a good teacher are?

BOX 1–1 TEACHERS OF THE YEAR

Edward J. Silver, Jr., 1996 Maryland Teacher of the Year—Third Grade

The overriding belief that governs my teaching is that all children can learn and naturally want to learn. Children desire to explore and make sense of the world around them. My responsibility as a teacher is to develop a learning environment that fosters this inclination. This involves five components.

1. *Learning must be meaningful.* School must be an engaging, motivating place that builds on children's natural curiosity. In my classroom I try to embed learning in meaningful, motivational activities. Instead of simply teaching a unit on the moon, the students enter an astronaut training program to prepare for a simulated mission. Students learn about erosion by studying how to improve a school playground with the goal of advising the principal about their findings. Students plan class parties, which requires them to make a budget, to create invitations, and to write out instructions for activities. Learning in a meaningful context nourishes students' natural curiosity.

2. *Learning must be "hands on."* Children learn best when manipulating their world. Activities that I employ are based on children exploring the world using concrete items. In science, I try to use experiments daily, while in math we use manipulatives to solidify students' understanding of concepts.

3. *Learning must build connections.* Children learn best when they see how all learning is interrelated. In my teaching, I build units around unified themes. If students understand that what they are learning is not isolated information but part of the fabric that they encounter in all subject areas, it allows them to learn with greater depth and thus acquire better understanding. This also involves writing and communication. When children are given time to write about their learning, they reflect on it and connect new understanding to existing knowledge.

4. *Learning must be collaborative.* Working cooperatively is both a means and an end. Children who discuss with others what they are learning are more actively involved in that learning and are more organized in their thinking. Children also need to learn how to work as a team to accomplish their goals. In my classroom, children work in groups in all subject areas. The learning experience involves discussion, group projects, and peer tutoring.

5. *Learning must be safe.* Learning is inherently risky because it involves questioning present understanding. If children are to move away from the commonplace, they need to be in a warm, accepting environment that fosters risk taking. I try to build such a community. My class becomes a family where we do not tolerate "put-downs," and where we emphasize kindness and encouragement.

Let me transport you to a day in my third grade class at Millington Elementary School.

The morning's energy level is high. Almost immediately there is a buzz of excitement as students check their science experiments from the day before. Other children are curled up in the reading corner with copies of a new book about the earth, still others finish their work publishing a class book of poetry. After a period of time, I give a signal and all the students gather on the rug for the day's orientation. As a class we are studying geology. Our theme, entitled "KOGEASI" (Kids On a Geological Exploration And Scientific Investigation), is built around a secret mission to be the first people to travel to the center of the earth. As a class we begin our study day with a theme song, a secret handshake, and a raucous salute (ROCK!). Enthusiastic about the mission, students brief the class on their learning projects. One group is finding information to chart the layers of the earth. Another group is designing the vehicle for the voyage. A third group is researching plate tectonics and designing a model of continental shift. Findings and problems are listed on chart paper taped to the wall. While the students report, my role is that of class facilitator.

Students then engage in a series of teacher-directed and student-initiated learning opportunities. Math is taught in a problem-solving format where skills are applied to solve the effects of ground cover on erosion. Students record measurements, graph and interpret data, and write about their findings. In reading, children read nonfiction books on the earth and learn to distinguish main ideas from supporting details. Social studies finds students in different parts of the room studying topographical maps. Throughout the day, students may write in a reflection journal about what they are learning, and often use technology (calculators and computers) as a tool to maximize their learning.

As the day ends, the class meets again on the rug to summarize the day's learnings and to help plan the next day's goals. My students are enthusiastic about learning and are becoming convinced that learning is an important and meaningful part of life.

John H. Funk, 1996 Utah Teacher of the Year—Kindergarten

As a kindergarten teacher, I have decided that how I begin my students' schooling career may determine the success of the rest of their education. My goals include providing a measure of stability in a perhaps unstable life, a safe, secure, and loving environment for each student, and an opportunity for a great start to the educational process. I make my room and my lesson plans as interesting and exciting as possible.

Kindergarten is the introduction to public education. Kindergarten teachers need to begin by teaching students about their surroundings and about how all of the academic skills they are learning will help them have a complete and happy life and better understand their world. The attitude toward school that kindergarten students develop can remain with them throughout their school career.

Students should be in school every day. Teachers are the catalysts to make school a place where children want to be. We are on a year-round schedule, attending for nine weeks followed by a three-week break. To help students develop a positive attitude about school, I make every effort to have that same attitude. Our classroom motto is, "I Like School." Whenever we are going on break, we don't say, "Hurrah, we get a vacation!" Instead, we always say, "Oh dear! We have to take a break from school. We would

rather keep going every day. This is where we want to be." Not only do the children look forward to returning to school, but so do I! We are excited to go to school each day. I have had a number of students call me at home to ask if we could come back to school. The rewards I have felt as a teacher center around my students' attitudes about wanting to be at school with me. How can you not feel fantastic when you have fifty best friends?

An effective teacher doesn't cease to care about students just because the school day is over. Teachers should be constant positive examples of caring. For me, personally caring and loving each child has yielded amazing results. I am much more conscientious about the contents of my lesson plans and more concerned about each child's success. Working with kindergarten students and studying the latest research has made me concerned about attending to the developmental stages of five-year-olds. As we approach academic skills we must remember their individual stages of development. Teachers shouldn't reflect the attitude, "Today we are learning addition. Put everything else away." Research tells us that young children learn best when *all* subjects are integrated together. We must begin teaching the "whole child."

Education can compete with other forms of excitement and entertainment in the world. Young students naturally become interested about and want to learn something new. My efforts are channeled to helping them achieve that harmony and love of learning, beginning their early school experience in a tactile and visual way. "Let's find everything in the world that is red. How does red feel? Taste? Smell? Sound? Look?"

My answer to critics of education is this: We must begin to teach our young children as *children* instead of as mini-adults. Giving our children hands-on, developmental experiences will help to build a strong foundation for their further education. Too many students are advancing through their school years with shaky and unsure foundations. Children who feel like failures at five will surely be failures at fifteen. My hope is that educators will teach children as *children* so that when they become adults they will *be* adults.

VOICES FROM THE FIELD

I can't remember a time when I didn't want to be a teacher. My parents tell stories of me "instructing" second grade friends for hours from my classroom on the steps of our front porch. While the details of those lazy afternoons elude me, I clearly remember an unwavering desire to become a real teacher.

While I grew up surrounded by teachers including my father and several aunts and uncles, my real passion for teaching was ignited by my students. My first practicum as an undergraduate student was with mentally challenged students. If someone had asked me at the time what I learned most from this experience, I would have replied that it uncovered my talent for analyzing concepts and breaking them down into fun, manageable steps. These special children taught me the pure, unselfish joy that comes from helping someone grasp a difficult concept, but I would realize later that they laid the foundation for a far more valuable lesson.

Another of my toughest, most defining experiences was student teaching in a classroom for emotionally disturbed children. Needless to say, they were not as eager as the "class" I greeted on the front steps of my childhood home. These often angry, distraught children taught me to look beyond the obvious. I still have a note from one of these students. It serves as a powerful, though humorous, reminder that every child can learn, but sometimes you have to meet other more basic needs first:

I am just about To lose my temper with that light
Sined Peter

Notes: I'm glad you did the right thing. You are a good worker! Please try to do your work.
                              Signed
                              Miss McKay

I cant That ligt Desterys me

Notes: Please try. The janitor will fix the light soon.
                              Signed
                              Miss McKay

I told you once and Im not going to tell you again.

I can not doo my work with that ligt.

Peter did complete his work that day, but even more remarkable, he was able to control his volatile temper by venting on paper instead of hitting and screaming. This note is a treasure I continue to save as an important record of my own growth. I was learning to listen with more than my ears. Writing was a new coping skill for Peter, and he needed acknowledgement of his efforts. Peter was teaching me to appreciate and value the learner as much as the learning.

These early learning experiences formed the cornerstone of my philosophy of education, summed up simply as "Children first." How lucky I was to discover this so early in my career—without this insight, the many demands in education might have become overwhelming. Instead, when inundated with a myriad of issues and events, I find direction by refocusing on solutions that most directly meet my students' needs.

If children first is the foundation of my philosophy, then "practice what you preach" is the framework around which I shape my instruction. I believe that all truly great teachers are themselves passionate learners. As a teacher, I am a partner in learning for my students, with my students, and through my students. Teaching is a new learning adventure each and every day.

Students often think of me as the *Ben Franklin* of the classroom, as I frequently quote proverbs or adages which reflect the principles I hold dear. For over ten years, the first words out of my mouth as I address a new class of students is the riddle "How do you eat an elephant?" As I go on to share the answer, "One bite at a time," I explain that even when something we are learning seems as large and overwhelming as an elephant, each one of them will learn it by taking it one step at a time. This lesson is intended to help them understand that though we won't all learn everything easily or at the same pace, we can all learn if we keep at it. I am a "can do" teacher and I know that students who learn the value of perseverance and determination face life with more confidence and self-assurance that they will find the answers they seek.

"If you give a man a fish, he eats for a meal. If you teach a man to fish, he eats for a lifetime." My role as a teacher is to help students become independent learners who can continue their quest for knowledge even without me. Every opportunity is used to point out when students exemplify what "good mathematicians," "good scientists," "good readers," or "good citizens" do to solve problems. For example, when a student reread a page to determine the meaning of an unknown word, I praised him and pointed out that he was doing what all good readers do: use picture clues, sound clues, and context clues to figure out words they don't understand. When another child discovered water on the floor by the drinking fountain and took the initiative to wipe it up before someone slipped, I complimented her on doing what good citizens do: look out for the welfare of others, as well as their own. It is important that children recognize their ability to learn and think for themselves. This builds self-reliance and provides a foundation for applying their knowledge in new situations. Being a risk-taker and a problem solver myself, I use a teaching approach that fosters a safe environment for students to take risks and solve problems, as well.

I hold high expectations for myself and for my students. It is never enough to do the minimum. Students are always encouraged to "Go the extra mile," to find and ask their own questions, then seek the answers using available resources. Activities have either a stated challenge or an open-ended challenge which invites students to continue learning beyond my lesson. My students don't just stay busy, they stay mentally engaged in learning. They actively seek knowledge and understanding.

This strong work ethic is reinforced by a story I tell about my childhood. When I was a little girl visiting my grandmother, she would let me have coffee. Actually it was more like milk with a teaspoon of coffee, but I felt quite grown up all the same. Every morning upon rising, my grandmother would say, "First we work, then we play." We would get dressed, make the beds, and pick up before enjoying biscuits and coffee together. Today Grandma's Rule prevails in my classroom, as well. My students begin most days gathered together at the back of the room to discuss the day's activities. Even though I have prepared lesson plans, I invite students to help sequence activities, set deadlines and establish goals for the day. This helps them learn how to prioritize and establish goals of their own. My students develop pleasure and pride in working hard and accomplishing difficult tasks.

Regardless of how supportive my classroom may be, sometimes students experience frustrations or setbacks. I cannot shield them from these disappointments, but I can teach them the value of a positive attitude. When something goes wrong or gets in the way of a goal of mine, an individual student, or the class, I cheerfully begin "Oh well . . ." and we repeat in unison "If life gives you lemons, make lemonade." Then we make a game of finding the good in the situation or creative ways to work around the problem. Learning requires perseverance and perseverance requires a positive attitude.

Still they sometimes lose sight of what's important. I've taught second graders for 24 years, so I consider myself somewhat of an authority on seven- and eight-year-olds. They are wonderful little people with expressive eyes and snaggle-tooth grins eager to burst from their lips at the slightest provocation. But they also experience disappointments with the same reckless abandon. Sometimes eight-year-old hands can't quite manage the grand ideas that an eight-year-old mind envisions, prompting quite a theatrical scene. When a child is in tears over a hole he just rubbed in his paper, I pull him up close and ask, "What's more important: people or things?" Though the child may be reluctant to admit it, I lead him to see that the paper is a thing. It can be fixed or replaced or forgotten. People are the only things in this world that are worth worrying about.

About five years ago, my principal gave everyone on our faculty a Children First pin which resulted in a ritual I perform each morning before declaring my primping complete. I do not skip this ritual no matter how late I may be running or how frustrated I feel over a bad-hair day. As I pick up my Children First pin to put it on, I pause to think about the little boy who seems to have lost his smile over the last few days, the little girl who's struggling with reading, or the child who is having trouble getting along. My thoughts become a prayer and a recommitment to put the children I touch before meetings, deadlines or even curriculum. My pin becomes a touchstone—a reminder that people are more important than things.

I want my students to see me as a teacher who finds joy in learning and who sees day-to-day challenges as exciting problems to solve, but who never loses sight of them as respected, cherished individuals. My philosophy is reflected in life lessons designed to take my students beyond knowledge and inspire them to set their own high expectations, to be unswervingly determined, and to maintain a positive outlook, I want my students to view their own learning as a life-long adventure that will bring them joy and enable them to bring joy into the lives of others, as well.

Norma Jackson—Texas Teacher of the Year 1998–1999

Ethical Standards for the Profession

A professional is an ethical person. The early childhood profession has a set of ethical standards to guide our thinking and behavior. As an early childhood professional, you will want to be a good teacher as judged by the profession. NAEYC has developed both a Statement of Commitment and a Code of Ethical Conduct (see Appendix B). Following is the Statement of Commitment from the code:

> As an individual who works with young children, I commit myself to furthering the values of early childhood education as they are reflected in the NAEYC Code of Ethical Conduct. To the best of my ability I will:
>
> - Ensure that programs for young children are based on current knowledge of child development and early childhood education.
> - Respect and support families in their task of nurturing children.
> - Respect colleagues in early childhood education and support them in maintaining the NAEYC Code of Ethical Conduct.
> - Serve as an advocate for children, their families and their teachers in community and society.
> - Maintain high standards of professional conduct.
> - Recognize how personal values, opinions, and biases can affect professional judgment.
> - Be open to new ideas and be willing to learn from the suggestions of others.
> - Continue to learn, grow, and contribute as a professional.
> - Honor the ideals and principles of the NAEYC Code of Ethical Conduct.[5]

WHAT DOES THE FUTURE HOLD FOR THE EARLY CHILDHOOD PROFESSIONAL?

As you prepare to undertake the professional challenges of the next century, the following are essential features of the future that will influence you and the profession:

- *Diversity.* The population of the United States will be even more diverse than it is today. Between 1974 and 1994, the percentage of white, non-Hispanic students enrolled in the public schools has decreased from 77.7 to 65.5 percent, while the enrollment of other ethnic groups continues to increase. The percentage of African-American students enrolled during this same time period has increased from 14.4 to 16.3 percent, the percentage of Hispanic students has increased from 6.3 to 13 percent, and the percentage of other ethnic groups has grown from 1.6 to 5.2 percent. Diversity training must be an essential part of the training of early childhood professionals, enabling them to work with children, parents, and families from all cultural and socioeconomic backgrounds.

- *Families.* Professionals will deliver services to children through the family. This means that early childhood professionals will need to know how to work with adults as well as children. Also, it means that professionals will have to rethink their concept of teaching.

- *Comprehensive services.* Early childhood programs will serve different types of children in different ways. There will be more young children with disabilities who will require programs designed to meet their and their families' needs. This means new programs will be developed, and teachers will be trained or retrained to provide appropriate services for a wide range of children with many and varied needs.

- *Public interest.* Early childhood education will continue to be a source of great interest and the focus of the public's attention. As a result, early childhood and children will continue to be a center of attention. Professionals have to be conversant with new ideas and practices and be willing and able to explain these to parents and the public.

- *Business and industry.* Business and industry will play larger roles than at present in the education of young children and their families, and in supporting services that achieve this goal. Professionals will also have to learn how to work with the business community.

- *Technology.* Technology will play an even greater role in learning at all levels. Part of professional development involves developing technological literacy in oneself and a willingness to foster technological literacy in children.

- *Professionalization.* We will see a stronger movement toward the professionalization of teaching, already evident from our previous discussion of professionalism. Professional roles will expand. A higher degree of professionalism will bring greater responsibility and decision making. The role of early childhood professionals will continue to be reconceptualized. Teachers will be trained to work with parents, design curriculum materials, plan programs for paraprofessionals, and work cooperatively with community agencies, including business and industry.

- *Respect for learning.* As an early childhood educator, you must be prepared to take your place in a world in which learning is valued and respected. You should also be prepared to devote your career to continually learning new skills and gaining new knowledge.

- *Community collaboration.* Professionals and community agencies will develop more collaborative, cooperative relationships. Teaching is an integral part of the broader range of human services and helping professions. The sharp lines that have traditionally separated social work, the health professions, and education are gradually blurring. There is also a trend toward resolving social problems through interdisciplinary programs, to which each profession contributes its particular expertise. A good way for you to keep updated on what the future holds is to read the daily newspaper, for in many respects, the future is here today.

ACTIVITIES FOR REFLECTION AND RESEARCH

1. Reflect about your best teachers. List their characteristics you would imitate.

2. What are five topics which you would benefit learning more about?

3. Write several paragraphs about why you think professional training is important in the field of early childhood education.

4. Reflect on your years in the primary grades. What experiences do you consider most meaningful? Why? Are these experiences you would want for children today? Why?

5. Share your philosophy of education with others. Have them critique it for comprehensiveness, clarity, and meaning. How do you feel about the changes they suggested?

6. List the reasons you have decided to become an early childhood professional.

7. Read the accounts of Teachers of the Year. What impressed you most about their experiences? What outstanding qualities do these teachers demonstrate? Why were they chosen as Teachers of the Year?

8. List five characteristics and qualities you think are essential for an early childhood professional. Compare your list with one written by one of your colleagues. How are they similar and different?

9. Read a local and a national newspaper for a week. Identify what you think are future trends that will influence early childhood education.

READINGS FOR FURTHER ENRICHMENT

Fujawa, Judy. *(Almost) Everything You Need to Know about Early Childhood Education: A Book of Lists for Teachers and Parents* (Washington, DC: Gryphon House, 1998).

Filled with the wisdom of over twenty years of teaching experience, this book of lists packs a great deal of information and insight into very few words. The author is a list maker whose entire teaching history is distilled in this compilation of what one needs to know and do to work successfully with children.

Hostetler, K., Hostetler, B., *Ethical Judgment in Teaching.* (Boston, MA: Allyn and Bacon, 1997).

This book is about helping teachers think carefully and knowledgeably about ethics in teaching, and to encourage them to talk to other people about it. Each chapter in the body of this text is organized around a pair of basic ethical concepts such as freedom and discipline, self and others, communities near and far, excellence and equality, unity and diversity, and faith and truth.

Palmer, P. J. *The Courage to Teach: Exploring the Inner Landscape of a Teacher's Life* (San Francisco: Jossey-Bass, 1998).

Parker Palmer takes teachers on an inner journey toward reconnecting with their vocation and their students—and recovering their passion for one of the most difficult and important of human endeavors.

RESEARCH ON THE INTERNET

The National Association for the Education of Young Children (NAEYC)

http://www.naeyc.org

The web site for the largest early childhood organization in the United States offers discussion of news and issues related to early childhood education, as well as links to early childhood resources organized by geographic area. You must be a member of NAEYC to access portions of this web site.

21st Century Teachers Website

http://www.21CT.org

"A national network of teacher leaders helping themselves and their colleagues through education technology." Enrollment in this organization is free, and gives access to its online news, library, and list of contacts.

Association for Supervision and Curriculum Development (ASCD)

http://www.ascd.org

Among other resources, ASCD offers its online newsletter *Education Bulletin* on its web site.

Center for Teaching Excellence

http://cte.uncwil.edu/

Hosted by the University of North Carolina at Wilmington, this site contains information on distance education and other teaching with technology issues, and also contains a link to an online interactive discussion board.

National Center to Improve Practice in Special Education

http://www.edc.org/FSC/NCIP/

Offers online workshops and video clips of special education students.

National Center to Improve the Tools of Educators

http://darkwing.uoregon.edu/~ncite/

Funded by the U.S. Office of Special Education Programs and housed at the University of Oregon, this site contains detailed information regarding the center.

National Council for Accreditation of Teacher Education (NCATE)

http://www.cpb.org/edtech/summits/ncate.html

Contains very basic information related to new standards proposed by NCATE, as well as contact information.

The Professional Development Partnership Projects

http://www.dssc.org/pdp/

Provides information regarding technical assistance and innovative ways in which to work with students with disabilities. Also contains an excellent state and national resource guide.

Systemic Reform—Perspectives on Personalizing Education

http://www.ed.gov/pubs/EdReformStudies/SysReforms/

Online compendium of articles written by various educators regarding the personalization of education.

NOTES

1. Barbara Willer and Sue Bredekamp, "A 'New' Paradigm of Early Childhood Professional Development,' " *Young Children,* 47(3), 1993, p. 64.

2. The New York State Early Childhood Career Development Initiative, *The New York State Early Childhood Education Core Body of Knowledge Framework: Essential Areas of Knowledge Needed for Working Effectively with Young Children, Birth through Age 8* (New York: Author, 1997), p. 8.

3. National Academy of Early Childhood Programs, *Accreditation Criteria and Procedures* (Washington, DC: National Association for the Education of Young Children, 1984), p. x.

4. National Association for the Education of Young Children, *Early Childhood Teacher Education Guidelines* (Washington, DC: Author, 1982), p. xii.

5. *Code of Ethical Conduct and Statement of Commitment* by S. Feeney and K. Kipnis, 1992, Washington, DC: The National Association for the Education of Young Children. Copyright © 1992 by NAEYC. Reprinted by permission.

CHAPTER

2

Contemporary Issues Affecting Early Childhood Education

FOCUS QUESTIONS

1. What contemporary influences are creating interest in early childhood education?
2. How does public policy influence early childhood education?
3. What are our views of children, and how do these views influence the education of young children?
4. How do social, political, economic, and educational issues influence child rearing and teaching?

Education is in part a matter of helping children and families live within contemporary society. Society makes demands on educational systems, and societal issues help establish the context in which we educate. As an early childhood professional, you must be aware of and take into account societal problems and issues, for they determine how you will teach and help children and families. Without a doubt, contemporary families and their structure have a tremendous influence on how you will practice your profession.

FAMILIES

How to best meet children's needs, in culturally appropriate ways, is always a primary goal of early childhood education. Today, early childhood professionals agree that a good way to meet children's needs is through their families, whatever that family unit may be (see Figure 2–1). Providing for children's needs through and within the *family system* makes sense for a number of reasons. First, the family has the primary responsibility for meeting many children's needs. So helping parents and other family members meet their children's needs in appropriate ways means that everyone stands to benefit. Helping people in a family unit—mother, father, grandparents, and others—be better parents helps them and their children.

Second, for children to be helped effectively, family problems and issues often must be addressed first. For example, helping parents gain access to adequate, affordable health care means that the whole family, including children, will be more healthy.

Third, early childhood professionals can do many things concurrently with children and their families that will benefit both at the same time. Literacy is a good example. Early childhood professionals are taking a family approach to helping children, their parents, and other family members learn how to read, write, speak, and listen. Teaching parents to read helps them understand the importance of supporting and promoting their children in the learning and teaching process.

Fourth, addressing the needs of children and their families as a whole, known as a *holistic* approach to education and the delivery of services, enables early childhood professionals and others to address a range of social

FIGURE 2–1
Two Models Illustrating a New
Paradigm for Providing Early
Childhood Services

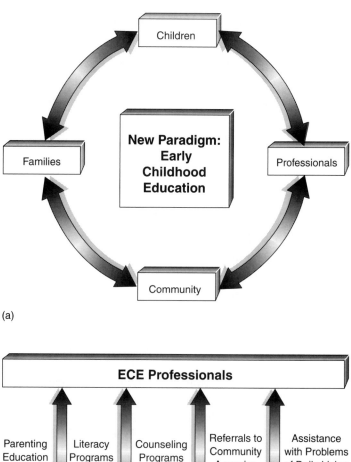

(a)

(b)

concerns at the same time. Literacy, health education and care, abuse prevention, AIDS education, and parenting programs are some examples of the family-centered approach to assisting and developing children and their families. Many programs such as Head Start and Even Start take a family approach to educating young children.

A major reason for new approaches to providing services to children and families is that families have changed and will continue to do so. Families are changing in the following ways:

Children's development begins in the family system. The family system, with the help and support of early childhood programs, provides for children's basic needs. It makes sense for early childhood professionals to work with and through the family system in the delivery of their services.

1.   *Structure.* Families include many kinds of arrangements other than what is typically referred to as a nuclear family—mother, father, and children. The definition of what a family is varies as society changes. Some of these changes result in

- single-parent families, headed by mothers or fathers
- extended families, which include grandparents, uncles, aunts, and other relatives or individuals not related by kinship

2.   *Roles.* As families change, so do the roles that parents and other family members perform. For example:

- More parents work today than in the past and so have less time for their children and family affairs.
- Working parents must combine many roles that go with being parents and employees. The many hats that parents wear increase as families change.

3.   Responsibilities. Responsibilities of families are also changing. As families change, many parents are not able to provide or cannot afford to pay for adequate and necessary care for their children. Other parents find that buffering their children from social ills such as drugs, violence, and delinquency is more than they can handle. Also, some parents are consumed by problems of their own, and so they have little time or attention to give their children. As families continue to change, early childhood professionals must continue to develop creative ways to meet the needs of children.

Changing family patterns create a need for child care (see Chapter 6). Both men and women are deciding to become parents—natural or adoptive—without marrying. According to the National Center for Health Statistics, over 1.2 million births—32 percent of all births—were among single mothers in 1996. This contrasts sharply with figures from 1980, at which time only 18 percent of all births were to single women. Of all women who had never been married in 1996, 21 percent had given birth to at least one child.

Interestingly, the sharpest increase in single parenthood is among affluent and well-educated women. For example, the percentage of unmarried women with one or more years of college who gave birth rose from 5.5 percent in

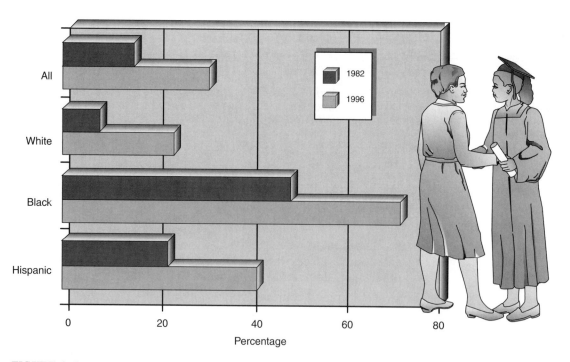

FIGURE 2–2
Percentage of Never-Married Women Age Eighteen to Forty-Four Who Have Children
Source: National Center for Health Statistics, *Monthly Vital Statistics Report,* 46 (11)(S), June 30, 1998.

1982 to 13.1 percent in 1994. According to the National Center for Health Statistics, educational level is the best predictor of birth rate; the highest birth rates are consistently among women with the lowest educational attainment (see Figure 2–2). Among women with college degrees, birth rates are highest for those in their early thirties. Figure 2–2 also shows the increase in never-married mothers from 1982 to 1996 for three major ethnic groups.

Welfare Reform

Welfare reform, which began in 1996, has had and will continue to have profound influence on children and families. In 1996, Congress passed the Personal Responsibility and Work Opportunity Reconciliation Act. This bill eliminated Aid to Families with Dependent Children (AFDC); JOBS, a work and training program for welfare recipients; and Emergency Assistance to Families with Children, a program designed to provide emergency help to families with children. These programs are replaced with a block grant of federal funds given to states.

Working Parents

More parents are working than ever before. Nearly 31 percent of all preschool-age children were cared for outside of the home while one or both parents worked in 1994, which created a greater need for early childhood programs. Between 1977 and 1994, the number of children in the United States with employed mothers increased from 4.4 million to 10.3 million. The increased demand for care facilities brings a beneficial recognition to early childhood programs and encourages early childhood professionals to meet parents' needs. Unfortunately, the urgent need for child care has encouraged some ill-prepared people, who do not necessarily have children's or parents' best interests in mind, to establish programs. Demand is high enough that good programs have not yet had a chance to drive inferior ones from the child care marketplace.

For their part, some parents are not able or willing to evaluate programs and select the best ones for their children, which also encourages poor-quality programs to stay in operation.

Single Parents

The number of one-parent families is increasing, while the number of two-parent households is declining, as shown in Figure 2–3. In 1997, nearly 28 percent of U.S. children were in families headed by a single parent. People become single parents for a number of reasons. Half of all marriages end in divorce. Some people choose single parenthood, and some, such as many teenagers, become parents by default. In addition, liberalized adoption

FIGURE 2–3

Living Arrangements of Children—1997
Source: U.S. Bureau of the Census, *Current Population Survey,* March 1997 (p. 20–509).

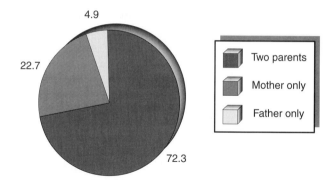

TABLE 2–1

Single Mothers with Children Living in Poverty—1997 (in Thousands)

Age of Mother	Number in Poverty	Percentage of Age Group
Total (all ages)	12,652	31.6
Less than 18 years	43	51.1
18–24 years	1,052	59.7
25–34 years	1,363	47.2

Source: Current Population Survey, Annual Demographic Survey 1998, Detailed Poverty (P60) Package, Table 1, "Poverty Status for Persons in 1997."

procedures, artificial insemination, surrogate childbearing, and general public support for single parents make this lifestyle an attractive option for some people. The reality is that more women are having babies without marrying. The most dramatic increase from 1990 to 1997 was the percentage of single-father households, which increased from 3.1 percent to 4.9 percent.

The need for affordable child care is influenced by the fact that in 1997, 31.6 percent of female-headed families were living below the poverty level (see Figure 2–4). The number of single mothers living in poverty, nearly 4 million, is better understood when compared with the 412,000 single fathers living in poverty in 1997. Single-parent mothers in poverty represent nearly 32 percent of their group, whereas single-parent fathers in poverty represent 20 percent of their group. A more detailed breakdown of mothers living in poverty is shown in Table 2–1.

Awareness of the growing number of single-parent families is not enough; we must also understand that within the population as a whole, certain cultural groups are disproportionately represented in single-parent families. Figure 2–5 on p. 36 illustrates these trends. These increases are attributable to several factors. First, pregnancy rates are higher among lower socioeconomic groups. Second, teenage pregnancy rates in poor white, Hispanic, and African-American populations are sometimes higher due to lower education

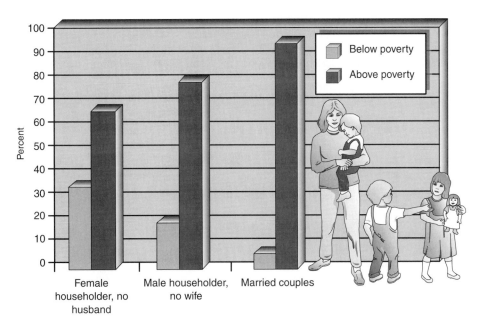

FIGURE 2–4
Families with Children Living in Poverty—1997
Source: U.S. Bureau of the Census, *Current Population Survey,* March 1997.

levels, economic constraints, and fewer opportunities for individuals. In addition, a complex interplay of personal issues, such as family, religious, and cultural conflicts, affects teenage pregnancy rates. In 1995, 37 percent of families were headed by females and 5 percent were headed by males.

Early professionals have always been concerned about how to assist and support single parents and their children, but today, more than ever, they recognize that these parents want and need their help. How well early childhood professionals meet the needs of single parents can make a difference in how successful single parents are in their new roles and how successful children are in life.

Teenage Parents: Children Having Children

Teenage pregnancies continue to be a problem. Each year nearly 500,000 teenagers give birth. The following facts about teenage pregnancy dramatically demonstrate its extent and effects:

• According to the National Center for Health Statistics, the rate of live births to teenage mothers in 1996 was 54.7 per 1,000 women aged 15–19 years, or 12.9 percent of all live births. While teenage pregnancies have decreased 16 percent from 1991 to 1997, the number is still significant. (Note

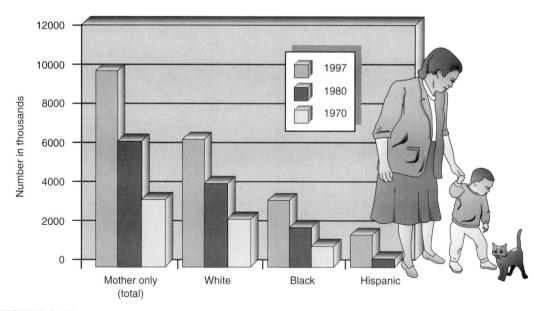

FIGURE 2–5A
Number of Single-Parent Families with Children by Race—Mother Only
Source: U.S. Bureau of the Census, *Historical Time Series,* Families (FM-2), May 1998.

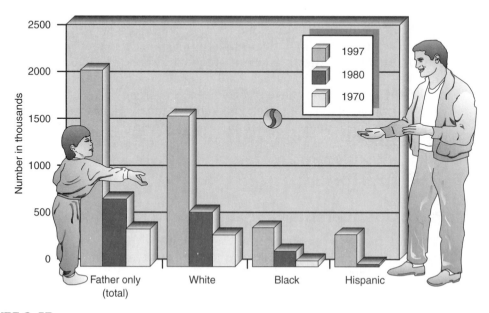

FIGURE 2–5B
Number of Single-Parent Families with Children by Race—Father Only
Source: U.S. Bureau of the Census, *Historical Time Series,* Families (FM-2), May 1998.

Teenage pregnancies continue to be a problem for a number of reasons. The financial costs of teenage childbearing are high, including costs to young mothers and their children. Teenage parents are less likely to complete their education and are more likely to have limited career and economic opportunities. How might early childhood programs help teenage parents meet their needs and the needs of their children?

that this is the *birth rate,* not the *pregnancy rate.* Many states do not report the number of teenagers who have had abortions, so there is really no way of determining the pregnancy rate for the nation as a whole.)

• The **estimated** pregnancy rate among teenagers in 1996 was 115 per 1,000 women aged 15–19 years, nearly twice the birth rate.

• The District of Columbia had the highest birth rate for teenagers in the United States in 1995, with 105.5 births per 1,000.

From an early childhood point of view, teenage pregnancies create greater demand for infant and toddler child care and programs to help teenagers learn how to parent. The staff of an early childhood program must often provide nurturance for both children and parents, because the parents themselves may not be emotionally mature. Emotional maturity is necessary for parents to engage in a giving relationship with children. When teenage parents lack parenting characteristics of any kind, early childhood professionals must help these parents develop them.

Concerned legislators and national leaders view teenage pregnancy as symptomatic of the problems of society in general. They worry about the demand for public health and welfare services, envision a drain on taxpayer dollars, and decry the loss of future potential because of school dropouts. From an early childhood point of view, teenage pregnancies create greater demand for infant and toddler child care and for programs to help teenagers learn how to be good parents. As noted above, early childhood professionals must nurture and help teenage parents who lack parenting characteristics of any kind.

Affluent Parents

On the other end of the continuum, some parents have sufficient disposable income and are willing to spend it on enriching their and their children's lives. Parents enroll themselves and their infants and toddlers in self-improvement programs promoted as physically and cognitively stimulating. Courses designed for expectant parents, new parents, and grandparents are now a standard part of the curriculum of many community colleges and schools. During one semester at a local community college, for example, parents could select from these courses: Parent/Infant Enrichment, Play Activities with the Preschool Child, Discipline Strategies That Work, Movement and Play Activities, Creative Learning—Storytelling/Drama, Toilet Learning, Choosing a Preschool for Your Child, Building Your Child's Self-Esteem, and Developmental Screening for Infants. Many of the courses required registration of both parents and their young children! It is obvious that early childhood professionals need to consider the needs of all parents and work with them accordingly.

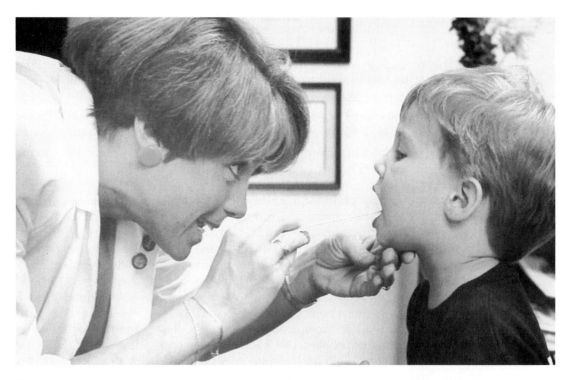

Readiness is now viewed as promoting children's learning and development in all areas. Readiness includes health and physical growth, such as being well rested, well fed, and properly immunized. The United Nations estimates that, worldwide, more than 8 million children a year die from five major diseases: pneumonia, diarrhea, measles, tetanus, and whooping cough.

Fathers

A continuing change in early childhood today is that fathers have rediscovered the joys of parenting and working with young children. Men are playing an active role in providing basic care, love, and nurturance to their children. In 1994, 41.9 percent of fathers were available to be the primary provider for their child 20 or more hours per week. The definition of fatherhood has changed; a father is no longer stereotypically unemotional, detached from everyday responsibilities of child care, authoritarian, and a disciplinarian. Fathers no longer isolate themselves from child rearing only because they are male. Men are more concerned about their role of fatherhood and their participation in family events before, during, and after the birth of their children. Fathers want to be involved in the whole process of child rearing. Because so many men feel unprepared for fatherhood, agencies such as hospitals and community colleges are providing courses and seminars to introduce fathers to the joys, rewards, and responsibilities of fathering.

Readiness also includes providing children with the right experiences at the time they need them. While experiences are important, it is also important to provide experiences that promote optimum brain development. For example, during the rapid period of language development from birth

---

Video Viewpoint

Children Growing Up without Fathers

Living in homes without fathers is a reality that affects the lives of growing numbers of children in the United States. In 25 percent of American households mothers are raising 40 million children alone. These are children that may never see or have contact with their biological fathers.

Reflective Discussion Questions: Why are we as a society so concerned about the absence of fathers in children's formative years? From your own background and experiences, what are some consequences for children being reared in homes without fathers? What does research show are some outcomes for children who are reared in homes without fathers? Why is having two parents in the home important for children? What are some critical behaviors that fathers role-model for their children? In what ways do fathers make a critical difference in the lives of children? Why is it important for mothers and fathers to tell their children "I love you"?

Reflective Decision Making: What can you as an early childhood professional do to make a difference in the lives of the children and their mothers living in homes without fathers? Make a list of community-based services that would be of help to families without fathers. How could you as an early childhood professional link children and their mothers to community-based services?

through age 3 it is important for parents and other caregivers to provide children with opportunities to hear and use language. Having the right experiences at the right time helps develop the brain and establishes the foundation for later learning. This is one reason there is so much interest in how the brain develops and in providing the appropriate experiences for brain development.

Brain Research

Although the field of neuroscience has been contributing to brain research for approximately twenty-five years, public interest in the application of this research to early childhood education has intensified recently. Media coverage of brain research and its implications for early childhood education is one factor contributing to this interest. Sharon Begley's *Newsweek* articles, "Your Child's Brain"[1] in 1996 and "How to Build a Baby's Brain"[2] in 1997, address the implications of brain research and how the findings of this research may be used in enhancing children's early years.

What specifically does brain research tell us about early childhood experiences? In many cases it affirms what early childhood educators have always known intuitively. Good parental care, warm and loving attachments, and positive age-appropriate stimulation from birth onward make a tremendous difference in children's cognitive development for a lifetime.

Brain research also tells us a great deal regarding stimulation and the development of specific areas of the brain. For example, brain research suggests that listening to music and learning to play musical instruments at very early ages stimulate brain cortical areas associated with mathematics and spatial reasoning. Brain research also suggests that gross motor activities and physical education should be included in a child's daily schedule throughout the elementary years. Regrettably, school systems often cut programs such as physical education and music in times of budget crisis, even though research shows that these programs are essential to a child's complete cognitive development.

New early childhood curricula are being developed based on the findings of brain research, and these programs strive to apply research findings in a practical way. One such program is Success for Life, developed by researchers and educators at the University of North Texas. The vision of Success for Life is to help children achieve a positive outlook on life through success in school and daily life. The goal of this interdisciplinary program is to integrate the findings of brain researchers with the best practices in early childhood education to provide support for healthy growth and to increase the cognitive and social competence of children. Children's needs—physical, social, emotional, cognitive, linguistic, nutritional, and health—are correlated with appropriate support and learning opportunities to create an optimal environment for growth and development.

CHILDREN WITH DISABILITIES

As a professional, you may well work with children with special needs. If so, you will need to know about laws that define terms and give special rights to children with special needs and their families. You will also need to use terms that apply to special needs children and to services provided for them. It is important for you to know these terms and to use them properly. For example, *children with disabilities* replaces terms such as *handicapped children.* Avoiding the reversals of phrases, such as *disabled children,* communicates to parents, children, and other professionals that you are sensitive to using more "people-first" language.

The Individuals with Disabilities Education Act

Prior to the implementation of the Individuals with Disabilities Education Act (IDEA) in 1975, approximately 1 million children with disabilities were excluded from the public school system, often resulting in unequal educational and employment opportunities for these special needs students. As a result of IDEA, three times the number of students with disabilities are enrolled in colleges and universities, and twice as many persons in their twenties with disabilities are working. Between 1990 and 1996, the number of children served by IDEA increased from 4.8 million to 5.6 million.

Congress continually amends the Individuals with Disabilities Education Act. The latest amendments were passed in 1997. While IDEA has significantly changed the lives of students with disabilities, statistics show more needs to be done:

- Twice as many children with disabilities than those without disabilities drop out of school.
- Dropouts usually do not return to school, have greater difficulty finding jobs, and often find themselves in the criminal justice system.
- Girls who drop out of school become unwed mothers at a much higher rate than their nondisabled peers.
- Many children with disabilities are excluded from the curriculum and assessments of their nondisabled peers, thus limiting their possibilities of performing to higher standards of performance.[3]

The 1997 IDEA amendments are designed to:

- Raise expectations for children with disabilities
- Increase parental involvement in the education of their children
- Ensure that regular education teachers are involved in planning and assessing children's progress

- Include children with disabilities in assessments, performance goals, and reports to the public
- Support quality professional development for all personnel who are involved in educating children with disabilities. IDEA defines "a child with a disability" as a child:

  with mental retardation, hearing impairments (including deafness), speech or language impairments, visual impairments (including blindness), serious emotional disturbance (hereinafter referred to as emotional disturbance), orthopedic impairments, autism, traumatic brain injury, other health impairments, or specific learning disabilities; and who, by reason thereof, needs special education and related services.[4]

The Americans with Disabilities Act (ADA) of 1990, defines *disability* as "a physical or mental impairment that substantially limits one or more of the major life activities."[5] This act mandates equal access by individuals with disabilities to both public and private schools. This law has had and will continue to have a profound effect on school architecture and equipment. For example, more schools and classrooms are wheelchair accessible and more playgrounds now have wheelchair-accessible equipment such as swings.

Table 2–2 shows the number of persons age six to twenty-one with disabilities in the various categories. In 1997, 8 percent of enrolled students had some sort of disability, a 17 percent increase from 1990.

TABLE 2–2
Number of Children Ages 6–21 Served Under IDEA by Disability: 1987–88 and 1996–97

1996–97	
Disability	**Number**
Specific Learning Disabilities	2,676,299
Speech or Language Impairments	1,050,975
Mental Retardation	594,025
Emotional Disturbance	447,426
Multiple Disabilities	99,638
Hearing Impairments	68,766
Orthopedic Impairments	66,400
Other Health Impairments	160,824
Visual Impairments	25,834
Autism	34,101
Deaf-Blindness	1,286
Traumatic Brain Injury	10,378
All Disabilities	5,235,952

Reporting on autism and traumatic brain injury was required under IDEA beginning in 1992–93.
Source: U.S. Department of Education, Office of Special Education Programs, Data Analysis System (DANS).

What Laws Help Children with Special Needs?

The landmark legislation providing for the needs of children with disabilities is PL 94-142. Section 3 of this law states:

> It is the purpose of this Act to assure that all handicapped children have available to them, within the time periods specified in section 612(2)(B), a free appropriate public education which emphasizes special education and related services designed to meet their unique needs, to assure that the rights of handicapped children and their parents or guardians are protected, to assist States and localities to provide for the education of all handicapped children, and to assess and assure the effectiveness of efforts to educate handicapped children.[6]

Public Law 94-142 provides for a free and appropriate education (FAPE) for all persons between the ages of three and twenty-one. The operative word is *appropriate*; the child must receive an education suited to his or her age, maturity, condition of disability, past achievements, and parental expectations. The common practice was to diagnose children with a disability and then put them in an existing program, whether or not that program was specifically appropriate. Now the educational program has to be appropriate for the child, which means that a plan must be developed for each child.

The child's education must occur within the least restrictive educational environment. *Least restrictive* means that environment in which the child will be able to receive a program that meets his or her specific needs—the regular classroom, if that is the environment in which the child can learn best. The least restrictive educational environment is not always the regular classroom; however, this law provides more opportunity to be with regular children.

The law requires *individualization of instruction* and *diagnosis*. Not only must the child's education be appropriate; it must also be individualized, taking into consideration the child's specific needs, disability, and preferences, as well as those of the parents. The key to the individualization process is another feature of the law that requires development of an *individualized educational plan (IEP)* for each child. This program must be in writing. In developing the IEP, a person trained in diagnosing disabling conditions, such as a school psychologist, must be involved, as well as a classroom professional, the parent, and, when appropriate, the child.

Several implications are associated with the IEP. One is that for the first time, on a formal basis, parents and children are involved in the educational determination of what will happen to the child. Second, the child must have a plan tailor-made or individualized for him or her. This approach assures accurate diagnosis and realistic goal setting, as well as responsible implementation of the program, which personalizes the process and increases the possibility of a more humane teaching-learning process.

The legislation specifies that parents and child will have a role in diagnosis, placement, and development of the IEP. Parents can state their desires for the child, and information that parents have about the child's learning style, interests, and abilities can be considered in developing the educational plan.

This process was not always possible or even considered necessary before passage of PL 94-142.

The law also provides for parents to initiate a hearing if they do not agree with the diagnosis, placement, or contents of the IEP. This provision gives the parents clout in encouraging public school personnel to provide a free and appropriate education for their child.

Using an individualized educational plan with all children, not just those with disabilities, is gaining acceptance with early childhood professionals. Individualizing objectives, methodology, and teaching helps ensure that the teaching process will become more accurate and accountable.

Public Law 99-457

In 1986, Congress passed PL 99-457, the Education of the Handicapped Act Amendments—landmark legislation relating to infants, toddlers, and preschoolers with disabilities. Public Law 99-457 amends PL 91-230, the Education of the Handicapped Act (EHA), which was passed in 1970. Public Law 99-457 authorizes two new programs: Title I, Program for Infants and Toddlers with disabilities (birth through age two years), and Title II, Preschool Grants Program (ages three through five years). The Preschool Grants Program extends to children who have disabilities and are between the ages of three and five the rights extended to the disabled under PL 94-142. This age group was included in PL 94-142 but often did not receive public school services because states had discretion over whether to provide services to this age group.

The legislation recognizes that families play a large role in delivering services to preschool children with disabilities. Consequently, PL 99-457 provides that, whenever appropriate and to the extent desired by parents, preschoolers' IEPs will include instruction for parents. The legislation also recognizes the desirability of variations in program options to provide services to preschoolers with disabilities. Variations may be part-day home based and part- or full-day center based.

The Program for Infants and Toddlers authorized by PL 99-457 establishes a state grant program for infants and toddlers with disabilities, from birth to two years, who (1) are experiencing developmental delays in one or more of the following areas: cognitive, physical, language and speech, psychosocial, or self-help skills; (2) have a physical or mental condition that has a high probability of resulting in delay (e.g., Down syndrome, cerebral palsy); or (3) are at risk medically or environmentally for substantial developmental delays if early intervention is not provided. This program provides for early intervention for all eligible children. Early intervention services provided under 99-457 include these:

- A multidisciplinary assessment and a written individualized family service plan (IFSP, detailed next) developed by a multidisciplinary team and the parents. Services must meet developmental needs and can include special education, speech and language pathology and audiology, occupational therapy, physical therapy, psychological services, parent and family training and counseling services, transition services, medical diagnostic services, and health services.

- An IFSP must contain

  a statement of the child's present levels of development

  a statement of the family's strengths and needs in regard to enhancing the child's development

  a statement of major expected outcomes for the child and family

  the criteria, procedures, and timeliness for determining progress

  the specific early intervention services necessary to meet the unique needs of the child and family

  the projected dates for initiation of services

  the name of the case manager

  transition procedures from the early intervention program into a preschool program

Since PL 99-457 requires an IFSP, professionals need to know what these plans consist of and what the procedures are for completing them. Although developing a program for individual children and/or their families is not the same as individualized instruction, it is important to know the differences between the two and how to conduct both processes.

Table 2–3 shows one page from an IFSP developed by Child Development Resources in Lightfoot, Virginia. Note that the IFSP is for the beginning implementation stage, which accounts for why the section "Parents' Report of Progress toward Outcome" is not yet filled in. As the plan is put into practice, this section will be completed. The following points should be kept in mind when striving for effective individual and family service plans.

- Methods and techniques of diagnostic and prescriptive teaching are essential as a basis for writing and implementing the IEP and the IFSP.

- Working with parents is an absolute must for every classroom professional. You should learn all you can about parent conferences and communication, parent involvement, and parents as volunteers and aides. In a sense, PL 94-142 and PL 99-457 mainstream parents as well as children.

- Working with all levels of professionals offers a unique opportunity for the classroom professional to individualize instruction. Since it is obvious that all professionals need help in individualizing instruction, it makes sense to involve all professionals in this process.

- As individual education becomes a reality for *all* children and families, professionals will need skills in assessing student behavior and family background and settings.

TABLE 2–3
Other Outcomes Desired by the Family

Outcome	Course of Action	Review/Modify (Date)	Parent's Report of Progress toward Outcome (Date)
1. Kevin will have a smooth transition from CDR to the public schools (Fall 1995)	1a. Kevin's family and Lara will visit the Play Center to observe classrooms, therapies, and to meet the staff.	Feb. 1995	
	1b. Kevin will be referred to the Play Center by Lara with parents' permission.	Mar. 1995	
	1c. Kevin's parents and Lara will attend eligibility and IEP meetings as needed.	May/June 1995	
	1d. Kevin will attend Developmental Play Group more frequently in the Spring to help him prepare for transition, if his parents desire.	Ongoing (starting late Spring 1995)	

Source: Child Development Resources, P.O. Box 299, Lightfoot, Virginia 23090. Used by permission.

• Professionals must know how to identify sources of, and how to order and use, a broad range of instructional materials, including media. One cannot hope to individualize without a full range of materials and media. Professionals must regularly be concerned with students' visual, auditory, and tactile/kinesthetic learning styles. Some children in a classroom may learn best through one mode, other children through another. The classroom professional can use media, in particular, to help make teaching styles congruent with children's learning modalities.

Sometimes in our reading, thinking, and discussion of the needs of children with disabilities, we forget or lose track of the laws which mandate specific services. The timeline in Box 2–1 will help you understand the chronological flow of laws influencing how children with disabilities are educated.

Inclusion and Full Inclusion

Inclusion is the practice of ensuring that all students with disabilities participate with other students in all aspects of the educational setting of which they are a part, including playgrounds, family day care centers, child care centers, preschools, and general education classrooms. Inclusion is becoming more

BOX 2–1   TIME LINE: SPECIAL NEEDS PROGRAMS

1963   PL 88-156 Maternal and Child Health Program is expanded.

1965   PL 89-313 Payments are made to states for children with disabilities, from birth to age twenty, in state-operated programs.

1965   PL 89-97 Medicaid Program is established.

1967   PL 90-248 Early and Periodic Screening, Diagnosis, and Treatment Program (EPSDT) is added to Medicaid Program.

1968   PL 90-538 Handicapped Children's Early Education Assistance Act creates Handicapped Children's Early Education Program (HCEEP); provides for model demonstration programs to acquaint public with problems and potentials of children with special needs.

1970   PL 91-230 Education of the Handicapped Act (EHA) is created; HCEEP is folded into Part C of EHA.

1974   PL 93-644 Head Start Program is amended to require that 10 percent of enrollment opportunities be made available to children with disabilities.

1975   PL 94-142 The Education for All Handicapped Children Act guarantees a free and appropriate education to children with disabilities ages five through twenty-one.

1983   PL 98-199 EHA is amended to allow use of funds for services to children with disabilities from birth.

1986   PL 99-457 authorizes the Federal Preschool Program, which extends rights under PL 99-142 to children ages three through five, and the Early Intervention Program, which establishes a state grant program for children from birth to two years old.

1990   Americans with Disabilities Act (ADA) requires access to public accommodations for all individuals regardless of disability. These public accommodations include child care centers and family child care homes.

1990   PL 101-476 Individuals with Disabilities Education Act (IDEA) provides services to children with disabilities from birth through age five.

1991   PL 102-119 Part H of IDEA is reauthorized and amended.

1992   Americans with Disabilities Act (ADA) establishes equal rights for people with disabilities in employment, state and local public services, and public accommodations including preschools, child care centers, and family child care homes.

1994   Improving America's School Act provides federal support for at-risk children to help them achieve challenging standards in core academic subjects.

1995   IDEA Amendments of 1995 specify in part that it be the policy of the United States that all children with disabilities have the opportunity to (1) meet developmental goals and, to the maximum extent possible, those challenging standards that have been established for all children; and (2) be prepared to lead productive, independent adult lives, again to the maximum extent possible.

1997   IDEA Amendments of 1997 are signed, and are designed to (1) raise expectations for children with disabilities; (2) increase parental involvement in the education of their children; (3) ensure that regular education teachers are involved in planning and assessing children's progress; (4) include children with disabilities in assessments, performance goals, and reports to the public; and (5) support quality professional development for all personnel who are involved in educating children with disabilities.

FIGURE 2–6
The Division for Early Childhood's Position Statement on Inclusion

Inclusion, as a value, supports the right of all children, regardless of their diverse abilities, to participate actively in natural settings within their communities. A *natural setting* is one in which the child would spend time had he or she not had a disability. Such settings include, but are not limited to, home and family, play groups, child care, nursery schools, Head Start programs, kindergartens, and neighborhood school classrooms.

DEC believes in and supports full and successful access to health, social service, and other supports and services for young children and their families that promote full participation in community life. DEC values the diversity of families and supports a family-guided process for determining services that are based on the needs and preferences of individual families and children.

To implement inclusive practices DEC supports:

a) The continued development, evaluation, and dissemination of full inclusion supports, services, and systems *so that options for inclusion are of high quality;*

b) The development of preservice and inservice training programs to prepare families, administrators, and service providers to develop and work within inclusive settings;

c) Collaboration among all key stakeholders to implement fiscal and administrative procedures in support of inclusion;

d) Research that contributes to our knowledge of state of the art services; and

e) The restructuring and unification of social, education, health, and intervention supports and services to make them more responsive to the needs of all children and families.

Source: Division for Early Childhood of the Council for Exceptional Children, adopted April 1993, revised December 1993. Used by permission.

and more prevalent, with 43.4 percent of disabled students attending school in regular classrooms in 1996. IDEA specifies that:

> *To the maximum extent appropriate, children with disabilities . . . are educated with children who are not disabled, and special classes, separate schooling, or other removal of children with disabilities from the regular environment occurs only when the nature or severity of the disability of a child is such that education in regular classes with the use of supplementary aids and services cannot be attained satisfactorily.*[7]

Services formerly provided in separate special education programs are now provided in inclusion programs in the natural environment by special educators and other special service providers. Review Figure 2–6 now as preparation for our further discussion of inclusion.

Full inclusion refers to the full-time inclusion of students with disabilities—even severe disabilities—in classrooms with students who do not have disabilities. While the term *inclusion* may imply that students with disabilities interact with students without disabilities for part of the school day, *full inclusion* indicates that there is no division whatsoever. Proponents of full inclusion not only cite the benefit of inclusion to students with disabilities, but point also to the benefit of teaching core values to students without disabilities through daily experience with disabled students.

Full inclusion receives a lot of attention and is the subject of great national debate for a number of reasons. First, court decisions and state and federal laws mandate, support, and encourage full inclusion. Many of these laws and court cases relate to extending to children and parents basic civil rights. For example, in the 1992 case, *Oberti v. Board of Education of the Borough of Clementon School District,* the judge ruled that Rafael, an eight-year-old with Down syndrome, should not have to earn his way into an integrated classroom but that it was his right to be there from the beginning.

Second, some parents of children with disabilities are dissatisfied with their children's attending separate programs. They view separate programs for their children as a form of segregation. In addition, they want their children to have the social benefits of attending classes in general education classrooms. On the other hand, some parents believe their children are best served in separate special education settings.

Third, some teachers feel they do not have the training or support necessary to provide for the disabilities of children who will be placed in their classrooms as a result of full inclusion. They also believe that they will not be able to provide for children with disabilities even with the assistance of aides and special support services.

Fourth, some people believe that the cost of full inclusion outweighs the benefits. On the other hand, some professionals think the cost involved in separate special education facilities and programs can be better used in inclusion programs. There is no doubt that educating students with disabilities costs more. The average cost of educating a regular classroom student nationally is $5,740, compared with $13,202 (2.3 times more) for an exceptional education student. This cost can be higher for some individual students and in some school districts.

Strategies for Teaching Children with Disabilities

Sound teaching strategies work well for all students, including those with disabilities. You must plan how to create inclusive teaching environments. The following ideas will help you teach children with disabilities and create inclusive settings that enhance the education of all students.

- *Accentuate the positive.*
- *Use appropriate assessment including work samples, cumulative records, and appropriate assessment instruments.*
- *Use concrete examples and materials.*
- *Develop and use multisensory approaches to learning.*

- *Model what children are to do rather than just telling them what to do.*
- *Let children practice or perform a certain behavior.*
- *Make the learning environment a pleasant, rewarding place to be.*
- *Create a dependable classroom schedule.*
- *Encourage parents to volunteer at school and to read to their children at home.*
- *Identify appropriate tasks children can accomplish on their own.*
- *Use cooperative learning* as a method in which children of various abilities work on a task together.
- *Use a circle of friends* in which children make and talk about friends, to help students develop friendships with their classmates.

PROGRAM IN ACTION

THE SUNRISE CHILDREN'S CENTER

The Sunrise Children's Center is an inclusionary center that serves children ages two to six years old. Sunrise, currently a 10,600 square-foot facility with eight classrooms, began as a self-contained regional preschool program housed within a local elementary school. As the need for inclusion became evident, teachers surveyed the area for existing child care programs or preschools that would "mainstream" children. Several challenges surfaced. Developmentally appropriate centers had long waiting lists and would not change their policy for children with special needs (who often are not identified until September). Many classes had large teacher-student ratios, and teachers were already challenged by the behaviors and concerns of their "typical" population. When approached, teachers often overreacted to children with special needs, feeling the need to do something "special" with their program. Sunrise began by hiring teachers and welcoming parents that believed in full inclusion. Their philosophy is that all children have strengths and areas of concerns, that all children deserve individual educational programs, and that typically developing children benefit in an inclusionary model as much as, if not more than, do children with special needs.

A Child's View of the Sunrise Center

Consistency is essential for all children. Every morning when I arrive I know exactly what is expected of me. I hang up my coat, put my lunch away, and get a big smile and greeting from my teacher and friends.

The room is sunny and well organized. Centers may change, but not without warning and preparation. I like it when I know about changes. One day we talked about changing the dress-up corner to a hospital, and before we did it we all talked about what we wanted to do.

Everything in the room has its place and there is lots of room to play. I look around the room and see a block area, a housekeeping center, a fine-motor play area, a reading corner, a sand table, a dress-up corner, and an art center.

Teachers always give plenty of time for transition from one activity to the next. My teacher starts singing the clean-up song and turns the timer over. The timer helps me know how long we have. Johnny isn't helping to clean up today, so my teacher starts to help me and encourages Johnny to put one block away. When he does she says, "Thank you!" so he wants to help more!

- *Use the Classwide Peer Tutoring Program (CWTP)* to involve whole class-rooms of students in tutoring activities that improve achievement and student engagement.
- *Develop a peer buddy system.*

A Transdisciplinary Team

For young children with special needs, a *transdisciplinary* team approach consists of interdisciplinary involvement across and among various health and social services disciplines. Members of this team can include any of the following professionals: early childhood educator, physical therapist, occupational therapist, speech communication therapist, psychologist, social worker, and pediatrician. The rationale for the transdisciplinary team is that a unified

Circle should be at the same time every day. Many children benefit from preteaching before circle begins. It's circle time and my teacher has the chairs out with our names on them. I have trouble with this but an assistant helps me. She sits in back of me during circle because I have trouble sitting still. She rubs my back hard (I like it!) and helps me when I get confused. Before circle we went over the songs, finger-plays, and book so I feel great that I know it.

The assistant needs to be discrete and non-verbal during circle to not distract from the teacher. I like the assistant in back of me, she's very quiet and not too pushy. After circle it's time to have snack.

Snack is a great time to encourage learning. During snack I practice talking to my friends. My assistant asks me lots of questions.

Therapy should be incorporated into daily group routine. Children should never feel singled out, different, or isolated from their peers. I have an oral motor program, but everyone does it with me. The teacher makes it into a game for all of us, saying, "Bring your tongue to the top of the house, to the basement," and so on.

Therapy should be provided in the setting that challenges the child. It's time for the bathroom and to get ready to go outside. I have trouble with the bathroom, but the assistant takes me in and asks me to use the toilet. My friends are there, too. I watch them and want to try! Getting my coat on is hard, but my teacher showed us all an easy way. The assistant helps me a little and I do the rest. We go out to the playground and a lady helps me play games with my friends. Our teachers warn us before it's time to line up and come inside.

Now it's time for activity centers. We gather on the rug and the teacher tells us about the different activities we can do. I feel overwhelmed, but the assistant suggests a table. I go to the table and another special person is playing a game that helps me with my speech. I have three other friends with me at the table. A bell rings and I go to another table where I learn to cut and paste. Sometimes I get to take friends to a special room and work with helper people.

It's time to go home now and we get back into a circle and sing, "It's time to say goodbye to our friends."

Contributed by Joanna Bogin, director, Sunrise Children's Center, Amherst, New Hampshire.

and holistic approach is the most effective way to provide resources and deliver services to children and their families.

Members of the team diagnose, prescribe, share information, and work cooperatively to meet children's needs. One of the members, usually the early childhood educator, heads the team, and other members act as consultants. The team leader carries out the instructions of other team members. A variation of this model is to have members of the team, such as the physical therapist, work directly with the child at specified times (e.g., twice a week) and provide activities and suggestions for the early childhood educator to implement at other times.

CHILD ABUSE

Many of our views of childhood are highly romanticized. We tend to believe that parents always love their children and enjoy caring for them. We also envision family settings full of joy, happiness, and parent-child harmony. Unfortunately for children, their parents, and society, these assumptions are not always true. The extent of child abuse is far greater than we might imagine.

- In 1996, almost 1 million children were the victims of substantiated or indicated child abuse and neglect, an 18 percent increase from 1990.
- The national rate of abuse was 15 cases per 1,000 children in the population in 1996.
- In 1995, Child Protective Services (CPS) investigated 2 million reports of abuse involving nearly 3 million children.
- An estimated 1,077 fatalities occurred as a result of child abuse in the 50 states and the District of Columbia in 1996. Figure 2–7 on page 55 further reveals the extent of abuse and neglect suffered by children today.

Causes of Abuse

Why do parents and guardians abuse children? Those who have been responsible for a group of young children will better understand the reasons for child abuse than those who do not know young children. Child rearing is hard work; it requires patience, self-control, understanding, and restraint. It is entirely likely that most parents, at one time or another, have come close to behavior that could be judged abusive. The following are the main reasons cited that provoke abuse:

- Stress is one of the most frequent causes of child abuse. Stressful situations arise from employment problems, divorce or separation, low income, poor quality of family life, moving, death of a family member, violations of law, sickness or injury, and other sources.

FIGURE 2–7
Substantiated Abuse and
Neglect Cases
Source: National Committee to
Prevent Child Abuse, 1996.

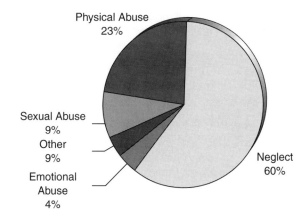

Physical Abuse
23%

Sexual Abuse
9%

Other
9%

Emotional
Abuse
4%

Neglect
60%

• Lack of parenting information is another reason parents abuse or neglect their children. Some parents do not know what to do or how to do it; these cases more frequently result in acts of omission or neglect than in physical violence.

• A third reason for child abuse is the parent's cognitive and emotional state. How people are reared and what parenting attitudes were modeled for them have a tremendous influence on how they will rear their own children.

• A fourth cause of abuse relates to unwanted and unloved children. We like to assume that every child is wanted and loved, but this is not the case. Some parents take out their frustration on their children, whom they view as barriers to their dreams and self-fulfillment.

• Some people believe a fifth reason for child abuse is the amount of violence in our society. Opponents of violence on television cite it as an example of people's callousness toward each other and decry it as poor role modeling for children.

• A sixth cause of abuse can be attributed to parental substance abuse. Substance abuse creates a chaotic environment in which children cannot tell what to expect from their parents. Children of parents who use or abuse alcohol or drugs are often neglected because the parent is emotionally or physically absent when drunk or high.

Seeking Help

What can be done about child abuse? There must be a conscious effort to educate, treat, and help abusers or potential abusers. The school is a good place to begin. Another source of help is the federal government's National Center on Child Abuse and Neglect, which helps coordinate and develop programs and policies concerning child abuse and neglect. For information, call or write to any of the following:

• The Administration for Children and Families, Department of Health and Human Services, 200 Independence Avenue, W., Washington, D.C. 20201. http://www.acf.dhhs.gov/

• Child Help USA handles crisis calls and provides information and referrals to every county in the United States. Its hotline is 800-422-4453. http://www.childhelpusa.org/

• The National Committee to Prevent Child Abuse (NCPCA) is a volunteer organization of concerned citizens that works with community, state, and national groups to expand and disseminate knowledge about abuse prevention. The NCPCA has chapters in all the states; the address for its national office is National Committee to Prevent Child Abuse, 332 S. Michigan Avenue, Suite 1600, Chicago, Illinois 60604; telephone 312-663-3520. http://www.childabuse.org/

Children today are subjected to many stressful situations, including community environments, home life, and television. As early childhood professionals, we must seek ways to reduce or eliminate stress in children's lives that imperils their lives and learning. How can you advocate for reducing violence in children's environments?

POLITICS AND EARLY CHILDHOOD EDUCATION

Whatever else can be said about education, one point holds true: Education is political. Politicians and politics exert a powerful influence in determining what gets taught, how it is taught, to whom it is taught, and by whom it is taught. Early childhood education is no exception. An important political and educational event occurred in 1989 when President George Bush and all governors of the fifty states met at the University of Virginia to set national education goals. A result of this meeting was the creation in 1990 of the National Education Goals Panel (NEGP) and the release in April 1991 of *America 2000: An Education Strategy.* The six original goals of *America 2000* have been expanded to the following eight goals:

Goal 1: Ready to Learn

By the year 2000, all children will start school ready to learn.

Goal 2: School Completion

By the year 2000, the high school graduation rate will increase to at least 90 percent.

Goal 3: Student Achievement and Citizenship

By the year 2000, all students will leave grades 4, 8, and 12 having demonstrated competency over challenging subject matter including English, mathematics, science, foreign languages, civics and government, economics, arts, history, and geography; and every school in America will ensure that all students learn to use their minds well, so they may be prepared for responsible citizenship, further learning, and productive employment in our Nation's modern economy.

Goal 4: Teacher Education and Professional Development

By the year 2000, the Nation's teaching force will have access to programs for the continued improvement of their professional skills and the opportunity to acquire the knowledge and skills needed to instruct and prepare all American students for the next century.

Goal 5: Mathematics and Science

By the year 2000, United States students will be the first in the world in mathematics and science achievement.

Goal 6: Adult Literacy and Lifelong Learning

By the year 2000, every adult American will be literate and will possess the knowledge and skills necessary to compete in a global economy and exercise the rights and responsibilities of citizenship.

Goal 7: Safe, Disciplined, and Alcohol- and Drug-Free Schools

By the year 2000, every school in the United States will be free of drugs, violence, and the unauthorized presence of firearms and alcohol and will offer a disciplined environment conducive to learning.

Goal 8: Parental Participation

By the year 2000, every school will promote partnerships that will increase parental involvement and participation in promoting the social, emotional, and academic growth of children.

A detailed discussion of each of these goals can be found on NEGP's web site (http://www.negp.gov). In addition, NEGP prepared in 1997 a *Special Early Childhood Report* specifically related to goal 1, the goal of readiness. This report is available through NEGP, or online at http://www.negp. gov/webpg720.htm#child.

These goals have generated a great deal of debate, particularly concerning what they mean and how best to achieve them. Goals 1, 2, 6, and 7 have had and will continue to have particular implications for early childhood education. Goal 1 obviously impacts children's readiness for school. Goal 2 is pertinent because the early childhood years are seen as the place to prevent school dropout. Many public school programs for three- and four-year-old children are funded with the specific purpose of beginning efforts to keep children in school at a later age. Goal 6 has encouraged many *intergenerational literacy and family literacy programs* in which children, their parents, and other family members are taught to read. Goal 7 supports the drug prevention programs implemented in early childhood programs, again on the premise that early prevention is much more effective than later treatment.

Public Policies

In early childhood education, policies made through legislation and agency guidelines affect and influence the lives of children, parents, and families. They are implemented through official statements, pronouncements, and legislation. Many child care programs and most public schools, for example, have policies that require full immunization against childhood diseases before entering the program. As you might suspect, several public policies determine what ages children can enter school, how child care programs should operate, and how early childhood professionals are to provide appropriate care and education for children with special needs. Throughout this text, you will find many instances in which public policy outlines specific kinds of programs for children and families and the circumstances and funding under which they are delivered.

Advocacy

Early childhood professionals advocate on behalf of children and families. Advocacy is working in the larger community, beyond one's immediate family or classroom, to improve conditions for children. An advocate seeks to provide a voice in the system for children who have no power to work on their own behalf. As early childhood professionals become increasingly involved in advocacy activities, they and their professional organizations issue position statements designed to influence public policy before its enactment and implementation. Child advocacy agencies draft position papers on topics ranging from developmentally appropriate practices for young children to the pros and cons of developing public school programs for four-year-olds. NAEYC, for example, is a strong advocate for developmentally appropriate practices in early childhood programs. Agencies such as the Children's Defense Fund influence national and state legislation for programs to help children and families.

At no time in U.S. history has there been so much interest and involvement on the part of professionals in the development of public policy. This political reality is beneficial to all—children, parents, families, and early childhood professionals—for it helps assure that the best interests of the children's families will be considered when decisions are made that affect them.

HOW DO BELIEFS ABOUT CHILDREN INFLUENCE EARLY CHILDHOOD EDUCATION?

Views of children determine how people teach and rear them. As you read about the different views of children, try to clarify and change, when appropriate, what you believe. Also, identify social, environmental, and political factors that tend to support each particular view. Sometimes, of course, views overlap, so it is possible to synthesize ideas from several perspectives into a particular personal view.

Miniature Adult

What early childhood professionals and parents identify as childhood has not always been considered a distinct period of life. During medieval times, the notion of childhood did not exist; little distinction was made between children and adults. The concept of children as miniature adults was logical for the time and conditions of medieval Europe. Economic conditions did not allow for a long childhood dependency. The only characteristics that separated children from adults were size and age. Children were expected to act as adults in every way, and they did so.

In many respects the twentieth century is no different, because children are still viewed and treated as adults. In many Third World countries of Latin America, Africa, and Asia, children are, of necessity, expected to be economically productive. They are members of the adult working world at age four, five, or six. The United Nations Educational, Scientific, and Cultural Organization (UNESCO) estimates that 100 million children around the world work and live in city streets. In many countries children are involved in war as active participants and casualties. Almost daily, newspapers show these children dead or wounded and waiting for help.

In the United States, where child labor laws protect children from the world of adult work and exploitation, some people advocate allowing children to enter the workplace at earlier ages and for lower wages. In some rural settings, young children still have economic value. Approximately 1 million migrant children pick crops and help their parents earn a livelihood. At the other end of the spectrum, child actors and models engage in highly profitable and what some call glamorous careers.

Encouraging children to act like adults and hurrying them toward adulthood causes conflicts between capabilities and expectations, particularly when early childhood professionals demand adultlike behavior from children and set unrealistic expectations. Problems associated with learning, behavior, and social skills can occur when children are constantly presented with tasks and activities that are developmentally inappropriate for them.

Competent Person

The 1960s ushered in a renewal of interest in very young children and how they learn. Many research studies have focused on the importance of the early years and challenged professionals and parents to reconsider the role early learning plays in lifelong learning. As a result of this renewed interest in the early years, parents placed great *intellectual* importance on early learning. This change in parental attitudes toward early learning resulted in the "concept of the competent infant." The image of the competent infant is promoted and reinforced by such social conditions as divorce, increasing numbers of single parents, and two-career families. For example:

> A competent infant can cope with the separation from parents at an early age. He or she is able to adjust with minimal difficulty to babysitters, day care centers, full-day nursery schools and so on. If some parents feel residual pangs of guilt about leaving their young offspring in out-of-home care, they can place their youngster in a high-pressure academic program. If the child were not in such a program, the parents tell themselves, he or she would fall behind peers and would not be able to compete academically when it is time to enter kindergarten. From this perspective, high pressure academic programs are for the young child's "own good."[8]

The view of the competent child is alive and well in the United States. Indeed, some parents believe that their children possess the competence and resiliency to deal with the problems associated with growing up along with divorce, poverty, and lack of health care.

Sinful Child

Based primarily on the religious belief in original sin, the view of the child as sinful was widely accepted in the fourteenth through eighteenth centuries, particularly in colonial North America during the Puritan era of the sixteenth and seventeenth centuries. Misbehavior was a sign of this inherent sin. Making children behave and using corporal punishment whenever necessary were emphasized. Misbehavior was taken as proof of the devil's influence, and beating the devil out of the child was an acceptable solution.

This view of inherent sinfulness persists, manifested in the belief that children need to be controlled through rigid supervision and insistence on unquestioning obedience to and respect for adults. Educational institutions are perceived as places in which children can be taught "right" behavior. The number of private and parochial or religious schools that emphasize respect, obedience, and correct behavior is growing because of parents' hopes of rearing children who are less susceptible to the temptation of crime, drugs, and declining moral values. Also, the Christian Right preaches a biblical approach to child rearing, encouraging parents to raise their children to obey them. Disobedience is viewed as sinful, and obedience is promoted, in part, through strict discipline.

Blank Tablet

The English philosopher John Locke (1632–1704) believed that children were born into the world as *tabula rasa,* or blank tablets. After extensive observations, Locke concluded, "There is not the least appearance of any settled ideas at all in them; especially of ideas answering the terms which make up those universal propositions that are esteemed innate principles."[9]

Locke believed that children's experiences, through sensory impressions, determined what they learned and consequently what they became. The blank tablet view presupposes no innate genetic code or inborn traits; that is, children are born with no predisposition toward any behavior except what is characteristic of human beings. The sum of what a child becomes depends on the nature and quality of experience; in other words, environment is the primary determinant of what a person becomes.

The blank tablet view has several implications for teaching and child rearing. If children are seen as empty vessels to be filled, the teacher's job is to fill them—to present knowledge without regard to needs, interests, or readiness for learning. What is important is that children learn what is taught. Children become what adults make of them.

This perspective of children de-emphasizes individual differences and assumes that as children are exposed to the same environmental influences, they will tend to behave and even think the same. This concept is the basis for many educational beliefs and practices in socialist countries. Children begin schooling early, often at six weeks of age, and are taught a standard curriculum that promotes a common political consciousness. They are expected to behave in ways that are consistent with and appropriate to how a citizen of the state should behave.

Growing Plant

A perennially popular view of children envisages them as growing plants, with the educator or parent acting as gardener. Classrooms and home are greenhouses in which children grow and mature in harmony with their natural growth patterns. A consequence of growth and maturing is that children *unfold,* much as a flower blooms under the proper conditions. In other words, what children are to become results from natural growth and a nurturing environment. Two key ingredients of this natural growth and unfolding are *play* and *readiness.* The content and process of learning are included in play, and materials and activities are designed to promote play.

Children become ready for learning through motivation and play. This concept prompts teaching subjects or skills when children reach the point at which they can benefit from appropriate instruction. Lack of readiness to learn indicates that the child has not sufficiently matured; the natural process of unfolding has not occurred.

Belief in the concept of unfolding is evident in certain social and educational policies, such as proposals to raise the age requirements for entry into kindergarten and first grade so that children have more time to mature and get ready for school. Many people also believe each child's maturation occurs in accordance with an innate timetable, that there is a "best time" for learning specific tasks. They feel it is important to allow time for children's inner tendencies to develop and that teachers and parents should not "force" learning. This maturation process is as important as, if not more so than, children's experiences. Many contemporary programs operate on the unfolding concept, whether or not it is explicitly stated.

Property

The view that children are property has persisted throughout history. Its foundation is that children are the property of their parents or institutions. This view is justified in part by the idea that, as creators of children, parents have a right to them and their labors. Children are, in a real sense, the property of their parents. Parents have broad authority and jurisdiction over their children. Interestingly, few laws interfere with the right of parents to control their children's lives, although this situation is changing somewhat as children are given more rights and the rights they have are protected.

Laws (although difficult to enforce) protect children from physical and emotional abuse. Where there are compulsory attendance laws, parents must send their children to school. Generally, however, parents have a free hand in dealing with their children. Legislatures and courts are reluctant to interfere in what is considered a sacrosanct parent-child relationship. Parents are generally free to exercise full authority over their children. Within certain broad limits, most parents feel their children are theirs to do with as they please. Parents who embrace this view see themselves as decision makers for their children and may place their own best interests above those of their children.

Investment in the Future

Closely associated with the notion of children as property is the view that children represent future wealth of potential for parents and a nation. Since medieval times, people have viewed child rearing as an investment in the future. Many parents assume (not always consciously) that when they are no longer able to work or must retire, their children will provide for them. Consequently, having children becomes a means to an end. Seeing that children are clothed and fed assures their future economic contribution to their parents.

This view of children as investments, particularly in their parents' future, is being dramatically played out in contemporary society. More middle-age adults are becoming parents to their aging and ill parents. This group, known as the "sandwich generation," is taking care of both their grandchildren, as a result of divorce, death, abandonment, and other circumstances, *and* their elderly parents. Many of these middle-age parents who thought they were investing in their future through their children may not have any investment at all.

Over the last several decades, several social policies in the United States have been based partly on the view that children are future investments for society in general. Many programs are built on the underlying assumption that preventing problems in childhood leads to more productive adulthood. An extension of this attitude is that preventing a problem is less expensive than curing one. Some local educational programs thus emphasize identifying the problems of children and their families early, to take preventive rather than remedial action. As professionals, we also know that besides being more expensive, remediation is not as effective as prevention.

Particularly during the 1960s, many federal programs were based on the idea of conserving one of the country's greatest resources—its children. Head Start, Follow Through, and child welfare programs are products of this view, which has resulted in a "human capital" or "investment" rationale for child care and other services.

The public believes a primary goal of education is to develop children who will be productive and help protect the nation against foreign competition. Therefore, the early education of young children in "good" programs is seen as one way to strengthen the United States economically. From this perspective, then, investing in children is seen as an investment in the country. Also, the view that children are our greatest wealth implies that we cannot and should not waste this potential.

Some believe, however, that this perspective of children as an investment in the future fails to consider children's intrinsic human worth. Trying to make a nation stronger through its children tends to emphasize national priorities over individuals. Also, solving a nation's "problems" is not and should not be viewed primarily as a "children's" problem.

Person with Rights

A contemporary legal and humanistic view recognizes children as individuals with rights of their own. While children are often still treated as economic commodities and individuals who need protection, their rights are beginning to be defined, promoted, and defended. Since children are not organized into political groups, others must act as their advocates. Courts and social service agencies are becoming particular defenders.

The National Education Association (NEA), the nation's largest teachers' professional organization, adopted this Bill of Rights for Children:

> We, the People of the United States, in order to achieve a more perfect society, fulfill our moral obligations, further our founding ideals and preserve the continued blessings of liberty, do hereby proclaim this Bill of Rights for Children.
>
> I.   No child in a land of abundance shall be wanting for plentiful and nutritional food.
>
> II. A society as advanced in medical knowledge and abilities as ours shall not deny medical attention to any child in need.
>
> III. Whereas security is an essential requirement for a child's healthy development, the basic security of a place to live shall be guaranteed to every child.
>
> IV. To ensure the potential of the individual and nation, every child at school shall have the right to a quality education.
>
> V.   The government, whose primary role is to protect and defend at all levels, shall assure that children are safeguarded from abuse, violence, and discrimination.

HOW ARE THE PUBLIC SCHOOLS INFLUENCING EARLY CHILDHOOD EDUCATION?

Traditionally, the majority of preschool programs were operated by private agencies or agencies supported wholly or in part by federal funds to help the poor, unemployed, working parents, and disadvantaged children. But times have changed. Many parents are exerting great pressure on public school officials and state legislatures to sponsor and fund additional preschool and early childhood programs. The public schools of many states are now providing some degree of funding for programs for three- and four-year-olds. Consequently, public school programs for these children are a growing reality.

Parents lobby for public support of early childhood education for a number of reasons. First, because working parents cannot find quality child care for their children, they believe the public schools hold the solution to child care needs. Second, the persistent belief that children are a nation's greatest wealth makes it seem sensible to provide services to young children to avoid future school and learning problems. Third, many people believe that early public schooling, especially for children from low-income families, is necessary if the United States is to promote equal opportunity for all. They argue that low-income children begin school already far behind their more fortunate middle-class counterparts, and the best way to keep them from falling hopelessly behind is for them to begin school earlier. Fourth, some parents cannot afford quality child care. They believe preschools, furnished at the public's expense, are a reasonable, cost-efficient way to meet child care needs. A fifth reason for the demand for public school involvement relates to the "competent child." Parents want academic programs for their children at an earlier age and look, naturally, to the public schools to provide programs that will help their children succeed in life. Sixth, today's parents are the best educated in U.S. history. These well-educated parents, many of whom hold high-paying jobs, are causing a boom in preschool programs that emphasize earlier and more comprehensive education for young children.

The alignment of the public schools with early childhood programs is becoming increasingly popular. Many public schools have already moved into the area of child care and preschool programs for three- and four-year-old children. Several arguments favor such an alignment. First, some professionals think it is not wise to train nonteachers for preschool positions when trained professionals are available. Second, some professionals think it makes sense to put responsibility for educating and caring for the nation's children under the sponsorship of one agency—the public schools. For their part, public school teachers and the unions that represent them are anxious to bring early childhood programs within the structure of the public school system.

HOW IS EARLY CHILDHOOD EDUCATION CHANGING?

From all that we have discussed in this chapter, the field of early childhood education appears in constant flux. It can truly be said about early childhood education that change, often dramatic change, is predictable. The changes in early childhood education that occurred within the past decade have resulted in some identifiable *paradigm shifts*. A *paradigm* is a model for how things occur or happen. The following are some of the critically important paradigm shifts occurring in early childhood education today, discussed earlier:

- *Family-centered programs.* Early childhood professionals are now working with families within the family system in order to provide the most meaningful education and services to children and their families.

- *Across-generation programs.* It is common now for early childhood professionals to work with children and families across generations. Early childhood professionals are helping children and their parents, and in many cases grandparents, develop literacy skills. Consequently, three-generation programs are becoming more commonplace.

- *Collaborative efforts with other agencies.* More and more early childhood professionals are working cooperatively and collaboratively with professionals from other agencies to combine resources and to work in an integrative manner.

NEW BEGINNINGS

New Beginnings is a collaborative effort involving San Diego, San Diego County, San Diego Schools, the San Diego Housing Commission, and the San Diego Community College District. These five public agencies, along with the University of California—San Diego and the Children's Hospital and Health Center, are engaged in a long-term effort of institutional change as well as providing school-linked direct services to children and families.

The New Beginnings concept of interagency collaboration began in 1988 in a series of conversations among executives from the major public agencies serving children and families in San Diego County. The executives agreed that children and families in poverty in their communities had urgent needs and that their agencies provided services to many of the same children and families. They were concerned that none of the agencies were able to focus effectively on preventing negative outcomes for children. From these initial conversations grew a commitment to refocus and restructure public services so that they would be more effective and accessible to families.

A needs study focused on the needs of families and children at Hamilton Elementary School, which serves nearly 1,300 children in grades K through 5 in a densely populated, ethnically diverse, low-income neighborhood of East San Diego. One aspect of the feasibility study placed a social worker from the Department of Social Services on the school site to work with families and children. Other components included interviews with families in their homes, meeting with families at the school, focus groups with line workers in each of the agencies, and a data match of clients served by multiple agencies. The information gathered was used to develop findings, conclusions, and a plan for implementation. A major conclusion of the study was that most of the constraints limiting integrated services are issues of policy or practice, not insurmountable legal obstacles.

New Beginnings is not a project or program to be taken as a package and implemented. Rather, it is a set of basic principles:

- Services and activities for families need to be focused on prevention.
- Services need to be for families as a whole, not fragmented by the presenting "problem" or a single "client."
- Services need to be responsive to the needs of families, not the convenience of agencies and their staff.
- Agencies need to reallocate and realign resources that already exist before looking for infusions of new money.
- Implementation of the collaborative process and the basic principles needs to be adapted to the needs of each community.

The first application of these concepts is at a demonstration site located on the campus of Hamilton Academic Achievement Academy. This is a multiservice center designed to provide easy, nonfragmented access to families in the school's attendance area. Services provided at the center, opened in September 1991, include information and referral, parenting and adult education classes, workshops, counseling, case management, family advocacy, and service planning. The center also provides basic health care, including immunizations, Child Health and Disability Prevention (CHDP) exams, and minor treatment, as well as mental health services for children. The staff at the center includes a coordinator, an administrative assistant, a secretary/receptionist, and three full-time and three part-time family service advocates. Coming from existing partner agencies to work in new roles, staff members form an interdisciplinary service team to help meet the many needs of families and children. Other members of the extended team remain in their home agencies but provide services specifically targeted to families in the Hamilton attendance area.

Contributed by Carrie Peery, principal, Hamilton Academic Achievement Academy—the site of New Beginnings, Integrated Services for Children and Families, San Diego, California.

- *An ecological/holistic approach.* Early childhood professionals now realize that they have to deliver a wide range of services to children and their families in family and community settings. They also recognize that today more than ever they have to provide for children's physical, social, and emotional needs as well as their cognitive needs.

- *Child-centered programs.* Increasingly, what early childhood professionals do in their programs focuses on the needs of children and their families rather than their own needs or those of their agencies. In addition, child-centered programs emphasize that children and their active involvement in learning is the preferred method of education and the process by which children learn best. Consequently, an emphasis is on involving children in their own learning, which enables them to develop their knowledge and intelligence. Today, the teaching-learning process centers on having children be active participants in their own learning and cognitive development as opposed to being passive recipients of knowledge through teacher-directed learning, worksheets, and the like. Active learning is in; passivity is out.

Evidence for the rebirth of child-centered approaches to early childhood education is also seen in such pedagogical practices as cooperative learning, having children make choices about what they will learn and how, and using activities and strategies to promote children's thinking. Other child-centered approaches very much in evidence are programs designed to promote children's self-esteem; multiage grouping; the practice of having professionals stay with the same group of children for more than one year; transition programs that help children move easily from program to program, grade to grade, and agency to agency; and concern for children's health, safety, and nutrition.

ACTIVITIES FOR REFLECTION AND RESEARCH

1. Tia attends a private preschool from 9:00 to 11:30 three days a week. There are eighteen children in the classroom, including Tia. There is a preschool teacher, an assistant teacher, and a facilitator who addresses tasks such as diapering, suctioning, and assisting Tia from one place to another. Currently Tia receives speech therapy for twenty minutes two times a week. The doctor has suggested Tia do breathing and speech exercises for twenty to thirty minutes every day. Tia receives occupational therapy two days a week for twenty minutes each. She also has a home health nurse visit for four hours on Thursdays.

The ECSE teacher visits and consults with the preschool teacher every Monday for one hour.

   - What kind of help might the preschool teacher require to meet Tia's needs?

2. Interview parents about how they view their children: as miniature adults, the competent child, the child as sinful, blank tablets, growing plants, property, investments in the future, or persons with rights. How do you think their view(s) influences their child-rearing patterns?

3. Contact agencies that provide services to single parents, teenage parents, and families in need. How do these programs influence early childhood education programs in your local community?

4. Interview single parents and ask what they think are the effects and influences of single parenting on children. In what ways is single parenting stressful to parents and children? How can early childhood programs support and help single parents?

5. The emphasis on early education has prompted some critics and experts to charge that parents and early childhood professionals are making children grow up too soon, too fast. Interview parents and preschool teachers to determine their views on this topic: Do you agree or disagree that society is making children grow up too soon too fast?

6. Casey is a 4 1/2 year old girl with Down syndrome. She wears glasses to correct severe strabismus, and is bilaterally hearing impaired. She is in the process of being fitted for hearing aids. Casey attends the school district's special education preschool in the morning and Bright Beginnings, a child care center located near several of the factories in town, in the afternoon. The center prides itself on its service to families. It provides flexible scheduling and twenty-four-hour service in an attempt to meet the needs of parents. Bright Beginnings has never served a child with disabilities before in its preschool, and while it has many questions, it is willing to try.

   • What are some things the Bright Beginnings staff will have to do to get ready for Casey?

7. Investigate the types of preschool programs available in your community. Who may attend them? How are they financed? What percentage of the children who attend have mothers working outside the home?

8. Over a period of several weeks or a month, collect articles from newspapers and magazines relating to infants, toddlers, and preschoolers, and categorize them by topic (child abuse, nutrition, etc.). What topics were given the most coverage? Why? What topics or trends are emerging in early education, according to this media coverage? Do you agree with everything you read? Can you find instances in which information or advice may be inaccurate, inappropriate, or contradictory?

9. Visit attorneys, legal aid societies, juvenile courts, and other agencies. List the legal rights children already have. Do you think children have some rights they should not have? Which ones? Why?

10. Visit corporations and businesses in your area, and determine what they are doing to support education and family programs.

READINGS FOR FURTHER ENRICHMENT

Chenoweth, K., ed. *Creating Schools for All Our Students: What 12 Schools Have to Say* (Reston, VA: Council for Exceptional Children, 1995).

> A report of the findings of a team of educators and parents brought together at the Working Forum on Inclusive Schools, a pioneering effort of ten major national educational organizations.

Darling-Hammond, Linda. *The Right to Learn: A Blueprint for Creating Schools That Work* (San Francisco: Jossey-Bass, 1997).

> In order to create schools that work, Darling-Hammond describes a need to raise professional standards for teachers, strategies for creating more resources for teachers and classrooms, and many other important issues concerning education today.

Morton-Young, T. *After-School and Parent Education Programs for At-Risk Youth and Their Families: A Guide to Organizing and Operating a Community-Based Center for Basic Educational Skills Reinforcement, Homework Assistance, Cultural Enrichment, and Parent Involvement Focus* (Springfield, IL: Charles C Thomas, 1996). 2 ed.

> A practical and useful guide for teachers and others as they consider ways to extend their involvement with families and their community.

Ravitch, D., and Viteritti, J. P. eds. *New Schools for a New Century: The Redesign of Urban Education* (New Haven, CT: Yale University Press, 1999).

Ten essays by distinguished scholars that examine educational issues and reform from many different perspectives. Included in the discussions are charter schools, contracting arrangements, and school choice.

Schlechty, Phillip C. *Inventing Better Schools: An Action Plan for Educational Reform* (San Francisco: Jossey-Bass, 1997).

The author calls for a radical rethinking of old rules, roles, and relationships in order to improve schools. Developing a mission statement, setting goals, assessing results, and creating the support for change are discussed.

RESEARCH ON THE INTERNET

Council for Exceptional Children

http://www.cec.sped.org/

Publishes extremely up-to-date news regarding education-related legislation and contains numerous links to other sites.

Frequently Asked Questions about Access to Technology for Students with Disabilities

http://www.resna.org/tap/aet_sfaq.htm

A list of numerous questions and detailed responses concerning technology and students with disabilities.

Information Resources for Human Communication Disorders

http://www.nih.gov/nidcd/director.htm

An extensive list of contacts related to specific communication disorders.

Individualized Education Plans

http://www.neat-schoolhouse.org/Library/ Special_Education/Individualized_Education_ Plans/Individualized_Education_Plans.html

Contains links to other online resources, as well as a list of papers and other materials available online.

Legal Issues Surrounding Disabilities

http://www.galaxy.com/galaxy/Law/Societal/ Disabilities.html

Articles and directories of information concerning legal issues related to disabilities.

Disability Net: Feedback

http://www.disabilitynet.co.uk/

An interactive forum where questions can be posted and others' questions and responses may be viewed.

DisABILITY: Consumer Law/Searchable Index

http://consumerlawpage.com/resource/ ability.shtml/

List of links to online resources and a searchable index. This site also offers the opportunity for users to submit links to be added to the directory.

NOTES

1.   S. Begley, "Your Child's Brain," *Newsweek,* 55–62, February 19, 1996.

2.   S. Begley, "How to Build a Baby's Brain," *Newsweek* (Special Ed.), 28–32, 1997. Special Issue Spring/Summer.

3.   U.S. Department of Education, *Individuals with Disabilities Education Act General Information,* 1997 [Online]. Available: http://www.ed.gov/offices/OSERS/IDEA/ overview.html.

4.   Ibid., p. 9.

5.   42 U.S.C. 12101, July 26, 1990.

6.   *United States Statutes at Large,* Col. 89 (Washington, DC: U.S. Government Printing Office, n.d.).

7.   U.S. Department of Education, Individuals with Disabilities Education Act Amendments of 1997, p. 30.

8.   David Elkind, "Formal Education and Early Education: An Essential Difference," *Phi Delta Kappan,* 67, 1986, p. 634.

9.   John Locke, *An Essay Concerning Human Understanding* (New York: Dover, 1959), pp. 92, 93.

CHAPTER

3

The Past: Prologue to the Present

The teacher is not in the school to impose certain ideas or to form certain habits in the child, but is there as a member of the community to select the influences which shall affect the child and to assist him in properly responding to these influences.

John Dewey

FOCUS QUESTIONS

1. Why is it important to know the ideas and theories of great educators?

2. What are the basic beliefs of Luther, Comenius, Locke, Rousseau, Pestalozzi, Owen, Froebel, Montessori, Dewey, Piaget, Vygotsky, Maslow, Erikson, and Gardner?

3. How have the beliefs and ideas of great educators influenced early childhood programs?

4. What are basic concepts that are essential to high-quality early childhood programs and education?

5. Why is it important to have an appreciation of great educators and their contributions to the field of early childhood education?

6. What events have significantly influenced the field of early childhood education?

7. How have people, agencies, and legislation influenced early childhood education?

WHY IS THE PAST IMPORTANT?

There are at least three reasons to know about the ideas and theories of great educators who have influenced the field of early childhood education.

- First, by reading of the hopes, ideas, and accomplishments of people our profession judges famous, we realize that today's ideas are not necessarily new. Old ideas and theories have a way of being reborn. Good ideas and practices persist over time and tend to be recycled through thought and practices in ten- to twenty-year periods. For example, many practices popular in the 1970s, such as family grouping, child-centered education, and active learning, are now popular again as the twenty-first century approaches.

- Second, many ideas of famous educators are still dreams, despite the advances we attribute to modern education. In this regard, we are the inheritors of a long line of great persons who dedicated their lives to education. We should acknowledge this inheritance and use it as a base to build meaningful teaching careers and lives for children and their families. We have an obligation to continue to build the dream.

- Third, ideas expressed by the early educators help us understand how to implement current teaching strategies, whatever they may be. For instance, Rousseau, Froebel, and Montessori all believed children should be taught with dignity and respect. This attitude toward children is essential to an understanding of good educational practice and often makes the difference between good and bad teaching.

HISTORICAL INFLUENCES

Martin Luther

While the primary impact of the Protestant Reformation was religious, other far-reaching effects were secular. Two of these were *universal education* and *literacy,* both topics very much in the forefront of educational practice today.

In Europe, the sixteenth century was a time of great social, religious, and economic upheaval, partly because of the Renaissance and partly because of the Reformation. Great emphasis was placed on formal schooling to teach children how to read, the impetus for which is generally attributed to Martin Luther (1483–1546) and the Reformation he spurred.

The question of what to teach is a question early childhood professionals wrestle with today. In the case of European education of that time, Luther emphasized the necessity of establishing schools to teach children to read. Simply stated, Luther replaced the authority of the hierarchy of the Catholic Church with the authority of the Bible. Believing that individuals were free to work out their own salvation through the Scriptures meant that people had to learn to read the Bible in their native tongue.

This concept marked the real beginning of teaching and learning in people's native language, or *vernacular,* as opposed to Latin, the official language of the Catholic Church. Before the Reformation, only the wealthy or those preparing for a religious vocation learned to read or write Latin. Luther translated the Bible into German. Other translations followed, finally making the Bible available to people in their own language. In this way, the Protestant Reformation encouraged and supported popular universal education.

Luther also argued for public support of education:

> Therefore it will be the duty of the mayors and council to exercise the greatest care over the young. For since the happiness, honor, and life of the city are committed to their hands, they would be held recreant before God and the world, if they did not, day and night, with all their power, seek its welfare and improvement. Now the welfare of a city does not consist alone in great treasures, firm walls, beautiful houses, and munitions of war; indeed, where all these are found, and reckless fools come into power, the city sustains the greatest injury. But the highest welfare, safety, and power of a city consists in able, learned, wise, upright, cultivated citizens, who can secure, preserve, and utilize every treasure and advantage.[1]

Out of the Reformation evolved other religious denominations, all interested in preserving the faith through education and schooling. Today, many churches and synagogues operate early childhood programs. A growing number of parents want an early childhood program that supports their values, beliefs, and culture.

John Amos Comenius

John Amos Comenius (1592–1670) spent his life serving as a bishop, teaching school, and writing textbooks. Of his many writings, those that have received the most attention are *The Great Didactic* and *Orbis Pictus* (*The World in Pictures*), considered the first picture book for children.

Comenius believed that humans are born in the image of God. Therefore, each individual has an obligation and duty to be educated to the fullest extent of one's abilities so as to fulfill this godlike image. Since so much depends on education, then, as far as Comenius was concerned, it should begin in the early years.

> It is the nature of everything that comes into being, that while tender it is easily bent and formed, but that, when it has grown hard, it is not easy to alter. Wax, when soft, can be easily fashioned and shaped; when hard it cracks readily. A young plant can be planted, transplanted, pruned, and bent this way or that. When it has become a tree these processes are impossible.[2]

Comenius also believed that education should follow the order of nature. Following this natural order implies a timetable for growth and learning, and early childhood professionals must observe this pattern to avoid forcing learning before children are ready. Comenius also thought that learning is best achieved when the senses are involved and that sensory education forms the basis for all learning:

> Everything should, as far as is possible, be placed before the senses. Everything visible should be brought before the organs of sight, everything audible before that of hearing. Odors should be placed before the sense of smell, and things that are testable and tangible before the sense of taste and of touch respectively. If an object can make an impression on several senses at once, it should be brought into contact with several.[3]

A broad view of Comenius's total concept of education is evident by examining some of his principles of teaching:

> Following in the footsteps of nature we find that the process of education will be easy
>
>   i. If it begins early, before the mind is corrupted.
>   ii. If the mind be duly prepared to receive it.
>   iii. If it proceeds from the general to the particular.
>   iv. And from what is easy to what is more difficult.

  v. If the pupil be not overburdened by too many subjects.

  vi. And if progress be slow in every case.

 vii. If the intellect be forced to nothing to which its natural bent does not incline it, in accordance with its age and with the right method.

 viii. If everything be taught through the medium of the senses.

  ix. And if the use of everything taught be continually kept in view.

  x. If everything be taught according to one and the same method.

These, I say, are the principles to be adopted if education is to be easy and pleasant.[4]

John Locke

John Locke (1632–1704) popularized the tabula rasa, or blank tablet, view of children. This and other of his beliefs still influence modern early childhood education and practice. Indeed, the extent of Locke's influence is probably unappreciated by many who daily implement practices based on his theories. More precisely, Locke developed the theory of and laid the foundation for *environmentalism*—the belief that it is the environment, not innate characteristics, that determines what children will become.

  Locke's assumption of human learning and nature was that there are no innate ideas. This belief gave rise to his theory of the mind as a blank tablet or "white paper." As Locke explains:

> Let us suppose the mind to be, as we say, white paper void of all characters, without ideas. How comes it to be furnished? Whence comes it by that vast store which the busy and boundless fancy of man has painted on it with an almost endless variety? Whence has it all the materials of reason and knowledge? To this I answer, in one word, from experience; in that all our knowledge is founded, and from that it ultimately derives itself.[5]

For Locke, then, environment forms the mind. The implications of this belief are clearly reflected in modern educational practice. The notion of the primacy of environmental influences is particularly evident in programs that encourage and promote early education as a means of overcoming or compensating for a poor or disadvantaged environment. Based partly on the idea that all children are born with the same general capacity for mental development and learning, these programs also assume that differences in learning, achievement, and behavior are attributable to environmental factors such as home and family conditions, socioeconomic context, early education, and experiences. Programs of early schooling, especially the current move for public schooling for three- and four-year-olds, work on the premise that disadvantaged children fail to have the experiences of their more advantaged counterparts. In fact, it is not uncommon to provide public funding for early schooling for those who are considered disadvantaged and to design such programs especially for them.

Because Locke believed that experiences determine the nature of the individual, sensory training became a prominent feature in the application of his theory to education. He and others who followed him believed that the best way to make children receptive to experiences was to train their senses. In this regard, Locke exerted considerable influence on others, particularly Maria Montessori, who developed her system of early education based on sensory training.

Jean-Jacques Rousseau

Jean-Jacques Rousseau (1712–1778) is best remembered by educators for his book *Émile,* in which he raises a hypothetical child from birth to adolescence. Rousseau's theories were radical for his time. The opening lines of *Émile* set the tone not only for Rousseau's educational views but for many of his political ideas as well: "God makes all things good; man meddles with them and they become evil."[6]

Rousseau advocated a return to nature and an approach to educating children called *naturalism.* To Rousseau, naturalism meant abandoning society's artificiality and pretentiousness. A naturalistic education permits growth without undue interference or restrictions.

Many contemporary practices stress naturalism in this approach regardless of whether practitioners are always aware of it. For example, family grouping seeks to create a more natural familylike atmosphere in schools and classrooms, literacy programs emphasize literature from the natural environment (e.g., using menus to show children how reading is important in their everyday lives), and conflict resolution programs teach children how to get along with others.

Rousseau believed, however, that although parents and others have control over education that comes from social and sensory experiences, they have no control over natural growth. In essence, this is the idea of *unfolding,* in which the nature of children—what they are to be—unfolds as a result of maturation according to their innate timetables. We should observe the child's growth and provide experiences at appropriate times. This idea is consistent with developmentally appropriate practice.

Johann Heinrich Pestalozzi

Johann Heinrich Pestalozzi (1746–1827) was greatly influenced by Rousseau and his *Émile.* In fact, Pestalozzi was so impressed by Rousseau's back-to-nature concepts that he purchased a farm and started a school called Neuhof. There Pestalozzi developed his ideas of the integration of home life, vocational education, and education for reading and writing.

Pestalozzi believed all education is based on sensory impressions and that, through the proper sensory experiences, children can achieve their natural potential. This belief led to "object lessons." As the name implies, Pestalozzi thought the best way to learn many concepts was through manipulatives, such as counting, measuring, feeling, and touching. Pestalozzi believed the best teachers were those who taught children, not subjects. He also believed in multiage grouping. Pestalozzi anticipated by about 175 years the many family-centered programs of today that help parents teach their young children in the home. He believed mothers could best teach their children and wrote two books, *How Gertrude Teaches Her Children* and *Book for Mothers,* detailing procedures to do this. He felt that "the time is drawing near when methods of teaching will be so simplified that each mother will be able not only to teach her children without help, but continue her own education at the same time."[7]

Robert Owen

Robert Owen (1771–1858) influenced education through his activities associated with New Lanark, Scotland, a model mill town he managed. Owen was an *environmentalist;* that is, he believed that the environment in which children are reared is the main factor contributing to their beliefs, behavior, and achievement. Consequently, he maintained that society and persons acting in the best interests of society can shape children's individual characters. Owen believed that by controlling the circumstances and consequent outcomes of child rearing, it was possible to build a new and perhaps more perfect society. Such a deterministic view of child rearing and education pushes free will to the background and makes environmental conditions the predominate force in directing and determining human behavior. This is how Owen explained it:

> Any character, from the best to the worst, from the most ignorant to the most enlightened may be given to any community, even to the world at large, by the application of proper means; which means are to a great extent at the command and under the control of those who have influence in the affairs of men.[8]

To implement his beliefs, Owen opened an infant school in 1816 at New Lanark, designed to provide care for about a hundred children aged eighteen months to ten years while their parents worked in his cotton mills. This led to the opening of the first infant school in London in 1818.[9]

Several things about Owen's efforts and accomplishments are noteworthy. First, his infant school preceded Froebel's kindergarten by about a quarter of a century. Second, Owen's ideas and practices influenced educators as to the importance of early education and the relationship between education and societal improvements, an idea much in vogue in current educational practice. In addition, early childhood professionals and other professionals today, not unlike during Owen's time, seek through education to reform society and provide a better world for all humankind.

Friedrich Wilhelm Froebel

Friedrich Wilhelm Froebel (1782–1852) developed a curriculum and methodology for educating young children. In the process, he earned the distinction as the "father of the kindergarten."

Froebel's primary contributions to educational thought and practice are in the areas of learning, curriculum, methodology, and teacher training. His concept of children and how they learn is based, in part, on the idea of unfolding, held by Comenius and Pestalozzi. The educator's role, whether parent or teacher, is to observe this natural unfolding and provide activities that will enable children to learn what they are ready to learn when they are ready to learn. The teacher's role is to help children develop their inherent qualities for learning. In this sense, the teacher is a designer of experiences and activities.

Consistent with his idea of unfolding, comparable to the process of a flower blooming from a bud, Froebel compared the child with a seed that is planted, germinates, brings forth a new shoot, and grows from a young, tender plant to a mature fruit-producing one. He likened the role of educator to that of gardener. In his kindergarten, or "garden of children," he envisioned children being educated in close harmony with their own nature and the nature of the universe. Children unfold their uniqueness in play, and it is in the area of unfolding and learning through play that Froebel made one of his greatest contributions to the early childhood curriculum.

Froebel believed and early childhood professionals believe today that play is a process through which children learn. Learning flows from play. These children are engaged in play that supports their growth and development. Froebel urged early childhood educators to support the idea that play is the cornerstone of children's learning.

All the great educators believed play is the basis for learning and incorporated play into their curriculum. When planning programs and activities, early childhood professionals should provide many opportunities for children to participate in play. What would you say to parents who asked you about the importance of play in their child's growth and development?

According to Froebel, the teacher is responsible for guidance and direction so children can become creative, contributing members of society. To achieve this end, Froebel developed a systematic, planned curriculum for the education of young children. Its bases were "gifts," "occupations," songs he composed, and educational games. Gifts were objects for children to handle and use in accordance with teachers' instructions, so they could learn shape, size, color, and concepts involved in counting, measuring, contrasting, and comparing. The first gift was a set of six balls of yarn, each a different color, with six lengths of yarn the same colors as the balls. Part of the purpose of this gift was to teach color recognition. The second gift was a cube, a cylinder, and a sphere.

Occupations were materials designed for developing various skills, primarily psychomotor, through activities such as sewing with a sewing board, drawing pictures by following the dots, modeling with clay, cutting, stringing beads, weaving, drawing, pasting, and folding paper. Many of the games or plays Froebel developed were based on his gifts.

Froebel is called the "father of the kindergarten" because he devoted his life to developing both a program for young children and a system of training for kindergarten teachers. Many of the concepts and activities of the gifts and occupations are similar to activities that many kindergarten and other early childhood programs provide.

Froebel's recognition of the importance of learning through play is reinforced by contemporary early childhood professionals who plan and structure their programs around play activities. Other features of Froebel's kindergarten that remain are the play circle, where children sit in a circle for learning, and the singing of songs to reinforce concepts taught with "gifts" and "occupations." Froebel was the first educator to develop a planned, systematic program for educating young children and the first to encourage young, unmarried women to become teachers.

Common Beliefs of Great Educators

All the educators discussed in this section held certain basic premises in common. First, they believed strongly in the important role of the family in educating children and laying the foundation for all future learning. Second, they believed in the importance of educating children early in life. Consequently, they advocated schooling either in the home or in a school setting. Third, they felt parents needed training and help to be good parents and their children's first teachers. They recognized that for education to begin early in life, it was imperative that parents have materials and training to do a good job (as we will discuss in Chapter 13). Educators and politicians are rediscovering how important parents are in the educational process. Parent involvement is being encouraged in public schools and other agencies, and we are learning what great educators have known all along: that parents are their children's first, and perhaps best, teachers.

MODERN INFLUENCES
Maria Montessori

If we were to single out one person to credit with a revival of early childhood education, it would be Maria Montessori. The Montessori method helped create and renew interest in early childhood education beginning about 1965. When parents and professionals were searching for exemplary early childhood programs, Montessori is one of the models they turned to. Maria Montessori (1870–1952) devoted her life to developing a system for educating young children that has influenced virtually all subsequent early childhood programs. The first woman in Italy to earn a medical degree, she was appointed assistant instructor in the psychiatric clinic of the University of

Rome. At that time, it was customary not to distinguish between the mentally retarded children and the insane, and her work brought her into contact with the mentally disabled children who had been committed to insane asylums. Although Montessori's first intention was to study children's diseases, she soon became interested in educational solutions for problems such as deafness, paralysis, and idiocy.

At that time she said, "I differed from my colleagues in that I instinctively felt that mental deficiency was more of an educational than medical problem."[10] Of her initial efforts at educating children, she said:

> I succeeded in teaching a number of the idiots from the asylums both to read and to write so well that I was able to present them at a public school for an examination together with normal children. And they passed the examination successfully.[11]

This was a remarkable achievement, which aroused interest in both Montessori and her methods. Montessori had the opportunity to perfect her methods and implement them with normal school-age children quite by chance. In 1906 she was invited by the director general of the Roman Association for Good Building to organize schools for young children of families who occupied the tenement houses constructed by the association. In the first school, named the *Casa dei Bambini,* or Children's House, she tested her ideas and gained insights into children and teaching that led to the perfection of her system.

John Dewey

John Dewey (1859–1952) represents a truly American influence on U.S. education. Dewey did more to alter and redirect the course of education in the United States than any other person.

Dewey's theory of schooling, usually called *progressivism,* emphasizes children and their interests rather than subject matter. From this child-centered emphasis comes the terms *child-centered curriculum* and *child-centered schools.* The progressive education philosophy also maintains that schools should be concerned with preparing children for the realities of today rather than some vague future time. As expressed by Dewey in *My Pedagogical Creed,* "education, therefore, is a process of living and not a preparation for future living."[12] Thus, out of daily life should come the activities in which children learn about life and the skills necessary for living.

What is included in Dewey's concept of children's interests? "Not some one thing," he explained. "It [interest] is a name for the fact that a course of action, an occupation, or pursuit absorbs the powers of an individual in a thorough-going way."[13] In a classroom based on Dewey's ideas, children are involved with physical activities, utilization of things, intellectual pursuits, and social interaction. Physical activities include running, jumping, and active involvement with materials. In this phase the child begins the process of education and develops other interest areas that form the basis for doing and learning. The growing child learns to use tools and materials to construct

Children are born to learn. Learning is not something children "get ready for" but is a continous process. What can professionals do to support children's learning? What factors do you think are critical to support children's readiness to learn?

things. Dewey felt that an ideal expression for this interest was daily living activities or occupations such as cooking and carpentry.

Although Dewey believed the curriculum should be built on the interests of children, he also felt it was the teacher's responsibility to plan for and capitalize on opportunities to integrate or weave traditional subject matter through and around the fabric of these interests. Dewey describes a school based on his ideas:

> All of the schools . . . as compared with traditional schools [exhibit] a common emphasis upon respect for individuality and for increased freedom; a common disposition to build upon the nature and experience of the boys and girls that come to them, instead of imposing from without external subject-matter standards. They all display a certain atmosphere of informality, because experience has proved that formalization is hostile to genuine mental activity and to sincere emotional expression and growth. Emphasis upon activity as distinct from passivity is one of the common factors.[14]

Teachers who integrate subjects, use thematic units, and encourage problem-solving activities and critical thinking are philosophically indebted to Dewey.

There has been much misinterpretation and criticism of the progressive movement and of Dewey's ideas, especially by those who favor a traditional approach that emphasizes the basic subjects and skills. Actually, Dewey was not opposed to teaching basic skills or topics. He did believe, however, that traditional educational strategies imposed knowledge on children, whereas their interests should be a springboard for involvement with skills and subject matter.

The accumulation and acquisition of information for purposes of reproduction in recitation and examination is made too much of. "Knowledge," in the sense of information, means the working capital, the indispensable resources of further inquiry; of finding out, or learning, more things. Frequently it is

---

PROGRAM IN ACTION

NEW CITY SCHOOL

You don't have to be in early childhood education very long to hear a teacher say, "That boy is just sooooo active." Indeed, this statement often has a "well, what can you do" tone to it. At New City School, an independent school in St. Louis with students 3 years old through 6th grade, both the tone and the words are different even though we certainly have lots of active boys. Our statement, "That's a very b-k kid," reflects our focus on Howard Gardner's Multiple Intelligences. We develop curriculum and look at children (and adults!) from the belief that there are at least 8 intelligences: Bodily-Kinesthetic, Spatial, Logical-Mathematical, Musical, Linguistic, Naturalistic, Intra-Personal and Inter-Personal. We believe children (and adults!) have strengths in all of these areas. We work to support children's growth in using their strengths and in understanding their particular strengths and those of others.

When New City teachers and administrators started working with Howard Gardner's Multiple Intelligences model about 10 years ago, we quickly agreed that our pre-school program had the fewest changes to make in

order to reflect the Multiple Intelligences. Indeed, pre-school programs in general with their use of centers and choice time have traditionally given children many opportunities to explore and create. Puzzle areas and art centers offer spatial choices; pretending provides many inter-personal options; games and manipulatives offer logical-mathematical, spatial and inter-personal choices; the list is long.

How then has our program changed? Two changes come quickly to mind. First, we now have a framework with which to plan centers and assessment. Our pre-school teachers use the Multiple Intelligences framework in planning centers and activities, checking themselves to make sure that children have opportunities to use and develop their various intelligences. Remember that b-k kid we talked about in the beginning? Rather than thinking about "containing him" with rules and time-outs, New City teachers plan centers making sure that there are bodily-kinesthetic activities available during choice time, not just at recess. Do we sud-

treated as an end itself, and then the goal becomes to heap it up and display it when called for. This static, cold-storage ideal of knowledge is inimical to educative development. It not only lets occasions for thinking go unused, but it swamps thinking. No one could construct a house on ground cluttered with miscellaneous junk. Pupils who have stored their "minds" with all kinds of material which they have never put to intellectual uses are sure to be hampered when they try to think. They have no practice in selecting what is appropriate, and no criterion to go by; everything is on the same dead static level.[15]

Dewey not only influenced educational thought and practice in the United States but also exerted a strong influence on the educational thought and practice of other countries that embrace his concept of incorporating work and education. The idea of "socially useful education" is still evident in contemporary China, Russia, and some Eastern European countries.

PROGRAM IN ACTION—continued

denly have an instant gym connected to our classroom? Definitely not! But, teachers now use adjacent halls and even classroom space for activities such as hopscotch, scooter boards, basketball, jumpropes and the like. Once children do activities, teachers provide parents and colleagues with assessment information using the Multiple Intelligence framework. Parents receive information about their children through multiple page progress reports and portfolio nights; here again, the Multiple Intelligences focus is used in showing the children's work and sharing their progress. So, the parents of that child with strong Bodily-Kinesthetic Intelligence learn that their child often chooses b-k related activities and that teachers use that bodily-kinesthetic strength in helping the child learn other things. Thus that child might practice counting while jumping rope or shooting baskets or learn letters by throwing bean bags at alphabet squares.

Secondly, we put a strong emphasis on the Personal Intelligences, Intra-Personal, knowing yourself, and Inter-Personal, knowing how to work and play with others. Believing strongly that these talents can be developed just as a musical or linguistic talent, New City teachers have developed activities and assessment techniques to support growth in the Personal Intelligences. In our 4/5s classrooms, for example, teachers regularly schedule "Buddy Days" during choice time. On a Buddy Day, children are paired up by the teachers and must then work together to choose activities for the morning. Teachers model, problem solve, comfort and support children as they learn to express their interests and accept the interests of their partners. Over the school year, these children learn to listen, negotiate, delay gratification and solve problems with a variety of peers. Parents recognize the importance we place on the Personals when they read our Progress Reports, where the first page is devoted entirely to the Personal Intelligences with assessment topics ranging from teamwork and appreciation for diversity to motivation and problem solving.

The Multiple Intelligences framework has allowed us to further develop an early childhood program where all of the Intelligences of the children are appreciated.

Contributed by Barbara James Thompson, New City School, St. Louis, Missouri.

Jean Piaget

Jean Piaget (1896–1980) studied in Paris, where he worked with Theodore Simon at the Alfred Binet laboratory, standardizing tests of reasoning for use with children. (Binet and Simon developed a scale for measuring intelligence.) This experience provided the foundation for Piaget's clinical method of interviewing, used in studying children's intellectual development. As Piaget recalls, "Thus I engaged my subjects in conversations patterned after psychiatric questioning, with the aim of discovering something about the reasoning process underlying their right, but especially their wrong, answers."[16] The emphasis on this method helps explain why some developers of a Piaget-based early childhood curriculum encourage the teacher's use of questioning procedures to promote thinking.

Following his work with children in Paris, which established the direction of his life work, Piaget became associated with the Institute J.J. Rousseau in Geneva and began studying intellectual development. Piaget's own three children played a major role in his studies, and many of his consequent insights about children's intellectual development are based on his observations and work with them. Using his own children in his studies caused some to criticize his findings. His theory, however, is based on not only his research but also literally hundreds of other studies involving thousands of children. We will discuss Piaget's theory in more detail in Chapter 4.

Lev Vygotsky

Lev Vygotsky (1896–1934), a contemporary of Piaget, increasingly inspires the practices of early childhood professionals. Vygotsky's theory of development is particularly useful in describing children's mental, language, and social development. His theory also has many implications for how children's play promotes language and social development.

Vygotsky believed that children's mental, language, and social development is supported and enhanced by others through social interaction. This view is opposite from the Piagetian perspective in which children are much more solitary developers of their own intelligence and language. For Vygotsky, development is supported by social interaction, and "learning awakens a variety of developmental processes that are able to operate only when the child is interacting with people in his environment and in collaboration with his peers. Once these processes are internalized, they become part of the child's independent developmental achievement."[17] Further, Vygotsky believed that beginning at birth, children seek out adults for social interaction, and development occurs through these interactions.

For early childhood professionals, one of Vygotsky's most important concepts is the *zone of proximal development,* which Vygotsky defines as

> that area of development into which a child can be led in the course of interaction with a more competent partner, either adult or peer. [It] is not some clear-cut space that exists independently of the process of joint activity itself. Rather, it is

the difference between what the child can accomplish independently and what he or she can achieve in conjunction with another, more competent person. The zone is thus created in the course of social interaction.[18]

Abraham Maslow

Abraham Maslow (1890–1970) developed a theory of motivation based on the satisfaction of needs. Maslow identified self-actualization or self-fulfillment as the highest need but maintained that self-actualization cannot be achieved until certain basic needs are met. These basic needs include life essentials, such as food, safety, and security; belongingness and love; achievement and prestige; and aesthetic needs.

Erik Erikson

Erik H. Erikson (1902–1994) developed an influential theory of psychosocial development. Cognitive development occurs hand in hand with social development; you cannot separate the two. This is why Erikson's theory is so important. According to Erikson, children's personalities and social skills grow and develop within the context of society and in response to society's demands, expectations, values, and social institutions, such as families, schools, and other programs, such as child care centers. Adults, especially parents and teachers, are principal components of these environments and therefore play a powerful role in helping or hindering children in their personality and cognitive development. For example, school-age children must deal with demands to learn new skills or risk a sense of incompetence—a crisis of "industry versus inferiority."

Howard Gardner

Howard Gardner (1943–) identifies eight intelligences: linguistic, musical, logical-mathematical, spatial, bodily-kinesthetic, interpersonal, intrapersonal, and naturalistic. This view of intelligence and its components has influenced and will undoubtedly continue to influence educational thought and practice. In Chapter 4 we discuss in greater detail Gardner's eight intelligences.

FROM LUTHER TO GARDNER: BASIC CONCEPTS ESSENTIAL TO GOOD EDUCATIONAL PRACTICES

As they relate to children

- Everyone needs to learn how to read and write.
- Children learn best when they use all their senses.
- All children are capable of being educated.

- All children should be educated to the fullest extent of their abilities.
- Education should begin early in life.
- Children should not be forced to learn but should be appropriately taught what they are ready to learn and should be prepared for the next stage of learning.
- Learning activities should be interesting and meaningful.
- Social interactions with teachers and peers are a necessary part of development.
- Children have multiple intelligences.

As they relate to teachers

- Teachers must show love and respect for all children.
- Teachers should be dedicated to the teaching profession.
- Good teaching is based on a theory, a philosophy, goals, and objectives.
- Children's learning is enhanced through the use of concrete materials.
- Teaching should move from the concrete to the abstract.
- Observation is a key means for determining children's needs.
- Teaching should be a planned, systematic process.
- Teaching should be child centered rather than adult or subject centered.
- Teaching should be based on children's interests.
- Teachers should collaborate with children as a means of promoting development.
- Teachers should diversify their approaches to teaching to account for children's multiple intelligences.
- Teachers should plan so they incorporate all eight intelligences in their planning and activities.

As they relate to parents

- The family is an important institution in children's education and development.
- Parents are their children's primary educators.
- Parents must guide and direct young children's learning.
- Parents should be involved in any educational program designed for their children.
- Everyone should have knowledge of and training for child rearing.
- Parents and other family members are collaborators in children's learning.
- Parents must encourage and support their children's many interests and their unique ways of learning.

HOW DOES THE RECENT PAST INFLUENCE EARLY CHILDHOOD EDUCATION?

As you prepare to consider how the recent past influences early childhood education, review the timeline of early childhood education in box 3.1. This timeline will put contemporary events into a historical context and will also help you understand that history is always in the making.

To fully understand the current basis for the public's interest in early childhood education and young children, we need to look back a half century to three significant events: (1) the general acceptance of claims that the public schools were not successfully teaching reading and related skills, (2) the growth of the civil rights movement and war on poverty, and (3) the launching of the satellite *Sputnik I* by the Soviet Union on October 4, 1957.

These events changed early childhood education in two important ways. First, in and of themselves, they influenced specific policies, programs, and legislation affecting young children and their families. Second, they affected people's attitudes toward and ways of thinking about what is best for young children.

How the United States educates its children and how well the schools fulfill their appointed tasks are always topics of national discussion and debate. Hardly a day passes that the schools are not criticized in some way. Schooling and public criticism go hand in hand.

During the 1950s, a host of articles and books detailed "why children cannot read," followed in 1955 by the publication of Rudolf Flesch's *Why Johnny Can't Read*. Flesch criticized the schools for the way reading was taught. His opinion of reading methods laid the groundwork for introducing the phonetic approach to reading, a system based on having children learn that letters represent sounds. As children learn such skills as initial consonant sounds, blends, digraphs (a pair of letters representing a specific speech sound), silent consonants, and medial and final consonants, they can "sound out" the majority of words they encounter. This phonetic method, championed by Jeanne Chall, replaced the "look-say" or "whole-word" method popular at the time. As you might expect, given the inevitable swing of the education pendulum, the phonetic approach is currently encountering criticism and challenges in the name of contemporary methods of teaching reading such as whole language and emerging literacy.

The Civil Rights Movement and War on Poverty

As a result of the 1960s civil rights movement, the rights of children and parents to public education were clarified and extended. Many of the new federal and state regulations and laws that affect children with disabilities, the disadvantaged, and abused children are essentially civil rights legislation rather than purely educational legislation.

BOX 3–1 TIME LINE: THE HISTORY OF EARLY CHILDHOOD EDUCATION

The following material summarizes key events cumulatively affecting early childhood education as we know it today.

1524   Martin Luther argued for public support of education for all children in his *Letter to the Mayors and Aldermen of All the Cities of Germany in Behalf of Christian Schools.*

1628   John Amos Comenius's *The Great Didactic* proclaimed the value of education for all children according to the laws of nature.

1762   Jean-Jacques Rousseau wrote *Émile,* explaining that education should take into account the child's natural growth and interests.

1780   Robert Raikes initiated the Sunday School movement in England to teach Bible study and religion to children.

1801   Johann Pestalozzi wrote *How Gertrude Teaches Her Children,* emphasizing home education and learning by discovery.

1816   Robert Owen set up a nursery school in Great Britain at the New Lanark Cotton Mills, believing that early education could counteract bad influences of the home.

1817   Thomas Gallaudet founded the first residential school for the deaf in Hartford, Connecticut.

1824   The American Sunday School Union was started with the purpose of initiating Sunday schools around the United States.

1836   William McGuffey began publishing the *Eclectic Reader* for elementary school children; his writing had a strong impact on moral and literary attitudes in the nineteenth century.

1837   Friedrich Froebel, known as the "father of the kindergarten," established the first kindergarten in Blankenburgh, Germany.

1837   Horace Mann began his job as secretary of the Massachusetts State Board of Education; he is often called the "father of the common schools" because of the role he played in helping set up the elementary school system in the United States.

1837   Édouard Seguin, influenced by Jean Itard, started the first school for the feebleminded in France.

1856   Mrs. Margaretha Schurz established the first kindergarten in the United States in Watertown, Wisconsin; the school was founded for children of German immigrants, and the program was conducted in German.

1860   Elizabeth Peabody opened a private kindergarten in Boston, Massachusetts, for English-speaking children.

1869   The first special education class for the deaf was founded in Boston.

1871   The first public kindergarten in North American was started in Ontario, Canada.

1873   Susan Blow opened the first public school kindergarten in the United States in St. Louis, Missouri, as a cooperative effort with William Harris, superintendent of schools.

1876   A model kindergarten was shown at the Philadelphia Centennial Exposition.

1880   First teacher-training program for teachers of kindergarten began in Oshkosh Normal School, Philadelphia.

1884   The American Association of Elementary, Kindergarten, and Nursery School Educators was founded to serve in a consulting capacity for other educators.

1892   The International Kindergarten Union (IKU) was founded.

1896   John Dewey started the Laboratory School at the University of Chicago, basing his program on child-centered learning with an emphasis on life experiences.

1905   Sigmund Freud wrote *Three Essays of the Theory of Sexuality,* emphasizing the value of a healthy emotional environment during childhood.

1907   Maria Montessori started her first preschool in Rome called Children's House; her now-famous teaching method was based on the theory that children learn best by themselves in a properly prepared environment.

1909 Theodore Roosevelt convened the first White House Conference on Children.

1911 Arnold Gesell, well known for his research on the importance of the preschool years, began child development study at Yale University.

1911 Margaret and Rachel McMillan founded an open-air nursery school in Great Britain, in which the class met outdoors and emphasis was on healthy living.

1912 Arnold and Beatrice Gesell wrote *The Normal Child and Primary Education.*

1915 Eva McLin started the first U.S. Montessori nursery school in New York City.

1915 The Child Education Foundation of New York City founded a nursery school using Montessori's principles.

1918 The first public nursery schools were started in Great Britain.

1919 Harriet Johnson started the Nursery School of the Bureau of Educational Experiments, later to become the Bank Street College of Education.

1921 Patty Smith Hill started a progressive, laboratory nursery school at Columbia Teachers College.

1921 A. S. Neill founded Summerhill, an experimental school based on the ideas of Rousseau and Dewey.

1922 With Edna Noble White as its first director, the Merrill-Palmer Institute Nursery School opened in Detroit, with the purpose of preparing women in proper child care; at this time, the Institute was known as the Merrill-Palmer School of Motherhood and Home Training.

1922 Abigail Eliot, influenced by the open-air school in Great Britain and basing her program on personal hygiene and proper behavior, started the Ruggles Street Nursery School in Boston.

1924 *Childhood Education,* the first professional journal in early childhood education, was published by the IKU.

1926 The National Committee on Nursery Schools was initiated by Patty Smith Hill at Columbia Teachers College; now called the National Association for the Education of Young Children, it provides guidance and consultant services for educators.

1926 The National Association of Nursery Education (NANE) was founded.

1930 The IKU changed its name to the Association for Childhood Education.

1933 The Work Projects Administration (WPA) provided money to start nursery schools so that unemployed teachers would have jobs.

1935 First toy-lending library, Toy Loan, was founded in Los Angeles.

1940 The Lanham Act provided funds for child care during World War II, mainly for day care centers for children whose mothers worked in the war effort.

1943 Kaiser Child Care Centers opened in Portland, Oregon, to provide twenty-four-hour child care for children of mothers working in war-related industries.

1944 The journal *Young Children* was first published by the NANE.

1946 Dr. Benjamin Spock wrote the *Common Sense Book of Baby and Child Care.*

1950 Erik Erikson published his writings on the "eight ages or stages" of personality growth and development and identified "tasks" for each stage of development; the information, known as "Personality in the Making," formed the basis for the 1950 White House Conference on Children and Youth.

1952 Jean Piaget's *The Origins of Intelligence in Children* was published in English translation.

1955 Rudolf Flesch's *Why Johnny Can't Read* criticized the schools for their methodology in teaching reading and other basic skills.

1957	The Soviet Union launched *Sputnik,* sparking renewed interest in other educational systems and marking the beginning of the "rediscovery" of early childhood education.
1958	The National Defense Education Act was passed to provide federal funds for improving education in the sciences, mathematics, and foreign languages.
1960	Katharine Whiteside Taylor founded the American Council of Parent Cooperatives for those interested in exchanging ideas in preschool education; it later became the Parent Cooperative Preschools International.
1960	The Day Care and Child Development Council of America was formed to publicize the need for quality services for children.
1964	At its Miami Beach conference, the NANE became the National Association for the Education of Young Children (NAEYC).
1964	The Economic Opportunity Act of 1964 was passed as the beginning of the war on poverty and the foundation for Head Start.
1965	The Elementary and Secondary Education Act was passed to provide federal money for programs for educationally deprived children.
1965	The Head Start program began with federal money allocated for preschool education; the early programs were known as child development centers.
1966	The Bureau of Education for the Handicapped was established.
1967	The Follow Through program was initiated to extend Head Start into the primary grades.
1968	B. F. Skinner wrote *The Technology of Teaching,* which outlines a programmed approach to learning.
1968	The federal government established the Handicapped Children's Early Education Program to fund model preschool programs for children with disabilities.
1970	The White House Conference on Children and Youth was held.
1971	The Stride Rite Corporation in Boston was the first to start a corporate-supported child care program.
1972	The National Home Start Program began for the purpose of involving parents in their children's education.
1975	Public Law 94-142, the Education for All Handicapped Children Act, was passed mandating a free and appropriate education for all children with disabilities and extending many rights to parents of such children.
1979	The International Year of the Child was sponsored by the United Nations and designated by Executive Order.
1980	The first American lekotek (toy-lending library) opened its doors in Evanston, Illinois.
1980	The White House Conference on Families was held.
1981	The Head Start Act of 1981 (Omnibus Budget Reconciliation Act of 1981, Public Law 97-35) was passed to extend Head Start and provide for effective delivery of comprehensive services to economically disadvantaged children and their families.
1981	The Education Consolidation and Improvement Act (ECIA) was passed, consolidating many federal support programs for education.
1981	Secretary of Education Terrell Bell announced the establishment of the National Commission on Excellence in Education.
1982	The Mississippi legislature established mandatory statewide public kindergartens.
1983	An Arkansas commission chaired by Hillary Clinton called for mandatory kindergarten and lower pupil-teacher ratios in the early grades.
1984	The High/Scope Educational Foundation released a study that it said documented the value of high-quality preschool programs for poor children. This study will

be cited repeatedly in coming years by those favoring expansion of Head Start and other early-years programs.

1985 Head Start celebrated its twentieth anniversary with a Joint Resolution of the Senate and House "reaffirming congressional support."

1986 The U.S. secretary of education proclaimed this the Year of the Elementary School, saying, "Let's do all we can this year to remind this nation that the time our children spend in elementary school is crucial to everything they will do for the rest of their lives."

1986 Public Law 99-457 (the Education of the Handicapped Act Amendments) established a national policy on early intervention that recognizes its benefits, provides assistance to states to build systems of service delivery, and recognizes the unique role of families in the development of their children with disabilities.

1987 Congress created the National Commission to Prevent Infant Mortality.

1988 Vermont announced plans to assess student performance on the basis of work portfolios as well as test scores.

1989 The United Nations Convention on the Rights of the Child was adopted by the UN General Assembly.

1990 The United Nations Convention on the Rights of the Child went into effect following its signing by twenty nations.

1990 Head Start celebrated its twenty-fifth anniversary.

1991 Education Alternatives, Inc., a for-profit firm, opened South Pointe Elementary School in Miami, Florida, the first public school in the nation to be run by a private company.

1991 The Carnegie Foundation issued "Ready to Learn," a plan to ensure children's readiness for school.

1994 The United Nations declared 1994 the Year of the Indigenous Child.

1995 Head Start Reauthorization established a new program, Early Head Start, for low-income pregnant women and families with infants and toddlers.

1999 As part of the effort to strengthen educational opportunities for America's 6 million students with disabilities, the Department of Education issued final regulations for implementing the individuals with Disabilities Education Act (IDEA) of 1997.

Included in this legislation, and undoubtedly the two most important for early childhood, are Public Law (PL) 94-142, the *Education for All Handicapped Children Act,* and PL 99-457, the *Education of the Handicapped Act Amendments,* both of which extend rights to educational and social services to special needs children and their parents and families. Both laws, with their tremendous educational implications, also broaden and extend civil rights. Consequently, children have been granted rights to a free, appropriate, individualized education, as well as humane treatment.

At the same time, the United States rediscovered the poor and recognized that not everyone enjoyed affluence. In 1964, Congress enacted the Economic Opportunity Act (EOA). The EOA was designed to wage a war on poverty on several fronts. Head Start, created by the EOA, attempted to break intergenerational cycles of poverty by providing education and social opportunities for preschool children of families living in poverty.

Head Start played as big a role, if not the biggest, as any other single force in interesting the nation in educating young children. Although programs for children had been sponsored by the federal government during the Great Depression and World War II, these were primarily designed to free mothers for jobs in defense plants. Head Start marked the first time that children and their families were the intended beneficiaries of the services.

Sputnik and the Research It Inspired

Spurred by the Soviet Union's launching of *Sputnik* in 1957, the U.S. government in 1958 passed the National Defense Education Act to meet national needs, particularly in the sciences. What made it possible for the Soviets to launch *Sputnik?* Examination of the Soviet educational system led to the conclusion that it provided educational opportunities at an earlier age than did the U.S. public schools. Some educators began to wonder if we too should not teach children at a younger age; a surge of interest in early education resulted.

At the same time that Soviet space achievements brought a reappraisal of our educational system, research studies were also influencing our ideas about how children learn, how they should be taught, and what they should learn. These studies led to a major shift in basic educational premises concerning what children can achieve. Research enabled early childhood professionals to arrive at these conclusions:

• The period of most rapid intellectual growth occurs before age eight. The extent to which children will become intelligent, based on those things by which we measure intelligence and school achievement, is determined long before many children enter school. The notion of promoting cognitive development implies that children benefit from home environments that are conducive to learning and early schoollike experiences, especially for children from environments that place them at risk of not developing their full potential.

• It is increasingly evident that children are not born with fixed intelligences. This outdated concept fails to do justice to people's tremendous capacity for learning and change. In addition, evidence supports developmental intelligence. The extent to which individual intelligence develops depends on many variables, such as experiences, child-rearing practices, economic factors, nutrition, and the quality of prenatal and postnatal environments. Inherited genetic characteristics set a broad framework within which intelligence will develop. Heredity sets the limits, while environment determines the extent to which individuals achieve these limits.

• Children reared in homes that are not intellectually stimulating may also lag intellectually behind their counterparts reared in more advantaged environments. Implications concerning the home environment are obvious. Experience shows that children who lack an environment that promotes learning opportunities may be at risk throughout life. On the other hand, homes that offer intellectual stimulation tend to produce children who do well in school.

ACTIVITIES FOR REFLECTION AND RESEARCH

1. Compare classrooms you attended as a child with early education classrooms you are now visiting. What are the major similarities and differences? How do you explain the differences?

2. Do you think most teachers are aware of the historic influences on their teaching? Why is it important for teachers to be aware of these influences?

3. Reflect on your experiences in elementary school. What experiences were most meaningful? Why? What teachers do you remember best? Why?

4. Interview the parents of children who attend a parochial school. Find out why they send their children to these schools. Do you agree or disagree with their reasons?

5. Reexamine Comenius's ten basic principles of teaching. Are they applicable today? Which do you agree with most and least?

6. Is it really necessary for children to learn through their senses? Why?

7. Why do society in general and education in particular not always follow the best educational practices advocated by many great educators?

8. List ways you have been or are being influenced by ideas and theories of the people and events discussed in this chapter. Do schools make a difference?

READINGS FOR FURTHER ENRICHMENT

Dewey, John. *Experience and Education* (New York: Collier, 1938; reprint, 1997).

Dewey's comparison of traditional and progressive education. Provides a good insight into what Dewey believed schools should be like.

Fogarty, R., Bellanca, J. *Multiple Intelligences: A Collection* (Boston, MA: Allyn and Bacon, 1998).

Contains research and writing about Howard Gardener's multiple intelligences theory. Students will find that the articles explore practical applications of the theory and provide supporting evidence that teaching to the multiple intelligences is effective with all learners.

Hymes, J. L., Jr. *Twenty Years in Review: A Look at 1971–1990* (Washington, DC: National Association for the Education of Young Children, 1991).

A treasure trove of detail about recent history in early childhood education. Each chapter chronicles a year's history.

Koetzsch, Ronald. *The Parents' Guide to Alternatives in Education* (Berkeley, CA: Shambhala Publications, 1997).

This in-depth guide investigates the alternatives to public school education and provides an overview of the development of education in North America. The author also surveys some current movements in education theory.

Monroe, Will S. *Comenius and the Beginnings of Educational Reform* (New Hampshire, Ayer Co. pub., 2000). 19th ed.

The author traces the reform movement in education before and up to Comenius, who was responsible for the movement's most significant contributions. He also discusses the life of Comenius and his educational writings.

Murphy, Daniel. *Comenius: A Critical Reassessment of His Life and Work* (Dublin: Irish Academic Press, 1995).

Murphy reexamines the principles of Comenius's pedagogic philosophy, giving particular attention to the learner-centered methods of teaching which constitute his main legacy to world education.

Winsor, Charlotte, ed. *Experimental Schools Revisited* (New York: Agathon, 1973).

A series of bulletins published by the Bureau of Educational Experiments, a group of professionals dedicated to the cooperative study of children, from 1917 to 1924. The book documents the roots of modern education and relates the first serious attempts to provide educational programs for toddlers and provide experiences based on children's maturational levels. Chapters dealing with play school and playthings demonstrate philosophical and methodological bases for learning through play.

RESEARCH ON THE INTERNET

Martin Luther

http://www.ic/net.org/pub/resources/text/wittenburg/wittenburg-luther.html

Links to many of Luther's writings online.

John Amos Comenius

http://www.moravian.org/lifemag.htm

Comenius was honored in *Life* magazine's 1997 "The Millennium" cover story under the event the editors deemed, "The Invention of Childhood."

John Locke

http://www2.msstate.edu/~src5/educator.html

A list of links to important works by Locke, including his personal epitaph, in which he states his philosophies of education.

Jean-Jacques Rousseau

http://www.infed.org/thinkers/et-rous.htm

Contains a brief statement by Rousseau on education, as well as a few links to other Rousseau sites.

Johann Heinrich Pestalozzi

http://www.infed.org/thinkers/et-pest.htm

From the same site as the above concerning Rousseau, a similar page about Pestalozzi.

Robert Owen

http://home.sprynet.com/sprynet/rlgreen/eps312r4.htm

A brief document describing the concept of universal education.

Friedrich Wilhelm Froebel

http://www.infed.org/thinkers/et-froeb.htm

Biography and bibliography of the father of the kindergarten.

Maria Montessori

http://www.3000.com/montessori_sf/index.htm

The web site of the Maria Montessori School and Teacher Training Center in San Francisco. This site contains brief descriptions of Montessori's ideas as they apply to various age groups.

John Dewey

http://www.siu.edu/~deweyctr/

The Center for Dewey Studies is housed at the University of Southern Illinois at Carbondale, and its web site offers online documents about Dewey, numerous links, and instructions for joining the John Dewey Internet mailing list.

Jean Piaget

http://www.piaget.org/

The Jean Piaget Society's web site is an excellent source of information regarding publications and conferences about the work and theories of Piaget.

Lev Vygotsky

http://www.bestpraceduc.org/people/LevVygotsky.html

An extensive bibliography of readings concerning Vygotsky.

Abraham Maslow

www.rebt.org/essays/achieve1.html

A detailed description of Maslow's concept of self-actualization.

Erik Erikson

http://idealist.com/children/cdw.html

This site contains a hypertext overview of Erikson's theories, as well as an overview of several education theories.

Howard Gardner

http://www.zephyrpress.com/gardner.htm

An April 1997 interview with Gardner, particularly regarding the eighth (naturalistic) intelligence.

NOTES

1. From F. V. N. Painter, *Luther on Education,* © 1928 Concordia Publishing House, pp. 180–81. Used by permission.

2. John Amos Comenius, *The Great Didactic of John Amos Comenius,* ed. and trans. M. W. Keating (New York: Russell & Russell, 1967), p. 58.

3. Ibid, pp. 184–185.

4. Ibid., p. 127.

5. John Locke, *An Essay Concerning Human Understanding,* ed. Peter H. Nidditch (Oxford: Oxford University Press, 1975), p. 104.

6. Jean-Jacques Rousseau, *Émile; Or, Education,* trans. Barbara Foxley (New York: Dutton, Everyman's Library, 1933), p. 5.

7. Ibid., p. 1691.

8. S. Bamford, *Passages in the Life of a Radical* (London: London Simpkin Marshall, 1844).

9. *The New Encyclopaedia Britannica in Thirty Volumes,* 15th ed. (Chicago: University of Chicago, 1978), vol. 14, p. 990.

10. Maria Montessori, *The Discovery of the Child,* trans. M. J. Costelloe (Notre Dame, IN: Fides, 1967), p. 22.

11. Maria Montessori, *The Montessori Method,* trans. Anne E. George (Cambridge, MA: Bentley, 1967), p. 38.

12. Reginald D. Archambault, ed., *John Dewey on Education—Selected Writings* (New York: Random House, 1964), p. 430.

13. Henry Suzzallo, ed., *John Dewey's Interest and Effort in Education* (Boston: Houghton Mifflin, 1913), p. 65.

14. Archambault, *John Dewey on Education,* pp. 170–171.

15. Reprinted with permission of Simon & Schuster from *Democracy and Education* by John Dewey. Copyright 1916 by Macmillan Publishing Company, renewed 1944 by John Dewey.

16. Edwin G. Boring et al., eds., *A History of Psychology in Autobiography* (Worcester, MA: Clark University Press, 1952; New York: Russell & Russell, 1968), vol. IV, p. 244.

17. L. S. Vygotsky, *Mind in Society* (Cambridge, MA: Harvard University Press, 1978), p. 90.

18. Jonathan R. H. Tudge, "Processes and Consequences of Peer Collaboration: A Vygotskian Analysis," *Child Development,* 63, 1992, p. 1365.

CHAPTER 4

Learning Theories: How Do Children Learn?

FOCUS QUESTIONS

1. What is learning, and how do theorists explain learning?
2. Why is it important for early childhood professionals to know how children learn?
3. How do learning theories influence how children learn?
4. How are learning theories similar and different?
5. Why is it important to know theories that explain how children learn?
6. What implications do learning theories have for early childhood professionals?

WHAT ARE LEARNING THEORIES?

Professionals use theories to explain how children learn. A *theory* consists of statements and assumptions about relationships, principles, and data designed to explain and predict children's learning. Theories are the raw material, the essential building blocks necessary for understanding how children learn and for making decisions about how to support and enhance that learning.

Learning: What Is It?

Learning means different things to different people. Think for a moment about how you would define learning and what learning means to you. For some, the ability to learn is a sign of intelligence. For others, it means the grades children bring home on their report cards. For many parents, learning is the answer to "What did you learn in school today?" For others, learning is reflected in the job someone has and how much money he or she earns.

However, for our purposes, none of these meanings or approximations will suffice. We will use a definition that professionals in the field agree on. *Learning* means "any relatively enduring change as a result of some experience."[1] Generally, when we talk about a change in children, we mean a change in behavior. This change or learning is determined in a number of ways: by observing what a child is doing, by noting how she is interacting with other children, by examining her results on an achievement test, or by reading his story of a visit to the zoo.

Indeed, the ways we can determine whether learning has occurred are numerous and a part of any discussion of early childhood programs. However, learning is the change that results from *experiences,* and the experiences that make up the curriculum are at the core of the learning process. How does this learning process occur? To help answer this question, we turn to experts who have spent their careers trying to answer this question.

Why Are Learning Theories Important?

Learning theories are important for several reasons. First, they help us think about how children learn. Second, they enable us to explain to others, especially parents, how learning occurs and what we can expect of children. Third, theories enable us to evaluate children's learning. Fourth, theories enable us to develop programs for children using the theoretical ideas as a foundation.

WHAT IS PIAGET'S THEORY?

Piaget's theory of intelligence is basically a logicomathematical theory; that is, intelligence is perceived as consisting primarily of logical and mathematical abilities. Compare this view with Vygotsky's view and Howard Gardner's theory of multiple intelligences presented later in the chapter.

Generally, the term *intelligence* suggests intelligence quotient or IQ—that which is measured on an intelligence test. This is not what Piaget meant by intelligence; rather, *intelligence* is the cognitive, or mental, process by which children acquire knowledge; hence, *intelligence* is "to know." It is synony-

Piaget's theory has many implications for how professionals interact with children and design learning experiences for them. Among the implications are that children think differently at different stages of cognitive development and that their thinking is not like adult thinking and should not be compared with it.

mous with *thinking* in that it involves the use of mental operations developed as a result of acting mentally and physically in and on the environment. Active involvement is basic to Piaget's cognitive theory; through direct experiences with the physical world, children develop intelligence. In addition, intelligence develops over time and children are *intrinsically* motivated to develop intelligence.

Piaget conceived of intelligence as having a biological basis; that is, all organisms, including humans, adapt to their environments. You are probably familiar with the process of physical adaptation, in which an individual, stimulated by environmental factors, reacts and adjusts to that environment; this adjustment results in physical changes. Piaget applied the concept of adaptation to the mental level, using it to explain how intellectual development occurs as a result of children's encounters with parents, teachers, siblings, peers, and the environment. The result is cognitive development.

Constructivism and Intellectual Development

Piaget's theory is a *constructivist* view of development. Children literally construct their knowledge of the world and level of cognitive functioning. "The more advanced forms of cognition are constructed anew by each individual through a process of 'self-directed' or 'self-regulated' activity."[2] The constructivist process

> is defined in terms of the individual's organizing, structuring and restructuring of experience—an ongoing lifelong process—in accordance with existing schemes of thought. In turn, these very schemes become modified and enriched in the course of interaction with the physical and social world.[3]

Children continuously organize, structure, and restructure experiences in relation to existing schemes of thought. Experiences provide a basis for constructing schemes. As a result, children literally build their own intelligence.

In explaining the role of constructivism, Constance Kamii, a leading Piaget scholar, states, "Constructivism refers to the fact that knowledge is built by an active child from the inside rather than being transmitted from the outside through the senses."[4]

Active Learning

Active learning as both a concept and process is an inherent part of constructivism. As a concept, *active learning* means that children develop—construct—knowledge through physical and mental activity. As a process, active learning means that children are actively involved with a variety of manipulative materials in problem-setting and problem-solving activities. The majority of early childhood professionals support active learning as the preferred practice in early childhood programs.

Intellectual Development and Adaptation

According to Piaget, the adaptive process at the intellectual level operates much the same as at the physical level. The newborn's intelligence is expressed through reflexive motor actions such as sucking, grasping, head turning, and swallowing. Through the process of adaptation to the environment via these reflexive actions, the young child's intelligence has its origin and is developed.[5]

Through this interaction with the environment resulting in adaptation, children organize sensations and experiences. The subsequent organization and processes of interaction are called *intelligence.* Obviously, therefore, the quality of the environment and the nature of children's experiences play a major role in the development of intelligence. For example, the child with various and differing objects available to grasp and suck, and many opportunities for this behavior, will develop differentiated sucking organizations (and therefore an intelligence) quite different from that of the child who has nothing to suck but a pacifier.

The Process of Adaptation

Piaget believed the adaptive process is composed of two interrelated processes, assimilation and accommodation. On the intellectual level, *assimilation* is the taking in of sensory data through experiences and impressions and incorporating them into knowledge of people and objects already created as a result of these experiences.[6]

Accommodation is the process by which individuals change their way of thinking, behaving, and believing to come into accord with reality. For example, a child who is familiar with cats because she has seen several at home may, upon seeing a dog for the first time, call it a cat. She has assimilated dog into her organization of cat. However, she must change (accommodate) her model of what constitutes "catness" to exclude dogs. She does this by starting to construct or build a scheme for dog and thus what "dogness" represents.[7]

The twin processes of assimilation and accommodation, viewed as an integrated, functioning whole, constitute *adaptation.*

Equilibrium is another process in Piaget's theory of intelligence. *Equilibrium* is a balance between assimilation and accommodation. Children cannot assimilate new data without to some degree changing their way of thinking or acting to fit those new data. People who always assimilate without much evidence of having changed are characterized as "flying in the face of reality." Yet individuals cannot always accommodate old ideas to all the information they receive. If this were the case, no beliefs would ever be maintained. A balance is needed between the two. Diagrammed, the process would look something like that in Figure 4–1.

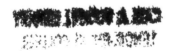

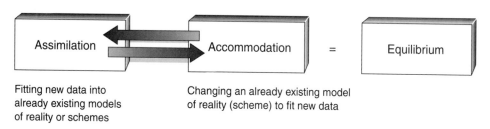

Fitting new data into
already existing models
of reality or schemes

Changing an already existing model
of reality (scheme) to fit new data

FIGURE 4–1
The Adaptation Process

Upon receiving new sensory and experiential data, children assimilate or fit these data into their already existing knowledge (scheme) of reality and the world. If the new data can be immediately assimilated, then equilibrium occurs. If unable to assimilate the data, children try to accommodate and change their way of thinking, acting, and perceiving to account for the new data and restore the equilibrium to the intellectual system. It may well be that a child can neither assimilate nor accommodate the new data; if so, he or she rejects the data entirely. Figure 4–2 and accompanying text illustrate the construction of a new concept.

Rejection of new information is common if what children are trying to assimilate and accommodate is radically different from their past data and experiences. This partially accounts for Piaget's insistence that new experiences must have some connection or relationship to previous experiences. Child care and classroom experiences should build on previous life and school experiences.

Schemes

Piaget used the term *scheme* to refer to units of knowledge that children develop through the adaptation process. (In reality, children develop many schemes.) Newborns have only reflexive actions. By using reflexive actions such as sucking and grasping, children begin to build their concept and understanding of the world.

When a child uses primarily reflexive actions to develop intellectually, he or she is in what Piaget called the *sensorimotor stage,* which begins at birth and usually ends between eighteen months and two years. Reflexive actions help children construct a mental scheme of what is suckable and what is not (what can fit into the mouth and what cannot) and what sensations (warm and cold) occur by sucking. Children also use the grasping reflex in much the same way to build schemes of what can and cannot be grasped.

FIGURE 4–2

All children have schemes consisting of thoughts and actions. This child has a scheme for identifying cats, which includes short ears and a fluffy tail. When he sees another animal, in this case a dog, that is similar to but different from his scheme for a cat, disequilibrium occurs, However, through the processes of assimilation and accommodation, he develops a new scheme for dog that is separate from cat.

Piaget believed that, developmentally, after children were capable of making one-to-one correspondence and classifying and ordering objects they were ready for higher level thinking activities such as those that involve numeration and time and spatial relationships. How do these activities contribute to children's intellectual development?

In the process of adaptation, Piaget ascribed primary importance to the child's physical activity. Physical activity leads to mental stimulus, which in turn leads to mental activity. Thus, it is not possible to draw a clear line between physical activity and mental activity in infancy and early childhood. Settings should provide for active learning by enabling children to explore and interact with people and objects. Early childhood professionals' understanding of this key concept helps explain their arranging infant and toddler settings so children can be active. It also helps explain the growth of programs that encourage and provide active learning for all children.

Everyone recognizes that children should play, but we have not always recognized the importance of play as the context in which children construct mental schemes to form a basis for all other schemes. Play, to Piaget, is a powerful process in intellectual development. Parents seem to sense this intuitively in wanting their children to play, particularly with other children. Many early childhood professionals have an understanding of the importance of play and include it in their curricula.

TABLE 4–1
Piaget's Stages of Cognitive Development

Stage	Characteristic
Sensorimotor (birth to 18 months/2 years)	Uses sensorimotor system of sucking, grasping, and gross-body activities to build schemes; begins to develop object permanency
Preoperational (2 to 7 years)	Dependent on concrete representations; uses the world of here and now as frame of reference; enjoys accelerated language development; internalizes events; is egocentric in thought and action; thinks everything has a reason or purpose; is perceptually bound; makes judgments primarily on basis of how things look
Concrete operations (7 to 12 years)	Is capable of reversal of thought process; able to conserve; still is dependent on how things look for decision making; becomes less egocentric; structures time and space; understands number; begins to think logically
Formal operations (12 to 15 years)	Is capable of dealing with verbal and hypothetical problems; can reason scientifically and logically; no longer is bound to the concrete; can think with symbols

Stages of Intellectual Development

Table 4–1 summarizes Piaget's developmental stages and provides examples of stage-related characteristics. Piaget contended that developmental stages are the same for all children, including the atypical child, and that all children progress through each stage in the same order. The ages are only approximate and should not be considered fixed. The sequence of growth through the developmental stages does not vary; the ages at which progression occurs do vary.

Sensorimotor Stage

During the period from birth to about two years, children use senses and motor reflexes to build knowledge of the world. They use their eyes to see, mouths to suck, and hands to grasp. Through these innate sensory and reflexive actions, they continue to develop an increasingly complex, unique, and individualized hierarchy of schemes. What children are to become physically and intellectually is related to these sensorimotor functions and interactions.

The sensorimotor period has these major characteristics:

- Dependency on and use of innate reflexive actions.
- Initial development of object permanency (the idea that objects can exist without being seen).
- Egocentricity, whereby children see themselves as the center of the world and believe events are caused by them.

- Dependence on concrete representations (things) rather than symbols (words, pictures) for information.
- By the end of the second year, children rely less on sensorimotor reflexive actions and begin to use symbols for things that are not present. (We will discuss intellectual development in infants, toddlers, preschoolers, and primary grade children in more detail in later chapters.)

Preoperational Stage

The *preoperational stage* begins at age two and ends at approximately seven years. Preoperational children are different from sensorimotor children in these ways:

- Language development begins to accelerate rapidly.
- There is less dependence on sensorimotor action.
- These children have an increased ability to internalize events and think by using representational symbols such as words in place of things.

Preoperational children continue to be egocentric, expressing ideas and basing perceptions mainly on how they perceive or see things. How things look to preoperational children is the foundation for several other stage-related characteristics. First, when children look at an object that has multiple characteristics, such as a long, round, yellow pencil, they will "see" whichever of those qualities first catches their eye. Preoperational children's knowledge is based mainly on what they are able to see, simply because they do not yet have operational intelligence or the ability to think using mental images.

Second, the absence of operations makes it impossible for preoperational children to *conserve,* or determine that the quantity of an object does not change simply because some transformation occurs in its physical appearance. For example, show preoperational children two identical rows of checkers (see Figure 4–3). Ask whether each row has the same number of checkers. The children should answer affirmatively. Next, space out the checkers in each row, and ask whether the two rows still have the same number of checkers. They may insist that more checkers are in one row "because it's longer." Children base their judgment on what they can see—namely, the spatial extension of one row beyond the other row. This example also illustrates that preoperational children are not able to *reverse* thought or action, which requires mentally putting the row back to its original length.

As preoperational children act as though everything has a reason or purpose, they believe everything happens for a specific purpose. This explains children's constant and recurring questions about why things happen and how things work.

Preoperational children also believe everyone thinks as they think and acts as they do for the same reasons. Preoperational children have a hard time putting themselves in another's place, and it is difficult for them to be sympathetic and empathetic.

FIGURE 4–3
The absence of operations in preoperational children makes it impossible for them to determine that the quantity of a group of objects does not change because some changes occur in how the objects look. Try this checker experiment with several children and see how they are thinking and making sense of their world based on how things look to them.

How preoperational children talk reflects their egocentrism. For example, in explaining about a dog that ran away, a child might say something like this: "And we couldn't find him . . . and my dad he looked . . . and we were glad." The child assumes you have the same point of view she does and know the whole story. The details are missing for you, not for the child. Young children's egocentrism also helps explain why they tend to talk at each other rather than with each other. This dialogue between two children playing at a day care center reveals egocentrism:

Jessica: My Mommy's going to take me shopping.
Mandy: I'm going to dress this doll.
Jessica: If I'm good I'm going to get an ice cream cone too.
Mandy: I'm going to put this dress on her.

The point is that egocentrism is a fact of cognitive development in the early childhood years. Our inability always to see clearly someone else's point of view is evidence that egocentrism in one form or another is part of the cognitive process across the life span.

Concrete Operations Stage

Piaget defined an *operation* as an action that can be carried out in thought as well as executed materially and that is mentally and physically reversible.

Children in the *concrete operations stage,* from about age seven to about age twelve, begin to use mental images and symbols during the thinking process and can reverse operations. Teachers can encourage the development of mental processes during this stage through the use of concrete or real objects when talking about and explaining concepts.

Keep in mind, however, that telling is not teaching. Professionals should structure learning settings so children have experiences at their level with real objects, things, and people. Teachers often provide activities that are too easy rather than too difficult. For example, instead of just giving the children a basket of beads to play with, ask them to sort the beads into a red group, a blue group, a yellow group, and a green group.

Concrete operational children begin to develop the ability to understand that change involving physical appearances does not necessarily change quality or quantity. They also begin to reverse thought processes, by going back over and "undoing" a mental action just accomplished. Other mental operations children are capable of during this stage are these:

- One-to-one correspondence
- Classification of objects, events, and time according to certain characteristics
- Classification involving multiple properties of objects
- Class inclusion operations
- Complementary classes

The concrete stage does not represent a period into which children suddenly emerge, after having been preoperational. The process of development from stage to stage is gradual and continual and occurs over a period of time as a result of maturation and experiences. No simple sets of exercises will cause children to move up the developmental ladder. Rather, on-going developmentally appropriate activities lead to conceptual understanding.

Formal Operations Stage

The second part of operational intelligence is *formal operations.* It begins at about twelve years of age and extends to about fifteen years. Children become capable of dealing with increasingly complex verbal and hypothetical problems and are less dependent on concrete objects to solve problems. Thinking ranges over a wide time span that includes past, present, and future. Children develop the ability to reason scientifically and logically, and they can think with all the processes and power of adults. How a child thinks is thus pretty well established by age fifteen, although adolescents do not stop developing new schemes.

Piaget came to these conclusions about early childhood education:

- Children play an active role in their own cognitive development.
- Mental and physical activity are important for cognitive development.
- Experiences constitute the raw materials necessary to develop mental structures.
- Children develop cognitively through interaction with and adaptation to the environment.
- Development is a continuous process.
- Development results from maturation and the *transactions* or interactions between children and the physical and social environments.

Early childhood professionals use these tenets to guide their planning and teaching.

WHAT IS THE BASIS OF THE MONTESSORI APPROACH?

The following principles form the basis for the Montessori theory of learning. They represent how Montessori ideas are translated into practice in many programs across the United States.

Respect for the Child

Respect for the child is the cornerstone on which all other Montessori principles rest. According to Montessori:

> As a rule, however, we do not respect children. We try to force them to follow us without regard to their special needs. We are overbearing with them, and above all, rude. Then we expect them to be submissive and well-behaved, knowing all the time how strong is their instinct of imitation and how touching their faith in and admiration of us. They will imitate us in any case. Let us treat them, therefore, with all the kindness which we would wish to help to develop in them. . . . Kindness consists in interpreting the wishes of others, in conforming one's self to them, and sacrificing, if need be, one's own desire.[8]

Educators and parents show respect for children in many ways. Helping children do things and learn for themselves, for example, encourages and promotes independence. At the same time, it also demonstrates a basic respect for their needs as individuals to be independent and self-regulating. When children have choices, they are able to develop the skills and abilities necessary for effective learning, autonomy, and positive self-esteem. These practices are so much more respectful of children than always doing for them or insisting that they do things as adults want them to.

> ### PROGRAM IN ACTION
>
> ## BILINGUAL MONTESSORI PRESCHOOL
>
> A unique integration of native language instruction, preschool education, and the Montessori method is taking place in more than twenty child development centers throughout California. Administered by the Foundation Center for Phenomenological Research in Sacramento, the centers serve nearly 1,900 Spanish-speaking children six weeks to six years of age.
>
> The Foundation Center provides a supportive learning environment for children through the Montessori method, home (i.e., native) language instruction, and multicultural environment. The staff relies exclusively on the child's primary language for instruction, interacting with the children only in Spanish throughout the day. Some children may respond occasionally in English, but staff members always use Spanish when communicating with the children.
>
> "If you respect a child's home language, the transition to the second language will happen miraculously," comments Antonia López, director of education and staff development for the Foundation Center. "A lot of people think that if a child learns to speak English sooner, they'll be better off. But they don't realize what you're doing is separating the child from its parents."
>
> All staff are recruited from the community the centers serve. After working as teaching assistants, they begin the process of being certified as Montessori teachers.

Children Are Children

Children are not adults. Children should be treated as children, and Montessori was firm in her belief that a child's life must be recognized as separate and distinct from that of adults. She believed adults restrict the education of young children when they impose their ideas and dreams on them, failing to distinguish between children's lives and their own.

The Absorbent Mind

Montessori believed children educate themselves. She said that children absorb knowledge directly from the environment. This is Montessori's concept of the absorbent mind.[9]

According to Montessori, there are unconscious and conscious stages in the development of the absorbent mind. From birth to three years, the *unconscious absorbent mind* develops the senses used for seeing, hearing, tasting, smelling, and touching. As a result, the child literally absorbs everything.

From three to six years, the *conscious absorbent mind* selects sensory impressions from the environment and further develops the senses. In this phase children are selective in that they refine what they know. For example, children in the unconscious stage merely see and absorb an array of colors without distinguishing among them; however, from three on, they develop the ability to distinguish, match, and grade colors. Montessori challenged teachers to think through the concept of the absorbent mind:

> How does a child, starting with nothing, orient himself in this complicated world? How does he come to distinguish things, by what marvelous means does he come to learn a language in all its minute details without a teacher but merely by living simply, joyfully, and without fatigue, whereas an adult is in constant need of assistance to orient himself in a new environment to learn a new language, which he finds tedious and which he will never master with the same perfection with which a child acquires his own mother tongue?[10]

Early childhood professionals in their work with young children are reemphasizing Montessori's and others' ideas that children are born able to learn and with an ongoing readiness and ability to learn.

Sensitive Periods

Montessori believed there are sensitive periods when children are more susceptible to certain behaviors and could learn specific skills more easily:

> A *sensitive period* refers to a special sensibility which a creature acquires in its infantile state, while it is still in a process of evolution. It is a transient disposition and limited to the acquisition of a particular trait. Once this trait or characteristic has been acquired, the special sensibility disappears. . . .
>
> A child learns to adjust himself and make acquisitions in his sensitive periods. These are like a beam that lights interiorly or a battery that furnishes energy. It is this sensibility which enables a child to come in contact with the external world in a particularly intense manner. At such a time everything is easy; all is life and enthusiasm. Every effort marks an increase in power. Only when the goal has been obtained does fatigue and the weight of indifference come on.
>
> When one of these psychic passions is exhausted, another area is enkindled. Childhood thus passes from conquest to conquest in a constant rhythm that constitutes its joy and happiness.[11]

The sensitive period for many learnings occurs early in life, during the time of rapid physical language and cognitive growth. At this time, parents and teachers must provide experiences necessary for optimum development. Through observation and practice, for example, Montessori was convinced the sensitive period for development of language was a year or two earlier than originally thought.

Once the sensitivity for learning a particular skill occurs, it does not arise again with the same intensity. For example, children will never learn languages as well as when the special sensitivity for language learning occurs. Montessori said, "The child grows up speaking his parent's tongue, yet to grownups the learning of a language is a very great intellectual achievement."[12]

Teachers must do three things: Recognize that there are sensitive periods, learn to detect them, and capitalize on them by providing the optimum learning setting to foster their development. Much of what early childhood professionals mean by *readiness* is contained in Montessori's concept of sensitive periods.

The Prepared Environment

Montessori believed children learn best in a prepared environment, which can be any setting—a classroom, room at home, nursery, or playground. The purpose of the prepared environment is to make children independent of adults. It is a place in which children can *do things for themselves.* The ideal classrooms Montessori described are really what educators advocate when they talk about child-centered education and active learning. In many respects, Montessori was the precursor of many practices in use today.

Following their introduction to the prepared environment, children can come and go according to their desires and needs, deciding for themselves which materials to work with. Montessori removed the typical school desks from the classroom and replaced them with tables and chairs at which children could work individually or in small groups. In a modern Montessori classroom, much of a child's work is done on the floor. Montessori saw no reason for a teacher's desk, since the teacher should be involved with the children where they are doing their work. She also introduced child-sized furniture, lower chalkboards, and outside areas in which children could take part, at will, in gardening and other outdoor activities.

Montessori's concept of a classroom was a place in which children could do things for themselves, play with material placed there for specific purposes, and *educate themselves.* She developed a classroom free of many of the inhibiting elements in some of today's classrooms. Freedom is an essential characteristic of the prepared environment. Since children are free, within the environment, to explore materials of their own choosing, they absorb what they find there.

Self-Education or Autoeducation

Montessori referred to *autoeducation* as the concept that children are capable of educating themselves. When children are actively involved in a prepared environment and exercising freedom of choice, they literally educate themselves.[13]

Our universal perception of the teaching-learning act is that the teachers teach and children learn, a view that overlooks that everyone learns a great deal through one's own efforts. Through the principle of autoeducation, Montessori focuses our attention on this human capability. The art of teaching includes preparing the environment so that children, by being actively involved in it, educate themselves. Think of the things you learned by yourself and the circumstances under which you learned them. Your reflections will remind you of the self-satisfaction that accompanies self-learning and the power it has to generate further involvement. This concept is fundamental to all quality early childhood programs.

WHAT IS VYGOTSKY'S THEORY?

Lev Vygotsky (1896–1934) believed that children's cognitive, language, and social development results from their social and cultural environments. This theory is a *social-cultural* view and is opposite from the Piagetian perspective in which children are much more solitary developers of their own intelligence and language. Further, Vygotsky believed that beginning at birth, children seek out adults for social interaction, and development occurs through these interactions. For Vygotsky, development is supported by social interaction, and

> learning awakens a variety of developmental processes that are able to operate only when the child is interacting with people in his environment and in collaboration with his peers. Once these processes are internalized, they become part of the children's independent developmental achievement.[14]

Further, Vygotsky believed that beginning at birth, children seek out adults for social interaction, and development occurs through these interactions.

For early childhood professionals, one of Vygotsky's most important concepts is the *zone of proximal development.* Vygotsky defined this zone as

> that area of development into which a child can be led in the course of interaction with a more competent partner, either adult or peer. . . .[It] is not some clear-cut space that exists independently of the process of joint activity itself. Rather, it is the difference between what the child can accomplish independently and what he or she can achieve in conjunction with another, more competent person. The zone is thus *created* in the course of social interaction.[15]

From Vygotsky's point of view:

> Learning is not development; however, properly organized learning results in mental development and sets in motion a variety of developmental processes that would be impossible apart from learning. Thus, learning is a necessary part and universal aspect of the process of developing culturally organized, specifically human, psychological functions.[16]

For Vygotsky, learning is directly related to the course of child development. *Intersubjectivity* is a second Vygotsky concept. Intersubjectivity is based on the idea that

> individuals come to a task, problem, or conversation with their own subjective ways of making sense of it. If they then discuss their differing viewpoints, shared understanding may be attained. . . . In other words, in the course of communication participants may arrive at some mutually agreed-upon, or intersubjective, understanding.[17]

Communication or dialogue between teacher and child literally becomes a means for helping children "scaffold," that is, develop new concepts and think their way to higher-level concepts.

This intersubjectivity is similar to Piaget's theory that disequilibrium sets the stage for assimilation and accommodation, and, consequently, new schemes develop. Furthermore, Vygotsky believed that as a result of teacher-child collaboration, the child uses concepts learned in the collaborative process to solve problems when the teacher is not present. As Vygotsky said, the child

> continues to act in collaboration even though the teacher is not standing near him. . . . This help—this aspect of collaboration—is invisibly present. It is continued in what looks from the outside like the child's independent solution of the problem.[18]

According to Vygotsky, social interactions and collaboration are essential ingredients in the processes of learning and development.

Many current practices such as cooperative learning, joint problem solving, coaching, collaboration, mentoring, and other forms of assisted learning are consistent with Vygotsky's theory of development.

Research shows that higher achievement results when children are engaged in cooperative learning tasks. Also, cooperative learning results in helping children see the world from other people's point of view. What are ways that you can include cooperative learning in your classroom practices?

FIGURE 4–4
The Intelligences, in Gardner's Words

• Linguistic intelligence is the capacity to use language, your native language, and perhaps other languages, to express what's on your mind and to understand other people. Poets really specialize in linguistic intelligence, but any kind of writer, orator, speaker, lawyer, or a person for whom language is an important stock in trade highlights linguistic intelligence.

• People with a highly developed logical-mathematical intelligence understand the underlying principles of some kind of a causal system, the way a scientist or logician does; or can manipulate numbers, quantities, and operations, the way a mathematician does.

• Spatial intelligence refers to the ability to represent the spatial world internally in your mind—the way a sailor or airplane pilot navigates the large spatial world, or the way a chess player or sculptor represents a more circumscribed spatial world. Spatial intelligence can be used in the arts or in the sciences. If you are spatially intelligent and oriented toward the arts, you are more likely to become a painter or a sculptor or an architect than, say, a musician or a writer. Similarly, certain sciences like anatomy or topology emphasize spatial intelligence.

• Bodily kinesthetic intelligence is the capacity to use your whole body or parts of your body—your hands, your fingers, your arms—to solve a problem, make something, or put on some kind of a production. The most evident examples are people in athletics or the performing arts, particularly dance or acting.

• Musical intelligence is the capacity to think in music, to be able to hear patterns, recognize them, remember them, and perhaps manipulate them. People who have a strong musical intelligence don't just remember music easily—they can't get it out of their minds, it's so omnipresent. Now, some people will say, "Yes, music is important, but it's a talent, not an intelligence." And I say, "Fine, let's call it a talent." But, then we have to leave the word *intelligent* out of *all* discussions of human abilities. You know, Mozart was damned smart!

• Interpersonal intelligence is understanding other people. It's an ability we all need, but is at a premium if you are a teacher, clinician, salesperson, or politician. Anybody who deals with other people has to be skilled in the interpersonal sphere.

• Intrapersonal intelligence refers to having an understanding of yourself, of knowing who you are, what you can do, what you want to do, how you react to things, which things to avoid, and which things to gravitate toward. We are drawn to people who have a good understanding of themselves because those people tend not to screw up. They tend to know what they can do. They tend to know what they can't do. And they tend to know where to go if they need help.

• Naturalist intelligence designates the human ability to discriminate among living things (plants, animals) as well as sensitivity to other features of the natural world (clouds, rock configurations). This ability was clearly of value in our evolutionary past as hunters, gatherers, and farmers; it continues to be central in such roles as botanist or chef. I also speculate that much of our consumer society exploits the naturalist intelligences, which can be mobilized in the discrimination among cars, sneakers, kinds of makeup, and the like. The kind of pattern recognition valued in certain of the sciences may also draw upon naturalist intelligence.

Source: "The First Seven . . . and the Eighth: An Interview with Howard Gardner," *Educational Leadership* (September 1997), p. 12.

WHAT IS THE THEORY OF MULTIPLE INTELLIGENCES?

Howard Gardner (1943–   ) has developed a theory of *multiple intelligences* (MI).

According to Piaget, mature biological thinking, or intelligence, consists of mainly logical-mathematical activities, such as classification, seriation, numeration, time, and spatial relations. This view of intelligence as a single set of mental skills, measurable by an intelligence test, is the way intelligence is generally conceived by educators and the public. Gardner, on the other hand, maintains:

> [A] human intellectual competence must entail a set of skills of problem solving—enabling the individual to *resolve genuine problems or difficulties* that he or she encounters and, when appropriate, to create an effective product—and must also entail the potential for *finding or creating problems* thereby laying the groundwork for the acquisition of new knowledge.[19]

Consequently, Gardner and MI theory postulate that instead of one intelligence, children have eight intelligences. They are explained in Gardner's words in Figure 4–4.

The educational implications of MI are tremendous. While all children will demonstrate intelligence in all eight, some will be better in some intelligences than others. This accounts for why children have a preferred learning style, different interests, different likes and dislikes, different habits, a preferred lifestyle, and different career choices. Teachers will have to support and teach to the intelligences of each child. Thus individual differences play a great role in MI theory.

Consequently, early childhood professionals should make efforts to accommodate their teaching styles, activities, and materials to children's learning styles. Table 4–2 will help you make this connection using Gardner's theory.

WHAT IS BEHAVIORISM?

Behaviorism plays down the roles of biology, maturation, and time in learning. Instead, behaviorists stress the role of the environment and the opportunity to learn. Behaviorists see development as a continuous set of changing behaviors governed by the principles of learning rather than as a series of age-bound behaviors. Age and stage descriptions of development are irrelevant because development results from children's interactions with the environment and the reward system of the environment. Change in behavior is a function of what the child learns in the environment.

Behaviorist Principles

Behaviorists believe the following principles govern how children learn:

1. The environment is everything. Experiences are a product of a child's interaction with the environment. Behaviorists also believe in controlling the order to shape behavior.

TABLE 4–2
Eight Styles of Learning

Type	Likes To	Is Good At	Learns Best By
Linguistic Learner *"The Word Player"*	read write tell stories	memorizing names, places, dates and trivia	saying, hearing and seeing words
Logical/Mathematical Learner *"The Questioner"*	do experiments figure things out work with numbers ask questions explore patterns and relationships	math reasoning logic problem solving	categorizing classifying working with abstract patterns/relationships
Spatial Learner *"The Visualizer"*	draw, build, design, and create things daydream look at pictures/slides watch movies play with machines	imagining things sensing changes mazes/puzzles reading maps, charts	visualizing dreaming using the mind's eye working with colors/pictures
Musical Learner *"The Music Lover"*	sing, hum tunes listen to music play an instrument respond to music	picking up sounds remembering melodies noticing pitches/rhythms keeping time	rhythm melody music
Bodily/Kinesthetic Learner *"The Mover"*	move around touch and talk use body language	physical activities (sports/dance/acting) crafts	touching moving interacting with space processing knowledge through bodily sensations
Interpersonal Learner *"The Socializer"*	have lots of friends talk to people join groups	understanding people leading others organizing communicating manipulating mediating conflicts	sharing comparing relating cooperating interviewing
Intrapersonal Learner *"The Individual"*	work alone pursue own interests	understanding self focusing inward on feelings/dreams following instincts pursuing interests/goals being original	working alone individualized projects self-paced instruction having own space
Naturalist *"The Investigator"*	investigate discover how things work make comparisons	identifying animals and plants collecting insects, etc. playing with and showing interest in dinosaurs	investigating doing project work, field, outside activities

Source: Chart from "Different Child, Different Style" by Kathy Faggella and Janet Horowitz in *Instructor,* September 1990, p. 52. Copyright © 1990 by Scholastic. Reprinted by permission. Naturalist addition by author.

2.   What children do is important, not what they think. Actions speak louder than words.

3.   Learning is gradual and continuous, not stage related. Development is an incremental sequence of specific conditioned behaviors.

4.   Behaviorist principles of learning are true for people of all ages, across the life span from birth to death.

Ivan Pavlov (1849–1936) was interested in how biological events such as digestion systematically relate to changes in the environment. The application of this interest to learning was truly revolutionary. Pavlov knew that a hungry dog salivates when presented with meat. The meat is the *unconditioned stimulus,* and the salivation is the *unconditioned response.* Pavlov conditioned, or trained, a dog's salivary response by providing meat simultaneously with the ringing of a bell. After several repetitions, Pavlov could merely ring a bell and the dog would salivate. The bell became a *conditioned stimulus* because it took the place of food, an unconditioned stimulus. Salivating became a *conditioned response,* because when the dog heard the bell—the conditioned stimulus—it salivated.

J. B. Watson (1878–1958) is considered the founder of behaviorism. He examined behavior and saw it to be a system of stimulus-response associations. Behaviorism views development as the culmination of an individual's learning experiences. Without learning experiences, there is no development, only physical growth.

Watson maintained that he could take any normal child and raise him to be just about any person he chose.

> Give me a dozen healthy infants, well-formed, and my own specified world to bring them up in and I'll guarantee to take any one at random and train him to become any type of specialist I might select—doctor, lawyer, artist, merchant-chief and, yes, even beggarman and thief, regardless of his talents, penchants, tendencies, abilities, vocations, and race of his ancestors.[20]

B. F. Skinner (1904–1990) did more than any other individual to spread the behaviorist theory through words and accomplishments. One of Skinner's major contributions is a detailed explanation of the process of *operant conditioning,* which describes the process of learning that occurs when responses are followed by reinforcers. The term *operant* means that children (individuals) operate or act in and on the environment. As a result of this operation of interaction, certain behaviors are reinforced, and learning results. Whereas Pavlov *created* a new stimulus-response relation, in operant conditioning, an *already existing* response is strengthened or weakened. A child must emit a response *before* the response is conditioned.

For example, Amanda would like her eighteen-month-old son, Matt, to learn names for things. She shows him many toys while saying their names. One day, much to Amanda's delight, Matt says, "Ball." She profusely praises Matt: "Great, fantastic, good for you, Matt! You know the name for 'ball.' "

Consequently, when Matt plays with his toy and touches, picks up, or otherwise interacts with a ball and says, "Ball," Amanda praises him. Through such operant conditioning (the operant response, "ball," is followed by a reinforcer, praise), Matt learns the name for "ball." It is in precisely this manner that behaviorists believe Matt will learn not only language but other behavior as well. Life is full of other such examples.

Social Learning Theory

Albert Bandura (1925–   ) describes *social learning theory* as "the explanation of human behavior in terms of a continuous reciprocal interaction between cognitive, behavioral, and environmental determinants."[21] Bandura believes that such a conception of behavior "neither casts people into the role of powerless objects by environmental forces nor free agents who can become whatever they choose. Both people and their environments are reciprocal determinants of each other."[22] Bandura believes children play a major role in the development of their behaviors. He and other learning theorists believe learning occurs primarily through modeling, observation, vicarious experiences, and self-regulation.

Self-regulation occurs when a child initiates new behavior or modifies existing behavior as a result of wanting to change based on things she has observed or read. Learning also occurs through reading and talking with others about experiences they have had. While a child cannot learn to ride a bicycle by reading about it, she can through reading be motivated to do so.

Observation plays a powerful role in learning. Children literally observe others to learn how to act. As children see, they do. This observation can be firsthand, e.g., observing parents, siblings, other family members, and teachers. And the observation can occur electronically via movies, videos, video games, and the Internet. This is why parents and others must monitor what children view.

Basically four processes are involved in modeling: (1) paying attention to people, (2) selecting behaviors to reproduce, (3) remembering the observed behavior, and (4) reproducing what was observed. Attention to people is based on their engaging qualities, their particular behaviors, and a child's frame of reference. Selecting what behaviors to reproduce is largely a matter of what the child values or what he sees others whom he admires valuing. Those behaviors that bring pleasure will more likely be modeled; whereas if a child sees a peer being punished for a particular behavior, he is less likely to model that behavior. Retention occurs through recalling the observed, because obviously if a child does not remember a behavior, he cannot be much influenced by it. Reproduction is more than a process of "monkey see, monkey do." Replication occurs best when a child has the requisite skills to perform the behavior and an opportunity to practice.

Learning theories play important roles in early childhood practice. As an early childhood professional, you will want to be knowledgeable with all the theories so that you can apply them to your teaching with young children.

ACTIVITIES FOR REFLECTION AND RESEARCH

1. Visit a Montessori classroom and compare the classroom arrangement and materials to those of the pre-school and kindergarten programs you attended. What are the similarities and differences?

2. What features of the Montessori program do you like best? Why? What features do you like least? Why? What features are best for children?

3. Interview Montessori teachers about their program. What do they believe are the basic features and strengths of the Montessori program?

4. Behavior modification and reinforcement techniques are very popular with teachers, caregivers, special educators, and others. Visit schools, programs, and agencies to determine how practitioners use behavior modification techniques in their everyday work with young children.

5. Some critics of education feel that schools have assumed (or have been given) too much responsibility for teaching too many things. Do you think certain subjects or services could be taught or provided through another institution or agency?

6. What evidence can you find that Piaget has influenced early childhood programs?

7. In addition to the recurring themes of the great educators presented in this chapter, are there others you would list? Tell why you selected other themes.

READINGS FOR FURTHER ENRICHMENT

Gordon, Cam. *Together with Montessori* (Minneapolis: Jola, 1993).

A practical guide to help teachers, administrators, and parents work cooperatively in developing quality Montessori programs.

Hainstock, E. G. *The Essential Montessori: An Introduction to the Woman, the Writings, the Method, and the Movement* (Plume, 1997).

The book has been relied upon for almost two decades as the definitive guide to the writings of Maria Montessori and to the teaching and application of her ideas in today's educational arena, as well as being an indispensable sourcebook for teacher training programs, advice on choosing schools, materials needed for the classroom, and much more.

Lillard, Paula Polk. *Montessori in the Classroom: A Teacher's Account of How Children Really Learn* (New York: Schocken Books, 1997).

What really happens inside a Montessori classroom? How do teachers teach? How do children learn? This day-by-day record in the year of the life of a Montessori classroom answers these questions and provides an illuminating and practical glimpse of the Montessori method in action.

Schunk, D. *Learning Theories: An Educational Perspective* (Upper Saddle River, NJ: Prentice Hall, 1996), 2nd ed.

The author provides students with an understanding of theories and research on learning and related processes and demonstrates their application in educational contexts. Important historical theories are initially discussed, followed by accounts of research.

Standing, E. M., Havis, L. *Maria Montessori: Her Life and Work* (Penguin USA, 1998).

Part biography and part exposition of her ideas, this engaging book reveals through her letters and personal diaries Maria Montessori's humility and delight in the success of her educational experiments and is an ideal introduction to the principles and practices of the greatest educational pioneer of the 20th century.

Stupiansky, S. *Building Understanding Together: A Constructivist Approach to Early Childhood Education* (Delmar Publishing, 1997).

A comprehensive and practical overview of Piaget's theory of constructivism and practical applications of this theory. This book is an excellent reference source for future and current teachers as well as parents, administrators, and policy makers.

NOTES

1. George M. Gazda, Raymond J. Corsini, and contributors, *Theories of Learning* (Itasca, IL: Peacock, 1980), p. 455.

2. Deanna Kuhn, "The Role of Self-Directed Activity in Cognitive Development," in *New Directions in Piagetian Theory and Practice,* ed. Irving E. Sigel, David M. Brodzinsky, and Roberta M. Golinkoff (Hillsdale, NJ: Erlbaum, 1981), p. 353.

3. David M. Brodzinsky, Irving E. Sigel, and Roberta M. Golinkoff, "New Dimensions in Piagetian Theory and Research: An Integrative Perspective," in *New Directions in Piagetian Theory and Practice,* ed. Irving E. Sigel, David M. Brodzinsky, and Roberta M. Golinkoff (Hillsdale, NJ: Erlbaum, 1981), p. 5.

4. Constance Kamii, "Application of Piaget's Theory to Education: The Preoperational Level," in *New Directions in Piagetian Theory and Practice,* ed. Irving E. Sigel, David M. Brodzinsky, and Roberta M. Golinkoff (Hillsdale, NJ: Erlbaum, 1981), p. 234.

5. Mary Ann Spencer Pulaski, *Understanding Piaget* (New York: Harper & Row, 1980), p. 9.

6. P. G. Richmond, *An Introduction to Piaget* (New York: Basic Books, 1970), p. 68.

7. Ibid.

8. Maria Montessori, *Dr. Montessori's Own Handbook* (New York: Schocken Books, 1965), p. 133.

9. Maria Montessori, *The Absorbent Mind,* trans. Clause A. Claremont (New York: Holt, Rinehart & Winston, 1967), p. 25.

10. Maria Montessori, *The Secret of Childhood,* p. 48.

11. Ibid., pp. 46, 49.

12. Montessori, *The Absorbent Mind,* p. 6.

13. Ibid., p. 84.

14. L. S. Vygotsky, *Mind in Society* (Cambridge, MA: Harvard University Press, 1978), p. 90.

15. Jonathan R. H. Tudge, "Processes and Consequences of Peer Collaboration: A Vygotskian Analysis," *Child Development,* 63, 1992, p. 1365.

16. Ibid.

17. Vygotsky, *Mind in Society,* p. 90.

18. Tudge, "Processes and Consequences," p. 1365.

19. Howard Gardner, *Frames of Mind* (New York: Basic Books, 1983), pp. 60–61.

20. J. B. Watson, *Behaviorism* (New York: Norton, 1924), p. 104.

21. A. Bandura, *Social Learning Theory* (Upper Saddle River, NJ: Prentice Hall, 1977), p. vii.

22. Ibid.

CHAPTER

5

Early Childhood Programs

FOCUS QUESTIONS

1. What are the basic features of models of early childhood education today?
2. What are the similarities, differences, and strengths of various models of early childhood education?
3. How are learning theories translated into practice through models of early childhood programs?
4. What are the implications that program models have for your practice as an early childhood professional?

THE HIGH/SCOPE EDUCATIONAL APPROACH: A PIAGET-BASED PROGRAM

The High/Scope Educational Research Foundation is a nonprofit organization that sponsors and supports the High/Scope Educational Approach. The program is based on Piaget's intellectual development theory and

> is an innovative, open-framework educational program that seeks to provide broad, realistic educational experiences for children. The curriculum is geared to the child's current stage of development to promote the spontaneous and constructive processes of learning and to broaden the child's emerging intellectual and social skills.[1]

Since part of the Piagetian theory of intellectual development maintains that children must be actively involved in their own learning through experiences and encounters with people and things, the High/Scope Educational Approach promotes children's active involvement in their own learning. The program identifies three fundamental principles:

- Active participation of children in choosing, organizing, and evaluating learning activities, which are undertaken with careful teacher observation and guidance in a learning environment replete with a rich variety of materials located in various classroom learning centers
- Regular daily planning by the teaching staff in accord with a developmentally based curriculum model and careful child observations
- Developmentally sequenced goals and materials for children based on the High/Scope Key Experiences[2]

Objectives

The High/Scope program strives to

> develop in children a broad range of skills, including the problem solving, interpersonal, and communication skills that are essential for successful living in a rapidly changing society. The curriculum encourages student initiative by provid-

ing children with materials, equipment, and time to pursue activities they choose. At the same time, it provides teachers with a framework for guiding children's independent activities toward sequenced learning goals.

The teacher plays a key role in instructional activities by selecting appropriate, developmentally sequenced material and by encouraging children to adopt an active problem-solving approach to learning. . . . This teacher-student interaction—teachers helping students achieve developmentally sequenced goals while also encouraging them to set many of their own goals—uniquely distinguishes the High/Scope Curriculum from direct-instruction and child-centered curricula.[3]

The High/Scope approach influences the arrangement of the classroom, the manner in which teachers interact with children, and the methods employed to assess children. The High/Scope curriculum can be defined by looking at the five interrelated components shown in Figure 5–1. Look at Figure 5–1 to see how active learning forms the hub of the "wheel of learning" and is supported by the key elements of the curriculum.

FIGURE 5–1
High/Scope Curriculum Wheel

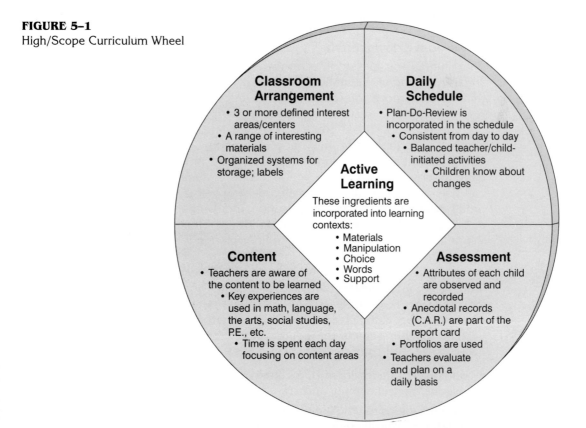

Source: Used with permission of David P. Weikart, president, High/Scope Educational Research Foundation, 600 N. River St., Ypsilanti, Michigan 48198-2898.

The Five Elements of the High/Scope Approach

Adults who use the High/Scope curriculum must be fully committed to providing settings in which children learn actively and construct their own knowledge. The child's knowledge comes from personal interaction with ideas, direct experience with physical objects, and application of logical thinking to these experiences. The adult's role is to supply the context for these experiences, to help the child think about them logically, and, through observation, to understand the progress the child is making. In a sense, children are expected to learn by the scientific method of observation and inference, at levels of sophistication consonant with their development.

Active Learning

At the center of the High/Scope curriculum is the idea that children are the mainspring of their own learning. The teacher supports children's active learning by stocking the classroom with a variety of materials, making plans and reviewing activities with children, interacting with and carefully observing individual children, and leading small- and large-group active learning activities.

Classroom Arrangement

The High/Scope classroom arrangement invites children to engage in personal, meaningful, educational experiences. In addition, the classroom contains five or more interest areas that encourage choice. You will want to review Figure 5–2 to see a room arrangement for kindergarten.

The plan-do-review process, detailed later in the chapter, is the child-initiated experience that implements the High/Scope Educational Approach. The organization of materials and equipment in the classroom supports the daily routine—children know where to find materials and what materials they can use, which encourages development of self-direction and independence. Small-group tables are used for seating, independent work space, center-time activities, and teacher-directed instruction. Flexibility and versatility contribute to the learning function. The floor plan in Figure 5–2 shows how room arrangement can support and implement the program's philosophy, goals, and objectives and how a center approach (books, blocks, computers, dramatic play, art, construction) provides space for large-group activities and individual work. In a classroom where space is at a premium, the teacher must work at making one area serve many difference purposes.

The teacher selects the centers and activities to use in the classroom based on several considerations:

- Interests of the children (e.g., kindergarten children are interested in blocks, housekeeping, and art)
- Opportunities for facilitating active involvement in seriation, number, time relations, classification, spatial relations, and language development
- Opportunities for reinforcing needed skills and concepts and functional use of those skills and concepts

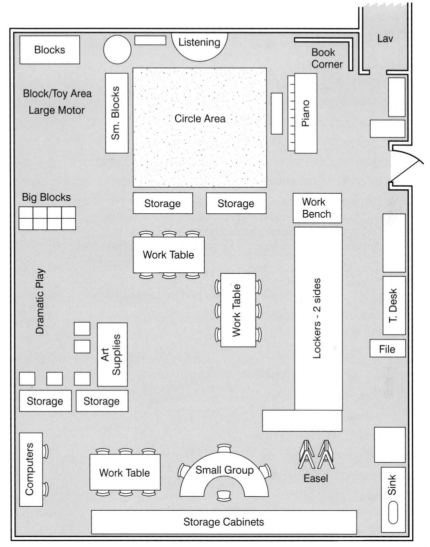

36′ × 30′ = 1,080 sq. ft.

FIGURE 5–2
A High/Scope Kindergarten Classroom Arrangement
Source: Used with permission of David P. Weikart, president, High/Scope Educational Research
Foundation, 600 N. River St., Ypsilanti, Michigan 48198-2898.

Daily Schedule

The schedule considers developmental levels of children, incorporates a
sixty- to seventy-minute plan-do-review process, provides for content areas,
is as consistent throughout the day as possible, and contains a minimum
number of transitions.

FIGURE 5–3
Key Experiences in Language and Literacy for a High/Scope K–3 Curriculum

Speaking and Listening
Speaking their own language or dialect

Asking and answering questions

Stating facts and observations in their own words

Using language to solve problems

Participating in singing, storytelling, poetic and dramatic activities

Recalling thoughts and observations in a purposeful context

Acquiring, strengthening, and extending speaking and listening skills
Discussing to clarify observations or to better follow directions
Discussing to expand speaking and listening vocabulary
Discussing to strengthen critical thinking and problem-solving activities

Writing
Observing the connections between spoken and written language

Writing in unconventional forms
Scribbles
Drawing
Letters—random or patterned, possibly including elements of names copied from the environment
Invented spelling of initial sounds and intermediate sounds

Writing in conventional forms

Expressing thoughts in writing

Sharing writing in purposeful context

Using writing equipment (e.g., computers, typewriters)

Writing in specific content areas

Acquiring, strengthening, and extending writing skills

Content

The curriculum content for planning comes in part from the key experiences, which are lists of observable learning behaviors (See Figure 5–3.)

Assessment

Teachers keep notes about significant behaviors, changes, statements, and things that help them better understand a child's way of thinking and learning. Teachers use two mechanisms to help them collect data, the key experience note form and the portfolio. The High/Scope Child Observation Record (see Chapter 7) is also used to assess children's development.

FIGURE 5–3,
continued

Letter formation
Sentence and paragraph formation
Capitalization, punctuation, and grammatical usage
Editing and proofreading for mechanics, content, and style

Expanding the forms of composition
    Expressive mode
    Transactional mode—expository, argumentative, descriptive
    Poetic mode—narrative mode

Publishing selected compositions

Reading
Experiencing varied genres of children's literature

Reading own compositions

Reading and listening to others read in a purposeful context

Using audio and/or video recordings in reading experiences

Acquiring, strengthening, and extending specific reading skills
    Auditory discrimination
    Letter recognition
    Decoding—phonetic analysis (letter/sound associations, factors affecting sounds, syllabication),
structural analysis (forms, prefixes, suffixes)
    Vocabulary development

Expanding comprehension and fluency skills
    Activating prior knowledge
    Determining purpose, considering context, making predictions
    Developing strategies for interpreting narrative and expository text
    Reading varied genres of children's literature

A Daily Routine to Support Active Learning

The High/Scope curriculum's daily routine is made up of a plan-do-review sequence and several additional elements. The plan-do-review sequence gives children opportunities to express intentions about their activities while keeping the teacher intimately involved in the whole process. The following paragraphs describe the elements of the daily routine.

Planning Time

It is not unusual for young children to make choices and to make decisions about implementing the choices. But in most preschool programs, children seldom think about these decisions systematically or reflect on the

HIGH/SCOPE IN PRACTICE

The High/Scope Educational Approach for three- to five-year-olds is a developmental model based on the principle of active learning. The following beliefs underlie this approach:

- Children construct knowledge through their active involvement with people, materials, events, and ideas, a process that is intrinsically motivated.

- While children develop capacities in a predictable sequence, adult support contributes to children's intellectual, social, emotional, and physical development.

- Consistent adult support and respect for children's choices, thoughts, and actions strengthen children's self-confidence, sense of responsibility, self-control, and knowledge.

- Careful observation of children's interests and intentions is a necessary step in understanding their level of development and planning and carrying out appropriate interactions with them.

In High/Scope programs these principles are implemented throughout the day, both through the structure of the daily routine and in the strategies adults use as they work with children. Staff of each program plan for the day's experiences, striving to create a balance between adult- and child-initiated activity.

As they plan activities, the staff considers five "factors of intrinsic motivation" that research indicates are essential for learning. These factors are enjoyment, interest, control, probability of success, and feelings of competence. During greeting and small-group times, staff members actively involve children in decisions about activities and materials as a way of supporting their intrinsic motivation to learn. This emphasis on child choice and control continues throughout the day, even during activities initiated by adults.

A Day at a High/Scope Program

Each program implements the High/Scope approach in a unique way. A typical day's activities at Giving Tree School follows:

The day begins with greeting time. Children gather as the teacher begins a well-known animal finger play, and join in immediately. Then the teacher suggests that the group make a circus of animals who are moving in many ways. Two children do not want to be animals, and the teacher suggests that these children may want to be the "audience." They get chairs and prepare to watch. Children suggest elephants, bears, and alligators as animals for the group to imitate. The children parade before the audience pretending to be animals and moving to the music. At the close of greeting time, the teacher suggests that children choose an animal to be as they move to the next activity, small-group time. During small-group time the children make "inventions" of their choice with recyclable materials a teacher has brought in and pine cones they collected the previous day.

As small-group time activities conclude, planning time begins. At this time, the teacher asks younger children to indicate their plans for work time by going to get something they will use in their play. She asks the older children to draw or copy the symbols or letters that stand for the area in which they plan to play (each play area is labeled with a sign containing both a simple picture symbol and words for the area).

To indicate his plan, Charlie, age three, gets a small hollow block and brings it to the teacher. "I'm going to make a train. That's all," he says. Aja, age four, gets a dress and a roll of tape. "I'm going to the playhouse to be the mommy, and then I'm going to the art area to make something with tape," she explains. Five-year-old Ashley shows the teacher her drawing of the tub table and the scoops she will use with rice at the table.

During work time, the teachers participate in children's play. Riding on Charlie's "train," one teacher shows Tasha how to make the numerals 3 and 5 for train "tickets," joins two children playing a board game, and listens to Aja as she explains how she made a doll bed out of tape and a box. Another teacher helps Nicholas and Charlie negotiate a conflict over a block, encouraging them by listening and asking questions until they agree on a solution.

As children play, teachers occasionally jot down short notes about significant play episodes. During the morning, they record five or six brief anecdotes they will use later for planning and child assessment. As work time draws to a close, they move through the room, reminding the children that in a few minutes the cleanup bell will ring. Ashley suggests that for cleanup they make two trains, moving around the room to music and pausing when the music stops to clean up an area. The children really enjoy this activity and cleanup is accomplished quickly.

At recall time, the children gather with the same groups they met with at planning time. Standing in a circle, each group rotates a hula hoop through their hands as they sing a short song. When the song ends, the child nearest the tape is the first to recall his or her work time experiences. Charlie tells about the train they made out of blocks. Nicholas describes the special "speed sticks" he played with. Aja shows her doll bed, and Tasha describes her "tickets." After snack time, the children get their coats on and discuss what they will do outside. "Let's collect more pine cones. We can use them for food for the baby alligators." "Let's go on the swings. I just learned how to pump." "Let's see if we can find more bugs hiding under the rocks. They go there for winter." The teacher responds, "I'd like to help you look for bugs."

Key Experiences

As children play, they are actively involved in solving problems and participate in many of the High/Scope "key experiences." There are fifty-eight key experiences that fall into ten categories: *social relations and initiative, language, creative representation, music, movement, classification, seriation, numbers, pace,* and *time.* Teachers use the fifty-eight key experiences as guides for understanding development, planning activities, and describing the thinking and actions involved in children's play.

The High/Scope approach to learning supports developmentally appropriate, active learning experiences for each child as it encourages decision making, creative expression, problem solving, and other emerging abilities.

Contributed by Betsy Evans, Director and Teacher, The Giving Tree School, Gill, Massachusetts, and Field Consultant, High/Scope Educational Research Foundation.

possibilities and consequences of their choices. In the High/Scope approach, planning time gives children a structured, consistent chance to express their ideas to adults and to see themselves as individuals who can act on decisions. They experience the power of independence and the joy of working to be conscious of their intentions, and this supports the development of purpose and confidence.

The teacher talks with children about the plans they have made before the children carry them out. This helps children to clarify their ideas and think about how to proceed. Talking with children about their plans provides an opportunity for the teacher to encourage and respond to each child's ideas, to suggest ways to strengthen the plans so they will be successful, and to understand and gauge each child's level of development and thinking style. Both children and adults receive benefits: Children feel reinforced and ready to start their work, while adults have ideas of what opportunities for extension might arise, what difficulties children might have, and where problem solving may be needed. In such a classroom, all are playing appropriate and important roles.

Key Experiences

The teacher must also continually encourage and support children's interests and involvement in activities, which occur within an organized environment and a consistent routine. Teachers plan from key experiences through which they may broaden and strengthen children's emerging abilities. Children generate many of these experiences on their own; others require adult guidance. Many key experiences are not limited to specific objects or places, but are natural extensions of children's projects and interests. Refer to Figure 5–3 to review key experiences that support learning in areas of speaking and listening, writing, and reading.

Work Time

This next part of the plan-do-review sequence is generally the longest single time period in the daily routine. Teachers new to the High-Scope curriculum sometimes find work time confusing because they are not sure of their role. Adults do not lead work-time activities—children execute their own plans of work—but neither do they just sit back and watch. The adult's role during work time is to observe children to see how they gather information, interact with peers, and solve problems, and then enter into the children's activities to encourage, extend, and set up problem-solving situations.

Cleanup Time

Cleanup time is naturally integrated into the plan-do-review sequence after the "doing." During cleanup time, children return materials and equipment to their labeled places and store their incomplete projects. This process restores order to the classroom and provides opportunities for the children to learn and use many basic cognitive skills. Of special importance is the way the learning environment is organized to facilitate children's use of the materials. All materials in the classroom that are for children's use are within reach and on open shelves. Clear labeling is essential; this usually consists of easy-to-understand representations of the various objects on each shelf. With this organizational plan, children can realistically return all work materials to their appropriate places. Knowing where everything is located also gives children a sense of control, ownership, and even mastery.

Recall Time

Recall time, the final phase of the plan-do-review sequence, is the time when children represent their work-time experience in a variety of developmentally appropriate ways. They might recall the names of the children they involved in their plan, draw a picture of the building they made, or describe the problems they encountered. Recall strategies include drawing pictures, making models, physically demonstrating how a plan was carried out, or verbally recalling the events of work time. The teacher supports children's linking of the actual work to their original plan.

This review permits children to reflect on what they did and how it was done. It brings closure to children's planning and work-time activities, allowing them to express insight into what they have experienced. Putting their ideas and experiences into words also facilitates children's language development.

WHAT IS THE MONTESSORI PROGRAM?

The Montessori system is attractive to parents and teachers for a number of reasons. First, Montessori education has always been identified as a quality program for young children. Second, parents who observe a *good* Montessori program like what they see: orderliness, independent children, self-directed learning, a calm environment, and *children* at the center of the learning process. Third, Montessori's approach is based on the premise that education begins at birth, and the idea of early learning remains popular with parents. Fourth, public schools include Montessori in their magnet programs, giving parents choices in the kind of program their children will have at a particular school. It is also used as a means of desegregation.

Over the past decade, the implementation of Montessori education has increased tremendously in public school early childhood programs. Montessori would probably smilingly approve of the contemporary use of her method once again to help change the nature and character of early childhood education.

What Is the Role of the Montessori Teacher?

The Montessori teacher should demonstrate certain behaviors to implement the principles of this child-centered approach. The teacher's roles include these:

1. *Making children the center of learning.* As Montessori said, "The teacher's task is not to talk, but to prepare and arrange a series of motives for cultural activity in a special environment made for the child."[4]

2. *Encouraging children to learn* through the freedom provided for them in the prepared environment.

3. *Observing children* to prepare the best possible environment, recognizing sensitive periods, and diverting inappropriate behavior to meaningful tasks.

Montessori believed, "It is necessary for the teacher to *guide* the child without letting him feel her presence too much, so that she may be always ready to supply the desired help, but may never be the obstacle between the child and his experience."[5]

How Does the Montessori Method Work?

In a prepared environment, certain materials and activities provide for three basic areas of child involvement: *practical life* or motor education, *sensory materials* for training the senses, and *academic materials* for teaching writing, reading, and mathematics. All these activities are taught according to a prescribed procedure.

Practical Life

The prepared environment emphasizes basic, everyday motor activities, such as walking from place to place in an orderly manner, carrying objects such as trays and chairs, greeting a visitor, learning self-care skills, and doing other practical activities. For example, the "dressing frames" are designed to perfect the motor skills involved in buttoning, zipping, lacing, buckling, and tying. The philosophy for activities such as these is to make children independent of the adult and develop concentration. Water activities play a large role in Montessori methods, and children are taught to scrub, wash, and pour as a means of developing coordination. Practical life exercises also include polishing mirrors, shoes, and plant leaves; sweeping the floor; dusting furniture; and peeling vegetables.

Montessorians believe that as children become absorbed in an activity, they gradually lengthen their span of concentration; as they follow a regular

Sensory training plays a major role in the Montessori method. What knowledge, skills, and concepts is this child learning through her involvement with these materials?

sequence of actions, they learn to pay attention to details. Montessori practitioners believe that without concentration and involvement through the senses, little learning takes place. Although most people assume that we learn practical life activities incidentally, a Montessori teacher shows children how to do these activities through precisely detailed instructions. Verbal instructions are minimal; the emphasis in the instructional process is on *showing how*—modeling and practice.

Montessori believed children's involvement and concentration in motor activities lengthen their attention span. In a Montessori classroom, it is not uncommon to see a child of four or five polish his shoes or scrub a table for twenty minutes at a time! The child finds the activity intrinsically rewarding and pleasurable.

Practical life activities are taught through four different types of exercises. *Care of the person* involves activities such as using the dressing frames, polishing shoes, and washing hands. *Care of the environment* includes dusting, polishing a table, and raking leaves. *Social relations* include lessons in grace and courtesy. The fourth type of exercise involves *analysis and control of movement* and includes locomotor activities such as walking and balancing. Figures 5–4, 5–5, and 5–6 are directions for some of the practical life activities in a Montessori classroom. Notice the procedures and the exactness of presentation.

Materials: Tray, rice, two small pitchers (one empty, the other containing rice)

Presentation: The child must be shown how to lift the empty pitcher with the left hand and with the right, raise the pitcher containing rice slightly higher. Grasping the handle, lifting, and tilting are practiced. The spout of the full pitcher must be moved to about the center of the empty pitcher before the pouring begins. Set down both pitchers; then change the full one to the right side, to repeat the exercise.

When rice is spilled, the child will set the pitchers down, beside the top of the tray, and pick the grains up, one at a time, with thumb and forefinger.

Purpose: Control of movement.

Point of Interest: Watching the rice.

Control of Error: Hearing the rice drop on the tray.

Age: 2$\frac{1}{2}$ years.

Exercise: A container with a smaller diameter, requiring better control of movement. Control the amount of rice for the smaller container.

Note: Set up a similar exercise, using colored popcorn instead of rice.

Rice or Popcorn

FIGURE 5–4

Pouring

Source: *A Montessori Teacher's Manual* by Elizabeth and Charles Caspari and Friends. © E. G. Caspari, 1974. All rights reserved. Used by permission.

Materials: Apron, green-leafed plant, sheet of white freezer paper, basket with small sponge, caster, bottle of plant polish, orange stick, cotton ball.

Presentation:
1. Lay out all the material in order of use from left to right.
2. Bring a plant to the table and place it on the paper.
3. Dampen the sponge at the sink and gently wipe off the top side of the leaf with forward strokes. Hold the leaf on the underside with the other hand. Stroke several leaves to remove the dust.
4. Pour small amount of polish into caster.
5. Wrap a small portion of the cotton ball on the orange stick.
6. Dip the stick in the polish and again stroke gently on the leaf in the manner described above.

Clean up:
1. Remove cotton from the stick and put it in the wastebasket.
2. Take the caster to the sink and wash and dry it.
3. Wash the sponge and bring it back to the table.
4. Place the material back in the basket.
5. Replace the plant on the shelf.
6. Fold the paper. Discard only if necessary.
7. Return basket and paper to the shelf.

Purpose: Coordination of movement; care of plants.

Point of Interest: Seeing the leaves get shiny.

Control of Error: Dull leaves and polish on white paper.

Age: 3 years and up.

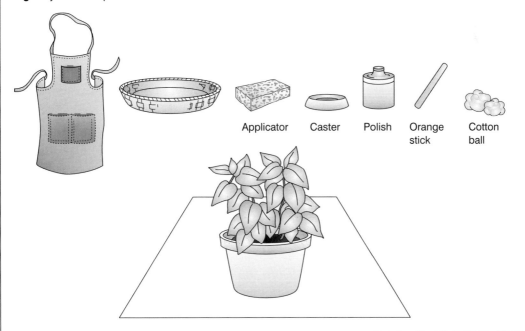

Applicator   Caster   Polish   Orange stick   Cotton ball

FIGURE 5–5

Plant Shining

Source: *A Montessori Teacher's Manual* by Elizabeth and Charles Caspari and Friends. © E. G. Caspari, 1974. All rights reserved. Used by permission.

Materials: Basket with a duster, soft brush, and feather duster; table to be dusted

Presentation:
Look for dust, with the eyes at the level of the surface of the table. Start with one half of the table, the one immediately in front of you.
Wipe the surface first, as most of the dust will be lying on the top and will give the greatest result.
Always dust away from the body, starting at one end working progressively to the other end, using circular movements.
After the top dust the sides, after the sides dust the legs. Don't forget the corners, the insides of the legs, and underneath the tabletop. The brush is to be used for the corners.
Shake the duster over the wastebasket or outdoors.

Purpose: Coordination of movements, care of the environment, indirect preparation for writing

Point of Interest: The dust to be found in the duster; shaking the dust off the cloth

Control of Error: Any spot of dust left behind

Age: $2\frac{1}{2}$ to $4\frac{1}{2}$ years.

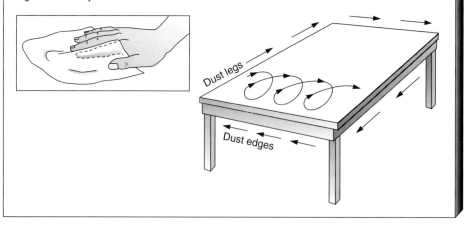

FIGURE 5–6

Dusting

Source: *A Montessori Teacher's Manual* by Elizabeth and Charles Caspari and Friends. © E. G. Caspari, 1974. All rights reserved. Used by permission.

Sensory Materials

For many early childhood educators the core of the Montessori program is the specialized set of learning materials that help children learn and which support Montessori's ideas about how to best facilitate children's learning. Many of these materials are designed to train senses. Sensory materials include brightly colored rods and cubes and sandpaper letters. One purpose of Montessori sensory materials is to train children's senses to focus on some obvious, particular quality. For example, with red rods, the quality is length; with pink tower cubes, size; and with bells, musical pitch. Montessori felt that children need help discriminating among the many stimuli they receive. Accordingly, the sensory materials help make children more aware of the capacity of their bodies to receive, interpret, and make use of stimuli. In this sense, the Montessori sensory materials are labeled *didactic,* designed to instruct.

Second, Montessori thought that perception and the ability to observe details were crucial to reading. The sensory materials help sharpen children's powers of observation and visual discrimination as readiness for learning to read.

A third purpose of the sensory materials is to increase children's ability to think, a process that depends on the ability to distinguish, classify, and organize. Children constantly face decisions about sensory materials: Which block comes next, which color matches the other, which shape goes where? These are not decisions the teacher makes, nor are they decisions children arrive at by guessing; rather, they are decisions made by the intellectual process of observation and selection based on knowledge gathered through the senses.

Finally, all the sensory activities are not ends in themselves. Their purpose is to prepare children for the occurrence of the sensitive periods for writing and reading. In this sense, all activities are preliminary steps in the writing-reading process.

Materials for training and developing the senses have these characteristics:

- *Control of error.* Materials are designed so that children can see whether they make a mistake. For example, if a child does not build the blocks of the pink tower in their proper order, she does not achieve a tower effect.
- *Isolation of a single quality.* Materials are designed so that other variables are held constant except for the isolated quality or qualities. Therefore, all blocks of the pink tower are pink because size, not color, is the isolated quality.
- *Active involvement.* Materials encourage active involvement rather than the more passive process of looking.
- *Attractiveness.* Materials are attractive, with colors and proportions that appeal to children.

Academic Materials for Writing, Reading, and Mathematics

The third area of Montessori materials is academic—specifically, items for writing, reading, and mathematics. Exercises are presented in a sequence that encourages writing before reading. Reading is therefore an outgrowth of writing. Both processes, however, are introduced so gradually that children are never aware they are learning to write and read until one day they realize they are writing and reading. Describing this phenomenon, Montessori said that children "burst spontaneously" into writing and reading. She anticipated contemporary practices such as the whole-language approach in integrating writing and reading and in maintaining that through writing children learn to read.

Montessori believed many children were ready for writing at four years of age. Consequently, a child who enters a Montessori system at age three has done most of the sensory exercises by the time he is four. It is not uncommon to see four- and five-year-olds in a Montessori classroom writing and reading. Following are examples of Montessori materials that lay the foundation for and promote writing and reading:

- *Ten geometric forms and colored pencils.* These introduce children to the coordination necessary for writing. After selecting a geometric inset, children trace it on paper and fill in the outline with a colored pencil of their choosing.
- *Sandpaper letters.* Each letter of the alphabet is outlined in sandpaper on a card, with vowels in blue and consonants in red. Children see the shape, feel the shape, and hear the sound of the letter, which the teacher repeats when introducing it.
- *Movable alphabet, with individual letters.* Children learn to put together familiar words.
- *Command cards.* These are a set of red cards with a single action word printed on each card. Children read the word on the card and do what the word tells them to do (e.g., *run, jump*).

Examples of materials for mathematics are the following items:

- *Number rods.* A set of red and blue rods varying in length from ten centimeters to one meter, representing the quantities one through ten. With the teacher's help, children are introduced to counting.
- *Sandpaper numerals.* Each number from one to nine in sandpaper on a card. Children see, touch, and hear the numbers as the teacher or they say them. They eventually match number rods and sandpaper numerals. Children also have the opportunity to discover mathematical facts by using these numerals.
- *Golden beads.* A concrete material for the decimal system. The single bead represents one unit. A bar made up of ten units in a row represents a ten, ten of the ten bars form a square representing one hundred, and ten hundred squares form the cube representing one thousand.

Additional Features

Other features of the Montessori system are *mixed-age grouping* and *self-pacing*. A Montessori classroom always contains children of different ages, usually from two-and-a-half to six years. This strategy is becoming more popular in many classrooms and has long been popular in the British infant schools. Advantages of mixed-age groups are that children learn from one another and help each other, a wide range of materials is available for all children, and older children become role models and collaborators for younger children. Contemporary instructional practices of student mentoring and cooperative learning all have their roots in and are supported by multi-age grouping.

In a Montessori classroom, children are free to learn at their own rate and level of achievement. They determine which activities to participate in and work at their own pace. However, children are not allowed to dally at a task. Through observation, the teacher determines when children have perfected one exercise and are ready to move to a higher level or different exercise. If a child does not perform an activity correctly, the teacher gives him or her additional help and instruction.

Table 5–1 outlines the basic characteristics of a good Montessori program that you can use as a guideline when you observe Montessori classrooms. Perhaps you can add other criteria you think make a good early childhood program. Regardless of the type of program you observe, remember, the development of the individual child is one hallmark of a quality program. Quality Montessori programs endeavor to promote children's development at all levels—the intellectual, social, emotional, and physical. This dedication to and success at treasuring the uniqueness of each child and promoting individual development helps to account for the enduring popularity of Montessori's ideas and the programs that bear her name.

Montessori and Contemporary Practices

The Montessori approach supports many methods used in contemporary early childhood programs.

1. *Integrated curriculum.* Montessori provides an integrated curriculum in which children are actively involved in manipulating concrete materials across the curriculum—writing, reading, science, math, geography, and the arts. The Montessori curriculum is integrated in other ways, across ages and developmental levels. Montessori materials are age appropriate for a wide age range of children.
2. *Active learning.* In Montessori classrooms, children are actively involved in their own learning. Manipulative materials provide for active and concrete learning.

TABLE 5–1

Basic Characteristics of a Montessori Program for Three- to Six-Year-Old Children

Growth in the Child	Program Organization	Adult Aspects
Toward independence and problem solving	Ungraded three-year age span: 2.6 to 6 years	Certified Montessori teachers at the 3- to 6-year level
Toward the enjoyment of learning	Parental commitment to a three-year cycle of attendance	Continuing professional development
Toward the development of order, concentration, and coordination	Five-day week with a minimum daily three hour session	Observational skills to match students' developmental needs with activities
Toward skills in oral communication	Personal and group instruction	Strategies to facilitate the unique and total growth of each individual
Toward respect for oneself, other people, and the planet	Child:adult ratio of 15:1	Leadership skills to foster a nurturing environment supportive of learning
	Observational records of the child	
	Regularly scheduled parent conferences	A partnership developed with parents
Toward responsible group membership	Public observation policy	Supervision and education of auxiliary classroom personnel

Learning Environment	Program Emphasis	Administrative Support
Diverse set of Montessori materials, activities, and experiences	To encourage intrinsic motivation, spontaneous activity, and self-education	Organized as a legally and fiscally responsible entity
Schedule that allows large blocks of uninterrupted learning time	To provide sensory education for intellectual development	Nondiscriminatory admissions policy
Classroom atmosphere that encourages social interaction	To encourage competencies through repetitive concrete experiences	Written educational policies and procedures
Space for personal, small-group, and whole-class learning activities	To encourage cooperative learning through peer teaching and social interaction	Adherence to state laws and health requirements
Lightweight, proportionate, movable child-sized furnishing	To provide learning opportunities through physical activity and outdoor work	Current school affiliation with AMS and other professional groups
Identifiable ground rules	To provide learning activities for creative expression	
Aesthetically pleasing environment		
Outdoor space to accommodate rigorous physical activity		

Source: American Montessori Society, *Basic Characteristics of a Montessori Program for Children Ages 3 to 6 Years*, pamphlet (New York: Author, 1991). Copyright April 1991. Used by permission.

A Montessori environment is characterized by orderliness, with a place for everything and everything in its place. The low shelving gives children ready access to and encourages use of the materials. Why is it important to have an organized environment?

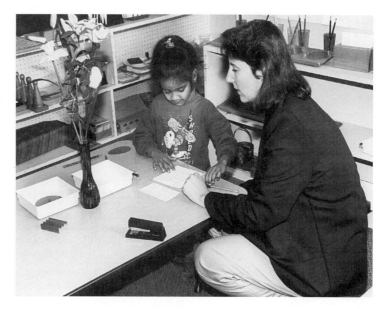

3. *Individualized instruction.* Curriculum and activities should be individualized for children. Montessori does this through individualizing learning for *all* children. Individualization occurs through children's interactions with the materials as they proceed at their own rates of mastery.

4. *Independence.* The Montessori environment emphasizes respect for children and promotes success, both of which encourage children to be independent. Indeed, independence has always been a hallmark of Montessori.

5. *Appropriate assessment.* Observation is the primary means of assessing children's progress, achievement, and behavior in a Montessori classroom. Well-trained Montessori teachers are skilled observers of children and adept at translating their observation into appropriate ways for guiding, directing, facilitating, and channeling children's active learning.

6. *Developmentally appropriate practice.* From the preceding illustrations, it is apparent that the concepts and process of developmentally appropriate curriculum and practice are inherent in the Montessori method. What is specified in developmentally appropriate practice (see Chapters 6 through 9) is included in Montessori practice. Indeed, it may well be that some of the most developmentally appropriate practices are conducted by Montessori practitioners. It is more likely that quality Montessori practitioners understand, as Maria Montessori did, that children are much more capable than some early childhood practitioners think.

WHAT IS THE REGGIO EMILIA APPROACH?

Reggio Emilia is a city in northern Italy. The excellent educational program the city offers its children, based on providing an educational environment that encourages learning, is known as the Reggio Emilia approach. Reggio Emilia sponsors infant programs for children three months to three years and programs for children three to six years. Loris Malaguzzi founded and for many years directed the Reggio Emilia system of municipal early childhood education.

Basic Principles of the Reggio Emilia Approach

The Image of the Child

The educators in Reggio Emilia first and foremost always speak about the image they have of the child. All children have preparedness, potentials, curiosity, and interest in engaging in social interaction, establishing relationships, constructing their learning, and negotiating with everything the environment brings to them. Teachers are deeply aware of children's potentials and construct all their work and the environment of the children's experience to respond appropriately.

Children's Relationships and Interactions within a System

Education focuses on each child and is conducted in relation with the family, other children, the teachers, the school, the community, and the wider society. Each school is viewed as a system in which all these interconnected relationships are reciprocal, activated, and supported.

The Three Subjects of Education: Children, Parents, and Teachers

Children's well-being is connected with the well-being of parents and teachers. Children's rights and needs are recognized. Children have a right to high-quality care and education that support the development of their potentials. Children have rights to the best that a society can offer, parents have rights to be involved in the life of the school, and teachers have rights to grow professionally.

The Role of Parents

Parents are considered to be an essential component of the program, and they are included in the advisory committee that runs each school. Parents' participation is expected and supported and takes many forms: day-to-day interaction, work in the schools, discussion of educational and psychological issues, special events, excursions, and celebrations. Parents are an active part of their children's learning experience and, at the same time, help ensure the welfare of all children in the school.

The Role of Space: An Amiable School

The infant-toddler centers and schools are, of course, the most visible aspect of the work done by teachers and parents in Reggio Emilia. They convey many messages, of which the most immediate is that this is a place where adults have thought about the quality and the instructive power of space.

The layout of physical space, in addition to welcoming whoever enters the schools, fosters encounters, communication, and relationships. The arrangement of structures, objects, and activities encourages choices, problem solving, and discoveries in the process of learning.

It is also true that the centers and schools of Reggio are simply beautiful. However, their beauty does not come from expensive furnishings but rather from the message the whole school conveys about children and teachers engaged together in the pleasure of learning. There is attention to detail everywhere: in the color of the walls, the shape of the furniture, the arrangement of simple objects on shelves and tables. Light from the windows and doors shines through transparent collages and weaving made by children. Healthy, green plants are everywhere. Behind the shelves displaying shells or other found or made objects are mirrors that reflect the patterns that children and teachers have created.

The environment is also highly personal. For example, in one of the halls, a series of small boxes made of white cardboard creates a grid on the wall. On each box the name of a child or a teacher is printed with rubber stamp letters. These boxes are used for leaving little surprises or messages for one another. Communication is valued and favored at all levels.

The space in the centers and schools of Reggio Emilia is personal in still another way: It is full of the children's own work. Everywhere there are paintings, drawings, paper sculptures, wire constructions, transparent collages coloring the light, and mobiles moving gently overhead. Their work turns up even in unexpected spaces like stairways and bathrooms.

The Value of Relationships and Interaction of Children in Small Groups

In preparing the space, teachers offer the possibility for children to be with the teachers and many of the other children, or with just a few of them, or even alone when they need a little niche to stay by themselves.

Teachers are always aware, however, that children learn a great deal in exchanges with their peers, especially when they can interact in small groups. Such small groups of two, three, four, or five children provide possibilities for paying attention, hearing and listening to each other, developing curiosity and interest, asking questions, and responding to them. It provides opportunities for negotiation and dynamic communication.

The Role of Time and the Importance of Continuity

Time is not set by a clock, and continuity is not interrupted by the calendar. Children's own sense of time and their personal rhythm are considered in planning and carrying out activities and projects. The full-day schedule provides sufficient time for being together among friends in a good environment and for getting things done with satisfaction.

Teachers get to know the personal time of the children and each child's particular characteristics because children stay with the same teachers and the same peer group for three-year cycles (infancy to three and three to six).

Teachers as Partners

To know how to plan or proceed with their work, teachers observe and listen to the children closely. Teachers use the understanding they gain in this way to act as a resource for them. They ask questions and discover the children's ideas, hypotheses, and theories. Then the adults discuss together what they have recorded through their own notes, or audio or visual recordings, and make flexible plans and preparations. Then they are ready to enter again into dialogues with the children and offer them occasions for discovering and also revisiting experiences since they consider learning not as a linear process but as a spiral progression. In fact, teachers consider themselves to be partners in this process of learning. The role of teachers, therefore, is considered to be one of continual research and learning, taking place with the children and embedded in team cooperation.

Cooperation and Collaboration as the Backbone of the System

Cooperation at all levels in the schools is the powerful mode of working that makes possible the achievement of the complex goals that Reggio educators have set for themselves. Teachers work in pairs in each classroom, not as head teacher and assistant but at the same level; they see themselves as researchers gathering information about their work with children by means of continual documentation. The strong collegial relationships that are maintained with all other teachers and staff rely on this information to engage in collaborative discussion and interpretation of both teachers' and children's work. These exchanges provide ongoing training and theoretical enrichment. This cooperative system is further supported by a team of pedagogical coordinators, called *pedagogisti,* who also support the relationships among all teachers, parents, community members, and city administrators.

The Many Languages of Children: Atelierista and Atelier

A teacher who is trained in the visual arts works closely with the other teachers and the children in every preprimary school (and visits the infant-toddler centers). This teacher is called an *atelierista,* and a special workshop or studio, called an *atelier,* is set aside and used by all the children and teachers as well as by the *atelierista.* The *atelier* contains a great variety of tools and resource materials, along with records of past projects and experiences.

The activities and projects, however, do not take place only in the *atelier.* Through the years the roles of the *atelier* and *atelierista* have expanded and become part of the whole school. Smaller spaces called *mini-ateliers* have been set up in each classroom; furthermore, teachers and *atelieristi* have been working more and more together, transferring to one another the reciprocal skills. What is done with materials and media is not regarded as art per se, because in the view of Reggio educators, the children's use of many media is not a separate part of the curriculum but an inseparable, integral part of the whole cognitive-symbolic expression involved in the process of learning.

The Power of Documentation

Transcriptions of children's remarks and discussions, photographs of their activity, and representations of their thinking and learning using many media are carefully arranged by the *atelierista,* along with the other teachers, to document the work (and the process of learning) done in the schools. This documentation has several functions. Among these are to make parents aware of their children's experience and maintain their involvement; to allow teachers to understand children better and to evaluate the teachers' own work, thus promoting their professional growth; to facilitate communication and exchange of ideas among educators; to make children aware that their effort is valued; and to create an archive that traces the history of the school and the pleasure of learning by many children and their teachers.

The Emergent Curriculum

The curriculum is not established in advance. Teachers express general goals and make hypotheses about what direction activities and projects might take; consequently, they make appropriate preparations. Then, after observing children in action, they compare, discuss, and interpret together their observations and make choices that they share with the children about what to offer and how to sustain the children in their exploration and learning. In fact, the curriculum emerges in the process of each activity or project and is flexibly adjusted accordingly through this continuous dialogue among teachers and with children.

Projects

Projects provide the backbone of the children's and teachers' learning experiences. They are based on the strong conviction that learning by doing is of great importance and that to discuss in small groups and to revisit ideas and experiences is the premier way of gaining better understanding and learning.

Ideas for projects originate in the continuum of the experience of children and teachers as they construct knowledge together. Projects can last from a few days to several months. They may start from either a chance event, an idea or a problem posed by one or more children, or an experience initiated directly by teachers. For example, a study of crowds originated when a child told the class about a summer vacation experience. Whereas teachers had expected the children to tell about their discoveries on the beach or in the countryside, a child commented that "crowd" was all that she remembered.

WHAT IS THE BANK STREET PROGRAM?

In 1919, Harriet Johnson started the Nursery School of the Bureau of Educational Experiments in New York, devoted to the study of children and educational practice. The bureau later became the Bank Street College of Education, which sponsors the Bank Street School for Children. The Bank Street early childhood program is based on a developmental-interactionist point of view. This approach to education has its roots in the philosophy of John Dewey, the preeminent American educator who did much to influence what is often called *progressive education,* which basically is a theory of schooling emphasizing children and their interests rather than subject matter. Because of this attention to children, the terms *child-centered, child-centered schools,* and *child-centered curriculum* are frequently used to denote early childhood programs designed with children's needs and interests in mind. Review in Chapter 3 how Dewey described the child-centered approach and his emphasis on respect for children and the need to develop curricula and activities based on their interests.

In a child-centered approach, learning initiatives come *primarily* from the children. The teacher's role is that of facilitating and providing an environment in which children can follow their interests and learn within the context of the activities resulting from these interests. Play is the primary context within which children discover, extend, and develop their interests. Thus, a predetermined curriculum is not imposed from the outside; rather the natural development of the child is the key.

The Bank Street Program represents this child-centered approach to learning and education, and it constitutes the "middle ground" or "center" of American preschool educational thought and practice. This child-centered focus maintains that children's development, needs, and natures, not adults' or society's, should determine the goals, objectives, and teaching practices of early childhood programs.

The developmental-interactionist model has the following four general goals:

1. *To enhance competence.* This goal includes the use of knowledge, self-esteem, self-confidence, resourcefulness, resilience, and a feeling of competence.

2. *To promote individuality or identity.* This goal includes identifying self-qualities and roles occupied, for example, worker, learner, member of group, and so forth.

3. *To promote socialization.* Two primary abilities are necessary to achieve this goal: first, sensitivity to others' points of view and the ability to engage in

cooperative relations in play, work, talk, and argument; and second, the ability to communicate in a variety of ways.

4. *To develop integration of functions and the ability to be open to a wide range of phenomena.*[6]

Barbara Biber (1903–), long a proponent of the whole-child approach and a leading spokesperson for the developmental-interactionist point of view, suggests the following eight developmental-educational goals and accompanying preschool activities:

1. To serve the child's need to make an impact on the environment through direct physical contact and maneuver.

   • Exploring the physical world: for example, equipment, space, and physical protection.
   • Constructive, manipulative activities with things (presymbolic): for example, a variety of materials—blocks, clay, sand, and wood.

2. To promote the potential for ordering experience through cognitive strategies.

   • Extending receptiveness and responsiveness: for example, variety of sensorimotor-perceptual experiences, focus on observation and discrimination.
   • Extending modes of symbolizing: for example, gestural representation; two-dimensional representation with pencil, crayons, paints; and three-dimensional representation with clay, blocks, and wood.
   • Developing facility with language: for example, word meanings and usage; scope of vocabulary; mastery of syntax; playful and communicative verbal expression.
   • Stimulating verbal-conceptual organization of experience and information: for example, verbal formulation; integration of present and nonpresent; accent on classification, ordering, relationship, and transformation concepts in varied experiential contexts.

3. To advance the child's functioning knowledge of his environment.

   • Observation of functions within school: for example, heating systems, water pipes, kitchen, and elevator.
   • Story-reading: for example, stories about nature, work processes, people's roles and functions.
   • Observation of functioning environment outside the school: for example, to observe work forces, natural processes—buildings, construction, traffic regulation; to visit police, fire fighters, farm and dairy.
   • Discussion of contemporary events that children hear about: for example, war, demonstrations, strikes, space activities, street violence, explorations, and earthquakes.

4. To support the play mode of incorporating experience.

   • Nourishing and setting the stage for dramatic play activity: for example, experiences, materials, and props.

- Freedom to go beyond the restraints of reality in rehearsing and representing.

5. To help the child internalize impulse control.

    - Communicating a clear set of nonthreatening controls: for example, limits, rules, and regulations.
    - Creating a functional adult authority role: for example, understandable restraints, alternative behavior patterns, and nonpunitive sanctions.

6. To meet the child's need to cope with conflicts intrinsic to this stage of development.

    - Dealing with conflict over possession displaced from the family scene: for example, fostering special relation of child to a single adult, guidance in learning to share things as well as people.
    - Alleviating conflict over separation related to loss of familiar context of place and people: for example, visits from people to school, interchange of home and school objects, and school trips to school neighborhoods.
    - Accepting ambivalence about dependence and independence: for example, selection of areas of curriculum most suited to independent exploration and acceptance of regressive dependent behavior under stress.

7. To facilitate the development of an image of self as a unique and competent person.

    - Increasing knowledge of self: for example, identity, family, and ethnic membership, and awareness of skills.
    - Clarifying sense of self: for example, as initiator, learner, and autonomous individual.
    - Advancing integration of self: for example, self-realization through reexpression in symbolic play, latitude for individual mix of fantasy with knowledge of objective reality.

8. To help the child establish mutually supporting patterns of interaction.

    - Building informal communication channels, verbal and nonverbal: for example, adult-child, child-child.
    - Cooperative and collective child-group relations: for example, discussion periods, joint work projects.
    - Creating supportive adult roles: for example, source of comfort, troubleshooter, solver of unknowns, investor in child's learning.[7]

Classroom practice is what really defines a child-centered approach. Consequently, the teacher in a Bank Street program has two fundamental roles. One is to act as a mediator between the world of the family and the world of the peer group and larger society. The second role is to foster the child's ego development and mental health.[8] These roles are accomplished by developing a sense of trust between the teacher and child. Above all, the teacher needs to be a trusting person. As a result of this trust bond, the teacher can promote the child's initiative in interacting with the world outside the family.

WHAT IS THE HEAD START MODEL?

To help overcome the negative effects of poverty on the lives of adults and children, the federal government in 1964 passed the Economic Opportunity Act. One of the main purposes of this act was to break intergenerational cycles of poverty by providing educational and social opportunities for children from low-income families. The act created Project Head Start. As you review Figure 5–7, you will see how many children are living in poverty.

History and Operating Principles

Head Start was implemented during the summer of 1965, and approximately 550,000 children in 2,500 child development centers were enrolled in the program. The first programs were designed for children entering first grade who had not attended kindergarten. The purpose of Head Start was literally to give children a head start on their first grade experience and, it was hoped, on life itself.

Today, the National Head Start program has an annual budget of nearly $4 billion and serves 752,000 low-income children and families. There are 1,440 Head Start programs nationwide, with a total of 16,636 centers and

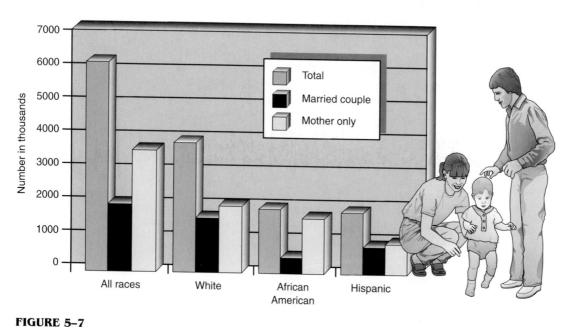

FIGURE 5–7

Families with Children Living in Poverty

Source: Lamison-White, Leatha, U.S. Bureau of the Census, Current Population Reports, Series PGO-198, *Poverty in the United States: 1997,* U.S. Government Printing Office, Washington, DC, 1998.

Head Start and other early childhood programs are dedicated to developing linkages between programs and families. All families and family members have to be involved in decisions regarding their children and program goals and objectives. How might this mother be involved in a Head Start program?

42,500 classrooms. The average cost per child of the Head Start program is $4,571 annually. Head Start has a paid staff of 146,200 and 1,249,000 volunteers. A total of 16,098,000 children have been served by Head Start since it began.[9]

Head Start is based on the premise that all children share certain needs, and that children of low-income families, in particular, can benefit from a comprehensive developmental program to meet those needs.

Goal and Purposes

The overall goal of Head Start is to bring about a greater degree of social competence in disadvantaged children. Social competence, in this context, is the child's everyday effectiveness in dealing with his environment and later responsibilities in school and life. Social competence takes into account the interrelatedness of cognitive and intellectual development, physical and mental health, nutritional needs, and other factors that enable a child to function optimally. Head Start is a comprehensive developmental approach to helping achieve social competence. To this end, Head Start goals provide for:

- *The improvement of the child's health and physical abilities.*
- *The encouragement of self-confidence, spontaneity, curiosity, and self-discipline which will assist in the development of the child's social and emotional health.*
- *The enhancement of the child's mental processes and skills with particular attention to conceptual and verbal skills.*

- *The establishment of patterns and expectations of success for the child, which will create a climate of confidence for his present and future learning efforts and overall development.*
- *An increase in the ability of the child and his family to relate to each other and to others in a loving and supporting manner.*
- *The enhancement of the sense of dignity and self-worth within the child and his family.*

The Head Start Program approach is based on the philosophy that (1) A child can benefit most from a comprehensive, interdisciplinary program to foster development and remedy problems as expressed in a broad range of services; and that (2) the child's entire family, as well as the community, must be involved.[10]

Head Start is intended to provide a comprehensive developmental program for children ages birth to five years from low-income families. The program is also dedicated to helping children achieve a positive outlook on life through success in school and daily life activities. Implementation of these objectives occurs through a comprehensive child development program delivered in center-based and home-based settings.

Program Design and Management

Head Start makes every effort to ensure that the management and governance of programs is conducted in such a way that supports the implementation of its published performance standards. Additionally, Head Start administrative services are designed to help local programs strengthen their administrative and management capabilities to bring about effective delivery of services. This component covers five major areas: program planning and management, personnel management, financial management, procurement and property management, and eligibility and enrollment.

With regard to program governance, *Head Start Program Performance Standards* state, "Agencies must establish and maintain a formal structure of shared governance through which parents can participate in policy making or in other decisions about the program."[11]

Parents and Families

Head Start requires that parents and community members must receive preference for employment vacancies for which they are qualified. Therefore, it is not uncommon to find parents employed as aides and teachers in Head Start. The belief is that helping parents learn helps their children learn. For example, parents who learn in the Head Start center that mealtime is a time for conversation are more likely to model this behavior by talking to their children at home. In this respect, a great deal of emphasis is placed on Head Start teachers modeling appropriate behavior for parents so parents can model for their children.

Increasing Parent Income, Responsibility, and Pride

Employing parents in Head Start centers is also a way to increase family incomes. Many parent volunteers have later been hired as bus drivers, cooks, aides, teachers, and directors. As a result of seminars and training programs, some parents have gained the skills necessary to assume positions of increased responsibility, such as assistant teacher, teacher, and program director. Jobs in Head Start are not viewed as dead-end positions.

Of course, pay and responsibility are not the only benefits; such work also enhances parents' self-image, an important factor in personal life.

Every Head Start program operates under policies established by a council that includes parents. Half the policy council members are selected from among parents with children in the program, and half from interested community agencies (day care, family services) and parents who have previously had children in Head Start. Policies established by the council include determining the attendance area for the center and the basis on which children should be recruited, helping develop and oversee the program budget, and acting as a personnel and grievance committee.

Head Start Services

Head Start offers the following program services: education, parent involvement, health services (including nutrition and mental health), family partnerships, staff development, and administration.

Effective January 8, 1998, all Head Start programs had to operate their programs and services according to new performance standards in order to continue receiving federal funds. It is informative to examine these standards for each area. The Head Start Bureau provides guidance on the performance standards to help each program implement them. However, local agencies are responsible for designing programs to best meet the needs of their children and families.

The performance standards encourage the integration of services across components and emphasize partnerships with families and communities. We list some of these standards in our discussion of each of the service areas. The full set of current Head Start Performance Standards appears in the November 5, 1996, issue of the *Federal Register.*

Implementation of Services

All Head Start programs are encouraged to explore ways to deliver services directly to children in their homes. This approach is based on the premise that the parent is the most important person in the child's life and the home the optimum place for growth and development. In brief, the local option encourages Head Start staff to plan programs that fit their needs and the needs of children and parents, while also taking into consideration the characteristics of the community they serve.

Local agencies may choose home-based programs as a means of delivering Head Start services. Today, 578 Head Start agencies operate home-based programs. Skilled home visitors assist parents in providing support services and developmental activities that children would normally receive in a center-based program. Presently, 4,396 home visitors serve more than 44,630 children and their families.

The primary difference between the options is that the home-based option focuses on parents in the home setting and is designed to help them be the primary educator of their child. It is augmented by group socialization activities conducted at the center, in one of the family's homes, or at another accessible location, such as a community center. The home-based option has these strengths:[12]

- Parent involvement is the very keystone of the program.
- Geographically isolated families have an invaluable opportunity to be part of a comprehensive child and family program.
- The individualized family plan is based on both a child and a family assessment.
- The family plan is facilitated by a home visitor who is an adult educator with knowledge and training related to all Head Start components.
- The program includes the entire family.

According to Glenna Markey of the Bear River Head Start in Logan, Utah, there are several keys to making a home-based option work:

- *The home visitor must work with the parent, not the child. When parents work with their children, the intended results of the home-based option are achieved.*
- *The home visitor must help the parent become a "child development specialist," which ultimately benefits the parents' children and grandchildren.*
- *The home visitor must try to do such a good job that the parent can do without him or her. In this sense, the home visitors put themselves out of a job!*
- *The home visitor must assist the parent in identifying resources in the home environment that can be adapted for use in helping children learn. When the home visitor supplies toys or materials and when these materials are no longer available, parents may think learning has to stop. Therefore, parents must be encouraged not to rely on commercial and store-bought materials. For example, brown grocery bags can be a coloring book, puzzles can be made out of cereal boxes, and tin cans can become musical instruments.*[13]

Education and Development for All Children

Performance standards for education and development for all children include the following:

> In order to help children gain the skills and confidence necessary to be prepared to succeed in their present environment and with later responsibilities in school and life, grantee and delegate agencies' approach to child development and education must:
>
> - Be developmentally and linguistically appropriate, recognizing that children have individual rates of development as well as individual interests, temperament, languages, cultural backgrounds, and learning styles;
> - Be inclusive of children with disabilities, consistent with their Individualized Family Service Plan (IFSP) or Individualized Education Program (IEP);
> - Provide an environment of acceptance that supports and respects gender, culture, language, ethnicity, and family composition;
> - Provide a balanced daily program of child-initiated and adult-directed activities, including individual and small group activities; and
> - Allow and enable children to independently use toilet facilities when it is developmentally appropriate and when efforts to encourage toilet training are supported by the parents.[14]

Child Development and Education Approach for Infants and Toddlers

> Programs of service for infants and toddlers must encourage:
>
> - The development of secure relationships in out-of-home care settings for infants and toddlers by having a limited number of consistent teachers over an extended period of time. Teachers must demonstrate an understanding of the child's family culture and, whenever possible, speak the child's language;
> - Trust and emotional security so that each child can explore the environment according to his or her developmental level; and
> - Opportunities for each child to explore a variety of sensory and motor experiences with support and stimulation from teachers and family members.
>
> Agencies must support the social and emotional development of infants and toddlers by promoting an environment that:
>
> - Encourages the development of self-awareness, autonomy, and self-expression; and
> - Supports the emerging communication skills of infants and toddlers by providing daily opportunities for each child to interact with others and to express himself or herself freely.
>
> Agencies must promote the physical development of infants and toddlers by:
>
> - Supporting the development of physical skills of infants and toddlers including gross motor skills, such as grasping, pulling, pushing, crawling, walking, and climbing; and

- *Creating opportunities for fine motor development that encourage the control and coordination of small, specialized motions, using the eyes, mouth, hands, and feet.*[15]

Child Development and Education Approach for Preschoolers

Grantee and delegate agencies, in collaboration with the parents, must implement a curriculum that:

- *Supports each child's individual pattern of development and learning;*
- *Integrates all educational aspects of the health, nutrition, and mental health services into program activities;*
- *Ensures that the program environment helps children develop emotional security and facility in social relationships;*
- *Enhances each child's understanding of self as an individual and as a member of a group; and*
- *Provides individual and small group experiences both indoors and outdoors.*
- *Staff must use a variety of strategies to promote and support children's learning and developmental progress based on the observations and ongoing assessment of each child.*[16]

Head Start agencies are permitted and encouraged to consider several program models and select the option best suited to their children's needs and staff's capabilities and resources. Program options available to local agencies are the center-based program option, the home-based program option, or approved locally designed variations.

Education Objectives

The child development and educational program of Head Start is guided by the following objectives:

- *Provide children with a learning environment and the varied experiences which will help them develop socially, intellectually, physically, and emotionally in a manner appropriate to their age and state of development toward the overall goal of social competence.*
- *Integrate the educational aspects of the various Head Start components in the daily program of activities.*
- *Involve parents in educational activities of the program to enhance their role as the principal influence on the child's education and development.*
- *Assist parents to increase their knowledge, understanding, skills, and experience in child growth and development.*
- *Identify and reinforce experiences which occur in the home that parents can utilize as educational activities for their children.*[17]

These educational objectives guide local agencies in developing their own programs that are unique and responsive to the children, families, and communities they serve. Thus, there is really no "national" Head Start curriculum.

Child Health and Safety

Head Start assumes an active role in children's health. Children's current health status is monitored and reported to parents, and corrective and preventive procedures are undertaken with their cooperation. For example, if a child needs glasses, corrective orthopedic surgery, or dental care, services may be provided through the Head Start budget, although the program usually works with social service agencies to provide services or money for health needs.

Regardless of the procedure, the parents' role in providing health care for the child is never bypassed. Although Head Start employees may take children to the doctor or dentist, every effort is made to see that parents receive support and assistance for securing appropriate services. For example, the community worker for the Head Start program might provide transportation for a parent, or might make arrangements if the parent has difficulty fixing an appointment with a specialist. The philosophy inherent in this process supports the right of the parent as the primary teacher. An associated rationale is that through involvement in providing health services, parents learn how to provide for future needs.

Daily Health Education

In addition to arranging medical examinations and care, each Head Start program teaches children how to care for their health, including the importance of eating proper foods and caring for their teeth.

Head Start also seeks to direct children and parents to existing mental health delivery systems such as community health centers. It does not intend to duplicate existing services but to help its clientele become aware of, and utilize, available services.

Health and Emergency Procedure Performance Standards

Agencies operating center-based programs must establish and implement policies and procedures to respond to medical and dental health emergencies with which all staff are familiar and trained. Additionally, agencies must do the following:

- *Make a determination as to whether or not each child has an ongoing source of continuous, accessible health care. If a child does not have a source of ongoing health care, agencies must assist the parents in accessing a source of care.*
- *Obtain from a health care professional a determination as to whether the child is up-to-date on a schedule of age appropriate preventive and primary health care which includes medical, dental and mental health.*[18]

Injury Prevention. Agencies must:

- *Ensure that staff and volunteers can demonstrate safety practices; and*

- *Foster safety awareness among children and parents by incorporating it into child and parent activities.*

Hygiene

- *Staff, volunteers, and children must wash their hands with soap and running water at least at the following times:*
  After diapering or toilet use;
  Whenever hands are contaminated with blood or other bodily fluids; and
  After handling pets or other animals.

- *Staff and volunteers must also wash their hands with soap and running water:*

  Before and after giving medications;
  Before and after treating or bandaging a wound (nonporous gloves should be worn if there is contact with blood or blood-containing body fluids); and
  After assisting a child with toilet use.

- *Nonporous (e.g., Latex) gloves must be worn by staff when they are in contact with spills of blood or other visibly bloody bodily fluids.*

- *Spills of bodily fluids (e.g., urine, feces, blood, saliva, nasal discharge, eye discharge, or any fluid discharge) must be cleaned and disinfected immediately in keeping with professionally established guidelines (e.g., standards of the Occupational Safety Health Administration, U.S. Department of Labor). Any tools and equipment used to clean spills of bodily fluids must be cleaned and disinfected immediately. Other blood-contaminated materials must be disposed of in a plastic bag with a secure tie.*

- *Agencies must adopt sanitation and hygiene procedures for diapering that adequately protect the health and safety of children served by the program and staff. Grantee and delegate agencies must ensure that staff properly conduct these procedures.[19]*

Nutrition

A basic premise of Head Start is that children must be properly fed to have the strength and energy to learn. This philosophy calls for teaching children good nutrition habits that will carry over for the rest of their lives and be passed on to their children. In addition, parents are given basic nutrition education so they, in turn, can promote good nutrition in their families. Such programs include seminars on buying food and reading and comparing grocery advertisements. One Head Start program in consumer education for parents and staff emphasized can sizes, number of servings per can, comparison of prices, nutritional value, and specific foods that can maximize dollar value.

Identification of Nutritional Needs

The following performance standards govern child nutrition services. Staff and families must work together to identify each child's nutritional needs, taking into account staff and family discussions concerning:

- *Any relevant nutrition-related assessment data (height, weight, blood analysis);*
- *Information about family eating patterns, including cultural preferences, special dietary requirements for each child with nutrition-related health problems, and the feeding requirements of infants and toddlers and each child with disabilities;*
- *For infants and toddlers, current feeding schedules and amounts and types of food provided, including whether breast milk or formula and baby food is used, meal patterns, new foods introduced, food intolerances and preferences, voiding patterns, and observations related to developmental changes in feeding and nutrition. This information must be shared with parents and updated regularly.[20]*

Nutritional Services

Agencies must design and implement a nutrition program that meets the nutritional needs and feeding requirements of each child, including those with special dietary needs and children with disabilities. Also, the nutrition program must serve a variety of foods which reflect cultural and ethnic preferences and which broaden the child's food experience.[21]

Services to Children with Disabilities

At least 10 percent of Head Start enrollment must consist of children with disabilities. Nationally, 13.4 percent of all children enrolled in Head Start have a disability—mental retardation, autism, traumatic brain injury, health impairments, visual impairments (including blindness), hearing impairments (including deafness), emotional-behavioral disorders, speech or language impairments, orthopedic impairments, and learning disabilities.

To provide adequately for these children, staff and parents receive training in procedures related to the particular disabilities. Head Start also trains staff in identification, treatment, and prevention of child abuse and neglect. (See Chapter 12 for more information on educating children with disabilities.)

Family and Community Partnerships

Parent Involvement

From the outset, Head Start has been dedicated to the philosophy that if children's lives are to improve, corresponding changes must be made in parents' lives. Part of the Head Start thrust is directed toward that end. Head Start has always conducted programs which provide a planned program of experiences and activities that support and enhance the parental role as the principal influence in the child's education and development. Additionally, Head Start provides a program that recognizes parents as (1) responsible guardians of their children's well-being, (2) prime educators of their children, and (3) contributors to the Head Start Program and to their communities.

All Head Start programs enroll children with disabilities. As a model for inclusion, Head Start is set up to give a head start to as wide a range of children as possible. Not only does Head Start provide services to families of children with disabilities, it also integrates services with other community agencies.

Family Partnerships

The Head Start performance standards for family partnerships include the following:

- *Grantee and delegate agencies must engage in a process of collaborative partnership-building with parents to establish mutual trust and to identify family goals, strengths, and necessary services and other supports. This process must be initiated as early after enrollment as possible and it must take into consideration each family's readiness and willingness to participate in the process.*

- *As part of this ongoing partnership, grantee and delegate agencies must offer parents opportunities to develop and implement individualized Family Partnership Agreements that describe family goals, responsibilities, timetables and strategies for achieving them. In home-based program options, this Agreement must include the above information as well as the specific roles of parents in home visits and group socialization activities.*[22]

Community Partnerships

Performance standards for community partnerships include the following:

- *Grantee and delegate agencies must take an active role in community planning to encourage strong communication, cooperation, and the sharing of information among agencies and their community partners and to improve the delivery of community services to children and families in accordance with the agency's confidentiality policies. Documentation must be maintained to reflect the level of effort undertaken to establish community partnerships.*

- *Grantee and delegate agencies must take affirmative steps to establish ongoing collaborative relationships with community organizations to promote the access of children and families to community services that are responsive to their needs, and to ensure that Early Head Start programs respond to community needs.*[23]

More than ever, Head Start is endeavoring to be in cooperative and collaborative relationships with families and communities.

Early Head Start

EHS is designed to enhance children's physical, social, emotional, and intellectual development; support both parents in fulfilling their parental roles; and help parents move toward economic independence. Programs are expected to offer certain core services, including high-quality early education (both in and out of the home) and family support services; home visits; parent education; comprehensive health and mental health services, including services for women prior to, during, and after pregnancy; nutrition; and child care. EHS programs have the flexibility to respond to the unique strengths and needs of their own communities and of each child and family within that community.

Among the program options are family child care, center-based care, and home visits. Several projects use combinations of these models. In response to specific needs identified in their communities, some projects emphasize certain program components such as services for teen parents, family literacy, life skills development, substance abuse treatment, and injury and accident prevention. All projects work with community partners to ensure early, continuous, and comprehensive services.[24]

While all of the models we have discussed are unique, at the same time they all have certain similarities. All of them, regardless of their particular philosophical orientation, have as a primary goal the best education for all children.

As an early childhood professional, you will want to do several things now. First, begin to decide which of the features of the program models you embrace. Second, think about which of the features of models you embrace that you can incorporate into your own practice. An ongoing rule of the early childhood professional is deciding what you believe is best for children and families and making decisions to accomplish that goal.

ACTIVITIES FOR REFLECTION AND RESEARCH

1. The High/Scope approach is very popular in early childhood programs. What accounts for this popularity? Would you implement this curriculum in your program? Why?

2. Explain why you think Head Start and other programs are emphasizing a two-generation approach to the delivery of services. What are the pros and cons of such a delivery system?

3. Visit several Head Start programs and compare and contrast what you see. How are they similar and different? How do you account for this?

4. What features of the Montessori program do you like best? Why? What features do you like least? Why? What features are best for children?

5. Write to the AMS, AMI, and NAMTA for information about becoming a certified Montessori teacher.

6. Do you think *all* early childhood professionals should have knowledge of the Montessori program? Why?

READINGS FOR FURTHER ENRICHMENT

Beaty, Janice J. *Skills for Preschool Teachers,* 6th ed. (Upper Saddle River, NJ: Merrill/Prentice Hall, 2000).

Designed specifically for the Head Start, day care, and kindergarten worker, this book parallels the Child Development Associate competencies; helpful for anyone contemplating this training program.

Lillard, P. P. *Montessori in the Classroom: A Teacher's Account of How Children Really Learn* (New York: Schocken, August, 1997).

What really happens inside a Montessori classroom? How do teachers teach? How do children learn? This day-by-day record in the year of the life of a Montessori classroom answers these questions by providing an illuminating and practical glimpse of the Montessori method in action.

Lillard, P. P. *Montessori Today: A Comprehensive Approach to Education from Birth to Adulthood* (New York: Schocken, 1996).

In detailed accounts of Montessori theory and practice, the author shows how children acquire the skills to answer their own questions, learn to manage freedom responsibly, and maintain a high level of intellectual curiosity. This is an essential handbook for parents and teachers interested in the Montessori alternative for older children.

Mills, Kay. *Something Better for My Children: The History and People of Head Start* (New York: Dutton, 1998).

Kay Mills examines Head Start programs from the inner-city Los Angeles neighborhood of Watts and affluent Montgomery County, Maryland. Also included are summaries of Head Start's history and policies.

Cadwell, Louise Boyd. *Bringing Reggio Emilia Home: An Innovative Approach to Early Childhood Education (Early Childhood Education Series)* (Teachers College Press, November 1997).

This book integrates the experiences of one American teacher on a year-long internship in the preschools of Reggio, with a four-year adaptation of American schools.

Zigler, Edward and Susan Muenchow. *Head Start: The Inside Story of America's Most Successful Educational Experiment* (New York: Basic Books, 1992).

An interesting, behind-the-scenes account of the beginning and survival of Head Start. The authors draw on the lessons of Head Start to address some of today's most crucial and controversial lessons in education.

RESEARCH ON THE INTERNET

The National Head Start Association

http://www.nhsa.org

The National Head Start Association, composed of Head Start directors, staff, and parents, was created to provide a unified national voice for the Head Start community. The web site contains information about the organization as well as the full text of the 1998 Head Start Amendments and other government documents related to Head Start.

Head Start of Santa Clara and San Benito counties

http://www.sccoe.k12.ca.us/child/headstar.htm

The web site belongs to one of the oldest and largest Head Start programs in the United States. Basic information about Head Start, enrollment procedures, and links to numerous documents are available.

High/Scope K–3 Curriculum

http://www.ed.gov/pubs/EPTW/eptw11/eptw1
1d.html

> Detailed description about the basics of the program, requirements, and the cost of implementation of the High/Scope curriculum in a K–3 program.

A Summary of Significant Benefits: The High/Scope Perry Preschool Study through Age 27

http://www.tyc.state.tx.us/prevention/
hiscope.htm

> Summary of a study tracing the long-term effects of educating students using the High/Scope approach versus educating those under a different program.

The Reggio Emilia Approach to Early Childhood Education

http://www.cmu.edu/hr/child-care/reggio.html

> An overview of the Reggio Emilia approach.

NOTES

1. High/Scope Education Research Foundation, *The High/Scope K–3 Curriculum: An Introduction* (Ypsilanti, MI: Author, 1989), p. 1.

2. Ibid.

3. Ibid., p. 3.

4. Maria Montessori, *The Absorbent Mind*, trans. Claude A. Claremont (New York: Holt, Rinehart & Winston, 1967), p. 8.

5. Maria Montessori, *Dr. Montessori's Own Handbook* (New York: Schocken Books, 1965), p. 131.

6. R. DeVries, *Programs in Early Education: The Constructivist View* (New York: Longman, 1987), pp. 303–304.

7. B. Biber, *Early Education and Psychological Development* (New Haven, CT: Yale University Press, 1984), pp. 245–254.

8. DeVries, *Programs in Early Education,* p. 310.

9. Administration on Children, Youth, and Families, *Project Head Start Statistical Fact Sheet* (Washington, DC: Author, May 1997), pp. 1–3.

10. U.S. Department of Health and Human Services, *Head Start Program Performance Standards* (45 CFR §1304) (Washington, DC: U.S. Government Printing Office, November 1984), p. 4.

11. *Federal Register,* vol. 61, no. 215 (1996), p. 57219.

12. E. Dollie Wolverton, "The Home-Based Option: Reinforcing Parents," *National Head Start Bulletin,* 12, p. 1.

13. Phone interview with author.

14. *Federal Register,* vol. 61, no. 215 (1996), p 57213.

15. Ibid.

16. Ibid., p. 57214.

17. U.S. Department of Health and Human Services, *Head Start Program Performance Standards,* pp. 8–9.

18. *Federal Register,* vol. 61, no. 215 (1996), p. 57212.

19. Ibid., p. 57214–57215.

20. Ibid., p. 57215.

21. Ibid.

22. Ibid., p. 57216.

23. Ibid., p. 57218.

24. *Early Head Start National Resource Center.* www.ehsnrc.org

CHAPTER

6

Meeting the Child Care Needs of Parents and Families

FOCUS QUESTIONS

1. What are families' needs for child care services?
2. What is the terminology used with child care?
3. What are the purposes of child care programs?
4. What is quality child care, and how do quality programs operate?
5. What are the types of child care services and programs?
6. How is child care funded?
7. How effective are child care programs in meeting the needs of children, parents, and families?
8. What are the reasons for the growth of proprietary child care?
9. What issues are associated with child care?
10. What are future trends in child care services and needs?

WHY IS CHILD CARE POPULAR?

Child care is popular and in the center of the public eye for a number of reasons. One reason is that a number of demographic features create a high demand for child care. There are more dual-income families and more working single parents than ever before. For example, over 65 percent of mothers with children under six are employed. Nearly 21.5 million employed parents have children under the age of six, and it is not uncommon for mothers to return to work as early as six weeks after giving birth. In 1997, approximately 35 million employed parents with young children reported significant work-family conflict, creating a great demand for infant and young child care.

Second, child care is an important part of many politicians' solutions to the nation's economic and social problems. In this regard, child care is an instrument of public policy. Child care can be used to address political and social issues. For example, child care is an essential part of work-training programs designed to get people off welfare and help them join the workforce. At the same time, many work-training programs train welfare recipients for child care jobs. So, many welfare recipients are moving from welfare to gainful employment as child care workers.

Quality child care is also seen by politicians and the public as a way of addressing many of the country's problems through early intervention in children's lives. The reasoning goes that if we provide children with quality programs and experiences early in life, we reduce the possibility that they will need costly social services later in life.

As the demand for child care increases, the challenge to you and other early childhood professionals is clear. You and the profession must participate in advocating for and creating quality child care programs that meet the needs of children and families.

WHAT IS CHILD CARE?

Although day care is a widely used and popular term, *child care* is preferable to *day care,* because children are the central focus of any program provided for them.

Child care is a *comprehensive* service to children and families that *supplements* the care children receive from their families. Care is supplemental in that parents delegate responsibility to caregivers for providing care and appropriate experiences in their absence. Care is comprehensive in that, although it includes custodial care such as supervision, food, shelter, and other physical necessities, it goes beyond these to include activities that encourage and aid learning and are responsive to children's health, social, and psychological needs. Child care is also educational. It provides for the intellectual needs of children and helps engage them in the process of learning that begins at birth. Quality child care does not ignore the educational needs of young children and incorporates learning activities as part of the curriculum. Furthermore, child care staff work with parents to help them learn how to support children's learning in the home. A comprehensive view of child care considers the child to be a whole person; therefore, the major purpose of child care is to facilitate optimum development of the whole child and support efforts of families to achieve this goal.

TYPES OF CHILD CARE PROGRAMS

Child care is offered in many places, by many persons and agencies that provide a variety of care and services. The options for child care are almost endless. However, regardless of the kinds of child care provided, the three issues of quality, affordability, and accessibility always are part of the child care landscape.

Child Care by Family and Relatives

Child care is most commonly arranged within nuclear and extended families or with friends (see Figure 6–1). Parents handle these arrangements in various ways. Some mothers and fathers work different shifts, so one parent cares for the children while the spouse is at work. These families do not need out-of-home care. In some cases, children are cared for by grandparents, aunts, uncles, or other relatives. These arrangements satisfy parents' needs to have their children cared for by people with similar lifestyles and values. Such care may be less costly, and compensation may be made in ways other than direct monetary payments. These types of arrangements allow children to remain in familiar environments with people they know. Child care by family members provides children with continuity and a sense of safety and security.

The number of children who are cared for through informal arrangements exceeds the number enrolled in centers or family day care for two primary

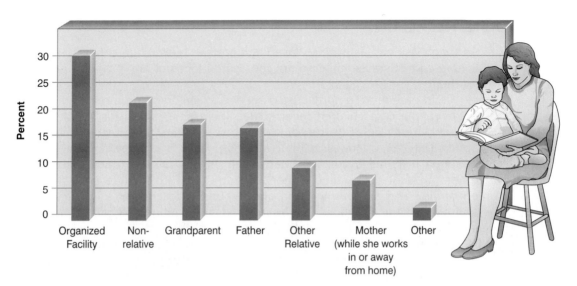

FIGURE 6–1
Caregivers of Children Under Age Five Whose Mothers Work
Source: U.S. Department of Education, National Center for Educational Statistics, 1996.

reasons. First, there is a lack of available quality child care programs. Second, many parents simply prefer to take care of their own children. When people search for child care, they often turn to people who are available and willing to take care of children. These two criteria, however, are not the best or only ones that people who provide child care or baby-sitting services should meet. There is a tremendous difference between placing a child in a high-quality, comprehensive program and placing that child with an individual who provides primarily custodial care.

Family Day Care

When child care is provided in a child's own family or familylike setting, it is known as *family day care*. In this arrangement an individual caregiver provides care and education for a small group of children in her or his home. Eleven percent of children under five in child care are in family day care. Family day care generally involves three types of settings: homes that are unlicensed and unregulated by a state or local agency, homes that are licensed by regulatory agencies, and homes that are licensed and associated with an administrative agency.

Many parents leave their children at unregulated and unlicensed homes, and the kind of care a child then receives depends on the person who provides it. Some family day care providers are motivated to meet state or local standards for child care so they can be licensed. Family day care providers

Family day care is the preferred method of child care. Parents like a program for their children that approximates a homelike setting. What are some characteristics of a homelike setting that you can incorporate into your classroom?

may also be associated with a child care agency. They meet state and agency standards for care and, in return, receive assistance, training, and referrals. The agency usually subsidizes the cost of children's care when parents are eligible for subsidies.

Both the quantity and the quality of specific services provided in family homes vary from home to home and from agency to agency. However, almost 50 percent of caregivers spend a substantial amount of their time in direct interaction with children. Read now the Program in Action, "Patrick's Day at Family Day Child Care," to see how good family day care is much more than baby-sitting.

Intergenerational Child Care

Intergenerational child care programs take two forms. One kind integrates children and the elderly into an early childhood and adult care facility. The elderly derive pleasure and feelings of competence from helping care for and interact with children, and young children receive attention and love from older caregivers. In today's mobile society, families often live long distances from each other, and children may be isolated from the care that grandparents can offer. Intergenerational programs blend the best of two worlds: Children and the elderly both receive care and attention in a nurturing environment.

PATRICK'S DAY AT FAMILY DAY CHILD CARE

I enjoy being a child care provider because I realize I can enhance a good family situation but cannot replace it. My home is open from 7:00 A.M. to 5:00 P.M. If these hours are not convenient for a family, other child care homes in my city have more flexible hours. I encourage parents to interview with as many child care providers as possible before they make a decision about a particular home.

The Day

7:45 a.m. Patrick is four and a half years old and has been coming to my Family Day Child Care home since he was ten weeks old. He is dropped off by his dad. Melanie, three and a half years; Bret, two and a half years; and Marina, four months, have already arrived. Marina has been fed and is napping. Bret and Melanie are playing with puzzles or stringing beads at the kitchen table. Patrick's dad chats a moment with Patrick and me, gives Patrick a kiss, and says goodbye. (I do not like sneak-out goodbyes; these can lead to distrust.) Patrick joins the activities at the table and after fifteen to twenty minutes goes to the blocks, as he loves to build. Tyler, twenty-three months, arrives and is fussy. He has been out ill for several days and has a rough time getting into the swing of things. I recommend that Tyler's dad make his good-bye quick and firm to end Tyler's turmoil. Tyler gets a hug and love from Dad and me, and tells me he would like to take a little rest. Five minutes later he wants to get up and play with his friends.

8:40–9:00 a.m. The children have breakfast. Patrick and Melanie help set the table, and everyone, even Tyler, helps clean up their own places after eating. Patrick leads everyone to the bathroom for wash-up time.

9:10 a.m. The children all help pick up toys, so we can get ready for music time, approximately twenty to thirty minutes of dancing, shaking, stomping, singing, and music making. I encourage the children to express their creativity, and each child gets a chance to perform individually. Melanie and Patrick love to use the wooden microphones and sing solo or duet. Tyler wants to copy everything anyone else does.

9:40 a.m. We have circle time, when everyone reviews the calendar, weather, shapes, and colors. Patrick reminds us he wants to do the alphabet mystery draw, where each child reaches into a bag and draws out a letter of the alphabet. One of the children draws a letter, and everyone tries to name it, even Tyler. Everyone helps him guess! Patrick loves this game and excels.

We then do fingerpaints, poster paints, felt pens, crayons, and chalking. Paper cutting and pasting is a constant favorite. Patrick will stick to a project until completed and then will "teach" a younger child how to complete his work. He is very kind and sincere in his efforts, and Bret appreciates the thoughtfulness. Tyler has to be included in all activities, or he will fuss until he is. His efforts are sincere, and he is very proud of himself. So are we all.

care providers. These services can be offered in-house (i.e., on-site) or through community or national resource and referral agencies.

- *On-site or near-site child care centers.* Corporations supply space, equipment, and child care workers. Some corporations contract with an outside agency to provide child care service. Some also maintain a list of family day care homes and contract for spaces. They may also assist in equipping the providers' homes for child care services.

- *Direct aid.* Some companies provide a flat subsidy—a specific amount to their employees to help cover the cost of child care. For example, NationsBank, the largest bank in the South, pays its associates with limited incomes up to $35 per week to pay for child care.

- *Voucher systems.* Corporations give employees vouchers with which to purchase services at child care centers.

- *Vendor systems.* Corporations purchase spaces at child care centers and make them available to employees either free or at reduced rates.

- *Contributions to a child care center.* In this case corporations pay a subsidy to help reduce rates for employees at a particular center.

- *Parent-family leave.* Some corporations provide paid or subsidized leaves of absence for parents in lieu of specific child care services.

- *Other arrangements.* Employers can offer a flexible work schedule, so parents may need less or no child care. They may also offer maternity leave extensions and paternity leaves, and allow sick leave use to include absence from work for a sick child.

Payroll Deductions for Child Care

Federal tax law allows employee payroll deductions for a flexible spending account for child care. The employee reimbursement system works either as a direct employee benefit or as a salary reduction plan, and does not limit the type of child care the employee can use.

As a benefit, the employee sets aside a certain amount of salary to be paid directly by the employer to the child care provider. Employee salary reductions are more common, which allow child care payments to be made from pretax earnings, often at a considerable discount for most employees. This plan provides a significant benefit to workers in higher tax brackets.

Under such plans, present tax law requires that employees forfeit any of the amount specifically set aside that they do not spend on child care by the end of the calendar year. Employees pay no federal or social security taxes on money spent for child care. The maximum salary reduction allowed is $5,000 per year.

NATIONSBANK CHILD CARE CENTER

NationsBank, the South's largest banking company, has earned national recognition as a leader in developing progressive and flexible programs for working parents. The results of an employee survey in the mid-1980s revealed child care to be the number one need. The company responded with an expanding and evolving array of work-family programs. The NationsBank Child Care Center in Charlotte, North Carolina, is a model representing an added dimension in the company's efforts to aid employees.

The center is designed with its primary users in mind: children. Natural lighting and play space are given priority. Each classroom opens directly to one of six outdoor playgrounds. Large, interior central foyers turn into recreational areas on foul-weather days.

The capacity for full-year child care is 160 children. Forty spaces (25 percent) are reserved for children of eligible tenants of the NationsBank Corporate Center. Also, there are thirty Back-Up Care spaces and ten Get Well Care spaces. Capacity may change based on enrollment demands. However, the anticipated enrollment structure is forty-eight infants (six groups of eight children), forty toddlers (four groups of ten children), and seventy-two preschoolers (four groups of eighteen children).

The Curriculum

Children enrolled in the center participate in a developmentally appropriate, individualized curriculum. Teachers understand the variety of learning styles and paces in children's normal development. Their job is to respond to each child's own style and pace.

At the heart is a warm, nurturing relationship with caring adults in a stimulating, developmentally designed environment. Thus, much of the teachers' planning revolves around the needs of the children—individually and as a group. Each day there is both indoor and outdoor activity, small-group and independent projects, and active and quiet play.

The program begins with an understanding that children are active learners and that there is no clear separation between learning and caring, play and work. The NationsBank Child Care Center is committed to promoting all aspects of development, including the following:

Motor development. Using large muscles for skills such as throwing and running as well as small muscles for activities such as stacking and writing

Perceptual development. For example, learning to look deliberately, thinking about what one sees, and distinguishing parts of a whole scene

Social/emotional development. How to be a constructive member of a group as well as an individual; recognizing and understanding feelings, how to act on or cope with them; allowing children to develop their unique, individual talents; developing a foundation that promotes success in school, including problem-solving skills, high self-esteem, and a love of learning; providing an environment that is free of racial and gender bias or stereotypes

*Language development.*Using words to express and understand needs, feelings, and ideas; reading and prereading skills; and appreciation for books and other written language

The center's yard, enclosed by a brick and wrought iron fence, has playground equipment for children to enjoy during recreation time. The ample exterior play space allows children to crawl, run, jump, skip, and enjoy outdoor activities on sunny days. Each of the six play areas serves as the "backyard" for children at their daytime home away from home.

Get Well Care

A program for children who are mildly ill is included among the services of the Full-Year Care. Parents receive detailed guidelines for Get Well Care on enrollment. When children in Full-Year Care are under the weather and not up to the demands of their regular activity, but well enough to leave home, child care can be provided in Get Well Care. This is a separate area, staffed by a full-time registered nurse.

Parent Involvement

NationsBank is committed to promoting active parent participation in the center. Parents are encouraged to visit the center and are welcome at any time. Extensive communication with parents about their child, their child's room, and the center is an important part of the program.

In addition to many written and verbal means of communication with parents, the parent representative system (parent reps) is a formal way parents can give feedback and input. Each month volunteer parent reps call other parents to learn how things are going and obtain ideas, questions, or suggestions about the center. Parent reps meet monthly to discuss these comments; these meetings are open to all parents.

Administration

Resources for Child Care Management (RCCM) manages and supervises NationsBank Child Care Center. RCCM's unique approach to the management of workplace child care centers ensures that NationsBank will have a strong influence on the program and policy at its center. This partnership is based on a mutual commitment to well-accepted standards of high-quality care.

Providing for children in developmentally appropriate ways is a major goal of NationsBank Child Care Center. Professionals respond to children's interests and learning styles in warm, nurturing ways. Corporations across the country are including child care in the benefits provided employees and their families and are leading the way in designing environments and programs that are child centered and family focused.

Proprietary Child Care

Some child care centers are run by corporations, businesses, and individual proprietors for the purpose of making a profit. Some for-profit centers provide custodial services and preschool and elementary programs as well. Many of these programs emphasize their educational component and appeal to middle-class families who are willing to pay for the promised services. About 35 percent of all child care centers in the United States are operated for profit, and the number is likely to grow. Child care is a big service industry, with more and more entrepreneurs realizing that there is money to be made in caring for the nation's children. A *New York Times* article from July 26, 1998, reported that the $30 billion child care industry is an "attractive growth sector" for investors.[1] Figure 6–2 shows the percentage of types of agencies that operate child care programs.

What Is Military Child Care?

The Army, Navy, Air Force, Marine Corps, and Coast Guard operate child development programs at over 700 locations within the United States and throughout the world. The armed services are the largest providers of employer child care services in the United States. The programs offer care of all kinds—hourly, part day, full day, before school and after school, evening, and weekend—to children of military families and other Department of Defense personnel. The services operate center programs ranging in size from 29 to 450 children. Infant care accounts for 40 percent of all child care services provided. These programs help family members meet their military responsibilities secure in the knowledge that their children are receiving quality care.

FIGURE 6–2

Percentage Distribution of Preschool Children under Six Years Old According to Type of Primary Arrangement: 1995.

Note: A child's "primary arrangement" was defined as the regular nonparental care arrangement or early childhood education program in which the child spent the most time per week.

Source: U.S. Department of Education, National Center for Education Statistics, National Household Education Survey, 1995, Early Childhood Program Participation Component.

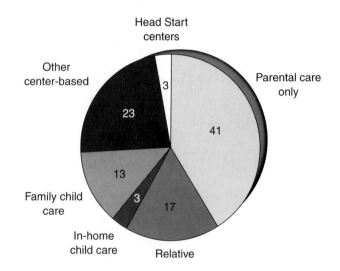

Military child care programs are funded through Department of Defense appropriations, participant fees, and funds from local programs. Department of Defense funds usually cover the costs of facilities, utilities, supplies, and equipment; participant fees cover the cost of staff salaries.

How Is Child Care Provided for Children with Medical Needs?

As child care becomes more popular, it also is becoming more specialized. Consequently, more and more programs are providing care for children with medical needs.

Ill Child Care

For most parents, balancing the demands of a job and the obligations of parenthood is manageable as long as children are healthy. But when children get sick, parents must find someone who will take care of them or must stay home. The National Child Care Survey data reveal that 35 percent of mothers employed outside the home reported that in the month previous to the survey their child was sick on a day they were supposed to work. Fifty-one percent of these women missed an average of 2.2 days of work per month because of sick children.[2]

Child care providers have begun to respond to parents' needs. Some centers provide care for sick children as part of their program, and other providers are opening centers exclusively for the care of ill children. Ill children are cared for in the following ways:

- *In the home.* Child care aides go into homes to care for ill children.
- *Hospital based.* Some hospitals have programs for providing for sick children.
- *Center based.* Ill child care is part of a center's program of services, usually in a separate room.
- *A separate facility.* This facility is specifically designed, built, and staffed to provide child care as needed for sick children.
- *Family care.* Ill children are provided for in a family day care home.

Before-School and After-School Care

In many respects, public schools are logical places for before-school and after-school care. They have the administrative organization, facilities, and staff to provide such care. Many taxpayers and professionals have always believed that schools should not sit empty in the afternoons, evenings, holidays, and summers. Using resources already in place for child care makes good sense. This is why in many communities public schools are helping meet the need for after-school child care. For example, the public schools in Dade County, Florida, provide before- and after-school care for over 22,000 students in 203 after-school and 111 before-school centers.

Many children come home after school to homes without parents or others to provide care and supervision. In order to help address this problem of latchkey children, more school districts are providing before- and afterschool child care programs. What are some advantages of these before- and afterschool programs?

Special needs students are mainstreamed at 83 schools with over 700 students in after-school care. Parents pay from $15 to $25 per week depending on the per-child cost at the individual school. Because the programs are school based and managed, the costs of services vary depending on the nature and cost of each program. Services begin at dismissal and end at 6 P.M. The curriculum includes Boy and Girl Scouts, 4-H, fun activities based on skills and concepts measured by state assessment tests for grades 3 and 5, drama, and ballet.

According to the National Study of Before and After School Programs, about 1.7 million children in kindergarten through grade 8 are enrolled in 49,500 programs.[3] The three most common sponsors of before- and after-school child care are the public schools, for-profit corporations, and nonprofit organizations.

Full-Service Child and Family Programs

While child care programs have traditionally focused on children's needs, the trend is toward providing a range of services to children and their families. Family-centered programs go beyond providing child care. They help parents cope with daily living problems (e.g., finding adequate housing) and enhance their parenting skills (e.g., providing parenting classes), and otherwise assist parents (e.g., connecting parents with health services). In this regard, child and family programs are linking up with other agencies, such as health clinics, so that they can meet children's, parents', and families' needs.

Child care is increasingly seen as a comprehensive service for *families*. This means that child care programs are not only providing services for children. They consider the entire family—children, parents, and extended relatives—as the recipients of their services. This expansion of services is in keeping with the trend by early childhood professionals to pay greater attention to the *ecology of early childhood*—the many environments in which children are reared and the influences these environments have on them and their families. These environments include family, home life and settings, siblings, community agencies, and so forth. All these influence children's growth and development. It makes sense to consider *family systems* when providing services to and for children.

How Much Should Child Care Cost?

Traditionally, child care has been a low-cost and low-paying operation. Many programs emphasize keeping costs low so that working and low-income parents will not be overburdened; this results in a very low pay scale for child care workers. Thus, as the cost of child care is kept low, the true cost is subsidized by low-paid workers. Yet if child care costs rise to provide workers with fairer wages, many families who can hardly afford what they now pay would be priced out of the services. Also, as more public schools offer programs for four-year-olds, many child care workers with degrees will be attracted to these programs by the higher salaries. This shift could tend to lower the quality of child care programs and further decrease salaries.

Two noteworthy efforts are currently under way to help address issues associated with the cost of child care and low child care worker wages, the Worthy Wage Coalition and the Full Cost of Quality program.

Worthy Wage Coalition

The Worthy Wage Coalition is an association of organizations whose primary focus is specifically to address issues of inadequate compensation in child care. Inadequate compensation for child care workers, which includes salaries and benefits, cannot be considered in isolation of other factors. These include quality care for children and affordability for families. The Worthy Wage Coalition is coordinated by the Child Care Employees Project, a national organization dedicated to improving child caregiver wages, working conditions, and access to training. Its address and phone number are 733 15th Street, NW, Suite 1037, Washington, D.C. 20005-2112; 202-737-7700.

Full Cost of Quality

The Full Cost of Quality program is an NAEYC initiative designed to highlight public awareness regarding what constitutes quality in early childhood services and the cost of fully meeting professional recommendations regarding high quality.

Parents need to know and understand that quality child care costs money. In addition, when parents understand what constitutes quality, they are more likely to seek it out and demand it. All early childhood professionals have an obligation to promote and provide high-quality programs, help parents understand the importance and cost of quality, and advocate to the public regarding quality child care. For more information about the Full Cost of Quality program, contact the Public Affairs Division of the National Association for the Education of Young Children, 1509 16th Street, NW, Washington, D.C. 20036; 800-424-2460.

HOW ARE EARLY CHILDHOOD PERSONNEL TRAINED AND CERTIFIED?

A major challenge facing all areas of the early childhood profession is the training and certification of those who care for and teach young children. Training and certification requirements vary from state to state, but more states are tightening standards for child care, preschool, kindergarten, and primary personnel. Many states have mandatory training requirements that individuals must fulfill before being certified as a child care worker. The curriculum of these training programs frequently specifies mandatory inclusion of topics. For example, in Texas, all child care personnel must complete a training course of four modules: state and local rules and regulations governing child care; health, safety, and nutrition; identifying and reporting child abuse and neglect; and child growth and development.

What Is the CDA National Credentialing Program?

At the national level, the Child Development Associate (CDA) National Credentialing Program offers early childhood professionals the opportunity to develop and demonstrate competencies for meeting the needs of young children. A CDA is one who is "able to meet the specific needs of children and who, with parents and other adults, works to nurture children's physical, social, emotional, and intellectual growth in a child development framework."[4]

The CDA program, begun in 1971, is a major national effort to evaluate and improve the skills of caregivers in center-based preschool settings, center-based infant-toddler settings, family day care homes, home visitor settings, and bilingual settings—programs that have specific goals for bilingual children. The CDA National Credentialing Program is operated by the Council for Early Childhood Professional Recognition. The council offers two options for obtaining the CDA credential. One option, the CDA Professional Preparation Program-P3, allows candidates to work in postsecondary institutions as part of the credentialing process. The second option is the direct assessment method, which is designed for candidates who have child care work experience in combination with some early childhood education training.

A candidate for the CDA credential in any setting must be eighteen years old or older and hold a high school diploma or equivalent. To obtain the CDA national credential, candidates under the direct assessment option must meet these additional eligibility requirements:

- 480 hours of experience working with children within the past five years
- 120 hours of formal child care education and training within the past five years

The candidate must then demonstrate competence in the six CDA competency areas (see Appendix B, "CDA Competency Goals and Functional Areas").

The CDA Professional Preparation Program

To obtain credentialing by means of this option, the candidate must meet the two general eligibility requirements of age and education and must also identify an advisor to work with during the year of study, which is made up of three phases.

The first phase is fieldwork. It involves study of the council's model curriculum, "Essentials for Child Development Associates Working with Young Children." This curriculum includes the six competency areas listed in Appendix B. The second phase is coursework, in which the candidate participates in seminars offered in community colleges and other postsecondary educational institutions. These seminars are designed to supplement the model curriculum and are administered by a seminar instructor. The third phase is the final evaluation, which takes place in the candidate's work setting or field placement.

The results of all three phases are sent to the council office for review and determination of whether the candidate has successfully completed all aspects of the CDA Professional Preparation Program. To date, more than 90,000 persons have been awarded the CDA credential.

Additional information about the CDA can be obtained from the Council for Early Childhood Professional Recognition, 1341 G Street, NW, Suite 400, Washington, D.C. 20005. The toll-free number is 800-424-4310; the fax number is 202-265-9161.

WHAT CONSTITUTES QUALITY CHILD CARE?

While there is much debate about quality and what it involves, we can nonetheless identify the main characteristics of quality child care programs.

Developmental Needs

Good child care provides for children's needs and interests at each developmental stage. For example, infants need good physical care as well as continual love and affection and sensory stimulation. Toddlers need safe surroundings and opportunities to explore. They need caregivers who support and encourage active involvement.

Appropriate and Safe Environment

At all age levels, a safe and pleasant physical setting is important. Such an area should include a safe neighborhood free from traffic and environmental hazards; a fenced play area with well-maintained equipment; child-sized equipment and facilities (toilets, sinks); and areas for displaying children's work, such as finger painting and clay models. The environment should also be attractive and pleasant. The rooms, home, or center should be clean, well lit, well ventilated, and cheerful.

Caregiver-Child Ratio

The ratio of adults to children should be sufficient to give children the individual care and attention they need. NAEYC guidelines for the ratio of caregivers to children are 1:3 or 1:4 for infants; 1:3 or 1:4 for toddlers; and 1:8 to 1:10 for preschoolers, depending on group size (see Table 6–1).

Developmentally Appropriate Programs

Programs should have written, developmentally based curricula for meeting children's needs. A program's curriculum should specify activities for children of all ages that caregivers can use to stimulate infants, provide for the growing independence of toddlers, and address the readiness and literacy skills of four- and five-year-olds. The program should go beyond good physical care to include social, emotional, and cognitive care as well. It should include a balance of activities, with time for playing indoors and outdoors and for learning skills and concepts.

Most of all quality programs use developmentally appropriate practices to implement the curriculum and achieve their programs goals. Figure 6–3 shows you the processes involved in developmentally appropriate practices.

TABLE 6–1
Recommended Staff-Child Ratios and Group Size

Age of Children	Group Size										
	6	8	10	12	14	16	18	20	22	24	28
Infants (birth to 12 mos.)	1:3	1:4									
Toddlers (12 to 24 mos.)	1:3	1:4	1:5	1:4							
2-year-olds (24 to 30 mos.)		1:4	1:5	1:6							
2 1/2-year-olds (30 to 36 mos.)			1:5	1:6	1:7						
3-year-olds					1:7	1:8	1:9	1:10			
4-year-olds						1:8	1:9	1:10			
5-year-olds						1:8	1:9	1:10			
6- to 8-year-olds								1:10	1:11	1:12	
9- to 12-year-olds										1:12	1:14

Note: Smaller group sizes and lower staff-child ratios have been found to be strong predictors of compliance with indicators of quality such as positive interactions among staff and children and developmentally appropriate curriculum. Variations in group sizes and ratios are acceptable in cases where the program demonstrates a very high level of compliance with criteria for interactions, curriculum, staff qualifications, health and safety, and physical environment.
Source: *Criteria for High Quality Early Childhood Programs with Interpretations* (Washington, DC: National Association for the Education of Young Children, 1994), p. 41.

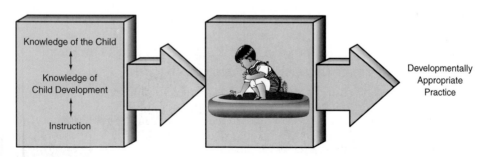

FIGURE 6–3
Applying Developmentally Appropriate Practice to Teaching

Family Education and Support

Parents and other family members should learn about the child care setting and their children's growth and development. Parents need encouragement to make the child care services part of their lives, so they are not detached from the center, its staff, or what happens to their children. Professionals must demonstrate to parents their competence in areas such as child development, nutrition, and planning and implementing developmentally appropriate curricula. They must also assure parents that they will maintain daily communication about the child's progress. Additionally, parents and professionals must agree on discipline and guidance procedures, and professionals and social service agencies need to guide parents about what constitutes good child rearing and appropriate discipline practices.

Staff Training and Development

Child care providers should be involved in an ongoing program of training and development. The CDA program is a good way for staff members to become competent and maintain the necessary skills. Program administrators should have a background and training in child development and early childhood education. Knowledge of child growth and development is essential for caregivers. Professionals need to be developmentally aware and child oriented rather than self- or center oriented.

Program Accreditation

In any discussion of quality, the question invariably arises, "Who determines quality?" Fortunately, NAEYC has addressed the issue of standards in its Center Accreditation Project (CAP). CAP is a national, voluntary accreditation process for child care centers, preschools, and programs that provide before- and after-school care for school-age children. Accreditation is administered through NAEYC's National Academy of Early Childhood Programs. NAEYC cites the following as benefits of accreditation:

- Accredited programs are recognized as quality programs.
- Parents will seek out accredited programs.
- The staff learns through the accrediting process.

The criteria addressed in the accreditation project are interactions among staff and children, curriculum, staff and parent interactions, administration, staff qualifications and development, staffing patterns, physical environment, health and safety, nutrition and food service, and program evaluation.[5]

WHAT ARE CRITICAL CHILD CARE ISSUES?

As in any profession, child care is not without controversies. The following sections explore some of the issues that confront society as a whole, child care professionals, and the profession.

Which Children Should Be Served?

Ultimately, a system of child care must be available to all parents and their children. Until this is possible, the United States needs priorities. Should child care be aimed at low-income parents who need to work or engage in work-training programs? Or should priority be given to abused and neglected children? Questions such as these are not easy to answer given the limited resources the United States allocates to quality child care; yet these are the questions faced by Head Start and other agencies as they seek to allocate the limited amount of care available. The United States is one of the few countries in the world that does not provide some form of direct child care support for all children. The U.S. system is often characterized as "patchwork" because it is not systematic and universal. It is, unfortunately, unlikely that this condition will change in the foreseeable future.

The Effects of Child Care on Children

The particular effects of child care on children is a much debated topic. In an effort to address conflicting research results and the profession's response to research studies, the National Center for Clinical Infant Programs (NCCIP), the National Academy of Science, and the Institute of Medicine issued the following statement:

> When parents have choices about the selection and utilization of supplementary care for their infants and toddlers and have access to stable child care arrangements featuring skilled, sensitive and motivated care givers, there is every reason to believe that both children and families can thrive. Such choices do not exist for many families in America today, and inadequate care poses risks to the current well-being and future development of infants, toddlers and their families.[6]

This statement makes it clear that federal, state, and individual programs must work together to develop ways to provide all U.S. children with high-quality child care offered by "skilled, sensitive and motivated" child care workers.

Recent research reveals that child care may have significant educational benefits for children. Evidence indicates that toddlers have a remarkable ability to learn new skills from each other, learning and remembering what they see other children do. Furthermore, what they learn in the play or child care group is retained outside the group setting.[7] This kind of research illustrates the increasing numbers of studies that attest to the positive benefits for children in quality preschool and child care programs.

State and National Licensing Standards

Some early childhood advocates maintain that one way, perhaps the only way, to increase the quality of child care is to have a system of national standards that all child care programs would have to meet. These standards would relate particularly to child-staff ratios, group size, and staff training. Advocates of such standards believe they would bring a badly needed uniformity to child care regulations. The closest that the United States comes to having a system of national standards is through programs that are federally funded and supported, such as Head Start.

At an early age, many children are in child care settings. In high-quality programs, children are engaged in active learning, interact with others, and experience a continuity of care that is beneficial to their development. What are some features of high-quality child care?

VIDEO VIEWPOINT

CAROL PORTER (FEEDING HUNGRY CHILDREN)

Carol Porter, ordinary citizen, extraordinary undertaking. Tired of the conditions she found in her city of Houston, Texas, Carol Porter organized an effort to feed hungry children. Carol's organization started out with just her family, who spent their life's savings to set up Kid Care. Now Carol and her volunteers load up vans and head for the poorest of Houston's neighborhoods and feed lunch daily to those who cannot feed themselves.

Reflective Discussion Questions: What are some conditions that some children live under which can be characterized as Third World conditions? Why is it that we as a nation will allow so many children to be hungry? What effects do hunger and undernourishment have on children's learning? Why is seeing that children are well fed becoming a part of the early childhood curriculum?

Reflective Decision Making: What can you do to help ensure that the children you teach are properly fed? What community agencies can you use to help your children receive the food they need?

As you might expect, not everyone agrees that a system of national standards is necessary or desirable. Some bemoan the federal control that standards would bring. Others think that child care is and should be a state- and locally regulated function. What will likely happen is that as more federal support is given to child care, attempts will be made to provide federal regulations as well.

The *NAEYC Position Statement on Licensing and Public Regulation of Early Childhood Programs* states:

1. Any program providing care and education to children from two or more unrelated families should be regulated; there should be no exemptions from this principle.

2. States should license all facilities that provide services to the public, including all centers, large family or group child care homes, and small family child care homes (i.e., grant permission to operate).

3. In addition to licensing facilities, states should establish complementary processes for professional licensing of individuals as teachers, caregivers, or program administrators (i.e., grant permission to practice).

4. Licensing standards should be clear and reasonable and reflect current research findings related to regulative aspects that reduce the risk of harm.

5. Regulations should be vigorously and equitably enforced.

6. Licensing agencies should have sufficient staff and resources to effectively implement the regulatory process.

7. Regulatory processes should be coordinated and streamlined to promote greater effectiveness and efficiency.

8. Incentive mechanisms should encourage the achievement of a higher quality of service beyond the basic floor.

9. Consumer and public education should inform families, providers, and the public of the importance of the early years and of ways to create environments that promote children's learning and development.

10. States should invest sufficient levels of resources to ensure that children's healthy development and learning are not harmed in early care and education settings.[8]

Quality Child Care for All

Although we talk a great deal about quality child care and identify the criteria that constitute quality, the fact remains that quality child care is not widely available to the majority of families. One challenge is determining how to provide quality programs that will enhance and promote families' optimum development. Not only does the quality of child care differ from program to program; it also varies among states, as we see in the variations in mandated adult-child ratios and the training guidelines required as a condition for employment.

Furthermore, when families and children at risk receive poor-quality child care, this places children in double jeopardy. While all children must have quality care, those who are at risk will benefit the most from quality care because it helps moderate the effects of risk factors. However, children from middle-class families are the most likely to receive poor-quality care because of the lack of quality care for this group. A constant challenge to all involved in the education and development of young children must be to upgrade all child care programs.

In addition, the comprehensive nature of good child care programs must be extended. Many still believe that if a program provides germ-free custodial care, it is a good one. Unfortunately, however, some of these programs have sterile philosophies and activities as well.

WHAT ARE FUTURE TRENDS IN CHILD CARE?

What does the future hold for child care? Some continuing trends are:

• The number of women who enter the workforce, full or part time, will increase. In particular, women with children under three will represent the fastest-growing group of parents seeking child care. For many working parents, staying home with their children is not an option or a desire.

• The number of employer-sponsored or -assisted child care programs will grow because of both employees' demands for child care and the obvious advantages to employers. The greater the benefits to employers, the more likely they will increase their involvement in child care.

• Public schools will participate to an even greater extent in providing child care, especially before-school and after-school care. Also, preschool programs for three- and four-year-olds are a rapidly growing part of public school programs. These programs ease parents' needs for child care. Within the next decade, programs for infants and toddlers may become part of the regular services of some public schools.

• Federal efforts at welfare reform, which aim to make permanent dependency on government funds a thing of the past, have tremendous implications for child care. Professionals are concerned that the increased demand for child care caused by taking parents off welfare, providing them with job training, and encouraging them to work will result in lower-quality care. Six and one-half million children under the age of thirteen live in homes that receive welfare.[9] These parents are desperate for child care. How to fill this need is a challenge for society and for the early childhood profession. You and other professionals will have to be very proactive in helping ensure that what parents say they want—quality child care—is a reality.

• The distinction between child care and preschool will further disappear until the two concepts are a unified whole. We already see evidence of this in many early childhood programs, and in many respects, Head Start is leading the way in this unified approach to early childhood education. Also, the public school entry into the child care arena, on an ever-accelerating scale, helps erode the boundaries between child care and preschool programs.

• Child care is big business, and big business will continue to enter the child care–education field as a means of providing services to parents and as a means of making a profit. Some of the current companies operating child care centers for profit are Knowledge Universe, New Horizons Kids Quest, Childtime Learning Centers, Bright Horizons, Kindercare, La Petite Academy, Corporate Family Solutions, and Child Care Network.

Probably one of the most significant changes in child care already under way is that child care will be more family centered and more dedicated to helping parents achieve their goals. As the child care system strives to involve families, it will also be more collaborative with other programs and agencies that can assist in family-centered programs. Both of these new directions will have many implications for new professional roles.

Child care represents, in many respects, the new frontier in early childhood education. Many more families need full-service, comprehensive programs. More opportunities for enhanced collaboration and greater linkages are apparent with each passing year. What is necessary is for early childhood professionals to continue to professionalize the field and create child care programs that can and are willing to provide for families' and children's needs.

ACTIVITIES FOR REFLECTION AND RESEARCH

1. Survey parents in your area to determine what services they desire from a child care program. Are most of the parents' child care needs being met? How is what they want in a child care program similar to and different from standards for quality child care discussed in this chapter?

2. Determine the legal requirements for establishing center and home child care programs in your state, city, or locality. What are the similarities and differences in regard to establishing home and center programs? What is your opinion of the guidelines? Why?

3. Invite people from child care programs, welfare departments, and social service agencies to speak to your class about

child care. Also, determine what qualifications and training are necessary to become a child care employee.

4. Visit various child care programs, including center and home programs, and discuss similarities and differences in class. Which of the programs provides the best services? What changes or special provisions need to be made to improve the success of these kinds of programs?

5. Gather information on four early childhood programs. What are the similarities and differences? In your opinion, what factors are necessary for the success of these kinds of programs?

6. Review the Yellow Pages of the telephone directory for child care programs. Call several for information. What conclusions can you draw from your calls?

7. Develop a checklist to show parents what to look for in a quality child care program.

8. Visit an employer-sponsored child care program and describe it to your classmates. List the pros and cons for parents and for employers of employer-sponsored child care.

9. Conduct a survey to learn the cost of child care services in your area. Arrange your data in a table. What conclusions can you draw?

10. Tell why or why not you would leave your six-week-old infant in center child care, and list the pros and cons for such care. Share this information with your classmates.

READINGS FOR FURTHER ENRICHMENT

Gormley, W. T. *Everybody's Children: Child Care as a Public Problem* (Washington, DC: Brookings Institution, 1995).

Presents an analysis of the state of American child care. It evaluates child care policies and the national attention given to young children and their families.

Kostelnik, Marjorie J., Anne K. Soderman, and Alice P. Whiren. *Developmentally Appropriate Curriculum: Best Practices in Early Childhood Education, 2/e* (Ohio: Prentice Hall, October 1998).

This book brings together the best information currently available for developing an integrated approach to curriculum and instruction in the early years. It is designed for current and future early childhood professionals working in formal group settings with young children ranging in age from three to eight.

Rab, V. Y. *Child Care and ADA: A Handbook for Inclusive Programs* (Baltimore, MD: Brooks, 1995).

Explains federal guidelines for program directors and child care personnel for daily practice and procedures when children with disabilities are admitted to child care programs.

INTERNET RESOURCES

The Annie E. Casey Foundation: Kids Count Data

http://www.aecf.org/kidscount

This site contains up-to-date statistics on various indicators of child welfare and factors affecting child care, organized and ranked on the state level as well as for the nation as a whole.

The U.S. Census Bureau: Child Care Statistics

http://www.census.gov/population/www/socdemo/childcare.html

Contains reports from the Census Bureau regarding trends in child care.

The Head Start Bureau

http://www.acf.dhhs.gov/programs/hsb/

The web site of Head Start includes a list of frequently asked questions concerning Head Start. Many of Head Start's research findings are viewable online.

U.S. Department of Education: Research and Statistics

http://www.ed.gov/stats.html

Searchable government statistics on child care, accountability, and numerous other topics.

NOTES

1. Andrea Adelson, "Baby, It's Hot Outside for Child Care Companies," *The New York Times,* July 26, 1998, p. BU8.

2. Sandra L. Hofferth, April Brayfield, Sharon Deich, and Pamela Holcomb,

National Child Care Survey 1990 (Washington, DC: Urban Institute Press, 1991), p. 355.

3.   U.S. Department of Education, Office of Policy and Planning. Internet address http://www.ed.gov/offices/OUS/eval/esed/b4&aft.html

4.   Carol Brunson Phillips, *Field Advisor's Guide for the CDA Professional Preparation Program* (Washington, DC: Council for Early Childhood Professional Recognition, 1991), p. 2.

5.   National Association for the Education of Young Children, *Accreditation by the National Academy of Early Childhood Programs* (Washington, DC: Author, 1991), p. 2.

6.   National Center for Clinical Infant Programs, *Infants, Families, and Child Care: Toward a Research Agenda* (Washington, DC: Author, 1988), p. 6.

7.   Daniel Goleman, "Baby Sees, Baby Does, and Classmates Follow," *The New York Times,* July 21, 1993, p. B7.

8.   National Association for the Education of Young Children, *Licensing and Public Regulations of Early Childhood Education Programs.* (1997). Available online at http://www.naeye-org/about/about_ index. htm

9.   J. Sexton, "Working and Welfare Parents Compete for Day Care Slots," *The New York Times,* March 28, 1997, p. A12.

CHAPTER

Developmentally Appropriate Practices

FOCUS QUESTIONS

1. What is assessment?
2. Why is it important for professionals to know how to assess?
3. What are the purposes and uses of assessment?
4. What is appropriate assessment?
5. What are some major ways to assess children's development, learning, and behavior?

The minutes, hours, and days are filled with assessment decisions. Questions abound: "What is Jeramy ready for now?" What can I tell Maria's parents about her language development?" "The activity I used in the large-group time yesterday didn't seem to work well. What could I have done differently?" Assessment will help you find the answers to these and many other questions relating to how to teach and what is best for children in all areas of development.

WHAT IS ASSESSMENT?

Much of children's lives are subject to and influenced by your assessment and the assessment of others. As an early childhood professional, assessment will influence your professional life and will be a vital tool of your professional practice. Assessment well done is one of your most important responsibilities.

Assessment is the process of collecting information about children's health, behavior, and academic progress and attainment in order to:

*   Identify what children know
*   Identify children's special needs
*   Determine appropriate placement
*   Select appropriate curricula to meet individual needs of children
*   Make lesson and activity plans
*   Select materials
*   Make decisions about how to implement learning activities
*   Report to parents about children's developmental status and achievement
*   Refer children and as appropriate their families for additional services to programs and agencies
*   Make policy decisions regarding what is and what is not appropriate for children

Assessment occurs primarily through observation, administration of commercial and teacher-made tests, and examination of students' products. You will probably use all three of these assessment procedures in your teaching.

Keep in mind that all assessment procedures should help you inform your instruction so you can provide the best for all children. Your goal is to help children be successful.

WHAT IS APPROPRIATE ASSESSMENT?

Today, early childhood professionals do their best to use assessment in appropriate ways, that is, to support children's learning. On the other hand, assessment and the results of assessment are often used inappropriately. One such example is the use of *high-stakes* assessment or testing to make life-changing decisions about children. Two examples are noteworthy. In some cases, children are either admitted or not admitted to kindergarten or first grade based on the outcome of a test. In some cases also, decisions about whether or not to promote children are based on the results of one national standardized test.

With so much emphasis on tests, it is understandable that the issue of testing and assessment raises many concerns on the part of the parents and professionals. Critics maintain that the standardized testing movement reduces teaching and learning to the lowest common denominator—teaching children what they need to know to get the right answers. Many early childhood professionals believe that standardized tests do not measure children's thinking, problem-solving ability, creativity, or responsibility for their own learning. Furthermore, critics believe that group-administered, objectively scored, skills-focused tests that dominate much of U.S. education do not support (indeed, may undermine) many of the curricular reforms taking place today.

WHAT IS AUTHENTIC ASSESSMENT?

Authentic assessment is also referred to as *performance-based assessment.* It is carried out through activities that require children to demonstrate what they know and are able to do. Meaningless facts and isolated information are considered unauthentic. Authentic assessment has the following traits:

- *Assesses children on the basis of their actual work.* Work samples—often in a portfolio—exhibitions, performances, learning logs, journals, projects, presentations, experiments, and teacher observations are essential processes in authentic assessment.

- *Provides for ongoing assessment over the entire school year.* Children's performance and achievement are continuously assessed, not just at the end of a grading period or at the end of the year through a standardized achievement test.

- *Is curriculum embedded.* Children are assessed on what they are actually doing in and through the curriculum.

- *Is a cooperative and collaborative process involving children, teachers, and in many cases parents.* This is an attempt to move away from teacher-focused assessment and make assessment more child centered.

- *Is intended to help professionals and parents learn more about children.* All areas—social-emotional, language, cognitive, and physical are assessed. The whole child is evaluated rather than a narrow set of skills. In this sense, it is child centered and humane.

- *Assesses what individual children are able to do.* Authentic assessment evaluates what they as individuals are learning, as opposed to comparing one child with another or children with children, as is so often the case.

- *Makes assessment part of the learning process.* For example, third grader Haydee Bolado, as part of a project on the community, visited the recycling center. She made a presentation to the class in which she used the overhead projector to illustrate her major points, displayed a poster board with pictures she had taken of the center, and presented several graphs to show which products were recycled most. In this way, she was able to demonstrate a broader range of what she had learned.

ASSESSMENT FOR SCHOOL READINESS

Because of federal mandates and state laws, school districts usually evaluate children in some way before or at the time of their entrance into school. Also, some type of screening occurs at the time of kindergarten entrance to evaluate learning readiness. Unfortunately, children are often classified on the basis of how well they perform on these screenings. When assessment is appropriate and the results are used to design developmentally appropriate instruction, it is valuable and worthwhile.

Screening Processes

Screening measures give school personnel a broad picture of what children know and are able to do, as well as their physical and emotional status. As gross indicators of children's abilities, screening procedures provide much useful information for decisions about placement for initial instruction, referral to other agencies, and additional testing that may be necessary to pinpoint a learning or health problem. Many school districts conduct a comprehensive screening program in the spring for children who will enter kindergarten in the fall, which can involve the following:

- Gathering information from parents about their children's health, learning patterns, learning achievements, personal habits, and special problems

- Doing a health screening, including a physical examination, a health history, and a blood sample for analysis

- Doing a vision, hearing, and speech screening

- Collecting and analyzing data from former programs and teachers, such as preschools and child care programs

- Administering a cognitive and/or behavioral screening instrument

EVALUATING THE LEARNING PROCESS

I have used student portfolios to evaluate my kindergarten students for fifteen years. Over time, however, I have redefined their purpose and identified several criteria to make more effective use of portfolios. I believe that the value of student portfolios is to provide a record of each student's process of learning and therefore collect student work based on the following criteria:

- Portfolio entries reflect a student's cognitive, social, emotional, and physical development.
- They provide a visual record of a student's process of learning over time.
- They encourage input from students, teacher, and parents.

My students and I together select the work samples. Each portfolio also includes a parent questionnaire, parent responses to conferences, individual assessment profiles, and anecdotal records. Because the volume of materials that can accumulate in a portfolio can become overwhelming, I use a table of contents in the format of a checklist stapled inside the folder, which makes examining the contents more practical and efficient. As work is added, I check the table of contents and can determine at a glance what data I have to make wise instructional decisions and what information I still need.

The success of student portfolios as an evaluation tool depends on the appropriate assessment of individual students, and accurate, conscientious documentation of student growth.

Appropriate Assessment

Appropriate assessment is the process of observing, recording, and documenting the work children do and how they do it. In my classroom, assessments are ongoing and occur as children perform daily classroom routines and participate in group time, share time, center time, and recess. I note which activities the children choose, how long they work on specific activities, and their process for completing activities. I observe students' learning styles, interest levels, skill levels, coping techniques, strategies for decision making and problem solving, and interactions with other children. Observations, however, have little value unless they are accurately documented.

Accurate Documentation

To manage documentation more accurately and efficiently, I have developed or adapted a variety of forms to make systematic assessments. Throughout the year, I use these assessment tools to systematically record information on individual children in each area of their development. I use a symbol system to date the occurrence of behaviors and describe and document skill proficiency as appropriate. Emphasis is on what each child can do, and each child's progress is compared with his or her prior work. As I review these individual assessments I am able to quickly detect areas of growth.

Symbol System

+ = Progress is noted

= Needs more time and/or experience

* = See comments

In addition to the individual student profiles, I have also developed several class evaluation forms that allow me flexibility in recording observations quickly yet accurately. These forms are especially useful in planning group and/or individual instruction and they provide additional documentation that supports the individual assessment records. For example, I make anecdotal records (on Post-It notes) of unanticipated events or behaviors, a child's social interactions, and problem-solving strategies. I transfer these Post-Its to a class grid so I can determine at a glance which children I have observed. The anecdotal records, along with the individual assessment profiles, become a part of each student's portfolio to be used for instructional planning and communicating with parents.

Throughout the year samples of students' work are dated and included in the portfolios. Quarterly work samples that I select include some illustrating abilities with cutting activities, writing numbers (each child decides how far he or she can write), writing letters of the alphabet, and any words or stories a child can write independently (using either invented or conventional spelling). The children select samples of artwork and creative writing (e.g., journal entries, letters or drawing they have done for parents).

Use of Information

I use the information from student portfolios to plan classroom instruction for individuals and groups, to identify children who may need special help, and to confer with parents and colleagues. During conferences, I share with parents the student's assessment profile for the different areas of development, and together we examine samples of the child's work that support the assessment. Even though the progress is visually obvious, I can also point out less-obvious progress as we view the samples. I give parents conference response forms and ask for comments or suggestions for additional portfolio entries. Using the portfolio, I am satisfied that I have gleaned an accurate assessment of and appreciation for each child's total development.

Contributed by Linda Sholar, Sangre Ridge Elementary School, Stillwater, Oklahoma.

Comprehensive screening programs are conducted in one day or over several days. Data for each child are usually evaluated by a team of professionals who make instructional placement recommendations and, when appropriate, advise additional testing and make referrals to other agencies for assistance.

Screening Instruments and Observational Records

Several screening instruments provide information for grouping and planning instructional strategies. Most can be administered by people who do not have specialized training in test administration. Parent volunteers often help administer screening instruments, many of which can be administered in about thirty minutes.

BRIGANCE K and 1 Screen

The BRIGANCE K and 1 screen is an evaluation instrument for use in kindergarten and grade 1. The kindergarten pupil data sheet for the BRIGANCE K and 1 screen shows the skills, behaviors, and concepts evaluated in the kindergarten portion of the screening instrument (Figure 7–1).

Many school districts conduct a comprehensive screening for children entering kindergarten which may include tests of vision, hearing, or speech.

FIGURE 7-1
A Completed Kindergarten Pupil Data Sheet from BRIGANCE® K and 1 Screen

A. Student's Name Colin Killoran

Parents/Guardian Kristin Killoran

Address 310 Locke Street

	Year	Month	Day
Date of Screening	97	6	15
Birth date	92	1	10
Age	5	5	5

School/Program Vinal School

Teacher Leslie Feingold

Assessor Dennis Dowd

B. Basic Screening Assessments

Page	Assessment Number	Skill (Circle the skill for each correct response and make notes as appropriate.)	C. Scoring — Number of Correct Responses	Point Value	Student's Score
3	1A	**Personal Data Response:** Verbally gives: ① first name ② full name ③ age 4. address (street or mailing) 5. birth date (month and day)	3 x	2 points each	6/10
4 & 5	2A	**Color Recognition:** ① red ② blue ③ green ④ yellow ⑤ orange 6. purple ⑦ brown ⑧ black ⑨ pink 10. gray	8 x	1 point each	8/10
6	3A	**Picture Vocabulary:** Recognizes and names pictures of: ① dog ② cat ③ key ④ girl ⑤ boy ⑥ airplane ⑦ apple ⑧ leaf 9. cup 10. car	8 x	1 point each	8/10
7	4A	**Visual Discrimination—Forms and Uppercase Letters:** Visually discriminates which one of four symbols is different: ①○ ②□ ③④ ⑤○ ⑥○ 7. I ⑧ P 9. V 10. X	7 x	1 point each	7/10
8	5A	**Visual-Motor Skills:** Copies: ① — ② ○ ③ + ④ □ 5. △	4 x	2 points ea.	8/10
9 & 10	6A	**Gross-Motor Skills:** ① Hops two hops on one foot. ② Hops two hops on the other foot. ③ Stands on one foot momentarily. ④ Stands on the other foot momentarily. ⑤ Stands on one foot for five seconds. ⑥ Stands on the other foot for five seconds. ⑦ Walks forward heel-to-toe four steps. 8. Walks backward toe-to-heel four steps. ⑨ Stands on one foot momentarily with eyes closed. 10. Stands on the other foot momentarily with eyes closed.	8 x	1 pt. ea.	8/10
11	7A	**Rote Counting:** Counts by rote to: (Circle all letters prior to the first error.) ① ② ③ ④ ⑤ ⑥ 7 8 9 10	6	.5 point each	3/5
12	8A	**Identifies Body Parts:** Identifies by pointing to or touching: ① chin ② fingernails ③ heels ④ ankles ⑤ jaw ⑥ shoulders ⑦ elbows 8. hips ⑨ wrists 10. waist	8 x	.5 point each	4/5
13 & 14	9A	**Follows Verbal Directions:** Listens to, remembers, and follows: ① one-step direction 2. two-step direction	1 x	2.5 points each	2.5/5
15	10A	**Numeral Comprehension:** Matches quantity with numerals: ② ① ④ ③ 5	4 x	2 points ea.	8/10
16	11A	**Prints Personal Data:** (Prints first name) Reversals: Yes No ✓	1 x	.5 points ea.	.5/5
17	12A	**Syntax and Fluency:** ① Speech is understandable. ② Speaks in complete sentences.	2 x	5 points ea.	10/10

Total Score: 77.5/100

D. Observations:
1. Handedness: Right ✓ Left ____ Uncertain ____
2. Grasps pencil with: Fist ____ Fingers ✓
3. Hearing appeared to be normal: (See p. vii) Yes ____ No ____ Uncertain ____
4. Vision appeared to be normal: (See p. vii) Yes ✓ No ____ Uncertain ____
5. Record other observations on another sheet.

E. Recommendations:
Ask nurse to check hearing. Below cutoff (<92).

Factor score 13.5 below at-risk guideline (<18).

Presence of risk factors. Rescreen in 6–9 months.

Source: From BRIGANCE® *K & 1 Screen* (revised 1997). Curriculum Associates, Inc. BRIGANCE® is a registered trademark of Curriculum Associates, Inc. Used by permission.

DIAL-R

The DIAL-R (Developmental Indicators for the Assessment of Learning—Revised) is an instrument designed for screening large numbers of prekindergarten children. Requiring approximately twenty-five to thirty minutes to administer, it involves individual observation for motor skills, concepts, and language skills. The screening team consists of a coordinator, an operator for each of the skills areas screened, and aides or volunteers to register parents and children.

The High/Scope Child Observation Record

The High/Scope Child Observation Record (COR) for Ages 2 1/2 to 6 is used by teachers or other observers to assess young children's development by observing their typical classroom activities.[1] The COR measures young children's progress in all facets of their development, whether or not the teacher is using the High/Scope curriculum. The High/Scope COR assesses the full variety of processes of young children's development of initiative, social relations, creative representation, music and movement, language and literacy, and logic and mathematics. It is not limited, as typical tests are, to language and mathematics questions that each have only one right answer. The teacher directs a test; using the COR, the teacher observes young children's self-initiated activities.

The teacher using the COR begins by observing children's activities throughout both the program day and the classroom, writing notes to describe these activities in developmental terms. In addition to identifying the date and the child, each note describes an activity succinctly but with relevant details. A typical note under "Initiative," for example, would be as follows:

(10/25) La Tanya wrote her name three times on the turn list so she could have three turns at the new mask computer game.

The teacher collects these notes throughout the reporting period, which could be as brief as a month or as long as a semester, recording them on forms supplied for this purpose or, in the computer version, in easily retrievable data files. Using a Parent Report Form, the teacher reports to parents selected notes about their young children's development. This report is an opportunity for conversations with parents about what their children are doing in the classroom and at home and how parents and teachers can work together as partners to contribute to young children's development.

After collecting the notes, the teacher also uses them to rate each child's development from level 1 to level 5 on each of thirty items. These items encompass the various aspects of development, from engaging in complex play and making friends to showing interest in reading, sorting, and counting objects. The item on expressing choices, for example, has the following five levels:

1. Child does not yet express choices to others.
2. Child indicates a desired activity or place of activity by saying a word, pointing, or some other action.
3. Child indicates desired activity, place of activity, materials, or playmates with a short sentence.
4. Child indicates with a short sentence how plans will be carried out ("I want to drive the truck on the road").
5. Child gives detailed description of intended actions ("I want to make a road out of blocks with Sara and drive a truck on it.")

The resulting scores indicate children's development in the various areas. Comparing children's developmental status at the beginning and end of a period indicates the progress during that period. In a study of sixty-four Head Start teaching teams, the High/Scope COR demonstrated evidence of its reliability and concurrent validity.[2]

Portfolios

Today many teachers use portfolios, a compilation of children's work samples, products, and teacher observations collected over time, as a basis for assessment. Decisions about what to put in portfolios vary, but examples include written work, artwork, audiotapes, pictures, models, and other materials that attest to what children are able to do. Some teachers let children put their best work in their portfolios; others decide with children what will be included; still others select for themselves what to include. An important point to remember, and one often overlooked, is that portfolios are only one part of children's assessment.

WHAT IS OBSERVATION?

There is only one basis for observation: The children must be free to express themselves and thus reveal those needs and attitudes which would otherwise remain hidden or repressed in an environment that did not permit them to act spontaneously. An observer obviously needs something to observe; and if he must be trained in order to be able to see and recognize objective truth, he must also have at his disposal children placed in such an environment that they can manifest their natural traits.[3]

Professionals recognize that children are more than what is measured by any particular test. Observation is an "authentic" means of learning about children and what they know and are able to do, especially as it occurs in more naturalistic settings such as classrooms, child care centers, playgrounds, and homes. *Observation* is the intentional, systematic act of looking at the behavior of a child or children in a particular setting, program, or situation. Observation is sometimes referred to as "kidwatching," and is an excellent way to find out about children's behaviors and learning.

OBSERVING WILL

Welcome to Ms. Liz's classroom. Will is the child you will be observing. He is the energetic young boy dressed in overalls and a yellow shirt. You are encouraged to learn as much as you can about Will, his peers, his teacher (Ms. Liz), and the classroom.

Before you focus on individual photographs, observe the classroom in general. Reflect on the following questions:

- What general statements would you make regarding classroom arrangement, organization, materials, and equipment? Based on your observation, what recommendations would you make if this were your classroom? Would you arrange your classroom differently?

- Based on your observation of the children's involvement with materials and their peers, what can you say about their development, social competence, and play behavior? How do the children and Ms. Liz get along?

- Do the children in the classroom feel comfortable taking risks, working together, and expressing emotions?

- Do you think Ms. Liz operates a child-centered classroom? How does your observation support your answer?

- Do you think the children spend more time participating in hands-on experiences or teacher-related experiences?

- Can Ms. Liz's classroom be characterized as an active learning environment? How and why?

- What can you infer regarding gender equity and how boys and girls are treated in Ms. Liz's classroom?

- List five things children learn from large motor activities. How does outdoor play support children's learning?

Literacy development is important in early childhood programs. In Photo A, what is Ms. Liz doing to support the children's literacy development? What can you infer from the children's behavior regarding their literacy development? Note in Photo B how Ms. Liz supports Will's autonomy and "what he can do for himself." Based on your observation of Photo C, what are five things Will knows about reading? What do you notice about the behavior of Will's peers? What does their behavior indicate to you?

Personal Reflection Focus once again on Photo B. Do you agree with Ms. Liz allowing Will to take the picture book from her? Would you have allowed Will to read the book to the other children? What can Ms. Liz do to involve the other children in Will's retelling of the story?

In Photo D, you see Will and his friend Ryan building a tall tower. What can you tell about Will's willingness to engage in cooperative play with other children? What can you infer from Will's behavior and facial expression about the activity? Observe how the top of the tower is falling on the child behind Will.

Personal Reflection Would you allow Will and his peers to build their tower as high as they are building it? Why or why not?

In Photo E, observe how Will responds to the accident of the falling tower. What does Will's behavior tell you? What can you tell about Ms. Liz's behavior? What can you say about the behavior of Ryan (the child in the background behind Ms. Liz)?

Personal Reflection As a classroom teacher, how would you handle a situation in which a child was not seriously injured?

Photo A

Photo B

Photo C

Photo D

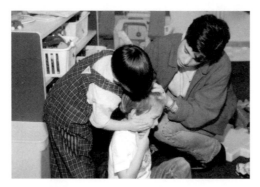

Photo E

continued

Personal Reflection How would you categorize Will and Megan's play behavior in Photo F? Based on your observation, what are some things that Will and Megan are learning? Are the materials appropriate for them to use?

Observe Will's determination and physical effort in Photo G. What are some things you can learn through observation in the outdoors? What developmental skills is Will enhancing through his outdoor play?

Personal Reflection What are some outdoor activities that you would include in your early childhood program? How would you provide for Will's safety and the safety of all children in outdoor play? What are some inferences you can make about outdoor safety?

During the parent-teacher conference depicted in Photo H, observe Will's facial expression and body language. What do they tell you? Does Will's mother seem supportive of him?

Personal Reflection Will is participating in the conference between Will's mother and Ms. Liz. Do you think he should or should not be involved in the parent-teacher conference? Why or why not? Do you think Ms. Liz and Will's mother value Will's participation? What are the pros and cons of Will participating in the conference?

Photo F

Photo G

Photo H

Merrill/Prentice Hall thanks Director Vicki Yun, Ms. Liz, Will Sims, and the children of LaPetite Academy of Dublin, Ohio, for allowing us to take photographs. Photos by Anthony Magnacca.

Observing children is an excellent way to find out about a child's behavior or how well they are learning.

Purposes of Observation

Observation is designed to gather information on which to base decisions, make recommendations, develop curriculum, plan activities and learning strategies, and assess children's growth, development, and learning. For example, sometimes when professionals and parents look at children, they do not really see or concern themselves with what children are doing or why children are engaged in a particular behavior or activity as long as children are safe and orderly. However, children's behaviors provide insight into children and their behaviors. The significance and importance of critical behaviors go undetected if observation is done casually and is limited to "unsystematic looking." The purposes of observation then include:

- *To determine the cognitive, linguistic, social, emotional, and physical development of children.* A developmental checklist (see Figure 7–2) is one way professionals can systematically observe and chart the development of children.

- *To identify children's interests and learning styles.* Today, teachers are very interested in developing learning activities, materials, and classroom centers based on children's interests, preferences, and learning styles.

- *To plan.* The professional practice of teaching requires planning on a daily, ongoing basis. Observation provides useful, authentic, and solid information enabling teachers to intentionally plan for activities rather than to make decisions on little or no information.

FIGURE 7–2

Emergent Literacy Behaviors Checklist

Use the following checklist to assess and date the student's progress as an emergent reader and writer.

Name:	Age:	Observed	Not Observed
demonstrates visual acuity			
demonstrates hearing acuity			
Print Concepts			
recognizes left-to-right sequencing			
recognizes top, down directionality			
asks what print says			
connects meaning between two objects, pictures			
models reading out loud			
models adult silent reading (newspapers, books, etc.)			
recognizes that print has different meanings (informational, entertainment, etc.)			
Comprehension Behaviors			
follows oral directions			
draws correct pictures from oral directions			
recognizes story sequence in pictures			
interprets pictures			
sees links in story ideas			
links personal experiences with text (story, title)			
logically reasons story plot/conclusions			
sees patterns in similar stories			
Writing Behaviors			
makes meaningful scribbles (attempts to make letter-like shapes)			
draws recursive scribbles (rows of cursive-like writing)			
makes strings of "letters"			
uses one or more consonants to represent words			
uses inventive spellings			

- *To meet the needs of individual children.* Meeting the needs of individual children is an important part of teaching and learning. Observation provides information about the individual needs of children. For example, a child may be advanced cognitively but be overly aggressive and lack the social skills necessary to play cooperatively and interact with others. Through observation, a teacher can gather information to develop a plan for helping the child learn how to play with others.

- *To determine progress.* Systematic observation, over time, provides a rich, valuable, and informative source of information about how individual children and groups of children are progressing in their learning and behavior.

- *To provide information to parents.* Professionals report to and conference with parents on an ongoing basis. Observational information adds to other information teachers have, such as test results and child work samples, and provides a fuller and more complete picture of individual children.

Observing a child at play lets a teacher learn about developmental levels, social skills, and peer interactions.

- *To provide self-insight.* Observational information can help professionals learn more about themselves and what to do to help children.

Advantages of Intentional, Systematic Observation

There are a number of advantages to gathering data through observation:

- One advantage to systematic, purposeful observation is that it enables professionals to collect information about children that they might not otherwise gather through other sources. A great deal of the consequences, causes, and reactions to children's behavior can only be assessed through observation. Observation enables you to gather data that cannot be assessed by formal, standardized tests, questioning, or parent and child interviews.

- Observation is ideally suited to learning more about children in play settings. Observation affords you the opportunity to note a child's social behavior in a play group and discern how cooperatively he or she interacts with peers. Observing a child at play gives professionals a wealth of information about developmental levels, social skills, and what the child is or is not learning in play settings.

- Observation allows you to learn a lot about children's prosocial behavior and peer interactions. It can help you plan for appropriate and inclusive activities to promote the social growth of young children. Additionally, your observations can serve as the basis for developing multicultural activities to benefit all children.

- Observation of children's abilities provides a basis for the assessment of what they are able to do developmentally. Many learning skills are developed sequentially, such as the refinement of large-motor skills before small-motor skills. Through observation, professionals can determine whether children's abilities are within a normal range of growth and development.

- Observation is useful to assess children's performance over time. Documentation of daily, weekly, and monthly observations of children's behaviors and learning provides a database for the cumulative evaluation of each child's achievement and development.

- Observation helps you provide concrete information for use in reporting to and conferencing with parents. Increasingly, reports to parents about children involve professionals' observations and children's work samples so parents and educators can collaborate to determine how to help children develop cognitively, socially, emotionally, and physically.

In summary, intentional observation is a useful, informative, and powerful means for informing and guiding teaching and helping ensure the learning of all children.

Steps for Conducting Observations

The steps involved in the process of systematic, purposeful observation, shown in Figure 7–3, include the following:

Step 1: Plan for Observation

Planning is an important part of the observation process. Everything you do regarding observation should be planned for in advance of the observation. A good guide to follow in planning is to ask the questions *who, what, where, when,* and *how.*

Setting goals for observation is an important part of the planning process. Goals allow you to reflect on why you want to observe and thus direct your efforts to what you will observe. Stating a goal focuses your attention on the

FIGURE 7–3
Four Steps for Effective
Observation

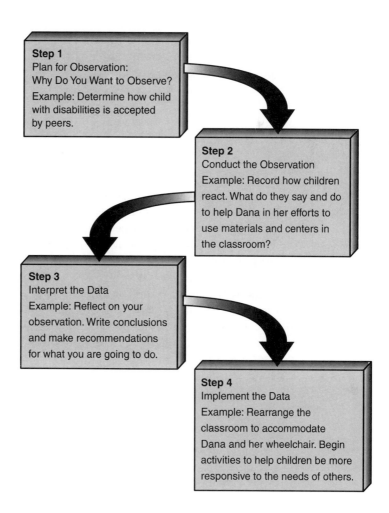

Step 1
Plan for Observation:
Why Do You Want to Observe?
Example: Determine how child
with disabilities is accepted
by peers.

Step 2
Conduct the Observation
Example: Record how children
react. What do they say and do
to help Dana in her efforts to
use materials and centers in
the classroom?

Step 3
Interpret the Data
Example: Reflect on your
observation. Write conclusions
and make recommendations
for what you are going to do.

Step 4
Implement the Data
Example: Rearrange the
classroom to accommodate
Dana and her wheelchair. Begin
activities to help children be more
responsive to the needs of others.

purpose of your observation. Goals, for example, that direct your attention to the effectiveness of your efforts in providing an inclusive classroom or program and in fully including an exceptional child into the classroom might read like this:

Goal 1: To determine what modifications might be necessary in the classroom to facilitate access to all parts of the classroom for Dana in her wheelchair

Goal 2: To assess the development of prosocial behavioral characteristics other children display to Dana while interacting in the classroom

Step 2: Conduct the Observation

While conducting your observation, it is imperative that you be objective, specific, and as thorough as possible. For example, during your observation of Dana and her peers you notice that there is not enough room for Dana to manipulate her wheelchair past the easel and shelf where the crayons are kept. None of her peers noticed that Dana could not reach the crayons and so did not help her get them. Dana had to ask one of the children to get the crayons for her.

Step 3: Interpret the Data

All observations can and should result in some kind of interpretation. Interpretation serves several important functions. First, it puts your observations into perspective, that is, in relation to what you already know and do not know of events and behaviors of your children. Second, interpretation helps you make sense of what you have observed and enables you to use your professional knowledge to interpret what you have seen. Third, interpretation has the potential to make you grow as a professional and learn to anticipate representative behavior indicative of normal growth and development under given conditions and to recognize what might not be representative of appropriate growth, development, and learning for each child. Fourth, interpretation forms the foundation for the implementation, necessary adaptations, or modifications in a program or curriculum. In this observation, you can note that Dana's only exceptionality is that she is physically disabled. Her growth in other areas is normal, and she displays excellent social skills in that she is accepted by others, knows when to ask for help, and is able to ask for help. When Dana asks for help, she receives it.

Step 4: Implement the Data

The implementation phase means that you commit to do something with the results of the "findings" of your observation. For example, although Dana's behavior in your observation was appropriate, many of the children can benefit from activities designed to help them recognize and respond to the needs of others. The physical environment of the classroom as well requires some modification in the rearrangement of movable furniture to make it more accessible for Dana. Also, implementation means you report to parents or others. Implementing, that is, doing something with the results of your observations, is the most important part of the process.

Using an Observational Guide

Observation is a valuable tool for all professionals and should help inform them and guide their teaching of young children. A sample observation form you can use is shown in Figure 7–4. You can also check other sources to develop more specific observation guides you could use as checklists to track developmental behaviors with individual children.

Reporting to and Communicating with Parents

A part of your responsibility as a professional is to report to parents about the growth, development, and achievement of their children. Some view reporting to parents as a bother and wish it was something they did not have to do. Nonetheless, reporting to and communicating with parents is one of the most

FIGURE 7–4
A Sample Observation Guide

Name: (Your Name) _____

Date: _____

Time: _____

Location: _____

Classroom or Setting: _____

Purpose of Observing: _____

Prediction or Expectations of Findings: _____

Significant Events During Observation:

Reflective Analysis of Significant Events: (This reflection should include what you have learned.)

List at least three ways you can use or apply what you observed to your future teaching.

important jobs of the early childhood professional. The following guidelines will help you meet this important responsibility of reporting your assessment information to parents:

- *Be honest and realistic with parents.* Too often, we do not want to hurt parents' feelings. Too often, we want to sugarcoat what we are reporting to parents. However, parents need your honest assessments about their children and what they know, are able to do, and will be able to do.
- *Communicate to parents so they can understand.* What we communicate to parents must make sense to them. They have to understand what we are saying. Reporting to parents often has to be a combination of written (in their language) and oral communication.
- *Provide parents with ideas and information that will help them help their children learn.* Remember that you and parents are partners in helping children be successful in school and life.

WHAT ARE ISSUES IN THE ASSESSMENT OF YOUNG CHILDREN?

As with almost everything that we have talked about and will talk about in this book, issues surround essential questions about what is good practice, what is inappropriate practice, and what is best for children and families. Assessment is no different regarding critical issues about what is considered best practice.

It is important to accurately and honestly report your assessment findings to the parents of your students.

Assessment and Accountability

Over the past decade, there has been a tremendous emphasis on testing and the use of tests to measure achievement and to compare children, programs, schools districts, and countries. This emphasis will continue for a number of reasons. First, the public, including politicians and legislatures, sees assessment as a means of making schools and teachers accountable for teaching the nation's children. Second, assessment is seen as playing a critical role in improving education. The view is that assessment results can be used as a guide for determining how the curriculum and instructional practices can be used to increase achievement. Therefore, as long as there is a public desire to improve teaching and achievement, we will continue to see an emphasis on assessment for accountability purposes.

High-Stakes Testing

We have previously talked about high-stakes testing. High-stakes testing occurs when standardized tests are used to make important and often life-influencing decisions about children. Standardized tests have specific and standardized content, administration and scoring procedures, and norms for interpreting scores. High-stakes outcomes include decisions about whether or not to admit children into programs, e.g., kindergarten, and whether or not to retain or promote children. Generally, the early childhood profession is opposed to high-stakes testing for children through grade 3. However, as part of the accountability movement, many politicians and school administrators view high-stakes testing as a means of making sure that children learn and that promotions are based on achievement. Many school critics maintain that in the pre-K and primary grades there is too much social promotion, that is, passing children from grade to grade merely to enable students to keep pace with their age peers.

As an early childhood professional, part of your responsibility is to be an advocate for the appropriate use of assessment. You will make ongoing, daily decisions about how best to assess your children and how best to use the results of assessment.

ACTIVITIES FOR REFLECTION AND RESEARCH

1. Develop a developmental checklist similar to that shown in Figure 7–2. Observe in an early childhood classroom and determine how effective you are at observing some aspect of children's development and learning.

2. Observe a particular child during play or other activity. Before your observation make sure you follow the steps for conducting observations reviewed in this chapter. Use the information you gathered through observation to plan a learning activity for the child. As you plan, determine what information you need that you didn't gather thorough observa-

tion. When you observe again, what will you do differently?

3. Interview several kindergarten and primary teachers. Ask them for ideas and guidelines for how to assess with portfolios. Ask them to let you review some of the children's portfolios. What ideas can you use to help you assess thorough portfolios?

4. Frequently in newspapers and magazines there are articles about assessment and testing. Over a two-week period review these sources and determine what assessment and evaluation issues are "in the news."

5. Observe in a program that is providing services for children with disabilities. The purpose of your observation is to determine what accommodations need to be made for the children with disabilities.

READINGS FOR FURTHER ENRICHMENT

Stiggins, R. J. *Student-Centered Classroom Assessment,* 2nd ed. (Upper Saddle River, N.J.: Merrill/Prentice Hall, 1997).

Explains a special philosophy about classroom assessment—a philosophy that places students at the center of the assessment equation. Offers information on understanding assessment context, methods, applications, and communicating student achievement.

Tombari, Martin. *Authentic Assessment in the Classroom: Applications and Practice.* (Upper Saddle River, NJ: Merrill Pub Co., 1998).

This book focuses on authentic assessment—what it is, how to do it, and what the issues surrounding it are (e.g., validity, reliability, and impacts on instruction). The author's intent is to excite teachers about the possibilities for learning in their classrooms and to indicate ways to communicate this learning to other teachers, parents, and learners.

Popham, J. W. *Classroom Assessment: What Teachers Need to Know.* (Boston, MA: Allyn and Bacon, 1998).

This book is intended to help classroom teachers deal with assessment on a daily basis, promoting the idea that the results of assessment activities should improve the quality of the decisions they make about their own students.

RESEARCH ON THE INTERNET

Assessment and Standards on the Web

http://www.kane.k12.il.us/Links/AssmtLinks.html#anchor41851014

Includes links to several websites on the topic of Assessment. Sites include Appropriate and Authentic Assessment as well as links to topics regarding current standards on this issue.

Pathways to School Improvement on the Web

http://www.ncrel.org/sdrs/areas/issues/students/earlycld/ea500.htm

A website containing information regarding current issues including assessment of the progress and attainments of young children, 3 to 8 years of age, and the uses and abuses of assessment.

NOTES

1. High/Scope Educational Research Foundation, *High/Scope Child Observation Record (COR) for Ages 2 1/2 to 6* (Ypsilanti, MI: Author, 1992).

2. L. J. Schweinhart, S. McNair, H. Barnes, and M. Larner, "Observing Young Children in Action to Assess Their Development: The High/Scope Child Observation Record Study," *Educational and Psychological Measurement,* 53, Summer, pp. 445–455.

3. M. Montessori, *The Discovery of the Child* (New York: Ballantine Books, 1980), p. 46.

CHAPTER

8

Foundation Years for Learning

FOCUS QUESTIONS

1. Why have infant and toddler programs increased in popularity?
2. What are important stages in infant and toddler development?
3. How does Piaget's cognitive theory explain infant and toddler development?
4. How do literacy and language develop in the early years?
5. What are the major features of Erikson's theory of psychosocial development in the infant and toddler years?
6. How can you provide developmentally appropriate programs for infants and toddlers?
7. What are issues involved in providing quality care and education for infants and toddlers?

Interest in infant and toddler care and education is at an all-time high and will continue at this level into the twenty-first century. This growing demand stems primarily from the large number of women in the labor force. It is also fueled by parents who want their children to have an "early start" and get off on the "right foot" so they can have an even better life than their parents. The acceptance of early care and education is also attributable to a changing view of the very young and the discovery that infants are remarkably competent individuals. Parents and early childhood professionals have combined forces to give infants and toddlers quality care and education without harmfully and needlessly pushing and hurrying them. This collaborative effort will continue.

PHYSICAL DEVELOPMENT

The infant and toddler years between birth and age three are full of developmental milestones and social events. Infancy, life's first year, includes the first breath, the first smile, first thoughts, first words, and first steps. Significant developments also occur during toddlerhood, the period between one and three years; two such developments are unassisted walking and rapid language development. Mobility and language are the cornerstones of autonomy that enable toddlers to become independent. These unique developmental events are significant for children as well as those who care for and teach them. How early childhood professionals and parents respond to infants' firsts and toddlers' quests for autonomy helps determine how children grow and master the life events that await them.

To fully grasp their roles as educators and nurturers, early childhood professionals need to understand the major events and processes of normal growth and development. To begin, we must recognize that infants and toddlers are not the miniature adults many baby product advertisements picture them to be. Children need many years to develop fully and become independent. This period of dependency and professionals' responses to it are critical

TABLE 8–1

Height and Weight of Infants and Toddlers

Age	Males		Females	
	Height (in.)	**Weight (lb.)**	**Height (in.)**	**Weight (lb.)**
3–6 months	25.5	16	24.5	14.5
6–9 months	27.5	19.75	26.75	18.5
9–12 months	29.75	22.5	28.75	20.5
1–1.5 years	31	24.25	30.75	23.5
1.5–2 years	33.25	27	32	24.75
2 years	36	30.5	35	29
3 years	39	34.75	38.5	33.25

Source: Based on data online, *Baby Bag Online,* http://www.babybag.com/articles/htwt_av.htm, Copyright 1996.

for the developing child. Professionals must constantly keep in mind that "normal" growth and development are based on averages, and the "average" is the middle ground of development. (Table 8–1 gives average heights and weights for infants and toddlers.) To assess children's progress, or lack of it, professionals must know the milestones of different stages of development. At the same time, to assess what is "normal" for each child, they must consider the whole child. They must look at cultural and family background, including nutritional and health history, to determine what is normal for that child. Professionals must also keep in mind that when children are provided with good nutrition, health care, and a warm, loving, safe and emotionally secure environment, development tends toward what is "normal" for each child.

MOTOR DEVELOPMENT

Motor development is important to infants and toddlers because it contributes to intellectual and skill development. Human motor development is governed by certain basic principles:

- Motor development is sequential (Table 8–2).
- Maturation of the motor system proceeds from gross (large) to fine behaviors. When learning to reach, for example, an infant sweeps toward an object with the whole arm; as a result of development and experiences, gross reaching gives way to specific reaching and grasping.
- Motor development is from cephalo to caudal—from head to foot (tail). This process is known as *cephalocaudal development.* The head is the most developed part of the body at birth; infants hold their heads erect before they sit, and sitting precedes walking.

- Motor development proceeds from the proximal (midline or central part of the body) to the distal (extremities), known as *proximodistal development*. Infants are able to control their arm movements before they can control finger movements.

Motor development plays a major role in social and behavioral expectations. For example, toilet training (also called *toilet learning* or *toilet mastery*) is a milestone of the toddler period. This process often causes a great deal of anxiety for parents, professionals, and toddlers. American parents want to accomplish toilet training as quickly and efficiently as possible, but frustrations arise when they start too early and expect too much of children. Toilet training is largely a matter of physical readiness, and most child-rearing experts recommend waiting at least until children are two years old before beginning. Although some parents claim that their children are trained as early as one year, it is probably the parent rather than the child who is trained.

The principle of toilet training is that parents and professionals are helping children develop control over an involuntary response. When an infant's bladder and bowel are full, the urethral and sphincter muscles open. The goal of toilet training is to teach the child to control this involuntary reflex and use the toilet when appropriate. Training involves maturational development, timing, patience, modeling, preparation of the environment, establishment of a routine, and development of a partnership between the child and parents/professionals. Another necessary partnership is between parents and profession-

TABLE 8–2

Infant and Toddler Motor Milestones

Behavior	Age of Accomplishment or 90% of Infants/Toddlers
Chin up momentarily	3 weeks
Arms and legs move equally	7 weeks
Smiles responsively	2 months
Sits with support	4 months
Reaches for objects	5 months
Smiles spontaneously	5 months
Rolls over	5 months
Crawls	7 months
Creeps	10 months
Pulls self to stand	11 months
Walks holding onto furniture	13 months

Source: William K. Frankenburg, William Sciarillo, and David Burgess, "The Newly Abbreviated and Revised Denver Developmental Screening Test," *Journal of Pediatrics,* 99, December 1981, p. 996. Used by permission.

als who are assisting in toilet training, especially when parents do not know what to do, are hesitant about approaching toilet training, or want to start the training too soon.

HOW DOES INTELLECTUAL DEVELOPMENT OCCUR?

As we learned in Chapter 4, children's first schemata (schemes) are sensorimotor. According to Piaget, infants do not have "thoughts of the mind." Rather, they come to know their world by actively acting on it through their senses and motor action. According to Piaget, infants construct (as opposed to absorb) schemes using sensorimotor reflexive actions.

Infants begin life with only reflexive motor actions that they use to satisfy biological needs. In response to specific environmental conditions, they modify these reflexive actions through accommodation and adaptation to the environment. Patterns of adaptive behavior initiate more activity, which leads to more adaptive behavior, which in turn yields more schemes. Consider sucking,

Motor development plays a major role in cognitive and social development. Learning to walk enables young children to explore their environment which in turns contributes to cognitive development. What are some ways that motor development enhances young children's ability to learn?

for example, an innate sensorimotor scheme. The child turns the head to the source of nourishment, closing the lips around the nipple, sucking, and swallowing. As a result of experiences and maturation, the infant adapts or changes this basic sensorimotor scheme to include both anticipatory sucking movements and nonnutritive sucking such as sucking a pacifier or blanket.

Children construct or create new schemes through the processes of assimilation and accommodation. Piaget believed children are active constructors of intelligence through assimilation (taking in new experiences) and accommodation (changing existing schemes to fit new information), which result in equilibrium.

STAGES OF COGNITIVE DEVELOPMENT

Sensorimotor Intelligence

Sensorimotor intellectual development consists of six stages, shown in Table 8–3 and described in the following subsections.

Stage 1: Reflective Action (Birth to One Month)

During this stage, infants suck and grasp everything. They are literally ruled by reflexive actions. Reflexive responses to objects are undifferentiated, and infants respond the same way to everything. Sensorimotor schemes help infants learn new ways of interacting with the world, and the new ways of interacting promote cognitive development. Grasping is a primary infant sensorimotor scheme. At birth, the grasping reflex consists of closing the fingers around an object placed in the hand. Through experiences and maturation, this basic reflexive grasping action becomes coordinated with looking, opening the hand, retracting the fingers, and grasping, thus developing from a pure, reflexive action to an intentional grasping action. As an infant matures in response to experiences, the grasping scheme is combined with a delightful activity of grasping and releasing things.

Stage 2: Primary Circular Reactions (One to Four Months)

The milestone of this stage is the modification of the reflexive actions of Stage 1. Sensorimotor behaviors not previously present in the infant begin to appear: habitually sucking the thumb (indicates hand-mouth coordination), tracking moving objects with the eyes, and moving the head toward sounds (indicates the beginning of the recognition of causality). Infants start to direct their own behavior rather than being totally dependent on reflexive actions. The first steps of intellectual development have begun.

Primary circular reactions begin during Stage 2. A circular response occurs when an infant's actions cause a reaction in the infant or another person that prompts the infant to try to repeat the original action. The circular reaction is similar to a stimulus-response, cause-and-effect relationship.

TABLE 8–3
Stages of Sensorimotor Intellectual Development

Stage	Age	Behavior
1. Reflexive action	Birth to 1 month	Reflexive actions of sucking, grasping, crying, rooting, swallowing
		Through experiences, reflexes become more efficient (e.g., amount of sucking required for nourishment)
		Little or no tolerance for frustration or delayed gratification
2. Primary circular reactions	1 to 4 months	Acquired adaptations form
		Reflexive actions gradually replaced by voluntary actions
		Circular reactions result in modification of existing schemes
3. Secondary circular reactions	4 to 8 months	Increased responses to people and objects
		Able to initiate activities
		Beginning of object permanency
4. Coordination of secondary schemes	8 to 12 months	Increased deliberation and purposefulness in responding to people and objects
		First clear signs of developing intelligence
		Continuing development of object permanency
		Actively searches for hidden objects
		Comprehends meanings of simple words
5. Experimentation (tertiary circular reactions)	12 to 18 months	Active experimentation begins through trial and error
		Spends much time "experimenting" with objects to see what happens; insatiable curiosity
		Differentiates self from objects
		Realization that "out of sight" is not "out of reach" or "out of existence"
		Beginning of understanding of space, time, and causality
6. Representational intelligence (intention of means)	18 to 24 months	Development of cause-effect relationships
		Representational intelligence begins; can mentally represent objects
		Engages in symbolic imitative behavior
		Beginning of sense of time
		Egocentric in thought and behavior

Stage 3: Secondary Circular Reactions (Four to Eight Months)

Piaget called this stage that of "making interesting things last." Infants manipulate objects, demonstrating coordination between vision and tactile senses. They also reproduce events with the purpose of sustaining and repeating acts. The intellectual milestone of this stage is the beginning of object permanence. When infants in Stages 1 and 2 cannot see an object, it does not exist for them—"out of sight, out of mind." During later Stage 3, however, awareness grows that things that are out of sight continue to exist.

Secondary circular reactions begin during this stage. This process is characterized by an infant's repeating an action with the purpose of getting the same response from an object or person; for example, an infant will repeatedly shake a rattle to repeat the sound. Repetitiveness is characteristic of all circular reactions. *Secondary* here means that the reaction is elicited from a source other than the infant. The infant interacts with people and objects to make interesting sights, sounds, and events last. Given an object, the infant will use all available schemes, such as mouthing, hitting, and banging; if one of these schemes produces an interesting result, the infant continues to use the scheme to elicit the same response. Imitation becomes increasingly intentional as a means of prolonging an interest.

Stage 4: Coordination of Secondary Schemes (Eight to Twelve Months)

During this stage, the infant uses means to attain ends. Infants move objects out of the way (means) to get another object (end). They begin to search for hidden objects, although not always in the places they were hidden, indicating a growing understanding of object permanence.

Stage 5: Tertiary Circulation Reactions (Twelve to Eighteen Months)

This stage, the climax of the sensorimotor period, marks the beginning of truly intelligent behavior. Stage 5 is the stage of experimentation. Toddlers experiment with objects to solve problems, and their experimentation is characteristic of intelligence that involves tertiary circular reactions, in which they repeat actions and modify behaviors over and over to see what will happen. This repetition helps develop an understanding of cause-and-effect relationships and leads to the discovery of new relationships through exploration and experimentation.

Physically, Stage 5 is also the beginning of the toddler stage, with the commencement of walking. Toddlers' physical mobility, combined with their growing ability and desire to experiment with objects, makes for fascinating and often frustrating child rearing. They are avid explorers, determined to touch, taste, and feel all they can. Although the term *terrible twos* was once used to describe this stage, professionals now recognize that there is nothing terrible about toddlers exploring their environment to develop their intelligence. Novelty is interesting for its own sake, and toddlers experiment in many different ways with a given object. For example, they will use any available item—a wood hammer, a block, a rhythm band instrument—to pound the pegs in a pound-a-peg toy.

Stage 6: Representational Intelligence (Eighteen Months to Two Years)

This is the stage of transition from sensorimotor to symbolic thought. Stage 6 is the stage of symbolic representation. Representation occurs when toddlers can visualize events internally and maintain mental images of objects not present. Representational thought enables toddlers to solve problems in a sensorimotor way through experimentation and trial and error and predict cause-and-effect relationships more accurately. Toddlers also develop the ability to remember, which allows them to try out actions they see others do. During this stage, toddlers can "think" using mental images and memories, which enables them to engage in pretend activities. Toddlers' representational thought does not necessarily match the real world and its representations, which accounts for a toddler's ability to have other objects stand for almost anything: A wooden block is a car; a rag doll is a baby. This type of play, known as *symbolic play,* becomes more elaborate and complex in the preoperational period.

In summary, we need to keep in mind several important concepts of infant and toddler development:

1. The chronological ages associated with Piaget's stages of cognitive development are approximate. In fact, as we discussed in Chapter 5, children can do things earlier than the ages Piaget assigned. Professionals should not be preoccupied with children's ages but should focus on cognitive behavior, which gives a clearer understanding of a child's level of development. This is the true meaning of developmentally appropriate caregiving.

2. Infants and toddlers do not "think" as adults do; they come to know their world by acting on it and need many opportunities for active involvement.

3. Infants and toddlers are actively involved in constructing their own intelligence. Children's activity with people and objects stimulates them cognitively and leads to the development of mental schemata (schemes).

4. Parents and early childhood professionals need to provide environments and opportunities for infants and toddlers to be actively involved. These are two important conditions for intellectual development. Reflexive actions form the basis for assimilation and accommodation, which enable cognitive structures to develop. Professionals must ensure that infants and toddlers have experiences that will enable successful intellectual construction.

5. At birth, infants do not know that there are objects in the world and, in this sense, have no knowledge of the external world. They do not and cannot differentiate between themselves and the external world. For all practical purposes, the infant is the world. All external objects are acted on through sucking, grasping, and looking. This acting on the world enables infants to construct schemes of the world.

6. The concept of causality, or cause and effect, does not exist at birth. Infants' and toddlers' concepts of causality begin to evolve only through acting on the environment.

7. As infants and toddlers move from one stage of intellectual development to another, later stages evolve from, rather than replace, earlier ones. Schemes developed in Stage 1 are incorporated into and improved on by the schemes constructed in Stage 2, and so forth.

HOW DOES LANGUAGE DEVELOP?

Language development begins at birth. Indeed, some argue it begins before birth. The first cry, the first coo, the first "da-da" and "ma-ma," the first word are auditory proof that children are participating in the process of language development. Language helps define us as human, and represents one of our most remarkable intellectual accomplishments. How does the infant go from the first cry to the first word a year later? How does the toddler develop from saying one word to several hundred words a year later? While everyone agrees that children learn language, not everyone agrees how. How does language development begin? What forces and processes prompt children to participate in one of the uniquely human endeavors? Let us examine some of the explanations.

Language Acquisition

Heredity plays a role in language development in a number of ways. First, humans have the respiratory and laryngeal systems that make rapid and efficient vocal communication possible. Second, the human brain makes language possible. The left hemisphere is the center for speech and phonetic analysis and the brain's main language center. But the left hemisphere does not have the exclusive responsibility for language. The right hemisphere plays a role in our understanding of speech intonations, which enables us to distinguish between declarative, imperative, and interrogative sentences. Without these processing systems, language as we know it would be impossible. Third, heredity plays a role in language development in that some theorists believe that humans are innately endowed with the *ability* to produce language.

A major theme throughout this text is that all children are different. While we can clearly identify progressive stages of development, as in this photograph, early childhood professionals must always provide for the individual needs of every child. In what ways are these children similar? In what ways are they different?

Noam Chomsky is one proponent of the theory that humans are born with the ability to acquire language. He hypothesizes that all children possess a structure or mechanism called a *language acquisition device* (LAD) that permits them to acquire language. The young child's LAD uses all the language sounds heard to process many grammatical sentences, even sentences never heard before. The child hears a particular language and processes it to form grammatical rules.

Eric Lenneberg has studied innate language acquisitions in considerable detail in many different kinds of children, including the deaf. According to Lenneberg,

> All the evidence suggests that the capacities for speech production and related aspects of language acquisition develop according to built-in biological schedules. They appear when the time is ripe and not until then, when a state of what I have called "resonance" exists. The child somehow becomes "excited," in phase with the environment, so that the sounds he hears and has been hearing all along suddenly acquire a peculiar prominence. The change is like the establishment of new sensitivities. He becomes aware in a new way, selecting certain parts of the total auditory input for attention, ignoring others.[1]

The fact that children generate sentences they have never heard before is often cited as proof of innate ability. What would language be if we were only capable of reproducing the sentences and words we heard? The ability of children in all cultures and social settings to acquire language at a relatively immature age tends to support the thesis that language acquisition and use is more than a product of imitation or direct instruction. Indeed, children learn language without formal instruction.

The idea of a sensitive period of language development makes a great deal of sense and had a particular fascination for Montessori, who believed there were two such sensitive periods. The first begins at birth and lasts until about three years. During this time, children unconsciously absorb language from the environment. The second period begins at three years and lasts until about eight years. During this time, children are active participants in their language development and learn how to use their power of communication.

Environmental Factors

Theories about a biological basis of language should not be interpreted to mean that children are born with the particular language they will speak. While the ability to acquire language has a biological basis, the content of the language—syntax, grammar, and vocabulary—is acquired from the environment, which includes other people as models for language. Development depends on talk between children and adults and between children and children. Optimal language development ultimately depends on interactions with the best possible language models. The biological process may be the same for all children, but the content of their language will differ according to environmental factors. Children left to their own devices will not learn a language as well as children reared in linguistically rich environments.

For example, Susan Curtiss writes of Genie, a modern-day "wild child." During her early days, Genie had minimal human contact, and her father and brother barked at her like dogs instead of using human language. She did not have an opportunity to learn language until she was thirteen-and-a-half years old, and even after prolonged treatment and care, Genie remained basically language deficient and conversationally incompetent.[2]

Early Childhood Professionals and Language Learning

People who care for children and are around them in the early stages of language learning greatly influence how and what they learn. Children's language experiences can make the difference in their school success. Many children enter a preschool or child care setting without much experience in talking and listening to other children or adults in different social settings.

Parents and professionals should focus on the content of language: learning names for things, how to speak in full sentences, and how to use and understand language. Many of these language activities relate directly to success in preschool, kindergarten, and first grade. The following guidelines will help you promote children's language development:

- Treat children as partners in the communication process. Many infant behaviors, such as smiling, cooing, and vocalizing, serve to initiate conversation, and professionals can be responsive to these through conversation.

- Keep in mind that conversations are the building blocks of language development. Attentive and caring adults are infants' and toddlers' best stimulators of cognitive and language development.

- Talk to infants in a soothing, pleasant voice, with frequent eye contact, even though they do not "talk" to you. Most mothers and professionals talk to their young children differently from the way they talk to adults. They adapt their speech so they can communicate in a distinctive way called "motherese." Mothers' language interactions with their toddlers are much the same as with infants. When conversing with toddlers who are just learning language, it is a good idea to simplify verbalization—not by using "baby talk," such as "di-di" for diaper or "ba-ba" for bottle, but rather by speaking in an easily understandable way. For example, instead of saying, "We are going to take a walk around the block so you must put your coat on," you would instead say, "Let's get coats on." Use children's names when interacting with them, to personalize the conversation and build self-identity.

- Use a variety of means to stimulate and promote language development, including reading stories, singing songs, listening to records, and giving children many opportunities to verbally interact with adults and other children.

- Encourage children to converse and share information with other children and adults.

- Help children learn to converse in various settings by taking them to different places so they can use their language with a variety of people. This approach also gives children ideas and experiences for using language.

- Have children use language in different ways. Children need to know how to use language to ask questions, explain feelings and emotions, tell what they have done, and describe things.

- Give children experiences in the language of directions and commands. Many children fail in school settings not because they do not know language but because they have little or no experience in how language is used for giving and following directions. It is also important for children to understand that language can be used as a means to an end—a way of attaining a desired goal.

- Converse with children about what they are doing and how they are doing it. Children learn language through feedback—asking and answering questions and commenting about activities—which shows children that you are paying attention to them and what they are doing.
- Talk to children in the full range of adult language, including past and future tenses.

HOW DOES PSYCHOSOCIAL DEVELOPMENT OCCUR?

Erik H. Erikson (1902–1994) is noted for his psychosocial theory of development. According to Erikson, children's personalities grow and develop in response to social institutions such as families, schools, child care centers, and early childhood programs. Of course, adults are principal components of these environments and therefore play a powerful role in helping or hindering children in their personality development.

Stages of Psychosocial Development

Erikson's theory has eight stages, which he also classifies as ego qualities. These qualities emerge across the human life span. Erikson maintains that psychosocial development results from the interaction between maturational processes such as biological needs and the social forces encountered in everyday living. Socialization provides the context for conflict and crisis resolution during the eight developmental stages. Four of these stages apply to children from birth to age eight.

Stage 1: Basic Trust versus Mistrust (Birth to about Eighteen Months)

During this stage, children learn to trust or mistrust their environments and professionals. Trust develops when children's needs are met consistently, predictably, and lovingly.

Stage 2: Autonomy versus Shame and Doubt (Eighteen Months to about Three Years)

This is the stage of independence, when children want to do things for themselves. Lack of opportunities to become autonomous and independent and professional overprotection result in self-doubt and poor achievement. As a result, instead of feeling good about their accomplishments, children come to feel ashamed of their abilities.

Stage 3: Initiative versus Guilt (Three Years to about Five Years)

During the preschool years children need opportunities to respond with initiative to activities and tasks, which gives them a sense of purposefulness and accomplishment. Erikson believes children can feel guilty when they are discouraged or prohibited from initiating activities and are overly restricted in attempts to do things on their own.

Stage 4: Industry versus Inferiority (The Elementary School Years)

In this period, children display an industrious attitude and want to be productive. They want to build things, discover, manipulate objects, and find out how things work. Productivity is important during this stage. They also want recognition for their productivity, and adult response to children's efforts and accomplishments helps develop a positive self-concept. Feelings of inferiority result when children are criticized, are belittled, or have few opportunities for productivity.

DEVELOPMENTALLY APPROPRIATE PROGRAMS

Many issues we have discussed in earlier chapters, particularly in Chapter 5, relate to infant and toddler education. First is the issue of *developmental appropriateness.* All early childhood professionals who provide care for infants and toddlers—indeed, for all children—must understand and recognize this important concept, which provides the solid foundation for any program. NAEYC defines *developmentally appropriate* as having three dimensions:

- what is known about child development and learning—knowledge of age-related human characteristics that permits general predictions within an age range about what activities, materials, interactions, or experiences will be safe, healthy, interesting, achievable, and also challenging to children

- what is known about the strengths, interests, and needs of each individual child in the group to be able to adapt for and be responsive to inevitable individual variation; and

- knowledge of the social and cultural contexts in which children live to ensure that learning experiences are meaningful, relevant, and respectful for the participating children and their families.[3]

As part of NAEYC's revised *Developmentally Appropriate Practice in Early Childhood Programs,* the following guidelines for making decisions about developmentally appropriate practice will help staff plan for activities:

Guidelines for Decisions about Developmentally Appropriate Practice

An understanding of the nature of development and learning during the early childhood years, from birth through age 8, generates guidelines that inform the practices of early childhood educators. Developmentally appropriate practice requires that teachers integrate the many dimensions of their knowledge base. They must know about child development and the implications of this knowledge for how to teach, the content of the curriculum—what to teach and when—how to assess what children have learned, and how to adapt curriculum and instruction to children's individual strengths, needs, and interests. Further, they must know the particular children they teach and their families and be knowledgeable as well about the social and cultural context.

BOX 8-1 A VIEW FROM THE CLASSROOM DOOR

What does good infant and toddler care and early education look like? Every center director spends at least some of her time each day looking into classroom doors or windows to see if things are going okay. What does she expect to see? What are the indicators that matter during this snapshot view? Here are some of those things for me.

Continuity of teachers and children in the group. By far the first thing I look for is a familiar scene. Is everyone who is supposed to be in the classroom there? Are the people present who are the most knowledgeable about the children in the group? Are all of the children in the group present?

Familiar faces of the adults who care for children and children who are in the group are crucial to high-quality care and early education for infants and toddlers. Continuity of caregiver and continuity of group together allow for an intense level of predictability and stability that facilitates children's adjustment to out-of-home care and increases the chance that the separation and reunion process will be predictable and pleasant.

I also look for continuity to remain stable over time. Keeping teachers and children together in primary groups for lengthy periods of time (up to three or more years) allows teachers of infants and toddlers to create an out-of-home caregiving experience that is compatible with their family experience.

A sense of peace and tranquility. Perhaps one of the most frightening aspects of out-of-home care for parents of infants and toddlers is the real concern that children's emotional needs will not be met. Parents report that they are afraid that their child will need attention and not get it because of the demands of having three or more infants and five or more toddlers in a group.

This fear is magnified by the separation and reunion process which, during the infant and tod- dler years, can often (and quite normally) be accompanied by crying and resistance. Parents may leave a crying child at the beginning of the day and return to a crying child at the end of the day—fueling fears that the time in the middle couldn't have been pleasant either.

So, classrooms for infants and toddlers need to have a sense of tranquility and peace—a sense that the underlying timbre of the classroom is calm and stable. I look for a classroom where crying children are getting a prompt response—at least a verbal connection ("I'm on my way as soon as I finish changing this diaper")—if not a physical one, and where actions speak as loud as words do. I look to see if teachers have ideas about what children need now as well as what they might need later. And, I look to see if teachers have planned for or are going about meeting those needs. (Are bottles being warmed? Are security items labeled and available?) I look for evidence that teachers know each child's individual daily routine and respect it by offering a bottle or lunch before the child is too hungry or beginning a calm-down routine before the child gets too tired. I also look for signs that the adults are calm, confident, relaxed, and unhurried.

A balance of novelty and predictability in a clean environment. In infant and toddler programs, cleanliness is crucial. Because infants and toddlers spend a great deal of time on the floor and exploring with their hands and mouths, the environment must be clean and without odors.

It must also be predictable, filled with familiar yet interesting things to look at and manipulate. Children need to be able to find things where they left them the last time they were here—the same place for sleeping, eating, and reading books. But I also look for novel and interesting things to do, objects to touch, places to be, things to dump and sort through, and things to be discovered by uncovering or unwrapping.

I look for space. Overcrowding is a real problem with infant and toddler care because required licensing standards often limit space, which in the infant environment particularly can be filled up with cribs and other furniture. Infants and toddlers need plenty of space—enough to always have another area to move or be moved to for exploration, visual and tactile stimulation, or experimentation, and they need to get away from stimulation and excitement to avoid over-stimulation.

Engagement between children and teachers. One of the most critical components of quality care and early education for infants and toddlers is the interactive environment.

I look for teachers to be where children are and children to be where teachers are. Sometimes this means physical engagement like sharing a book in a comfortable rocking chair or playing together on the floor. Sometimes this means emotional engagement such as that involving routine activities like diapering and eating.

It means seeing evidence of emotional contact and connectedness—quick responses to cries, looking where the child looks and commenting on what is seen, checking to see if you're needed, verbal exchanges that lead children to believe you mean what you say, and a sense of caring about what children are seeing, feeling, and doing.

I look to see if teachers treat children respectfully—asking a child if she is ready to be picked up before doing it, using language to talk "to" children rather than "at" them, narrating what is going to happen before it happens and as it happens, etc.

I also look to see if teachers are observing children. Careful observation is the source of recognition of developmental progress and the way to discover emergent skills and interests. It also ensures that teachers register and make changes as children change so that boredom does not set in.

Pace changes across the day. Because infants and toddlers in full day care and early education can spend a majority of their day in out-of-home care, pace changes are crucial—both for children and the adults who care for them.

I look to see that things change across the day. Positions are changed for young infants. All children get opportunities to go outside, music sometimes fills the air, window blinds are closed to create a sense of calm, then opened to let the sun shine in! I look to see if the pace picks up and becomes energetic and active and then quiets down to become intimate and soothing.

Help with social problem solving. Children under three in out-of-home care are not yet able to interact intensely for long periods of time in groups without facilitation and support. In the beginning this looks a lot like protection from others—keeping fingers out of mouths, helping children crawl around rather than over, supporting side by side play, and giving infants and toddlers opportunities to look at and watch other children doing interesting things. Later on, it includes facilitating emerging social skills like sharing resources, taking turns, perfecting skills like using an outstretched hand to ask for a toy nonverbally, and using language to communicate needs and wants.

To make this happen, teachers need to be close to where children are—physically near them—so they are available to model, guide, or support children's initial and subsequent interactions. So I look for teachers to be on the floor where children are, at the table when children are eating, participating in the process of picking up and putting down interesting toys, and supporting emerging skills by example as well as with verbal and physical guidance.

The view from the door is often a snapshot—and certainly not an in-depth program evaluation. But high quality care and early education for infants and toddlers is very observable—the components that create a positive experience for both children and their teachers can be seen in a view from the door.

Kay Albrecht, Ph.D., is the executive director of HeartsHome Early Learning Center, a nationally accredited care and early education program in Houston, Texas, which serves over 60 infants and toddlers.

Increasing numbers of children are in infant and toddler care. When making decisions about child care, parents and others must consider four essential factors that determine the quality of infant/toddler care: the environment, the caregivers, the nature of the care, and the curriculum.

The following guidelines address five interrelated dimensions of early childhood professional practice: creating a caring community of learners, teaching to enhance development and learning, constructing appropriate curriculum, assessing children's development and learning, and establishing reciprocal relationships with families. (The word *teacher* is used to refer to any adult responsible for a group of children in any early childhood program, including infant/toddler caregivers, family child care providers, and specialists in other disciplines who fulfill the role of teacher.)

1. Developmentally appropriate practices occur within a context that supports the development of relationships between adults and children, among children, among teachers, and between teachers and families.

    A. The early childhood setting functions as a community of learners in which all participants consider and contribute to each other's well-being and learning.

    B. Consistent, positive relationships with a limited number of adults and other children are a fundamental determinant of healthy human development and provide the context for children to learn about themselves and their world and also how to develop positive, constructive relationships with other people.

    C. Social relationships are an important context for learning. Each child has strengths or interests that contribute to the overall functioning of the group. When children have opportunities to play together, work on projects in small groups, and talk with other children and adults, their own development and learning are enhanced.

    D. The learning environment is designed to protect children's health and safety and is supportive of children's physiological needs for activity, sensory stimulation, fresh air, rest, and nourishment. The program protects children's psychological safety; that is, children feel secure, relaxed, and comfortable rather than disengaged, frightened, worried, or stressed.

    E. Children experience an organized environment and an orderly routine that provides an overall structure in which learning takes place; the environment is dynamic and changing but predictable and comprehensible from a child's point of view.

2. Adults are responsible for ensuring children's healthy development and learning.

    A. Teachers respect, value, and accept children and treat them with dignity at all times.

    B. Teachers make it a priority to know each child well.

    C. Teachers create an intellectually engaging, responsive environment to promote each child's learning and development.

    D. Teachers make plans to enable children to attain key curriculum goals across various disciplines, such as language arts, mathematics, social studies, science, art, music, physical education, and health.

    E. Teachers foster children's collaboration with peers on interesting, important enterprises.

F. Teachers develop, refine, and use a wide repertoire of teaching strategies to enhance children's learning and development.

G. Teachers facilitate the development of responsibility and self-regulation in children.

3. Constructing appropriate curriculum

The content of the early childhood curriculum is determined by many factors, including the subject matter of the disciplines, social or cultural values, and parental input. In developmentally appropriate programs, decisions about curriculum content also take into consideration the age and experience of the learners. Achieving success for all children depends, among other essentials, on providing a challenging, interesting, developmentally appropriate curriculum. Constructing appropriate curriculum requires attention to at least the following guidelines for practice:

A. Developmentally appropriate curriculum provides for all areas of a child's development: physical, emotional, social, linguistic, aesthetic, and cognitive.

B. Curriculum includes a broad range of content across disciplines that is socially relevant, intellectually engaging, and personally meaningful to children.

C. Curriculum builds upon what children already know and are able to do (activating prior knowledge) to consolidate their learning and to foster their acquisition of new concepts and skills.

D. Effective curriculum plans frequently integrate across traditional subject-matter divisions to help children make meaningful connections and provide opportunities for rich conceptual development; focusing on one subject is also a valid strategy at times.

E. Curriculum promotes the development of knowledge and understanding, processes and skills, as well as the dispositions to use and apply skills and to go on learning.

F. Curriculum content has intellectual integrity, reflecting the key concepts and tools of inquiry of recognized disciplines in ways that are accessible and achievable for young children, ages 3 through 8.

G. Curriculum provides opportunities to support children's home culture and language while also developing all children's abilities to participate in the shared culture of the program and the community.

H. Curriculum goals are realistic and attainable for most children in the designated age range for which they are designed.

I. When used, technology is physically and philosophically integrated in the classroom curriculum and teaching.

4. Assessing children's learning and development

Assessment of individual children's development and learning is essential for planning and implementing appropriate curriculum. In developmentally appropriate programs, assessment and curriculum are integrated, with teachers continually engaging in observational assessment for the purpose of improving teaching and learning.

A. Assessment of young children's progress and achievements is ongoing, strategic, and purposeful.

B. The content of assessments reflects progress toward important learning and developmental goals.

C. The methods of assessment are appropriate to the age and experiences of young children. Therefore, assessment of young children relies heavily on the results of observations of children's development, descriptive data, collections of representative work by children, and demonstrated performance during authentic, not contrived, activities. Input from families as well as children's evaluations of their own work are part of the overall assessment strategy.

D. Assessments are tailored to a specific purpose and used only for the purpose for which they have been demonstrated to produce reliable, valid information.

E. Decisions that have a major impact on children, such as enrollment or placement, are never made on the basis of a single developmental assessment or screening device but are based on multiple sources of relevant information, particularly observations by teachers and parents.

F. To identify children who have special learning or developmental needs and to plan appropriate curriculum and teaching for them, developmental assessments and observations are used.

G. Assessment recognizes individual variation in learners and allows for differences in styles and rates of learning. Assessment takes into consideration such factors as the child's facility in English, stage of acquisition, and whether the child has had the time and opportunity to develop proficiency in his or her home language as well as in English.

H. Assessment legitimately addresses not only what children can do independently but what they can do with assistance from other children or adults. Teachers study children as individuals as well as in relationship to groups by documenting group projects and other collaborative work.

5. Establishing reciprocal relationships with families

Developmentally appropriate practices derive from deep knowledge of individual children and the context within which they develop and learn. The younger the child, the more necessary it is for professionals to acquire this knowledge through relationships with children's families.

A. Reciprocal relationships between teachers and families require mutual respect, cooperation, shared responsibility, and negotiation of conflicts toward achievement of shared goals.

B. Early childhood teachers work in collaborative partnerships with families, establishing and maintaining regular, frequent two-way communication with children's parents.

C. Parents are welcome in the program and participate in decisions about their children's care and education. Parents observe and participate and serve in decision-making roles in the program.

D. Teachers acknowledge parents' choices and goals for children and respond with sensitivity and respect to parents' preferences and concerns without abdicating professional responsibility to children.

E. Teachers and parents share their knowledge of the child and understanding of children's development and learning as part of day-to-day communication and planned conferences. Teachers support families in ways that maximally promote family decision-making capabilities and competence.

F. To ensure more accurate and complete information, the program involves families in assessing and planning for individual children.

G. The program links families with a range of services, based on identified resources, priorities, and concerns.

H. Teachers, parents, programs, social service and health agencies, and consultants who may have educational responsibility for the child at different times should, with family participation, share developmental information about children as they pass from one level or program to another.[4]

The full text of the *NAEYC Position Statement on Developmentally Appropriate Practice in Early Childhood Programs* is found in Appendix C.

Early childhood professionals must also understand the importance of providing programs for infants and toddlers that are uniquely different from programs for older children. NAEYC states the following about the necessity for unique programming for infants and toddlers:

Developmentally appropriate programs for children from birth to age 3 are distinctly different from all other types of programs—they are not a scaled-down version of a good program for preschool children. These program differences are determined by the unique characteristics and needs of children during the first 3 years:

- Changes take place far more rapidly in infancy than during any other period in life.
- During infancy, as at every other age, all areas of development—cognitive, social, emotional, and physical—are intertwined.
- Infants are totally dependent on adults to meet their needs.
- Very young children are especially vulnerable to adversity because they are less able to cope actively with discomfort and stress.

Infants and toddlers learn through their own experience, trial and error, repetition, imitation, and identification. Adults guide and encourage this learning by ensuring that the environment is safe and emotionally supportive. An appropriate program for children younger than three invites play, active exploration, and movement. It provides a broad array of stimulating experiences within a reliable framework of routines and protection from excessive stress. Relationships with people are emphasized as an essential contribution to the quality of children's experiences.[5]

Based on these dimensions, professionals must provide different programs of activities for infants and toddlers. To do so, early childhood professionals must get parents and other professionals to recognize that infants, as a group, are different from toddlers and need programs, curricula, and facilities specifically designed for them. It is then necessary to design and implement developmentally appropriate curricula. The early childhood education profession is leading the way in raising consciousness about the need to match what professionals do with children to children's development as individuals. We have a long way to go in this regard, but part of the resolution will come with ongoing training of professionals in child development and curriculum planning.

Finally, we will want to match professionals to children of different ages. Not everyone is emotionally or professionally suited to provide care for infants and toddlers. Both groups need adults who can respond to their particular needs and developmental characteristics. Infants need especially nurturing professionals; toddlers, on the other hand, need adults who can tolerate and allow for their emerging autonomy and independence.

VIDEO VIEWPOINT

FIRST THREE YEARS OF LIFE

Children between the ages of zero and three change rapidly. The Carnegie Corporation has released a study of how important these years are for stimulation and nurturing and what being deprived of certain experiences and opportunities in the first three years of life can mean for the future of our children and our nation. This is called the "quiet crisis."

Reflective Discussion Questions: Why is the quiet crisis such an important issue for early childhood professionals? For parents? What is the consequence for our nation of not fully providing for children's development in the critical early years? How does poverty negatively influence children's environments and prevent them from fully developing in the early years?

Reflective Decision Making: What are some things that you can do to improve the quality of children's environments in the first three years of life? What advice would you give parents concerning the quality of their home environments or how they could improve the quality of their home environments? Review this and other chapters in this book, and list some things you can do to provide infants and toddlers with appropriate attention and stimulation. In Chapter 5, we discuss Early Head Start. How can this and other early intervention programs provide children with the stimulation and attention they need?

Curricula for Infants and Toddlers

Curricula for infants and toddlers consist of all the activities and experiences they are involved in while under the direction of professionals. Consequently, early childhood professionals plan for all activities and involvements: feeding, washing, diapering/toileting, playing, learning and stimulating interactions, outings, involvements with others, and conversations. Professionals must plan the curriculum so it is developmentally appropriate. In addition to ideas derived from the NAEYC guidelines quoted previously, curriculum planning may include the following concepts:

- Self-help skills
- Ability to separate from parents
- Problem solving
- Autonomy and independence
- Assistance in meeting the developmental milestones associated with physical, cognitive, language, personality, and social development

Providing Multicultural Environments and Activities

As noted previously, NAEYC endorses multicultural experiences, materials, and equipment as an integral part of developmentally appropriate practices. NAEYC validates multicultural education in this way:

Providing a wide variety of multicultural, nonstereotyping materials and activities helps ensure the individual appropriateness of the curriculum and also

1. enhances each child's self-concept and esteem,
2. supports the integrity of the child's family,
3. enhances the child's learning processes in both the home and the early childhood program by strengthening ties,
4. extends experiences of children and their families to include knowledge of the ways of others, especially those who share the community, and
5. enriches the lives of all participants with respectful acceptance and appreciation of differences and similarities among them.

Multicultural experiences should not be limited to a celebration of holidays and should include foods, music, families, shelter, and other aspects common to all cultures.[6]

Early childhood professionals in all programs must endeavor to make their programs as multicultural and nonsexist as possible. The following ideas will help you achieve this goal:

Translating these theories and ideas into practice can be difficult at best. When you work in a program with a number of infants or toddlers it becomes very easy to get caught up in routine "custodial" duties and to forget you are dealing with unique individuals. The following suggestions will help bring multicultural education into the infant/toddler classroom:

- Create classrooms that are less conforming and more individualized. Is it really necessary for all toddlers to sit during "circle," or could there be a quiet option for those who would prefer it?

- Make an effort to recognize the special qualities of each child.

- Learn the background and culture of each family. The importance of continuity between center and home can't be overemphasized.

- Build self-esteem by allowing the child to feel competent. Encourage independence and allow the child to do things for him/herself. Plan this into the day—it takes twice as long but it's worth the effort.

- Encourage creativity. Allow children to do their own work regardless of how you think it looks.

- Allow them to be pleased and satisfied with their own work.

- Encourage creative and unique responses to questions.

- Portray both genders in nurturing roles. Let toddlers visit and help with infants on a regular basis.

- Avoid gender-stereotyped toys, puppets, puzzles and books.

- Use different types of music in programs. Classical, country and popular music is often important in homes. Use music from other countries as well. Tapes of the parents singing or reading can also be effective.

- Talk about feelings often. Give labels to emotions. Research indicates that acquiring labels for emotions appears to be important for children to identify their own experiences as well as develop empathy for others.

- Be aware that toddlers from families whose first language is not English may be learning two languages simultaneously. Allow children to become competent in their first language. Expose them to English, but don't push. For example, write their names in both languages and ask parents to provide translations of frequently used phrases.

- Put up pictures of different experiences, ethnic groups and customs in the infant/toddler area.

- Show different ways of meeting the same needs.

- Encourage positive attention seeking behavior in both genders. Give boys the words to get their needs for nurturance met.

- Be sure your materials represent many cultures and lifestyles. Dolls, books, puppets, music and dramatic play materials are just some of the things that can be easily adapted.[7]

IMPORTANT HEALTH ISSUES IN EARLY CHILDHOOD PROGRAMS

The spread of diseases in early childhood programs is a serious concern to all who care for young children (Figure 8–1). Part of the responsibility of all caregivers is to provide healthy care for all children. One of the most effective ways to control the spread of disease in early childhood programs and promote the healthy care of young children is by washing your hands and having children wash their hands before and after eating and toileting.

FIGURE 8–1
Spread of Contamination
in Child Care Centers

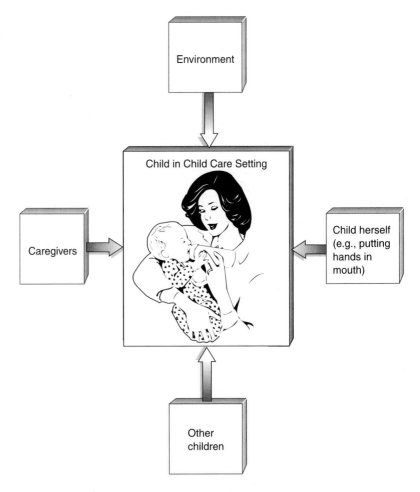

It is important for early childhood professionals to protect themselves and the children from AIDS. Here are some basic guidelines:

- Staff and children should wash their hands before eating
- Staff and children should wash their hands before and after using the toilet
- Staff should wash their hands before and after changing a diaper
- Staff should wash their hands before and after treating a cut or wound
- Staff should wear gloves if there is contact with blood or blood-containing body fluids or tissue discharge[8]

It sounds trite, but health in child care and preschool programs truly begins with the people who conduct the programs. Hand-washing policies, diapering procedures, and AIDS precautions, however well stated and intended, will do little good if not followed. It is important, therefore, for caregivers and teachers to do all that they can to protect and promote the health of children. Infants and toddlers are interesting and remarkably competent individuals. The developmental and educational milestones of these years are the foundations of all that follow throughout life. All professionals must use their knowledge, understanding, energy, and talents to ensure that this foundation is the best it can be.

ACTIVITIES FOR REFLECTION AND RESEARCH

1. Visit at least two programs that provide care for infants and toddlers. Observe the curriculum in each to determine whether it is developmentally appropriate. What suggestions would you make for improving the curriculum? Explain what you liked most and least about each program.

2. You have been asked to speak to a group of parents about what they can do to promote their children's language development in the first two years of life. Outline your presentation, and list five specific suggestions you will make. Use the online resources to help you in your research.

3. Observe children between the ages of birth and eighteen months. Identify the six stages of sensorimotor intelligence by describing the behaviors you observed. Cite specific examples of secondary and tertiary reactions. For each of the six stages, list two activities that would be cognitively appropriate.

4. Why is motor development important in the early years? What are five things early childhood educators can include in their programs to promote motor development?

5. Visit centers that care for young children of different cultures. List the differences you find. What areas are most similar?

6. Interview professionals who work in family day care homes and others who work in child care centers. How does the care for infants and toddlers differ in the two settings? In which kind of program would you prefer to be a professional? Why?

READINGS FOR FURTHER ENRICHMENT

Bornstein, M. *Parenting Infants* (Mahwah, NJ: Lawrence Erlbaum Associates, 1995).

> This book features a brief history of interest in parenting infants followed by the theoretical significance attached to parenting infants. The book also describes the characteristics of infants and infant development that are meaningful for parenting.

Carnegie Task Force on Meeting the Needs of Young Children. *Starting Points: Meeting the Needs of Our Youngest Children* (New York: Carnegie Corporation of New York, 2000).

> This report focuses attention on the "quiet crisis" affecting millions of children under three and their families. It challenges professionals to create integrated programs for developing responsible parenthood, guaranteeing quality child care choices, ensuring basic health and protection, and mobilizing communities to support young children and their families.

Koop, C. *Baby Steps: The "Whys" of Your Child's Behavior in the First Two Years* (New York: Freeman, 1993).

> In this book, the author begins with the newborn and traces the changes that occur in physical, motor, mental, and social-emotional development.

Shatz, M. *A Toddler's Life: Becoming a Person* (New York: Oxford University Press, 1995).

> This intimate account of a toddler's development from one to three is an odyssey conveyed through detailed and well-chosen observations as he participates in routine and special events.

Turner, P. H. and T. J. Turner. *Child Development and Early Education: Infancy through Preschool* (Boston, MA: Allyn and Bacon, 1998).

> This book addresses the major theoretical approaches in simple terms, and is packed with application ideas that practitioners can use in their programs for young children.

Watson, L. D. and M. Watson, and L. C. Wilson. *Infants and Toddlers: Curriculum and Teaching* (Delmar, 1998).

> This comprehensive, fourth edition includes the skills necessary to provide high-quality care for infants and toddlers in any child care setting. The book emphasizes individual care and includes helpful information on incorporating individualized techniques and activities for each child in care.

RESEARCH ON THE INTERNET

Early Childhood News

http://www.earlychildhoodnews.com

> *Early Childhood News* is a 50+ page, full-color magazine published six times a year by the Peter Li Education Group. More than 20,000 early childhood professionals across the United States and Canada subscribe to *Early Childhood News,* with a total readership of over 250,000.

Early Childhood Educators' and Family Web Corner

http://www.nauticom.net/www/cokids/index.html

> Provides links to teacher pages, family pages, articles, and staff development resources.

NOTES

1. Eric H. Lenneberg, "The Biological Foundations of Language," in *Readings in Applied Transformational Grammar,* ed. Mark Lester (New York: Holt, Rinehart & Winston, 1970), p. 8.

2. Susan Curtiss, *Genie: A Psycholinguistic Study of a Modern-Day "Wild Child"* (New York: Academic Press, 1977).

3. Sue Bredekamp and Carol Copple, eds., *Developmentally Appropriate Practice in Early Childhood Programs,* rev. ed. (Washington, DC: National Association for the Education of Young Children, 1997), p. 9, © 1997 by NAEYC. Used by permission.

4. Sue Bredekamp and Carol Copple, eds., *Developmentally Appropriate Practice in Early Childhood Programs,* rev. ed. (Washington, DC: National Association for the Education of Young Children, 1997), pp. 16–22.

5. National Association for the Education of Young Children, *Developmentally Appropriate Practice in Early Childhood Programs Serving Infants* (Washington, DC: Author, 1989), no. 547.

6. Sue Bredekamp, ed., *Developmentally Appropriate Practice in Early Childhood Programs Serving Children from Birth through Age 8,* expanded ed. (Washington, DC, National Association for the Education of Young Children, 1987), p. 2.

7. Kimberlee Whaley and Elizabeth Blue Swadener, "Multicultural Education in Infant and Toddler Settings," *Childhood Education,* 66 (4), pp. 239–240. Reprinted by permission of K. Whaley and E. B. Swadener and the Association for Childhood Education International, 11501 Georgia Ave., Suite 315, Wheaton, MD. Copyright 1990 by the Association.

8. National Academy of Early Childhood Programs, "Preventing HIV/AIDS Transmittal," *Newsletter of the National Academy of Early Childhood Programs,* 66(2), p. 5.

CHAPTER

9

Transitions and New Encounters

FOCUS QUESTIONS

1. How has the history of preschool education influenced contemporary practice?
2. What reasons account for the current interest in preschool programs?
3. What are the characteristics of preschoolers' growth and development?
4. How does play promote children's learning?
5. What are the purposes of play in preschool programs?
6. What are important issues concerning preschool programs?

Early childhood professionals view the preschool years as a cornerstone of learning. Parents view the preschool years as the time children "get ready" to enter kindergarten or first grade, and begin "formal" schooling. Others still think of the preschool years, the years from three to five, as a time when children should be unburdened by learning and allowed to play and enjoy life. For many children, though, the preschool years are the beginning of a critical period spanning fourteen years during which their lives will be dramatically influenced by teachers and schooling.

WHAT IS PRESCHOOL?

The traditional use of the term *preschool years* to describe the period before children enter school is rapidly becoming obsolete. Today, it is common for many children to be in a school of some kind beginning as early as age two or three, and child care beginning at six weeks is becoming de rigueur for children of working parents. Many states, including Texas, Florida, California, New York, and North Carolina, have public preschool programs for four-year-olds; the term *preschool* hardly applies to threes and fours anymore. For our purposes, preschools are programs for two- to five-year-old children, before kindergarten.

THE HISTORY OF PRESCHOOL EDUCATION

The history of preschool education is really the history of nursery school education, which cannot be separated from the history of kindergarten education. Nursery schools originated in Great Britain. In 1914, Margaret and Rachel McMillan started an open-air nursery emphasizing health care, healthy living, and cognitive stimulation.

In 1914, Caroline Pratt opened the Play School (now the City & Country School) in New York City. One of the nation's first truly progressive schools, it was patterned on the philosophy of John Dewey and designed to take advantage of what Pratt called children's "natural and inevitable" desire to learn.

Patty Smith Hill started a laboratory school at Columbia Teachers College in New York in 1921. Abigail Eliot started the Ruggles Street Nursery School in Boston in 1922. Meanwhile, also in 1922, the Merrill-Palmer Institute Nursery School opened in Detroit, under the direction of Edna White.

In 1940, the Lanham Act provided money for child care for mothers employed in defense-related industries. For example, the Kaiser Child Service Centers, with the help of government money, were built by Edgar Kaiser to provide child care for children of workers in the Kaiser shipyards. Each center was designed to provide care for about 1,000 children between the ages of 18 months and 6 years. Open 364 days a year, 24 hours a day, these centers were staffed by people with degrees in child development. This support ended when the war ended in 1945.

From the 1940s to the present, many preschools have been private, sponsored by parent cooperatives, churches, and other agencies. Federal involvement in preschool education through Head Start and support for child care programs directed at low-income families and children has been the major reason for the growth of preschool programs.

Why Are Preschools Growing in Popularity?

The acceleration of preschool programs began with Head Start in 1965. This trend continues to grow, with greater numbers of four-year-olds entering preschools, many operated by public schools (Figure 9–1).

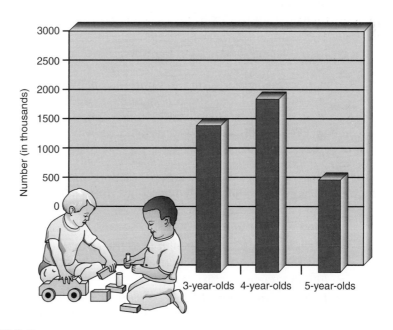

FIGURE 9–1

Preschool Enrollment

Source: U.S. Department of Education, National Center for Education Statistics, Primary Enrollment. (Table prepared July 1996.)

Additionally, the following reasons help explain the current popularity of and demand for preschool programs, particularly public programs for three- and four-year-olds:

- Changing family patterns, especially single-parent families.
- Changing economic patterns, with more women in the workforce.
- Changing attitudes toward work and careers. The shift away from home-making as a career to outside employment and careers causes the early childhood profession to provide more programs and services, including programs for threes and fours.
- Public policy and legislation such as welfare reform that causes greater demand for all kinds of early childhood programs.
- The view by parents, public policy planners, and researchers that intervention programs (to deal with such problems as substance abuse) work best in the early years. Research verifies the positive short- and long-term benefits to children and society of quality preschool programs.
- Growing concern on the part of corporations and businesses about the quality of the contemporary and future workforce. They see early education as one way of developing a literate workforce.
- Advocacy for publicly supported and financed preschools as a means of preventing the exclusion of poor children and their families from the early education movement.
- The increasingly popular notion that three- and four-year-old children are ready, willing, and able to learn.

A number of significant changes in programs and purposes have occurred in the 1990s. The predominant purpose of preschools used to be to enhance children's social-emotional development and get them ready for school. Preschools are now promoted as ways to accomplish the following objectives:

- *Support and develop children's innate capacity for learning.* The responsibility for "getting ready for school" has shifted from being primarily a child's and parent's responsibility to being a cooperative venture between child-family-home and school.
- *Provide a centralized agency (i.e., the school) and a support system (i.e., school personnel) to deliver services at an early age to children and their families.*
- *Deliver a full range of health, social, economic, and literacy services to families.* Thus, family welfare is also seen as a justification for operating preschools.
- *Solve or find solutions for pressing social problems.* The early years are viewed as a time when interventions are most likely to have long-term

positive influences. Preschool programs are seen as ways of lowering the number of dropouts, improving children's health, and reducing substance abuse and delinquency.

Public Preschools

More public schools now operate preschool programs. There are a number of reasons for this. First, public schools and their infrastructure (teachers, cafeteria workers, custodians, and administration) are already in place. Second, as long as parents pay taxes to support public schools, they often conclude that these schools should provide services for their children rather than their paying other programs to do so. Third, public schools are viewed as institutions that can offer all children equal access to educational and other services. If the public schools enroll three- and four-year-old children, other programs that traditionally offer programs to this age group will turn their attention to serving the needs of children from birth to age two.

WHAT ARE PRESCHOOLERS LIKE?

Today's preschoolers are not like the children of previous decades. Many have already attended one, two, or three years of child care or nursery school. They have watched hundreds of hours of television. Many have experienced the trauma of family divorces or the psychological effects of abuse. Both collectively and individually, the experiential backgrounds of preschoolers are quite different from those of previous generations. But it is precisely the impact and implications of this background that early childhood professionals must understand to meet preschoolers' needs effectively.

Physical and Motor Development

Understanding of preschoolers' physical and motor development enables you to acknowledge why active learning is so important. There is a noticeable difference between preschoolers and their infant and toddler counterparts. Preschoolers have lost most of their baby fat and taken on a leaner, lankier look. This "slimming down" and increasing motor coordination enables preschoolers to participate with more confidence in the locomotor activities so vitally necessary during this stage of growth and development. Girls and boys continue to grow several inches per year throughout the preschool years (Table 9–1).

Preschool children are learning to use and test their bodies. Locomotion plays a large role in motor and skill development and includes activities of moving the body through space—walking, running, hopping, jumping, rolling, dancing, climbing, and leaping. Children use these activities to investigate and explore the relationships between themselves, space, and objects in

TABLE 9–1
Average Height and Weight of Preschoolers

	Males		Females	
Age	Height (inches)	Weight (pounds)	Height (inches)	Weight (pounds)
3 years	38.0	32.4	37.6	30.7
4 years	40.5	36.8	40.0	35.2
5 years	43.3	41.2	42.7	38.9

Source: Based on data from P. V. V. Hamill et al., "Physical Growth: National Center for Health Statistics Percentiles," *American Journal of Clinical Nutrition 32,* 1979, pp. 607–629.

space. Preschoolers also like to participate in fine-motor activities such as drawing, coloring, painting, cutting, and pasting. They need programs that provide action and play, supported by proper nutrition and healthy habits of plentiful rest and good hygiene.

Although learning self-control is part of preschoolers' socialization process, developmentally appropriate practices call for activity. It is also important to incorporate health education and activities that promote good hygiene and nutrition into programs for three-, four-, and five-year-olds. Preschool and elementary curricula should incorporate lifelong goals and objectives for healthy living so children develop good habits early in life rather than grow up using bad habits.

Cognitive Development

Preschoolers are in the preoperational stage of intelligence. As we saw in Chapter 4, characteristics of the preoperational stage are (1) children grow in their ability to use symbols, including language; (2) children are not capable of operational thinking (an operation is a reversible mental action), which explains why Piaget named this stage *preoperational;* (3) children center on one thought or idea, often to the exclusion of other thoughts; (4) children are unable to conserve; and (5) children are egocentric.

Preoperational characteristics have particular implications for early childhood professionals. Early childhood professionals can promote children's learning during the preoperational stage of development by doing the following:

• *Furnish concrete materials to help children see and experience concepts and processes.* Children learn more from touching and experimenting with an actual object than they do from a picture, story, or video. If children are learning about apples, bring in a collection of apples for children to touch, feel, smell, taste, discuss, classify, manipulate, and explore.

Physical activities contribute to children's physical, social, emotional, linguistic, and cognitive development. It is essential that programs provide for children to engage in active play both in indoor and outdoor settings. What are some things that children can learn through participation in playground activities?

•   *Use hands-on activities that give children opportunities for active involvement in their learning.* When you encourage children to manipulate and interact with the world around them, they begin to construct concepts about relationships, attributes, and processes. Through exploration, preoperational children begin to collect and organize data about the objects they manipulate. For example, when children engage in water play with funnels and cups, they learn about concepts such as measurement, volume, sink/float, bubbles and the prism, evaporation, and saturation.

•   *Give children many and varied experiences.* Diverse activities and play environments lend themselves to teaching different skills, concepts, and processes. Children should spend time daily in both indoor and outdoor activities. Give consideration to the types of activities that facilitate large- and fine-motor, social, emotional, and cognitive development. For example, outdoor play activities and games such as tag, hopscotch, and jumprope enhance large-motor development; whereas fine-motor activities include using scissors, stringing beads, coloring, and writing.

•   *Model appropriate tasks and behaviors, as the preoperational child learns to a great extent through modeling.* Children should see adults reading and writing daily. It is also helpful for children to view brief demonstrations by peers or professionals on possible ways to use materials. For example, after children have spent a lot of time in free exploration with math manipulatives, teachers and others can show children patterning techniques and strategies they may want to experiment with in their own play.

• *Provide a print-rich environment to stimulate interest and development of language and literacy in a meaningful context.* The physical environment should display room labeling, class stories and dictations, children's writing, and charts of familiar songs and fingerplays. There should be a variety of literature for students to read including books, magazines, and newspapers. Paper and writing utensils should be abundant and assorted to motivate children to create. Daily literacy activities should include opportunities for shared, guided, and independent reading and writing; singing songs and fingerplays; and creative dramatics. Children should be read to every day.

• *Allow children periods of uninterrupted time to engage in self-chosen tasks.* Children benefit more from large blocks of time provided for in-depth exploration in meaningful play than they do from frequent, brief ones. It takes time for children to become deeply involved in play, especially imaginative and fantasy play. The morning and afternoon schedules should each contain at least two such blocks of time.

Language Development

Children's language skills grow and develop rapidly during the preschool years. Vocabulary increases, and sentence length increases as children continue to master syntax and grammar. During the preschool years, children's language development is diverse and comprehensive, and it constitutes a truly impressive range of learning. An even more impressive feature of this language acquisition is that children learn intuitively, without a great deal of instruction, the rules of language that apply to words and phrases they use.

HOW PRESCHOOLERS LEARN THROUGH PLAY

Children's play results in learning. Therefore, *play* is the process through which children learn. In this sense, play is a tool for learning.

The notion that children learn through play begins with Froebel, who built his system of schooling on the educative value of play. As discussed in Chapter 3, Froebel believed that natural unfolding (development) occurs through play. Since his time, most early childhood programs have incorporated play into their curricula or have made play a major part of the day.

Montessori thought of play as children's work and of the home and preschool as "workplaces" where learning occurs through play. Montessori viewed children's active involvement with materials and the prepared environment as the primary means through which they absorb knowledge and learn. John Dewey also advocated and supported active learning and believed that children learn through play activities based on their interests.

Dewey also thought that children should have opportunities to engage in play associated with everyday activities (e.g., the house center, post office, grocery store, doctor's office). He felt that play helps prepare children for adult occupations. Many curriculum developers and teachers base play activities, such as a dress-up corner, around adult roles.

Piaget believed play promotes cognitive knowledge and is a means by which children construct knowledge of their world. He identified three kinds of knowledge: physical, logical-mathematical, and social. According to Piaget, through active involvement, children learn about things and the physical properties of objects; increase their knowledge of the environment and their role(s) in it; and gain logical-mathematical knowledge—numeration, seriation, classification, time, space, and number. Piaget believed children learn social knowledge, vocabulary, labels, and proper behavior from others.

Unlike Piaget, Vygotsky viewed the social interaction that occurs through play as essential to children's development. He believed that through social interactions with others, children learn language and social skills—cooperation and collaboration—that promote and enhance their cognitive development (see Chapter 3). Viewed from Vygotsky's perspective, adults' play with children is as important as children's play with their peers. Thus, play promotes cognitive development and provides for a way to develop social skills.

What Do Preschoolers Learn through Play?

Play activities help preschoolers:

- Learn concepts
- Develop social skills
- Develop physical skills
- Master life situations
- Practice language processes
- Develop literacy skills (see description later)
- Enhance self-esteem
- Prepare for adult life and roles (e.g., learn how to become independent, think, make decisions, cooperate, and collaborate with others)

Play serves an important process for promoting children's learning and development. Play enhances social interaction and the development of social skills—learning how to share, getting along with others, taking turns, and generally learning how to live in a community. Play promotes physical development and body coordination and develops and refines small- and large-motor skills.

Play assists in personality and emotional development because it enables children to try out different roles, release feelings, express them-

THE VALUE OF PLAY

Early childhood educators have long recognized the value of play for social, emotional, and physical development. Recently, however, play has attracted greater importance as a medium for literacy development. It is now recognized that literacy develops in meaningful, functional social settings rather than as a set of abstract skills taught in formal pencil-and-paper settings.

Literacy development involves a child's active engagement in cooperation and collaboration with peers; it builds on what the child already knows with the support and guidance of others. Play provides this setting. During observations of children at play, especially in free-choice, cooperative play periods, one can note the functional uses of literacy that children incorporate into their play themes. When the environment is appropriately prepared with literacy materials in play areas, children have been observed to engage in attempted and conceptional reading and writing in collaboration with other youngsters. In similar settings lacking literacy materials, the same literacy activities did not occur.

To demonstrate how play in an appropriate setting can nurture literacy development, consider the following classroom setting in which the teacher has designed a veterinarian's office to go along with a class study on animals, focusing in particular on pets.

The dramatic play area is designed with a waiting room including chairs; a table filled with magazines, books, and pamphlets about pet care; posters about pets; office hour notices; a "No Smoking" sign; and a sign advising visitors to "Check in with the nurse when arriving." On a nurse's desk are patient forms on clipboards, a telephone, an address and telephone book, appointment cards, and a calendar. The office contains patient folders, prescription pads, white coats, masks, gloves, a toy doctor's kit, and stuffed animals for patients.

Ms. Meyers, the teacher, guides students in using the various materials in the veterinarian's office during free-play time. For example, she reminds the children to read important information they find in the waiting area or to fill out forms about their pet's needs, to ask the nurse for appointment times, or to have the doctor write out appropriate treatments or prescriptions. In addition to giving directions, Ms. Meyers also models behaviors by participating in the play center with the children when first introducing materials.

This play setting provided a literacy-rich environment with books and writing materials; modeled reading and writing by the teacher that children could observe and emulate; provided the opportunity to practice literacy in a real-life situation that had meaning and function; and encouraged children to interact socially by collaborating and performing meaningful reading and writing activities with peers. The following anecdotes relate the type of behavior Ms. Meyers observed in the play area.

- Jessica was waiting to see the doctor. She told her stuffed animal dog, Sam, not to worry, that the doctor would not hurt him. She asked Jenny, who was waiting with her stuffed animal cat, Muffin, what the kitten's problem was. The girls agonized over the ailments of their pets. After a while they stopped talking, and Jessica picked up the book *Are You My Mother?* and pretended to read to her dog, Sam. Jessica showed Sam the pictures as she read.

- Preston examined Christopher's teddy bear and wrote a report in the patient's folder. He read his scribble writing out loud and said, "This teddy bear's blood pressure is twenty-nine points. He should take sixty-two pills an hour until he is better and keep warm and go to bed." At the same time he read, he showed Christopher what he had written so he could understand what to do.

When selecting settings to promote literacy in play, choose those that are familiar to children and relate them to themes currently being studied. Suggestions for literacy materials and settings to add to dramatic play areas include the following:

- A fast-food restaurant, ice cream store, or bakery suggests menus, order pads, a cash register, specials for the day, recipes, and lists of flavors or products.

- A supermarket or local grocery store can include labeled shelves and sections, food containers, pricing labels, cash registers, telephones, shopping receipts, checkbooks, coupons, and promotional flyers.

- A post office to serve for mailing children's letters needs paper, envelopes, address books, pens, pencils, stamps, cash registers, and labeled mailboxes. A mail carrier hat and bag are important for children who deliver the mail and need to identify and read names and addresses.

- A gas station and car repair shop, designed in the block area, might have toy cars and trucks, receipts for sales, road maps for help with directions to different destinations, automotive tools and auto repair manuals for fixing cars and trucks, posters that advertise automobile equipment, and empty cans of different products typically found in service stations.

Contributed by Lesley Mandel Morrow, professor and Coordinator of Early Childhood Elementary Programs, Rutgers University.

selves in a nonthreatening atmosphere, and consider the roles of others. Play enhances and promotes development in the cognitive, affective, and psychomotor areas. It helps children learn, acquire information, and construct their own intelligence. Through play, children develop schemes, find out how things work (and what will not work), and lay the foundation for cognitive growth.

Children's play is full of opportunities for learning, but there is no guarantee that children will learn all they need to know when they need to know it through play. Providing opportunities for children to choose among well-planned, varied learning activities enhances the probability that they will learn through play.

Kinds of Play

Social Play

Much of children's play occurs with or in the presence of other children. Social play occurs when children play with each other in groups. Mildred Parten developed the most comprehensive description and classification of the types of children's social play:

- *Unoccupied play.* The child does not play with anything or anyone; the child merely stands or sits, without doing anything observable.

- *Solitary play.* Although involved in play, the child plays alone, seemingly unaware of other children.

- *Onlooker play.* The child watches and observes the play of other children; the center of interest is others' play.

- *Parallel play.* The child plays alone but in ways similar to and with toys or materials similar to those of other children.

- *Associative play.* Children interact with each other, perhaps by asking questions or sharing materials, but do not play together.

- *Cooperative play.* Children actively play together, often as a result of organization of the teacher (the least frequently witnessed play in preschools).

Social play supports many important functions. First, it provides the means for children to interact with others and learn many social skills. Play provides a context in which children learn how to compromise ("OK, I'll be the baby first and you can be the mommy"), gain impulse control ("I can't always do what I want when I want to do it"), learn to be flexible ("We'll do it your way first and then my way"), resolve conflicts, and continue the process of learning who they are. Children learn what skills they have, such as those relating to leadership. Second, social play provides a vehicle for practicing and developing literacy skills. Children have others with whom to practice language and learn from. Third, play helps children learn give and take; they realize they cannot always do whatever they want. And fourth, in giving a child other children with whom to interact, social play negates isolation and helps children learn the social interactions so vital to successful living.

Cognitive Play

Froebel, Montessori, and Piaget recognized the cognitive value of play. Froebel through his gifts and occupations, and Montessori through her sensory materials, saw children's active participation with concrete materials as a direct link to knowledge and development. Piaget's theory influences contemporary thinking about the cognitive basis for play. From a Piagetian perspective, play is literally cognitive development (see Chapter 5 and the High/Scope curriculum description).

Piaget's Stages of Play

Piaget describes four stages of play through which children progress as they develop: functional play, symbolic play, playing games with rules, and constructive play.

Puppets and plays provide many opportunities for children to learn and interact with others. Indeed, the props that professionals provide for children to play with contribute to all of children's learning, but in particular their literacy development. What literacy skills are these children learning?

Functional Play. Functional play, the only play that occurs during the sensorimotor period, is based on and occurs in response to muscular activities and the need to be active. Functional play is characterized by repetitions, manipulations, and self-imitation. Piaget described functional play (which he also called *practice play* and *exercise play*) this way: "The child sooner or later (often even during the learning period) grasps for the pleasure of grasping, swings [a suspended object] for the sake of swinging, etc. In a word, he repeats his behavior not in any further effort to learn or to investigate, but for the mere joy of mastering it and of showing off to himself his own power of subduing reality."[2]

Functional play allows children to practice and learn physical capabilities while exploring their immediate environments. Very young children are especially fond of repeating movements for the pleasure of it. They engage in sensory impressions for the joy of experiencing the functioning of their bodies. Repetition of language also is common at this level.

Symbolic Play. The second stage is symbolic play, which Piaget also referred to as the "let's pretend" stage of play. During this stage, children freely display their creative and physical abilities and social awareness in a number of ways, for example, by pretending to be something else, such as an animal. Symbolic play also occurs when children pretend that one object is another—that a building block is a car, for example—and may also entail pretending to be another person—a mommy, daddy, or caregiver. As toddlers and preschoolers grow older, their symbolic play becomes more elaborate and involved.

Playing Games with Rules. This third stage of play begins around age seven or eight. During this stage, children learn to play within rules and limits and adjust their behavior accordingly, and can make and follow social agreements. Games with rules are very common in middle childhood and adulthood.

Constructive Play. Piaget's fourth stage develops from symbolic play and represents children's adaptations to problems and their creative acts. Constructive play is characterized by children engaging in play activities in order to construct their knowledge of the world. They first manipulate play materials and then use these materials to create and build things (a sand castle, a block building, a grocery store) and experiment with the ways things go together.

Dramatic (Pretend) Play

Dramatic play allows children to participate vicariously in a wide range of activities associated with family living, society, and their and others' cultural heritage. Dramatic play is generally of two kinds: *sociodramatic* and *fantasy.* Sociodramatic play usually involves everyday realistic activities and events, whereas fantasy play typically involves fairy tale and superhero play. Dramatic play centers often include areas such as housekeeping, dress-up, occupations, dolls, school, and other situations that follow children's interests. A skillful professional can think of many ways to expand children's interests and then replace old centers with new ones. For example, after a visit to the police station, a housekeeping center might be replaced by an occupations center.

Professionals must assume a proactive role in organizing and changing dramatic play areas. They must set the stage for dramatic play and participate with children. They must also encourage those who "hang back" and are reluctant to play and involve those who may not be particularly popular with the other children. Surprisingly, because of their background and environment, some children have to be taught how to play.

Outdoor areas should be safe for children to play. Usually, states and cities have regulations requiring the playground to be fenced and have a source of drinking water, a minimum number of square feet of play area for each child, and equipment that is in good repair.

Rough-and-Tumble Play

All children, to a greater or lesser degree, engage in rough-and-tumble play. One theory of play says that children play because they are biologically programmed to do so; that is, it is part of children's—and adults'—genetic heritage to engage in play activities. Rough-and-tumble play activities enable children to learn about themselves; e.g., lead/follow, develop physical skills, experiment and practice roles physically and vicariously.

Outdoor Play

Children's play outside is just as important as inside. Outdoor environments and activities promote large- and small-muscle development and body coordination as well as language development, social interaction, and creativity. Professionals should plan for a particular child or group of children to move through progressively higher skill levels of running, climbing, and throwing. The outdoor area is a learning environment, and as such, the playground should be designed according to learning objectives.

Many teachers also enjoy bringing the indoor learning environment "outdoors," using easels, play dough, or dramatic play props to further enhance learning opportunities. In addition, taking a group of children outdoors for story or music time, sitting in the shade of a tree, brings a fresh perspective to daily group activities. As with indoor activities, provisions for outdoor play involve planning, supervising, and helping children be responsible for their behavior.

Early Childhood Professionals' Roles in Promoting Play

Early childhood professionals are the key to promoting meaningful play. You and other early childhood education professionals have the following responsibilities for supporting a quality play curriculum:

- Plan to implement the curriculum through play and integrate specific learning activities with play to achieve specific learning outcomes. Play activities should match children's developmental needs and be free of gender and cultural stereotypes. Professionals have to be clear about curriculum concepts and ideas they want children to learn through play.

- Provide time for learning through play and include it in the schedule as a legitimate activity in its own right.

- Structure time for learning through play. Create both indoor and outdoor environments that encourage play and support its role in learning.

- Organize the classroom or center environment so that cooperative learning is possible and active learning occurs.

- Provide materials and equipment that are appropriate to the children's developmental level and support a nonsexist and multicultural curriculum.

- Educate assistants and parents in how to promote learning through play.

- Supervise play activities and participate in children's play. In these roles, professionals help, show, and model when appropriate and refrain from interfering when appropriate.

- Observe children's play. Teachers can learn how children play and use the learning outcomes of play in planning classroom activities.

- Question children about their play, discuss what children did during play, and "debrief" children about what they have learned through play.

- Provide for safe play indoors and out.

THE PRESCHOOL CURRICULUM

How do we determine an appropriate curriculum for three- and four-year-olds? Some say the curriculum should stress academic skills related to reading, writing, and math and social skills such as getting along with others. Others say the curriculum should be based on what children will learn and do in kindergarten and first grade. Still others say that individual children should determine the curriculum according to what each knows or does not know; thus, the starting place is the needs and interests of children.

Appropriate Preschool Goals

Most quality preschools plan goals in these areas: social and interpersonal skills, self-help and intrapersonal skills, the building of self-esteem, academics, thinking skills, learning readiness, language and literacy, and nutrition.

Although we want children to be involved in child-initiated and active learning, sometimes it is necessary to directly teach children certain concepts and skills. What concepts or skills is this teacher directly teaching the children?

Social and Interpersonal Goals

- Helping children learn how to get along with other children and adults and how to develop good relationships with teachers
- Helping children learn to help others and develop caring attitudes

Self-Help Skills and Intrapersonal Goals

- Modeling for children how to take care of their personal needs such as dressing (tying, buttoning, zipping) and knowing what clothes to wear
- Eating skills (using utensils, napkins, and a cup or glass; setting a table)
- Health skills (how to wash and bathe, how to brush teeth)
- Grooming skills (combing hair, cleaning nails)

Self-Esteem Goals
- Promoting self-help skills to help children develop good self-images and high self-esteem
- Helping children learn about themselves, their family, and their culture
- Developing a sense of self-worth by providing experiences for success and competence
- Teaching about body parts and their function

Academic Goals
- Teaching children to learn their names, addresses, and phone numbers
- Facilitating children's learning of colors, sizes, shapes, and positions such as under, over, and around
- Facilitating children's learning of numbers and prewriting skills, shape identification, letter recognition, sounds, and rhyming
- Providing for small-muscle development

Thinking Goals
- Providing environments and activities that enable children to develop the skills essential to constructing schemes in a Piagetian sense—classification, seriation, numeration, and knowledge of space and time concepts. These form the basis for logical-mathematical thinking.
- Giving children opportunities to respond to questions and situations that require them to synthesize, analyze, and evaluate

Learning Readiness Goals
- Facilitating readiness skills related to school success, such as following directions, learning to work alone, listening to the teacher, developing an attention span, learning to stay with a task until it is completed, staying in one's seat, and controlling impulses

Language and Literacy Goals
- Providing opportunities for interaction with adults and peers as a means of developing oral language skills
- Helping children increase their vocabularies
- Helping children learn to converse with other children and adults
- Building proficiency in language
- Developing emergent literacy skills (prewriting and reading skills)

Nutrition Goals
- Providing experiences that enable children to learn the role of good nutritional practices and habits in their overall development

- Providing food preparation experiences
- Introducing children to new foods, a balanced menu, and essential nutrients

THE PRESCHOOL DAY

Although there are various ways to implement a preschool's goals, most preschools operate according to a play-oriented program that includes self-selection of activities and learning centers. The following sections illustrate a typical preschool daily schedule.

Opening Activities

As children enter, the teacher greets each individually. Daily personal greetings make the child feel important, build a positive attitude toward school, and provide an opportunity to practice language skills. They also give the teacher a chance to check each child's health and emotional status.

Children usually do not arrive all at one time, so the first arrivals need something to do while others are arriving. Free selection of activities or letting children self-select from a limited range of quiet activities, such as puzzles, pegboards, or markers to color with, is appropriate. Some teachers further organize this procedure by having children use an "assignment board" to help them make choices, limit the available choices, and practice concepts such as colors, shapes, or recognition of their own names. Initially, the teacher may stand beside the board when children come and tell each child what the choices are. The teacher may hand children their name tags and help them put them on the board. Later in the year, children can find their own tags and put them up. At the first of the school year, each child's name tag can include her or his picture (use an instant camera) or a symbol or shape the child has selected.

Group Meeting/Planning

After all children arrive, they and the teacher plan together and talk about the day ahead. This is also the time for announcements, sharing, and group songs.

Learning Centers

After the group time, children are free to go to one of various learning centers, organized and designed to teach concepts. Table 9–2 lists types of learning centers and the concepts each is intended to teach.

Bathroom/Hand Washing

Before any activity in which food is handled, prepared, or eaten, children should wash and dry their hands.

TABLE 9–2
Learning Centers

Center	Concepts	Center	Concepts
• Housekeeping	Classification Language skills Sociodramatic play Functions Processes	• Woodworking (pinewood, cardboard, Styrofoam)	Following directions Functions Planning Whole/part
• Water/sand	Texture Volume Quantity Measure	• Art	Color Size Shape Texture
• Blocks	Size Shape Length Seriation Spatial relations	 • Science	Design Relationships Identification of odors Functions
• Books/language	Verbalization Listening Directions How to use books Colors, size Shapes Names	 • Manipulatives	Measure Volume Texture Size Relationships Classifications
• Puzzles/perceptual development	Size Shape Color Whole/part Figure/ground Spatial relations		Spatial relationships Shape Color Size Seriation

Snacks

After center activities, a snack is usually served. It should be nutritionally sound and something the children can serve (and often prepare) themselves.

Outdoor Activity/Play/Walking

Ideally, outside play should be a time for learning new concepts and skills, not just a time to run around aimlessly. Children can practice climbing, jumping, swinging, throwing, and body control. Teachers may incorporate walking trips and other events into outdoor play.

Bathroom/Toileting

Bathroom/toileting times offer opportunities to teach health, self-help, and intrapersonal skills. Children should also be allowed to use the bathroom whenever necessary.

Lunch

Lunch should be a relaxing time, and the meal should be served family style, with professionals and children eating together. Children should set their own tables and decorate them with placemats and flowers they can make in the art center or as a special project. Children should be involved in cleaning up after meals and snacks.

Relaxation

After lunch, children should have a chance to relax, perhaps to the accompaniment of stories, records, and music. This is an ideal time to teach children breathing exercises and relaxation techniques.

Nap Time

Children who want or need to should have a chance to rest or sleep. Quiet activities should be available for those who do not need to or cannot sleep on a particular day. Under no circumstances should children be forced to sleep or lie on a cot or blanket if they cannot sleep or have outgrown their need for an afternoon nap.

Bathroom/Toileting

See the previous comments.

Snack

See the previous comments.

Centers or Special Projects

Following nap time is a good time for center activities or special projects. (Special projects can also be conducted in the morning, and some may be more appropriate then, such as cooking something for snack or lunch.) Special projects might be cooking, holiday activities, collecting things, work projects, art activities, and field trips.

Group Time

The day can end with a group meeting to review the day's activities. This meeting develops listening and attention skills, promotes oral communication, stresses that learning is important, and helps children evaluate their performance and behavior.

This preschool schedule is for a whole-day program; many other program arrangements are possible. Some preschools operate half-day, morning-only programs five days a week; others operate both a morning and afternoon session; others operate only two or three days a week. In still other programs, parents choose how many days they will send their children. Creativity and meeting parent needs seem to be hallmarks of effective preschool programs.

IMPORTANT CONSIDERATIONS FOR SELECTING A GOOD EARLY CHILDHOOD PROGRAM

Parents often wonder how to select a good early childhood program. Early childhood professionals can use the following guidelines to help others arrive at an appropriate preschool decision:

- What are the physical accommodations like? Is the facility pleasant, light, clean, and airy? Is it a physical setting you would want to spend time in? (If not, children will not want to, either.) Are plenty of materials available for the children to use?

- Do the children seem happy and involved or passive? Is television used as a substitute for a good curriculum and quality professionals?

- What kinds of materials are available for play and learning?

- Is there a balance of activity and quiet play and of individual, small-group, and group activities?

- Is there a balance of child-directed and professional-directed activities? Indoor and outdoor play?

- Is the physical setting safe and healthy?

- Does the school have a written philosophy, objectives, and curriculum? Does the program philosophy agree with the parents' personal philosophy of how children should be reared and educated? Are the philosophy and goals age appropriate for the children being served?

- Does the staff have written plans? Is there a smooth flow of activities, or do children wait for long periods "getting ready" for another activity? Does the curriculum provide for skills in self-help; readiness for learning; and cognitive, language, physical, and social-emotional development? Lack of planning indicates lack of direction. Although a program whose staff does not plan is not necessarily a poor program, planning is one indicator of a good program.

- What is the adult-child ratio? How much time do teachers spend with children one to one or in small groups? Do teachers take time to give children individual attention? Do children have an opportunity to be independent and do things for themselves?

- How does the staff relate to children? Are the relationships loving and caring?

- How do staff members handle typical discipline problems, such as disputes between children?

- Are positive guidance techniques used? Are indirect guidance techniques used, for example, through room arrangement, scheduling, and appropriate activity planning? Is there a written discipline philosophy that agrees with the parents' philosophy?

- Are staff personnel sensitive to the gender and cultural needs and backgrounds of children and families?

- Are there opportunities for outdoor activities?

- How is lunchtime handled? Are children allowed to talk while eating? Do staff members eat with the children?

- Is the staff stable?

- What kind of education or training does the staff have? The staff should have training in the curriculum and teaching of young children. The director should have at least a bachelor's degree in childhood education or child development (refer to Chapter 1).

- Is the director well trained? Can she or he explain the program? Describing a typical day can be helpful. Is she or he actively involved in the program?

- How does the staff treat adults, including parents? Does the program address the needs of children's families?

- Is the program affordable? If a program is too expensive for the family budget, parents may be unhappy in the long run. Parents should inquire about scholarships, reduced fees, fees adjusted to income level, fees paid in monthly installments, and sibling discounts.

- Are parents of children enrolled in the program satisfied?

- Are parents allowed to "drop-in" or visit unexpectedly—that is, anytime they wish?

- Do the program's hours and services match parents' needs?

- What are the provisions for emergency care and treatment? What procedures are there for taking care of ill children?

THE FUTURE OF PRESCHOOL EDUCATION

The further spread of public preschools for three- and four-year-old children is inevitable. This growth, to the point where all children are included, will take decades but will happen. Most likely, the public schools will focus more on programs for four-year-old children and then, over time, include three-year-olds. A logical outgrowth of this long-term trend will be for the public schools to provide services for even younger children and their families. One thing is certain: Preschool as it was known a decade ago is not the same today, and ten years from now, it will again be different.

ACTIVITIES FOR REFLECTION AND RESEARCH

1. Visit preschool programs in your area. Determine their philosophies and find out what goes on in a typical day. Which would you send your children to? Why?

2. Piaget believed that children construct schemes through play. Observe children's play, and give examples of schemes developed through play.

3. Identify the basic purposes of a preschool program. Ask your classmates to rank these in order. What conclusions can you draw from their rankings?

4. Survey preschool parents to learn what they expect from a preschool program. How do parents' expectations compare with the goals of preschool programs you visited?

5. Tell how you would promote learning through a specific preschool activity. (For example, what learning outcomes would you have for a sand/water area?) What, specifically, would be your role in helping children learn?

6. Write a philosophy of a preschool program, and develop goals and objectives for it. Write a daily schedule that would support your goals.

7. Visit a preschool program, and request to see the program goals. How do they compare with those listed in this chapter? What would you change, add, or delete?

8. Read and review five articles that relate to today's trend in establishing quality preschool programs. What are the basic issues discussed? Do you agree with these issues?

9. Develop a file of activities you can use in a preschool program. Use the following headings to help organize your file: Activity Name, Objective, Description, Materials Needed. Is it easier to find materials for some areas than for others? Why?

READINGS FOR FURTHER ENRICHMENT

Beaty, J. *Prosocial Guidance for the Preschool Child* (Upper Saddle River, NJ: Prentice Hall, 1998).

This book reflects the new approach to guidance in the preschool classroom, focusing on positive rather than inappropriate behaviors. It provides future and current teachers with the skills to create a prosocial physical environment, to anticipate and prevent inappropriate behavior from happening, and to help children manage their own behavior.

Hohmann, M. and D. Weikart. *Educating Young Children: Active Learning Practices for Preschool and Child Care Programs* (Ypsilanti, MI: High/Scope, 1995).

This book reviews the basic concepts of the High/Scope preschool curriculum and its development, implementation, and effectiveness.

Hughes, F. *Children, Play, and Development* (Boston, MA: Allyn and Bacon, 1998).

All children play. But many people don't know the importance of play and its relationship to child development. This book offers important research on the topic of play, stressing its significant role in children's lives.

Trister, D.D., Bickart, T.S., Scherr, C. *Preschool for Parents: What Every Parent Needs to Know About Preschool.* (Sourcebooks Trade, 1998).

Preschool for Parents is an informative guide for finding and selecting a great, safe preschool and giving children the best opportunity to learn, play and grow.

RESEARCH ON THE INTERNET

Professional Association for Childhood Education (PACE)

http://www.pacenet.org

PACE is a nonprofit tax-exempt organization established in 1955 to advance the profession of all who provide quality child care and early childhood education. PACE is a statewide association which serves all categories of licensed and regulated child care centers.

World Association of Early Childhood Educators

http://www.waece.com/

Organization for educators of children from birth to six years of age. In Spanish and English.

NOTES

1. Mildred Parten, "Social Play among Preschool Children," *Journal of Abnormal and Social Psychology,* 27, pp. 243–69.

2. Jean Piaget, *Play, Dreams and Imitations in Childhood* (London: Routledge & Kegan Paul, 1967), p. 162.

CHAPTER

10

Learning All You Need to Know

FOCUS QUESTIONS

1. What is the history of kindergarten programs from Froebel to the present?
2. What are issues surrounding readiness for learning?
3. How does age influence entrance for kindergarten?
4. What are appropriate goals and objectives for kindergarten programs?
5. What is the nature of developmentally appropriate kindergarten curricula?
6. What are the strengths and weaknesses of kindergarten screening and assessment programs?
7. Why are transitions important for kindergarten children?
8. What issues confront kindergarten education today?
9. How does your personal philosophy of kindergarten education influence the way you will teach?

Perhaps the title of this chapter struck you as a little odd or puzzling. Read it again. I got the idea for it from Robert Fulghum's best-selling book, *All I Really Need to Know I Learned in Kindergarten.* Fulghum says that the following suggestions form the essentials of kindergarten education:

> Share everything.
>
> Play fair.
>
> Don't hit people.
>
> Put things back where you found them.
>
> Clean up your own mess.
>
> Don't take things that aren't yours.
>
> Say you're sorry when you hurt somebody.[1]

It is doubtful anyone would argue with these kindergarten learning outcomes. But today, most people would expect more of kindergarten. Kindergarten is seen as an essential year, perhaps the essential year, in the schooling experience. And it is for this reason that expectations are high for children to learn the essentials and be successful.

THE HISTORY OF KINDERGARTEN EDUCATION

Froebel's educational concepts and kindergarten program were imported into the United States in the nineteenth century virtually intact by individuals who believed in his ideas and methods. Froebelian influence remained dominant for almost half a century, until John Dewey and his followers challenged it in the early 1900s. While Froebel's ideas still seem perfectly acceptable today, they were not acceptable to those in the mid-nineteenth century who subscribed to the notion of early education. Especially innovative and hard to accept was that learning could be based on play and children's interests—in

Today, kindergarten is a universal part of schooling, enrolling children from different cultures and socioeconomic backgrounds and subsequently, different life experiences. Thus, kindergarten children are not all at the same level developmentally, so the kindergarten program should not be the same for all children. How can professionals help ensure that kindergarten experiences meet the unique needs of children?

other words, that it could be child-centered. Most European and American schools were subject oriented and emphasized teaching basic skills. In addition, Froebel was the first to advocate a communal education for young children outside the home. Until Froebel, young children were educated in the home, by their mothers. Although Froebel advocated this method too, his ideas for educating children as a group in a special place outside the home were revolutionary.

Credit for establishing the first kindergarten in the United States is accorded to Margarethe Schurz. After attending lectures on Froebelian principles in Germany, she returned to the United States and in 1856 opened her kindergarten at Watertown, Wisconsin. Schurz's program was conducted in German, as were many of the new kindergarten programs of the time, since Froebel's ideas of education appealed especially to bilingual parents. Schurz also influenced Elizabeth Peabody, the sister-in-law of Horace Mann, when, at the home of a mutual friend, Schurz explained the Froebelian system. Peabody was not only fascinated but converted.

Peabody opened her kindergarten in Boston in 1860. She and her sister, Mary Mann, also published a book, *Kindergarten Guide*. Peabody almost immediately realized that she lacked the necessary theoretical grounding to implement Froebel's ideas adequately. She visited kindergartens in Germany and then returned to the United States to popularize Froebel's methods. Peabody is generally credited as kindergarten's main promoter in the United States.

One event that also helped advance the kindergarten movement was the appearance of appropriate materials. In 1860, Milton Bradley, the toy manufacturer, attended a lecture by Peabody, became a convert to the concept of kindergarten, and began to manufacture Froebel's gifts and occupations.

The first public kindergarten was founded in St. Louis, Missouri, in 1873 by Susan E. Blow, with the cooperation of the St. Louis superintendent of schools, William T. Harris. Elizabeth Peabody had corresponded for several years with Harris, and the combination of her prodding and Blow's enthusiasm and knowledge convinced Harris to open a public kindergarten on an experimental basis. Endorsement of the kindergarten program by a public school system did much to increase its popularity and spread the Froebelian influence within early childhood education. In addition, Harris, who later became the U.S. commissioner of education, encouraged support for Froebel's ideas and methods.

Were Froebel alive today, he would probably not recognize the program he gave his life to developing. Many kindergarten programs are subject-centered rather than child-centered as Froebel envisioned them. Furthermore, he did not see his program as a "school" but a place where children could develop through play. Although kindergartens are evolving to meet the needs of society and families, we must not forget the philosophy and ideals on which the first kindergartens were based.

WHO GOES TO KINDERGARTEN?

Froebel's kindergarten was for children three to seven years of age; in the United States, kindergarten has been considered the year before children enter first grade. Since the age at which children enter first grade varies, the age at which they enter kindergarten also differs. People tend to think that kindergarten is for five-year-old children rather than four-year-olds, and most professionals tend to support an older rather than a younger entrance age because they think older children are more "ready" for kindergarten and will learn better. Whereas in the past children had to be five years of age prior to December 31 for kindergarten admission, today the trend is toward an older admission age; many school districts require that children be five years old by September 1 of the school year.

SHOULD KINDERGARTEN BE COMPULSORY?

There is wide public support for compulsory and tax-supported public kindergarten. On one recent Gallup poll, 80 percent of respondents favored "making kindergarten available for all those who wish it as part of the public school system," 71 percent favored compulsory kindergarten attendance, and 70 percent thought children should start school at ages four or five (29 percent favored age four and 41 percent favored age five).[2] In keeping with this national sentiment, most children attend kindergarten, though it is mandatory in only twelve states (Arkansas, Delaware, Florida, Oklahoma, South Carolina, Ohio, Kentucky, Maryland, New Mexico, Rhode Island, West Virginia, and Tennessee) and the District of Columbia. Kindergarten has rapidly become universal for the majority of the nation's five-year-olds. Today, kindergarten is either a whole- or half-day program and within the reach of most of the nation's children. The number of children attending kindergarten has risen steadily and will continue to rise (Figure 10–1).

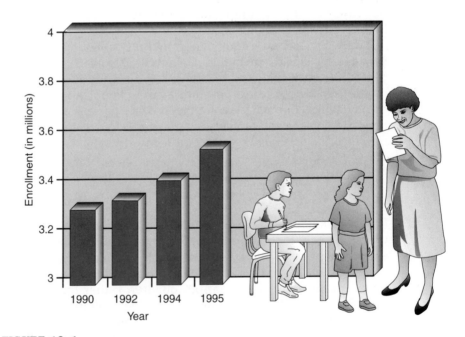

FIGURE 10–1

Kindergarten Enrollment

Source: U.S. Department of Education, National Center for Educational Statistics, Statistics of Public Elementary and Secondary School Systems, 1998.

SCHOOL READINESS: WHO GETS READY FOR WHOM?

School readiness is a major topic of debate in discussions of preschool and kindergarten programs. Raising entrance ages for admittance to kindergarten and first grade is based on the reasoning that many children are "not ready," and teachers therefore have difficulty teaching them. The early childhood profession is reexamining "readiness," its many interpretations, and the various ways the concept is applied to educational settings and children.

For most parents, readiness means the child's ability to participate and succeed in beginning schooling. From this perspective, it includes a child's ability, at a given time, to accomplish activities and engage in processes associated with schooling, whether nursery school, preschool, kindergarten, or first grade. Readiness does not exist in the abstract—it must relate to something. Readiness is measured against the process of formal public schooling. By the same token, a child's lack of readiness may be considered a deficit and detriment, because it indicates a child does not have the knowledge and skills for success in kindergarten and first grade.

However, as we discussed in Chapter 2, goal 1 of the Goals 2000: Educate America Act, Ready to Learn, states, "By the year 2000, all children in America will start school ready to learn." Goal 1 has three subgoals that merit our attention:[3]

- All children who are disadvantaged or who have disabilities will have access to high-quality and developmentally appropriate preschool programs that help prepare children for school.

- Every parent in the United States will be a child's first teacher and will devote time each day helping his or her preschool child learn; parents will have access to the training and support they need.

- Children will receive the nutrition and health care needed to arrive at school with healthy minds and bodies, and the number of low-birthweight babies will be significantly reduced through enhanced prenatal systems.

Discussions about readiness have changed our definition of it and attitude about what it means. Today, the term *readiness* is being replaced with the concept of early development and learning. Readiness is no longer seen as consisting of a predetermined set of capabilities children must attain before entering kindergarten or first grade. Furthermore, responsibility for children's early learning and development is no longer placed solely on the child or parents but rather is seen as a shared responsibility among children, parents, families, early childhood professionals, and communities.

The skills and behaviors kindergarten teachers believe are essential for kindergarten success are shown in Figure 10–2. How do these indicators

FIGURE 10–2
What Kindergarten Teachers Believe Are Important Factors for Kindergarten Readiness

- The student is physically healthy, rested, and well nourished
- Able to finish task
- Can count to 20 or more
- Takes turns and shares
- Has good problem-solving skills
- Is enthusiastic and curious in approaching new activities
- Is able to use pencils or paint brushes
- Is not disruptive of the class
- Knows the English language
- Is sensitive to other children's feelings
- Sits still and pays attention
- Knows the letters of the alphabet
- Can follow directions
- Identifies primary colors and basic shapes
- Communicates needs, wants, and thoughts verbally in child's primary language

Source: U.S. Department of Education, National Center for Educational Statistics, Kindergarten Teacher Survey on Student Readiness, 1995.

compare with our discussion of readiness? To your beliefs about readiness? NAEYC has adopted the following position statement on school readiness:

> The National Association for the Education of Young Children (NAEYC) believes that those who are committed to promoting universal school readiness must be committed to:
>
> 1. addressing the inequities in early life experience so that all children have access to the opportunities which promote school success;
> 2. recognizing and supporting individual differences among children; and
> 3. establishing reasonable and appropriate expectations of children's capabilities upon school entry.[4]

Maturation and Readiness

Some early childhood professionals and many parents believe that time cures all things, including a lack of readiness. They think that as time passes, a child grows and develops physically and cognitively and, as a result, becomes ready to achieve. This belief is manifested in school admissions policies that advocate children's remaining out of school for a year if they are not ready for school as measured by a readiness test. Assuming that the passage of time will bring about readiness is similar to the concept of unfolding, popularized by Froebel. Unfolding implies that development is inevitable and certain and that a child's optimum degree of development is determined by heredity and a biological clock. Froebel likened children to plants and parents and teachers to gardeners whose task is to nurture and care for children so they can mature according to their genetic inheritance and maturational timetable. The concept of unfolding continues to be a powerful force in early childhood education, although many challenge it as an inadequate, outmoded concept.

Important Readiness Skills

In all the rhetoric associated with readiness, readiness skills and behaviors are frequently overlooked. These skills and behaviors include language, independence, impulse control, interpersonal skills, experiential background, and physical and mental health (see Figure 10–2).

Language

Language is the most important readiness skill. Children need language skills for success in both school and life. Important language skills include receptive language, such as listening to the teacher and following directions; expressive language, demonstrated in the ability to talk fluently and articulately with teacher and peers, the ability to express oneself in the language of the school, and the ability to communicate needs and ideas; and symbolic language, knowing the names of people, places, and things, words for concepts, and adjectives and prepositions.

Independence

Independence means the ability to work alone on a task, take care of oneself, and initiate projects without always being told what to do. Independence also includes mastery of self-help skills, including but not limited to dressing skills, health skills (toileting, hand washing, using a handkerchief, and brushing teeth), and eating skills (using utensils and napkins, serving oneself, and cleaning up).

Impulse Control

Controlling impulses includes working cooperatively with others and not hitting others or interfering with their work, developing an attention span that permits involvement in learning activities for a reasonable length of time, and being able to stay seated for a while. Children who are not able to control their impulses are frequently (and erroneously) labeled hyperactive or learning disabled.

Interpersonal Skills

Interpersonal skills are those of getting along and working with both peers and adults. When asked why they want their child to attend a preschool program, parents frequently respond, "To learn how to get along with others." Any child care or preschool program is an experience in group living, and children have the opportunity to interact with others so as to become successful in a group setting. Interpersonal skills include cooperating with others, learning and using basic manners, and most important, learning how to learn from and with others.

Experiential Background

Experiential background is important to readiness because experiences are the building blocks of knowledge, the raw materials of cognitive development. They provide the context for mental disequilibrium, which enables children to develop higher levels of thinking. Children must go places—the grocery store, library, zoo—and they must be involved in activities—creating things, painting, coloring, experimenting, discovering. Children can build only on the background of information they bring to a new experience. If they have had limited experiences, they have little to work with and cannot develop well.

Physical and Mental Health

Children must have good nutritional and physical habits that will enable them to participate fully in and profit from any program. They must also have positive, nurturing environments and caring professionals to help them develop a self-image for achievement.

Dimensions of Readiness

Readiness has many dimensions that make it much more than a skill-focused process.

- *Readiness is never ending.* It does not exist only in the preschool and kindergarten years, although we often think of it this way. Readiness is not something children do or do not have, but rather is a continuum throughout life—the next life event is always just ahead, and what experiences children are currently engaging in should prepare them for it.

- *All children are always ready for some kind of learning.* Children always need experiences that will promote learning and get them ready for the next step. As early childhood educators, we should constantly ask such questions as, "What does this child know?" "What can I do to help this child move to the next level of understanding?"

- *Schools and professionals should promote readiness for children, not the other way around.* In this regard, schools should get ready for children and offer a curriculum and climate that allows for children's inevitable differences. Rather than subscribe only to notions of what learning is about, early childhood professionals should rededicate themselves to the ideal that schools are for children. Public schools that want children to be ready for predetermined programs have their priorities reversed. Schools should provide programs based on the needs of children and families, not on preconceived notions of what children ought to be able to do.

- *Children's readiness for learning should be viewed as a collaborative effort among children, the school, early childhood professionals, families, and the community.* (In this regard we can define the "community" as local, state, and national.) No longer can we or should we place the primary responsibility for children's readiness solely on children themselves or on their families. We all, individually and collectively, are responsible for helping children gain all they can from the process of schooling while assuring that they can be all they are capable of becoming.

- *Readiness is individualized.* Five- and six-year-old children exhibit a range of abilities. While we have said previously that all children are ready for particular learning experiences, not all children are ready for the same thing. It is not abnormal for some children to be behind in certain skills and behaviors and others to be ahead. What is abnormal is to expect all children to be the same.

- *Readiness is a function of culture.* Professionals have to be sensitive to the fact that different cultures have different values regarding the purpose of school, the process of schooling, children's roles in the schooling process, and what the family's and culture's roles are in promoting readiness. Professionals must learn about other cultures, talk with parents, and try to find a match between the process and activities of schooling and families' cultures.

Making Readiness a National Agenda

Ernest L. Boyer (1928–1995) and the Carnegie Foundation for the Advancement of Teaching set a national agenda for helping ensure that all children will enter school ready to learn. They proposed a seven-step agenda for achieving this goal.[5] The steps are listed here with some of the suggested subgoals:

Step 1:   *A healthy start.* Good health and good schooling are inextricably interlocked, and every child, to be ready to learn, must have a healthy birth and be well nourished and protected in the early years of life. As part of step 1, Boyer proposed a network of neighborhood-based ready-to-learn clinics in every underserved community to ensure basic health care for all mothers and preschool children.

Step 2: *Empowered parents.* The home is the first classroom. Parents are the most essential teachers; all children, as a readiness requirement, should live in a secure environment in which empowered parents encourage language development. Boyer recommended a new ready-to-learn reading series with recommended books for preschoolers, prepared under the leadership of the American Library Association.

Step 3: *Quality preschool.* Since many young children are cared for outside the home, high-quality preschool programs are required that not only provide good care but also address all dimensions of school readiness. Boyer suggested that every school district establish a preschool program as an optional service for all three- and four-year-olds not participating in Head Start.

Step 4: *A Responsive workplace.* If each child in the United States is to come to school ready to learn, we must have workplace policies that

PROGRAM IN ACTION

LONGFELLOW ELEMENTARY SCHOOL FOR THE VISUAL AND PERFORMING ARTS

An excellent example of restructuring at work in the early childhood arena is Longfellow Elementary School in Kansas City, Missouri, a magnet school for the visual and performing arts. Yvonne Clay's twenty-two kindergartners engage in an all-day program of basic skill instruction and drama, dance, music, and movement. Visual arts include painting, sketching, modeling with clay, and creative writing; the performing arts entail music, theater, and dance.

Drama plays a significant role in the curriculum and life of the kindergarten classroom. As Yvonne explains, "Drama and the other performing arts give children exposure to and experience with topics and people they would not otherwise have. Drama is in many ways a mirror of real-life events. I use drama to help children learn many important skills, concepts, and values. Drama is also a natural way of helping children learn through their bodies."

Yvonne gives these examples of drama activities in her kindergarten: "One of my groups reads in their basal reader a story of the rabbit and the hare. After the reading, the children acted out the story. We emphasized expression and how the human voice—their voices—sounds in certain situations. Also, during Black History Month in February, the children did a 'Readers Theater' of the *Rosa Parks Story.* One group read the story and another group acted out the events. The children had a lot of fun getting ready. They made bus stop signs, made costumes out of clothing from the Salvation Army, and made a bus out of cardboard boxes with chairs for seats. I revised an existing script for the children and worked with the parents of the children who had reading parts. It was a great learning activity!"

Yvonne teaches readiness skills, reading (many of the children are reading at a first grade level or above by the end of the school year), math, social studies, science, writing, and creative movement—all integrated with drama. Support teachers provide instruction in art, music, physical education, computers and Suzuki violin.

"I integrate academics into everything I do," explains Yvonne. "The visual and per-

are family-friendly, ones that offer child care services and give parents time to be with their young children.

Step 5: *Television as teacher.* Next to parents, television is the child's most influential teacher. School readiness requires television programming that is both educational and enriching. In this area, Boyer proposed a ready-to-learn cable channel, working collaboratively with public television, to offer programming aimed exclusively at the educational needs and interests of preschool children.

Step 6: *Neighborhoods for learning.* Since all children need spaces and places for growth and exploration, safe and friendly neighborhoods are necessary. Efforts to achieve this goal would include a network of well-designed outdoor and indoor parks in every community to give preschoolers opportunities for exercise and exploration.

forming arts give children experiences to build their academics on. The arts also give children a chance to appreciate their self-worth at many levels and in different ways. Take, for example, a child like Alex, who struggles in reading. He really excels in dance. The experiences of being good in this area are a great benefit to him."

A number of important activities support the curriculum and make this kindergarten program unique.

Artist-in-Residence Program

The school district has an artist-in-residence program through which artists come into the school and classrooms to perform and teach. For example, a local, well-known puppeteer gave a performance, then taught the children about puppets. He worked with the children in making puppets and helped them give a performance with their puppets.

Field Trips

The kindergarten children go every other month to various performing arts functions.

These include trips to the ballet, symphony orchestra, plays, and other performances throughout the Kansas City area. Following the field trips, children's experiences are integrated into the curriculum. For example, after a trip to the zoo, some children may create an art product and others may choose to write about the experience.

Community support for the Longfellow Magnet School is strong. According to Dee Davis, coordinator, early childhood, for the Kansas City Public Schools, "Families are enthusiastic about schools of choice for their children. They want and like to make choices on behalf of their children. Parents feel children do better in school when they study what interests them most." The curriculum of the kindergarten program, with its focus on song and dance, is in many ways reminiscent of that supported by Froebel and other great educators. It is also significant that a school named for one of the nation's most celebrated poets—Henry Wadsworth Longfellow—should be involved in promoting learning through the arts.

Step 7: *Connections across the generations.* Connections across the generations will give children a sense of security and continuity, which will contribute to their readiness in the fullest sense. Boyer envisioned a "grand-teacher program" in communities across the country in which older people participate as mentors in day care centers and preschools.

The readiness goal is a popular one with professionals and parents. Popularity is not enough, however. It will take the concerted efforts of all—professionals, parents, communities, state governments, the federal government, business, and citizens—to move from rhetoric to reality.

WHAT SHOULD KINDERGARTEN BE LIKE?

When making decisions about what kindergarten should be like, we can apply the critical ideas and philosophies of the historic figures discussed in Chapter 2 to contemporary practice. Consider Froebel, for example:

The Kindergarten is an institution which treats the child according to its nature; compares it with a flower in a garden; recognizes its threefold relation to God, man and nature; supplies the means for the development of its faculties, for the training of the senses, and for the strengthening of its physical powers. It is the institution where a child plays with children.[6]

By comparing Froebel's vision of the kindergarten with today's kindergartens, we see that many of today's kindergartens are much different from what Froebel envisioned. This situation is entirely appropriate in many ways, for society is vastly different today than it was in Froebel's time. However, we still need to remember Froebel's and others' visions of what kindergartens can be like.

Additionally, NAEYC identifies the following ten signs of a good kindergarten:

1. Children are playing and working with materials or other children. They are not aimlessly wandering or forced to sit quietly for long periods of time.

2. Children have access to various activities throughout the day, such as block building, pretend play, picture books, paints, and other art materials, and table toys such as Legos, pegboards, and puzzles. Children are not all doing the same things at the same time.

3. Teachers work with individual children, small groups, and the whole group at different times during the day. They do not spend time only with the entire group.

4. The classroom is decorated with children's original artwork, their own writing with invented spelling, and dictated stories.

5. Children learn numbers and the alphabet in the context of their everyday experiences. Exploring the natural world of plants and animals, cooking, taking attendance, and serving snack are all meaningful activities to children.

6. Children work on projects and have long periods of time (at least one hour) to play and explore. Filling out worksheets should not be their primary activity.

7. Children have an opportunity to play outside every day that weather permits. This play is never sacrificed for more instructional time.

8. Teachers read books to children throughout the day, not just at story time.

9. Curriculum is adapted for those who are ahead as well as those who need additional help. Because children differ in experiences and background, they do not learn the same things at the same time in the same way.

10. Children and their parents look forward to school. Parents feel safe sending their child to kindergarten. Children are happy; they are not crying or regularly sick.[7]

Developmentally Appropriate Practice

This book has emphasized that in all things early childhood professionals do for and with children, their efforts should be developmentally appropriate. Developmentally appropriate practice—that is, teaching and caring for young children—facilitates learning that is in accordance with children's physical, cognitive, social, and linguistic development. Understanding professionals will help children learn and develop in ways that are compatible with their age and who they are as individuals (e.g., their background of experiences, culture). Those early childhood professionals who embody the qualities of good kindergarten teachers (Box 10–1) will tend to be those who teach in developmentally appropriate ways.

BOX 10–1 QUALITIES OF A GOOD KINDERGARTEN TEACHER

1. Loves children (acceptance of various backgrounds and ability levels), respects children and parents

2. Patient, kind, caring, and understanding

3. Is a good listener

4. Promotes active learning, includes children's interests in the curriculum

5. Keeps up with current/new trends in education

6. Attends workshops and seminars regarding early childhood

7. Has a love for teaching kindergarten

8. Plans for learning, has a daily schedule, and is a short- and long-range planner

9. Is well organized

10. Has good classroom management

11. Has a good rapport with colleagues, parents, and children

12. Uses learning centers and has a child-centered classroom

13. Is innovative/creative

14. Can provide for all levels of students from enrichment to remedial

15. Instills a love of learning in students

16. Willing to give many extra hours

17. Has desire and motivation to do a good job

18. Has a goal of wanting to ensure that each child is successful

Contributed by the kindergarten teachers at Croissant Park Elementary School, Broward County, Florida.

Talking about developmentally appropriate practice is one thing; implementing it is another. Here are some of the implications of such practice for kindergarten programs (indeed, all programs involving young children):

- *Learning must be meaningful to children and related to what they already know.* Children find things meaningful when those things are interesting to them and they can relate to them.

- *Children do not learn in the same way or are interested in learning the same thing as everyone else all the time.* Thus, teachers must individualize their curriculum as much as possible. Montessori understood this point (see Chapter 5), and the High/Scope educational approach provides for it (see Chapter 5).

- *Learning should be physically and mentally active.* Children should be actively involved in learning activities by building, making, experimenting, investigating, and working collaboratively with their peers.

- *Children should be involved in hands-on activities with concrete objects and manipulatives.* Emphasis is on real-life activities as opposed to workbook and worksheet activities.

Full- or Half-Day Kindergarten

Both half- and full-day kindergarten programs are available. A school district that operates a half-day program usually offers one session in the morning and one in the afternoon, so that one teacher can teach two classes. Although many kindergartens are half-day programs, there is no general agreement that this system is best. Those who argue for it say that this is all the schooling the five-year-old child is ready to experience and that it provides an ideal transition to the all-day first grade. Those in favor of full-day sessions generally feel that not only is the child ready for and capable of a program of this length, but also such an approach allows for a more comprehensive program.

Although kindergartens are about evenly divided between whole- and half-day programs across the United States, the general trend is toward full-day kindergarten programs for all five-year-old children. This is in line with the thinking of a group of early childhood experts, who met recently to discuss issues on kindergarten education. They recommended that kindergarten should be full day. Their rationale was that full-day programs involve fewer transitions for children and enable teachers to get better acquainted with children and parents.[8]

However, essentially two factors stand in the way of a more rapid transition to full-day programs: tradition and money. Kindergartens are historically and traditionally half-day programs, although there is ample evidence of full-day programs for four- and five-year-old children. As time passes and society's needs begin to point to full-day programs to prepare children for living in an increasingly complex world, more kindergarten programs will become full day.

Money is the most important obstacle to the growth of full-day kindergarten programs. Without a doubt, it takes twice as many teachers to operate full-day programs as half-day programs. But as society continues to recognize the benefits of early education and as kindergartens and early childhood programs are seen as one means for solving societal problems, more funding will be forthcoming.

LITERACY EDUCATION AND YOUNG CHILDREN

Literacy education is "in." We hear about it in virtually all educational circles, and almost every early childhood educator is talking about how to promote it. It has replaced reading readiness as the main objective of many kindergarten and primary programs. *Literacy* means the ability to read, write, speak, and listen, with emphasis on reading and writing well. To be literate also means reading, writing, speaking, and listening within the context of one's cultural and social setting.

Literacy education is a hot topic in educational circles for a number of reasons. First, the National Adult Literacy Survey estimates that over 50 million Americans are functionally illiterate—at or below a fifth grade reading level. Furthermore, when we compare the U.S. literacy rate with that of other countries, we do not fare too well—many industrialized countries have higher literacy rates.[9] Consequently, educators and social policy planners are always concerned about the inability of the schools to teach all children to read at more than a functional level.

Today there is a great deal of emphasis on literacy development. The nation has set a goal of having all children read and write at or above level by grade 3. What are some activities and practices you can implement that will help ensure that all children achieve this national goal?

Second, businesses and industry are concerned about how unprepared the nation's workforce is to meet the demands of the workplace. Critics of the educational establishment maintain that many high school graduates do not have the basic literacy skills required for many of today's high-tech jobs. Therefore, schools, especially at the early grades, are feeling the pressure to adopt measures that will give future citizens the skills they will need for productive work and meaningful living.

Cultural and Social Processes of Literacy Education

Literacy is viewed as a process that involves both cognitive and social activities. Some reading and writing practices focus primarily on the cognitive—they are designed to give children mental skills such as word recognition or sound-word relationships. Teachers teach children to read using methods such as whole-word and phonetic analysis; these methods constitute the major portion of the reading program. Reading and writing are frequently taught as isolated, separate subjects and skills. Furthermore, reading and writing are often taught in ways that give them little meaning to children. Treating reading and writing as processes and skills that are separate from children's daily and immediate lives can lead to failure and to retention in kindergarten. Fortunately, this approach to literacy is changing.

Emergent Literacy

Today, early childhood professionals use the term *emergent literacy* when talking about reading, writing, speaking, and listening. Professionals view literacy as a process that begins at birth, perhaps before, and continues to develop across the life span, through the school years and into adulthood. Thus, with the first cry, children are considered to begin language development (see Chapter 8 for a discussion of linguistic development).

Emergent literacy themes emphasize using environmental and social contexts to support and extend children's reading and writing. Children want to make sense of what they read and write. The meaningful part of reading and writing occurs when children talk to each other, write letters, and read good literature or have it read to them. All of this occurs within a print-rich environment, one in which children see others read, make lists, and use language and the written word to achieve goals. Proponents of the whole-language approach maintain that this environment is highly preferable to previous approaches to literacy development.

The process of becoming literate is also viewed as a natural process; reading and writing are processes that children participate in naturally, long before they come to school. No doubt you have participated with or know of toddlers and preschoolers who are literate in many ways. They "read" all kinds of signs (McDonald's) and labels (Campbell's soup) and scribble with and on anything and everything.

The emergent literacy model views reading and writing acquisition as a continuum of development. Hence, children are always thought of as being on a continuous journey towards gaining full literacy development. How is this philosophy similar to or different from a philosophy that views some children as non-readers and illiterate?

The concept of emergent literacy, then, is based on the following beliefs about literacy and about how children learn:

- Reading and writing involve cognitive and social abilities that children employ in the processes of becoming literate and gaining meaning from reading, writing, speaking, and listening.

- Most children begin processes involved in reading and writing long before they come to school; they do not wait until someone teaches them. They should not have to wait to be taught. (Remember what Montessori said about early literacy.)

- Literacy is a social process that develops within a context in which children have the opportunity to interact with and respond to printed language and to other children and adults who are using printed language. In this context, children bring meaning to and derive meaning from reading and writing. Teachers and classrooms should encourage discussing and sharing knowledge and ideas through reading and writing.

- The cultural group in which children become literate influences how literacy develops and the form it takes. Children should also have opportunities to read the literature of many cultural groups in addition to their own.

Developing Literacy in Young Children

Literacy is certainly a worthy national and educational goal, not only for young children, but for everyone. However, how best to promote literacy has always been a controversial topic. One popular approach is "skill and drill," which involves repeated teaching of carefully planned sequential lessons. Many basal reading programs (fundamental materials used to teach literacy) that use this approach are still widely used in early childhood classrooms.

Basal approaches and materials used for literacy development often emphasize a particular method. One of the most popular methods is the *sight word approach* (also called *whole-word* or *look-say*) in which children are presented with whole words (*cat, bat, sat*) and develop a "sight vocabulary" that enables them to begin reading and writing. Many early childhood professionals label objects in their classrooms (door, bookcase, etc.) as a means of teaching a sight vocabulary.

A second popular basal approach is based on *phonics* instruction, which stresses teaching letter-sound correspondence. By learning these connections, children are able to combine sounds into words (*C-A-T*). The proponents of phonics instruction argue that letter-sound correspondences enable children to make automatic connections between words and sounds and, as a result, to sound out words and read them on their own. From the 1950s up until the present time there has been much debate about which of these two approaches to literacy development is best. Today, there is a decided reemphasis on the use of phonics instruction.

Another method of literacy development, the *language experience approach,* follows the philosophy and suggestions inherent in progressive education philosophy. This approach is child centered and maintains that literacy education should be meaningful to children and should grow out of experiences that are interesting to them. Children's own experience is a key element in such child-centered approaches. Many teachers transcribe children's dictated "experience" stories and use them as a basis for writing and for reading instruction.

Beginning about 1980, early childhood practitioners in the United States were influenced by literacy education approaches used in Australia and New Zealand as well as by approaches from Great Britain that were popular during the open education movement of the 1960s. These influences gradually developed into what is known as the *whole-language approach* to literacy development. Since whole language is a philosophy rather than a method, its definition often depends on who is using the term. This approach nonetheless advocates using all aspects of language—reading, writing, listening, and speaking—as the basis for developing literacy. Children learn about reading and writing by speaking and listening; they learn to read by writing, and they learn to write by reading. Basic philosophical premises of whole language follow:

- It is child-centered—children, rather than teachers, are at the center of instruction and learning. Thus, children's experiences and interests serve as the context for topics and as a basis for their intrinsic motivation to read, write, and converse. In this way, literacy learning becomes meaningful and functional for children.

- Social interaction is important and part of the process of becoming literate. Lev Vygotsky (see Chapter 4) stressed the social dimensions of learning. He proposed that through interaction with others, especially with more confident peers, and through interactions and conversations with teachers, children are able to develop higher cognitive learning. This process of learning through social interaction is referred to as *socially constructed knowledge.*

- Spending time on the processes of reading and writing is more important than spending time on learning skills for getting ready to read. Consequently, from the moment they enter the learning setting children are involved in literacy activities, that is, being read to; "reading" books, pamphlets, magazines, etc.; scribbling; "writing" notes and so forth.

- Reading, writing, speaking, and listening are taught as an integrated whole, rather than in isolation.

- Writing begins early (review our discussion in Chapter 11).

- Children's written documents are used as reading materials.

- Themes or units of study are used as a means of promoting interests and content. Generally, themes are selected cooperatively by children and teachers and are used as means of promoting ongoing intrinsic interest in literary processes.

Whole language dominated early childhood practice from about 1990 through 1995. However, growing numbers of critics of this approach, including parents and the public, maintain that because it is a philosophy rather than a specific approach, it does not teach children skills necessary for good reading. Additionally, some teachers have difficulty explaining the whole-language approach to parents, and some find it difficult to implement as well. Further, some research has indicated that whole-language approaches do not result in the high levels of reading achievement claimed by its supporters. As a result, proponents of phonics instruction are aggressively advocating a return to this approach as one which will best meet the needs of parents, children, and society. As with most things, a balanced approach is probably the best, and many early childhood advocates are encouraging literacy approaches that provide a balance between whole-language methods and phonics instruction and that meet the specific needs of individual children. It is likely that the debate over "the best approach" will continue. At the same time, there will be increased efforts to integrate the best of all approaches into a unified whole in order to make literacy education a reality for all children.

Additionally, what happens to children before they come to kindergarten influences the nature and success of their transitions. Three areas are particularly important in influencing the success of transitional experiences: children's skills and prior school-related experiences, children's home lives, and preschool and kindergarten classroom characteristics. Research demonstrates the following in relation to these three areas:[10]

- Children who are socially adjusted have better transitions. For example, kindergarten children whose parents initiate social opportunities for them are better adjusted socially.
- Rejected children have difficulty with transitions.
- Children with more preschool experiences have fewer transition adjustments to make.
- Children whose parents expect them to do well in kindergarten do better than children whose parents have low expectations for them.
- Developmentally appropriate classrooms and practices promote easier and smoother transitions for children.

The nature, extent, creativity, and effectiveness of transitional experiences for children, parents, and staff will be limited only by the commitment of all involved. If we are interested in providing good preschools, kindergartens, and primary schools, then we will include transitional experiences in the curricula of all these programs.

ISSUES RELATED TO KINDERGARTEN

In addition to readiness and transition issues, a number of other issues swirl around kindergarten practices and challenge professionals to make the kindergarten experience a meaningful one for all children.

The Pushed-Down Curriculum

Perhaps you have visited a kindergarten program and left thinking, "Wow, a lot of what they're doing in kindergarten I did in first grade!" Many early childhood professionals would agree. The *pushed-down curriculum* is what happens when professionals teach kindergarten children as first graders and expect them to act like first graders and when the kindergarten curriculum resembles that of first grade. The kindergarten curriculum should challenge all children to do their best and provide them with social and cognitive skills they need for success, but it should also be appropriate for them.

A number of reasons account for the pushed-down curriculum (also referred to as the *escalated* and *hot-house* curriculum). First, beginning in the 1980s there has been a decided emphasis on "academics" in U.S. education, particularly early childhood education (see Chapter 3). Second, some parents believe an academic approach to learning is the best way to succeed in school and the work world. They may also see academics as one of the ways to compensate for the lack of experiences and opportunities prior to their child's school entry. The challenge for early childhood professionals in this regard is to educate parents about what is and is not appropriate for young children's learning. Third, some first grade teachers are demanding children who are grounded in academics. And fourth, more teachers prepared to teach elementary and upper elementary grades are teaching in kindergarten.

Retention

Along with the benefits of early education and universal kindergarten come disturbing and potentially disastrous side effects for children. Retained children, instead of participating in kindergarten graduation ceremonies with their classmates, are destined to spend another year in kindergarten. Many of these children are retained or failed because teachers judge them to be immature, or they fail to measure up to the district's or teachers' standards for promotion to first grade. Children are usually retained in the elementary years because of low academic achievement or low IQ. (In comparison, reasons for retention are different at the junior high level, at which students are generally retained because of behavior problems or excessive absences.)

When well-meaning early childhood education professionals fail children, they do so in the belief that they are doing them and their families a favor. These professionals feel that children who have an opportunity to spend an extra year in the same grade will do better the second time around. Teachers' hopes, and consequently parents' hopes, are that these failed children will go on to do as well as (many teachers hold out the promise that they will do even better than) their nonretained classmates. But is this true? Do children do better the second time around?

Despite our intuitive feelings that children who are retained will do better, the research evidence is unequivocally to the contrary: Children do not do better the second time around. In addition, parents report that retained children have a more pessimistic attitude toward school, with a consequently negative impact on their social-emotional development.[11]

The ultimate issue of retention is how to prevent failure and promote success. To achieve those goals, professionals will have to change their views about what practices are best for children and how to prevent the risk factors that create a climate for unsuccessful school experiences. Some school districts have banned retention in kindergarten and first grade. As alternatives to retaining children in a grade, many school districts are implementing two kinds of programs: One is the developmental kindergarten, which, in essence, gives children two years to complete one year of kindergarten work. The second is transitional classes between kindergarten and first grade. However, these programs are controversial.

TECHNOLOGY AND LITERACY

It is the challenge of every teacher to think about using computers in a way that allows children the opportunity to gain experience and knowledge about technology and also supports the curriculum in a substantive and meaningful way. On a large scale, computer use is becoming a better part of every day reality, and the more students experience computers in the classroom, the better equipped they will be in their future academic and career pursuits.

How computers are used in the classroom varies greatly from kindergarten to the upper grades. Although older students use them for term papers, science, math, and research, young students face limitations imposed by their prereading and prewriting levels. As a result, early childhood teachers face a unique challenge integrating computers into their curriculum in a way that accommodates the children's developing reading and writing skills as the year progresses. This can be done by emphasizing programs or projects utilizing computer technology in a way that is developmentally appropriate and which helps to achieve reading fluency in the early years as the foundation for future success in education.

Our challenge, as we saw it, was to use the computer to promote both computer literacy and reading skills without inhibiting creativity. In order to accomplish this we shifted our focus from educational software and its inherent limitations, onto what could be accomplished by exploiting the mass storage and instant retrieval capabilities of the hardware. We then used the appropriate software to facilitate our goals, rather than letting the software define them.

In our kindergarten classroom we looked for ways in which technology would enhance or expand, in substantive ways, the limits of what could be accomplished. We were looking to do more than use a word processor to transcribe children's words, or a drawing program to replace traditional handmade story books. Though we were aware that developing computer literacy would be a result of such a project, we were searching for ways in which the computer could creatively facilitate reading and writing literacy, other than by imitating the traditional methods. We were also hoping that through the use of technology we could expand the type of projects possible in the classroom.

We used digital cameras to document trips and special projects, science experiments, and work done with blocks and in the creative play area as well as with math manipulatives. The children continually surprised us with the skills they acquired. They learned how to take pictures with the camera, download the pictures to the computer, use software to crop and alter their photos, sometimes adding an element of humor or surrealism to their work. These photos provided an immediate record of experiences while they were still fresh in the children's minds and could be reflected upon later the same day. They also stimulated conversation that often led to the expansion and refinement of an earlier project.

On a trip to Wave Hill Botanical Garden in the Bronx, we used this technique by having our students photograph the visit, print the pictures and annotate them. We used these pictures to create a bulletin board and later a book to share with their parents. Later in the year, after the children had gained enough keyboard proficiency and reading and writing skills to work more independently, we photographed a cooking class and produced a photo book that the students captioned using the computer—a project that lasted several weeks. In addition, the book became an extended exercise not only in literacy but also in recall, verbalization of ideas, and creative writing practice—especially when the children condensed their commentary into captions that synthesized their thoughts and experiences. In another instance, we used this process to help a child who was a fluent reader but was reluctant to write. We encouraged him to make a photo essay of his school birthday party. This was enough to motivate him to experiment with the written word.

An important feature of these projects was that digital photos could be taken, downloaded and printed in a matter of fifteen minutes. This allowed experiences to be on paper while they were still fresh in the children's minds. Some children learned to open their own files and start their own portfolios. However, this more advanced literacy led to questions of ethical behavior, integrity, honesty and privacy. Children needed to be taught to work only on their own projects and not use their newfound computer proficiency to wreak havoc on a classmates' file.

Toward the end of the school year we utilized Kid Pix Companion Slide Show to create a presentation from photographs we'd taken, documenting the kindergarten experience. The slide show was an overview of the year's activities which the children and parents could recall and reflect upon. While the teachers initially set up the program as some students looked on, the students gradually took control of the program. As they learned, the children tutored each other on the workings of making a slide show. Each child in the class selected a photograph from our growing collection that was particularly relevant to her/him, brought the photograph into the program, and recorded an oral description of the activity pictured. This then became the student's personal frame in the show. The children also programmed the style of movement from one frame to the next. The entire class was enthusiastically involved in this project. The presentation that resulted was then shared with the parents at the annual Academic Fair. The children were able to show their parents their own personal slide show frame, as well as those of their classmates, and instruct the adults on the way to navigate the program.

For us as teachers, this project marked a milestone in attaining our goal of more creative use of technology in the classroom. Numerous benefits were reaped from this experience, including the following:

1. The project involved ALL the children. Many of those formerly intimidated by computers became active, enthusiastic participants in this project. This was particularly true for a group of girls in the class, who were initially less experienced and more reticent computer users.

2. It gave the children a chance to highlight what they believed represented their interests, strengths and talents.

3. It gave the parents a window into school life.

4. It allowed immediate documentation of learning experiences which stimulated dialog among the children. These discussions often led to an analysis or critique of the experience and stimulated expansion and refinement of their work.

5. Digital photography captured images of experiences on the screen or on paper while they were still fresh in the children's minds. This became a great stimulus to writing.

6. It allowed the children to express their artistic sensibilities through photography, image alteration and layout.

7. Through the manipulation of the software, the children became more comfortable using the computer and were able to explore the capabilities of the technology. The project stimulated the use of problem solving strategies to overcome some of the technical challenges they faced.

8. The children derived great satisfaction from their work. They were excited to share their school lives, through this media, with their families. The families were similarly excited to have a chance to see what went on during the school year.

Although educational software has its place in education, computers used in other ways can help expand and enhance creativity and imagination—of both students and teacher. Digital photography, especially, can play a valuable role in the early childhood classroom for two reasons. First, it offers children a way to preserve and reproduce special moments for reflection—a potent stimulus to writing. Second, teachers can use the selected moments for further discussion and possible curriculum expansion, as well as share classroom experiences with parents.

For this to happen, teachers must be sensitive to children's needs when constructing a computer area, remain open-minded about the endless possibilities, and stay flexible about making changes to ensure equitable use by everyone. One must remain alert to the emergence of gender issues around allocation of computer time and design projects which generate interest across gender lines. It isn't necessary to know a lot about technology to embark on this journey. Computers are just another tool, and their use can be modified to fit the needs of both teachers and students.

Contributed by Ella Pastor, Emily Kearns, and Paula Reddy. Ella Pastor is Head Teacher of a kindergarten class at Riverdale Country School, 5250 Fieldston Road, Bronx, New York 10471-2999 (e-mail: epastor@juno.com). Emily Kearns is an Assistant Teacher at the school (e-mail: ekerns5285@aol.com). Paula Reddy, a computer specialist at the school, provided technical support for the projects.

High-Stakes Testing

Some kindergarten children still face *high-stakes testing*—testing that determines whether they will be promoted to first grade. High-stakes tests, also known as *benchmark tests,* are an effort to reduce social promotion, in which children are promoted so they can keep up with their age-mates, their social peers. There are a number of reasons for movement away from high-stakes testing. First, such tests do not fit well with the newer curriculum approaches such as whole language and with assessment processes such as portfolios. Second, high-stakes tests do not necessarily test what children really know. Third, these tests may be inappropriate for children of particular cultures. Fourth, many early childhood professionals believe it is not fair to children or their families to make a decision for or against promotion on the basis of one test.

The Graying of Kindergarten

There is a growing tendency for upwardly mobile parents to hold their children (especially sons) out of kindergarten for a year, for several reasons. First, when boys, who tend to be less mature than girls, have a birthday that makes them one of the youngest children in the class, they may not do as well as their parents expect. These parents want their children to be the oldest members of the kindergarten class, not the youngest. They reason that the older children will be the class leaders, will get more attention from the teacher, and will have another year of school under their belt and therefore will be able to better handle the pushed-down curriculum. In other words, these children will be at the top of their class in all respects.

Second, parents who keep their children out of kindergarten for a year can afford to do this. Less well-to-do parents, on the other hand, want their children in school because they cannot afford day care or baby-sitters.

Until society and schools really implement goal 1 of Goals 2000 ("All children will start school ready to learn") and until schools commit themselves to providing every child with the opportunity to learn to his or her fullest potential, the graying of kindergarten will likely continue.

THE FUTURE OF KINDERGARTEN

From our discussions in this chapter, you may have several ideas about how kindergarten programs will evolve as we move into the twenty-first century. Add your ideas to the ones cited here:

- The trend in kindergarten education is toward full-day, cognitive-based programs. Kindergartens give public schools an opportunity to provide children with the help they need for later success in school and life. Children come to kindergarten programs knowing more than their counterparts of twenty years ago. Children with different abilities and a society with different needs require that kindergarten programs change accordingly.

- Kindergarten curricula will include more writing and reading. This literacy emphasis is appropriate and flows naturally out of whole-language programs. The challenge for all professionals is to keep literacy development from becoming a rigid, basic skills approach.

- Technology will be included more in both preschool and kindergarten programs. This technology inclusion is in keeping with the current growth of technology in all grade levels. However, as with many things, we think that earlier is better, so introducing technology early is seen as one way of making children in the United States computer literate. Keep in mind the following ideas about technology: (1) Technology as an instructional model exists in growing numbers of early childhood programs, (2) Technology is no longer something that can be feared or ignored by early childhood professionals, and (3) Children are and can be very comfortable with and adept at technological applications to their lives and learning.

- Kindergarten will be viewed less as a place in which children get ready for school—and fail if they are not ready—and more as a place in which children learn and develop as part of the pre-K–12 schooling process.

ACTIVITIES FOR REFLECTION AND RESEARCH

1. Interview parents to determine what they think children should learn in kindergarten. How do their ideas compare with the ideas in this chapter and with your ideas?

2. As a teacher, would you support an earlier or later entrance age to kindergarten? If your local legislator wanted specific reasons, what would you tell him or her? Ask other teachers and compare their viewpoints.

3. How might culture, socioeconomic background, and home life affect what should be taught to children in kindergarten?

4. Give examples from your observations of kindergarten programs to support one of these opinions: (1) Society is pushing kindergarten children. (2) Many kindergartens are not teaching children enough.

5. Compare the curriculum of a for-profit kindergarten, a parochial school kindergarten, and a public school kindergarten. What are the similarities and differences? Which would you send your child to? Why?

6. Do you think kindergarten should be mandatory for all five-year-old children? At what age should it be mandatory?

7. Should the results of a readiness test be the final word on whether a child is admitted to kindergarten? Explain your answer.

8. What are reasons for the current interest in helping children make transitions from one setting or agency to another? What are other transitions that early childhood educators should help children make, besides those mentioned in this chapter?

9. You have been asked to speak to a parent group about the pros and cons of contemporary approaches to literacy development in kindergarten. What major topics would you include?

10. Develop a list of suggestions for how parents can promote literacy in the home.

READINGS FOR FURTHER ENRICHMENT

Fisher, B. and Holdaway, D. *Joyful Learning in Kindergarten* (Portsmouth, NH: Heinemann, 1998).

Joyful Learning demonstrates how to link student-center theory and practice in the preschool and kindergarten classroom.

Stull, E. C. *Kindergarten Teacher's Survival Guide* (Upper Saddle River, N.J.: Prentice Hall, 1998).

This book contains more than 100 activities to enrich reading readiness, language development, math, science, social studies, art, music, drama, and physical education.

Piper, T, *Language and Learning: The Home and School Years, 2 ed.* (Upper Saddle River, N.J.: Prentice Hall, 1999).

This book takes an integrative approach to how children learn language, how it is taught, and how the two are sometimes at odds. This book gives balanced treatment to theory and practice, to first and second language acquisition, and to showing and telling.

Feldman, R. S. *Child Development: A Topical Approach* (Upper Saddle River, N.J.: Prentice Hall, 1999).

This book captures the discipline in a way that excites readers about the field, draws them into its perspective, and molds their understanding of developmental issues.

RESEARCH ON THE INTERNET

ECEOL Website

http://www.ume.maine.edu/~cofed/eceol/curr.html

Collaborative effort of early childhood educators in building a site with well thought-out content; growing site with global early childhood perspective.

EarlyChildhood.com

http://www.earlychildhood.com/

Site for getting advice from experts in the early childhood field, expanding your collection of creative projects, and sharing ideas and questions with the early childhood community.

Early Childhood News

http://www.earlychildhoodnews.com/

Features sample articles from the print magazine for professionals who work with young children.

NOTES

1.   From *All I Really Need to Know I Learned in Kindergarten* by Robert L. Fulghum (New York: Villard, 1988), p. 6. Copyright © 1986, 1988, by Robert L. Fulghum. Reprinted by permission of Villard Books, a division of Random House, Inc.

2.   Alec M. Gallup, "The 18th Annual Gallup Poll of the Public's Attitudes toward Public Schools," *Phi Delta Kappan,* 68(1), 1987, pp. 55–56.

3.   *Goals 2000: Educate America Act* (Washington, DC: U.S. Government Printing Office, 1994).

4.   National Association for the Education of Young Children, "NAEYC Position Statement on School Readiness," *Young Children,* 46(1), November 1990, p. 21.

5.   Ernest L. Boyer, *Ready to Learn: A Mandate for the Nation* (Princeton, NJ: Carnegie Foundation for the Advancement of Teaching, 1992), pp. 136–43. Used by permission.

6.   Friedrich Froebel, *Mother's Songs, Games and Stories* (New York: Arno, 1976), p. 136.

7.   Copyright © 1996 by the National Association for the Education of Young Children, Early Years Are Learning Years Series, "Top Ten Signs of a Good Kindergarten Classroom," on NAEYC web site at http://www.naeyc.org/naeyc.

8.   "Reporter's Notebook: Experts Tackle Transition to Kindergarten," *Educational Week,* March 4, 1998, p. 12.

9.   Literacy Volunteers of America, *Facts on Literacy* (Syracuse, NY: Author, 1994).

10. K. L. Maxwell and S. K. Elder, "Children's Transition to Kindergarten," *Young Children,* 49(6), 1995, pp. 56–63.

11. P. Mantzicopoulos and D. Morrison, "Kindergarten Retention: Academics and Behavioral Outcomes through the End of Second Grade," *American Educational Research Journal,* 29(1), 1993, pp. 182–98.

CHAPTER

11

Preparation for Lifelong Success

FOCUS QUESTIONS

1. How are the primary years important for children, families, and the profession?
2. What are the similarities and differences among preschool, kindergarten, and primary grade children?
3. What are the physical, cognitive, language, psychosocial, and moral developmental characteristics of primary children?
4. How do instruction and learning processes used in the primary grades influence teaching and learning?
5. What contemporary issues are involved in primary education?
6. How is education in the primary years changing?

In contrast to the renewed interest in infants and preschoolers discussed in the previous chapters, one might almost say that the years from six to eight are the forgotten years of early childhood. In many ways, primary children are frequently overlooked in terms of early childhood education. Although the profession defines early childhood as the period from birth to age eight, children from birth through kindergarten receive most of the attention; primary grade children are more often thought of as belonging to the elementary years. Indeed, the years from six to twelve are often referred to as the *middle years* or *middle childhood,* the years between early childhood and adolescence.

Accordingly, one of the major challenges facing the early childhood profession is to reclaim the years from ages six through eight. We cannot focus research and training almost exclusively on the years up to age five as we presently do. Lives are shaped not only in the early years, but in the primary years as well.

WHAT ARE PRIMARY CHILDREN LIKE?

Throughout this text, we stress the uniqueness and individuality of children. Although we discuss in this and other chapters what children are like, and the common characteristics they share, as an early childhood professional you must always remember that each child is unique.

Physical Development

Two words describe the physical growth of primary age children: *slow* and *steady.* Children at this age do not make the rapid and obvious height and weight gains of the infant, toddler, and preschooler. Instead, they experience continual growth, develop increasing control over their bodies, and explore the things they are able to do.

From ages five to seven, children's average weight and height approximate each other. For example, at six years, boys weigh forty-six pounds and are forty-six inches tall, while girls weigh forty-three pounds and are forty-five inches tall. At age seven, boys weigh fifty pounds and are forty-eight inches tall, and girls, forty-eight pounds and forty-eight inches. The weight of boys and girls tends to be the same until about age nine, when girls pull ahead of boys in both height and weight. Wide variations appear in both individual rates of growth and development and among the sizes of children in each classroom. These differences in physical appearance result from genetic and cultural factors, nutritional intake and habits, health care, and experiential background.

Motor Development

Primary children are adept at many motor skills. The six-year-old is in the initiative stage of psychosocial development; seven- and eight-year-old children are in the industry stage. Not only are children intuitively driven to initiate activities, but they are also learning to be competent and productive individuals. The primary years are thus a time to use and test developing motor skills. Children at this age should be actively involved in activities that enable them to use their bodies to learn and develop feelings of purpose and competence. Their growing confidence and physical skills are reflected in games of running, chasing, and kicking. A nearly universal characteristic of children in this period is their almost constant physical activity.

Differences between boys' and girls' motor skills during the primary years are minimal—their abilities are about equal. Teachers therefore should not try to limit either boys' or girls' activities on the basis of gender. We see evidence of continuing refinement of fine-motor skills in children's mastery of many of the tasks they previously could not do or could do only with difficulty. They are now able to dress themselves relatively easily and attend to most of their personal needs, such as using utensils, combing their hair, and brushing their teeth. They are also more proficient at school tasks that require fine-motor skills, such as writing, doing artwork, and using computers.

Cognitive Development

Children's cognitive development during the primary school years enables them to do things as first, second, and third graders that they could not do as preschoolers. A major difference between these two age groups is that older children's thinking has become less egocentric and more logical (see Chapter 9). The cognitive milestone that enables children between seven and eleven to think and act as they do is concrete operational thought. Logical operations, although more sophisticated than in preoperational children, still require concrete objects and referents in the here and now. Abstract reasoning comes later, in the formal operations stage during adolescence.

Many of the skills learned in the primary grades are directly related to what children need for success in school, success in work and success in life. The curriculum of the preschool should encourage and support children's learning of basic skills and other skills that will help them succeed. What are some skills that you would include in a first-grade curriculum?

THE SIGNIFICANCE OF THE PRIMARY YEARS

The primary years of early childhood education are significant because children are further inducted into the process of formal schooling. The preschool experience is often viewed as preparation for school. Increasingly with kindergarten and especially with first grade, the process of schooling begins. How this induction goes will, to a large extent, determine how well children learn and whether they like school.

Children's attitudes toward themselves and their lives are determined at this time. The degree of success now sets limits on lifelong success as well as school success. Preparation for dealing with, engaging in, and successfully completing school tasks begins long before the primary grades, but it is during the primary grades that children encounter failure, grade retention, and negative attitudes. Negative experiences during this period have a profound effect on their efforts to develop a positive self-image. Primary children are in Erik Erikson's industry versus inferiority stage (see Chapter 8). They want and need to be competent, and they should be given the opportunities to be so.

HOW RESTRUCTURING IS AFFECTING THE PRIMARY GRADES

In Chapter 2 we discuss the restructuring of early childhood programs in the United States today. Nowhere is this restructuring more evident than in the primary grades. Grassroots efforts, led by parents, teachers, and building- or program-level administrators, are aimed at changing how schools operate

**VIDEO
VIEWPOINT**

THEY ARE WHAT THEY EAT

Children are not born with a taste for high-fat foods. It is a learned behavior. But, often, children are not given better choices. When children are let loose in a supermarket to make their own choices, parents are appalled at what their children do not know about good nutrition—and at food manufacturers who do not necessarily offer the healthiest of choices in their kid-attractive packages.

Reflective Discussion Questions: Why do you think it is that when given the opportunity, children select high-calorie, high-fat foods rather than "healthy foods"? Why do you think it is that manufacturers produce and sell foods with higher-fat content for children than adults? How are children's cartoons and cartoon characters used to market children's foods? How does television advertising steer children toward "bad food choices"? What are some reasons that children are eating more "unhealthy" foods? What is your reaction to the comment that "there are no good or bad foods; that eaten in moderation, any food is part of a well-balanced diet"?

Reflective Decision Making: Visit a local supermarket and read the fat, salt, and sugar content for foods marketed specifically for children. Make a list of the top fat, salt, and sugar foods for children. How can you work with parents to help them provide good nutritional meals for their children and other family members? What can you do in preschool and other early childhood settings to help children learn good nutritional practices? Conduct a survey of the foods that young children eat during the day. How many total grams of fat do you estimate they eat during a typical day? How does this compare with the 50 to 60 grams of fat recommended by nutritionists? Give specific examples of how manufacturers use food to promote and sell a particular product. What could you do as an early childhood educator to get children to eat more fruits and vegetables rather than fatty snacks?

and are organized, how teachers teach, how children are taught and evaluated, and how schools involve and relate to parents and the community. Accountability and collaboration are in; schooling as usual is out.

REASONS FOR RESTRUCTURING PRIMARY EDUCATION

Education in the primary grades is changing. Schooling in the elementary years in the United States has become a serious enterprise, for political, social, and economic reasons. First, educators, parents, and politicians are realizing that solutions to illiteracy, a poorly prepared workforce, and many social problems begin in the first years of school or even before. Second, the public is not happy about continuing declines in educational achievement. It wants the schools to do a better job teaching children the skills business and industry will need in the twenty-first century. Third, parents and the public in general want the schools to help solve many of society's problems (substance abuse, crime, violence, etc.) and turn around what many see as an abandonment of traditional American and family values.

THE CONTEMPORARY PRIMARY SCHOOL

A lot of change has occurred in the primary grades since the 1980s, with more on the way. Single-subject teaching and learning are out; integration of subject areas through such practices as whole language, thematic approaches, and literature-based programs is in. Students sitting in single seats, in straight rows, solitarily doing their own work are out; cooperative learning is in. Textbooks are out; projects and hands-on, active learning are in. Paper-and-pencil tests are out; student work samples and collaborative discussion of achievements are in. The teacher as director of all and "the sage on center stage" is out; facilitation, collaboration, cooperative discipline, and coaching are in. Letter grades and report cards are out; narrative reports, in which professionals describe and report on student achievement, checklists, which describe the competencies students have demonstrated, parent conferences, and other ways of reporting achievement are in.

In many respects, Dewey's progressive education ideas are finding fertile ground once again in the hearts and minds of early childhood professionals and parents who desire more personalized and developmental programs for young children. Many businesses and industries are operating exemplary and nationally acclaimed child care and preschool programs. Why can't they accomplish the same things for public education? Why not, indeed! This is but one of the many questions you should ask as you read about the model programs and consider how public agencies are helping change how schools operate. In the answers to your questions lie the future directions of many early childhood programs and the future of your career, as well.

THE NEW CURRICULUM FOR THE PRIMARY GRADES

In Chapters 8, 9, and 10 we identified child-centered practices and programs. The child-centered movement also is alive and well in the primary grades. We discuss some of these practices in this section.

The Self-Esteem Movement

In Chapter 3, we examined Maslow's hierarchy of needs. One of these needs is for self-esteem, a positive feeling of self-worth and self-image. The self-esteem movement began in the 1980s as a way of improving children's achievement. The argument is that children do not or cannot achieve because of poor self-worth. Proponents maintain that programs and practices to enhance self-esteem are particularly important for certain groups of children: minorities, females, and those at risk. Further, they maintain that children's self-esteem is lessened by uncaring teachers and an indifferent school system.

Efforts to enhance students' self-esteem have resulted in a number of practices:

- Praise is used as a means of recognizing and rewarding achievement. It also is used to make children feel special and comfortable with learning and to try to get children to do their best. Advocates of praising as a means of promoting self-esteem say it places less importance on the product and more on children's efforts. Unfortunately, in some cases, teachers have used praise too much, too often, and without a basis in solid achievement.

- Schools have been established that are specifically designed to promote self-esteem and increase achievement through identity with one's culture.

- Mentoring, role modeling, and "shadowing" programs have begun, in which students are given opportunities to interact with successful people.

Not everyone, however, agrees that the self-esteem movement is in children's best interests. Critics claim that teachers overpraise children, reward them for little effort and achievement, and substitute praise and rewards for teaching. Further, they maintain that true self-esteem results from achievement, not from hollow praise.

Prosocial Behavior

There is a growing feeling among early childhood professionals that schools can teach children the fundamentals of peaceful living, kindness, helpfulness, and cooperation. You and other educators can do several things to foster development of prosocial skills in the classroom:

- *Be a good role model for children.* You must demonstrate in your life and relationships with children and other adults the behaviors of cooperation and kindness that you want to encourage in children.

- *Provide positive feedback and reinforcement when children perform prosocial behaviors.* When children are rewarded for appropriate behavior, they tend to repeat that behavior. ("I like how you helped Tim get up when you accidentally ran into him. I bet that made him feel better.")

- *Provide opportunities for children to help and show kindness to others.* Cooperative programs between primary children and nursing and retirement homes are excellent opportunities to practice helping and kind behaviors.

- *Conduct classroom routines and activities so they are as free as possible of conflict.* Provide opportunities for children to work together and practice skills for cooperative living. Design learning centers and activities for children to share and work cooperatively.

- *When real conflicts occur, provide practice in conflict resolution skills.* These skills include taking turns, talking through problems, compromising, and apologizing. A word of caution regarding apologies: Too often, an apology is a perfunctory response on the part of teachers and children. Rather than just saying the often empty words, "I'm sorry," it is far more meaningful to help one child understand how another is feeling. Encouraging empathic behavior in children is a key to the development of prosocial behavior.

- *Conduct classroom activities that are based on multicultural principles and that are free from stereotyping and sexist behaviors (see Chapter 12).*

- *Read stories to children that exemplify prosocial behaviors, and provide such literature for them to read.*

- *Counsel and work with parents to encourage them to limit their children's television viewing, especially concerning programs that contain violence.*

- *Help children feel good about themselves, build strong self-images, and be competent individuals.* Children who are happy, confident, and competent feel good about themselves and are more likely to behave positively toward others.

Teaching Thinking

The back-to-basics movement has been a dominant theme in U.S. education and will likely continue as a curriculum force. We generally think of basic skills as reading, writing, and arithmetic, and many elementary schools allot these subjects the lion's share of time and teacher emphasis. Yet some critics of education and advocates of basic education do not consider the "three Rs" the ultimate "basic" of sound education. Rather, they feel, the real basic of education is thinking. The rationale is that if students can think, they can meaningfully engage in subject matter curriculum and the rigors and demands of the workplace and life. Increasingly, thinking and problem-solving skills are coming to be regarded as no less "basic" than math facts, spelling, knowledge of geography, and so on.

As a result, teachers are including the teaching of thinking in their daily lesson plans, using both direct and nondirect methods of instruction to teach learning skills. A trend in curriculum and instruction today is to infuse the teaching of thinking across the curriculum and to make thinking a part of the culture of a classroom.

To talk about a classroom culture of thinking is to refer to a classroom environment in which several forces such as language, values, expectations,

PROGRAM IN ACTION

LEARNING ABOUT PARTNERSHIPS, TEAMS, AND SHARING LEARNING

Sharing the responsibility of educating our youth is an emphasis goal at Lexington Park Elementary School in St. Mary's County, Maryland. Because we are located near the Naval Air Warfare Center Aircraft Division at Patuxent River, Maryland, we are involved in a community partnership with the Naval Aviation Depot Operations Center (NADOC). Personnel from NADOC volunteer time at our school as tutor buddies. Students identified under Title 1 are placed with tutors initially. However, any student showing need can receive support and assistance from a NADOC volunteer. For example, tutors will reread stories with children, listen to stories children read, and review comprehension questions.

Partnerships are also evident within our school in the way teachers team together to coordinate teaching efforts and learning experiences. Music, media/computer lab, physical education, and art teachers coordinate their lessons with studies developed in individual classrooms. For example, the art teacher will help us make handmade paper from egg cartons because, in our study of Japan, we learned that papermaking was a Japanese enterprise.

Partnerships, teams, and *sharing* are terms used frequently throughout our school. In addition to team teaching experiences, students benefit from a program entitled Roots and Wings from the New American Schools Development Corporation. The goal of the New American School Development Corporation is to support school restructuring efforts. Roots and Wings is one of eight grants funded nationally, and St. Mary's County Schools and Johns Hopkins University were jointly awarded a grant to initiate the program in our schools.

Math Wings is a pilot component of the Roots and Wings program. Piloting this math program provides for a unique teaching and learning experience. The units and lessons are sent from Johns Hopkins, and the program involves cooperative learning teams. The daily plan includes class discussion, team investigation, partnered practice, and individual reinforcement with homework. The program allows students to invent their own methods to solve problems. Students have begun to accept ownership of Math Wings because their comments and concerns are welcomed and encouraged from Johns Hop-

and habits work together to express and reinforce the enterprise of good thinking. In a classroom culture of thinking, the spirit of good thinking is everywhere. There is the sense that "everyone is doing it," that everyone including the teacher is making the effort to be thoughtful, inquiring, and imaginative, and that these behaviors are strongly supported by the learning environment.[1]

In classrooms that emphasize thinking, students are encouraged to use their power of analysis, and teachers ask higher-level questions. Teachers are being encouraged to challenge their children to think about classroom information and learning material rather than to merely memorize acceptable responses. Instead of asking children to recall information, teachers are ask-

kins. Students are free to provide constructive criticism about the lessons. Most students support the program. They are particularly fond of the use of manipulatives to reinforce the skills taught.

In the afternoon, our theme of partnership extends from individual classrooms to every third, fourth, and fifth grade classroom. All three grade levels work together to teach Cooperative Integrated Reading and Composition (CIRC), yet another component of the Roots and Wings program. This program, involving the use of cooperative learning teams, allows third, fourth, and fifth grade students to be placed in a group at their individual reading level. My own third graders enjoy working with students at different age and grade levels. Once students are grouped, their focus is to work together to achieve a common goal. The hour-and-a-half CIRC block involves whole-class discussion, cooperative groupings, partnering activities, as well as individual assignments. This component of Roots and Wings has been in place for two years. Teaching and reading and writing through the CIRC process has proven to be effective in increasing student self-esteem as well as student achievement.

Our day has just about come to a close. Students return to their homeroom classrooms and prepare for dismissal. In the last few minutes of the school day, students unwind with a book, debrief with a friend, or jot down events of the day in their journals. Unless a child is picked up by a parent, all students ride a bus home from school. As the last bus is called, a few students are left behind who are involved in after-school programs. Still another component of Roots and Wings is available for students who want to and can be involved in after-school programs. These students may enroll in a computer club, homework center, tutoring, and even drama club, all of which are made available four days a week.

As a third grade teacher, I expect to see children go through remarkable changes as they grow and learn. I have observed how the partnerships, teamwork, and shared learning experiences my students are able to engage in at Lexington Park Elementary help them develop strong roots grounded in effective instructional practice. I also have witnessed how students grow in self-esteem, learn to respect one another's ideas, and find their wings as they discover who they are and what the world has to offer them.

Contributed by Barbara Lord, Lexington Park Elementary School, Lexington Park, Maryland.

ing them to think critically about information, solve problems, and reflect, teaching them skills such as those on the following list:

Commonly Taught Thinking Skills

- *Analyzing*—examining something methodically; identifying the parts of something and the relationships between those parts
- *Inferring*—drawing a reasonable conclusion from known information
- *Comparing and contrasting*—noting similarities and differences between two things or events
- *Predicting*—forecasting what will happen next in a given situation, based on the circumstances

- *Hypothesizing*—developing a reasonable explanation for events, based on an analysis of evidence
- *Critical thinking*—examining evidence and arguments carefully, without bias, and reaching sound conclusions
- *Deductive reasoning*—applying general principles to specific cases
- *Inductive reasoning*—deriving general principles from an analysis of individual cases
- *Organizing*—imposing logical order on something
- *Classifying*—putting things into groups based on shared characteristics
- *Decision making*—examining alternatives and choosing one, for sound reasons
- *Problem solving*—analyzing a difficult situation and thinking creatively about how to resolve it[2]

Inductive and Deductive Reasoning

Other basic building blocks are reasoning skills, which include the following intellectual activities:[3]

- Enumeration, listing
- Grouping
- Labeling, categorizing
- Identifying critical relationships
- Making inferences
- Predicting consequences, explaining unfamiliar phenomena, hypothesizing
- Explaining and/or supporting predictions and hypotheses
- Verifying predictions

These skills are used both in inductive reasoning, thinking from the particular to the general or drawing a logical conclusion from instances of a case, and in deductive reasoning, inferring specifics from a general principle or drawing a logical conclusion from a premise.

Critical Thinking Skills

Critical thinking skills are used in everyday life activities to help determine the accuracy of information and to make decisions regarding choices. Critical thinking is the process of logically and systematically analyzing problems, data, and solutions in order to make rational decisions about what to do or believe. Skills involved in critical thinking include the following:

- Identify central issues or problems
- Compare similarities and differences
- Determine which information is relevant

- Formulate appropriate questions
- Distinguish among facts, opinion, and reasoning judgment
- Check consistency
- Identify unstated assumptions
- Recognize stereotypes and cliches
- Recognize bias, emotional factors, propaganda, and semantic slanting
- Recognize different value systems and ideologies
- Evaluate the adequacy of data
- Predict probable consequences[4]

The goal of teaching critical thinking is to encourage students to question what they hear and read and to examine their own thinking. Teachers cultivate critical thinking by providing learning environments in which divergent perspectives are respected and free discussion is allowed.

Creative Problem-Solving Strategies

Problem solving in any content area rests on thinking skills and critical thinking. Problem-solving skills can be taught directly through process strategies. For example, one system teaches problem-solving strategies using the acronym IDEAL as a mnemonic for a five-step process:

I   Identify the problem.

D   Define and represent the problem.

E   Explore possible strategies.

A   Act on the strategies.

L   Look back and evaluate the effects of your activities.[5]

Other effective problem-solving strategies include teaching students brainstorming techniques, imaging strategies, and ways to represent problems visually as an aid to finding a solution.

Implications for Professionals

Professionals who want to promote critical and creative thinking in children need to be aware of several things. First, children need the freedom and security to be creative thinkers. Many teachers and school programs focus on helping children learn the right answers to problems, so children soon learn from the process of schooling that there is only one right answer. Children may be so "right answer" oriented that they are uncomfortable with searching for other answers or consider it a waste of time.

Second, the environment must support children's creative efforts. Teachers must create classroom cultures in which children have the time, opportunity, and materials with which to be creative. Letting children think creatively only when all their subjects are completed, or scheduling creative thinking for certain times, does not properly encourage it.

Third, creative and critical thinking must be integrated into the total curriculum, so that children learn to think across the curriculum, the entire school day, and throughout their lives.

Cooperative Learning

You can probably remember how, when you were in primary school, you competed with other kids. You probably tried to see whether you could be the first to raise your hand. You leaned out over the front of your seat, frantically waving for your teacher's attention. In many of today's primary classrooms, however, the emphasis is on cooperation, not competition. Cooperative learning is seen as a way to boost student achievement and enhance self-esteem.

Cooperative learning is an instructional and learning strategy that focuses on instructional methods in which students are encouraged or required to work together on academic tasks. Students work in small, mixed-ability learning groups of usually four members wherein each member is responsible for learning and for helping all members learn. In one form of cooperative learning, called "Student Teams-Achievement Division," four students—usually one high achiever, two average students, and one low achiever—participate in a regular cycle of activities, such as the following:[6]

- The teacher presents the lesson to the group.
- Students work to master the material using worksheets or other learning materials. Students are encouraged not only to complete their work but also to explain their work and ideas to group members.
- Students take brief quizzes.

Children in a cooperative learning group are assigned certain responsibilities; for example, there is a group leader, who announces the problems or task; a praiser, who praises group members for their answers and work; and a checker. Responsibilities rotate as the group engages in different tasks. Children are also encouraged to develop and use interpersonal skills, such as addressing classmates by their first names, saying "Thank you," and explaining to their groupmates why they are proposing an answer. On the classroom level, teachers must incorporate five basic elements into the instructional process for cooperative learning to be successful:[7]

1. *Positive independence.* The students have to believe they are in the learning process together and that they care about one another's learning.
2. *Verbal, face-to-face interaction.* Students must explain, argue, elaborate, and tie what they are learning now to what they have previously learned.

3. *Individual accountability.* Every member of the group must realize that it is his or her own responsibility to learn.

4. *Social.* Students must learn appropriate leadership, communication, trust-building, and conflict resolution skills.

5. *Group processing.* The group has to assess how well its members are working together and how they can do better.

Proponents and practitioners of cooperative learning are enthusiastic about its benefits:[8]

- It motivates students to do their best.
- It motivates students to help one another.
- It significantly increases student achievement.

Supporters of cooperative learning maintain that it enables children to learn how to cooperate and that children learn from each other. And because schools are usually such competitive places, it gives children an opportunity to learn cooperative skills.

Not all teachers agree that cooperative learning is a good idea, however. They maintain that it is too time-consuming, because a group may take longer than an individual to solve a problem. Other critics charge that time spent on cooperative learning takes away time from learning the basic skills of reading, writing, and arithmetic.

Given the new approaches in primary education, it makes sense that professionals would want to use a child-centered approach that increases student achievement. Furthermore, school critics say that classrooms are

Learning how to work with and get along well with others is considered an essential workplace skill. Attitudes towards working cooperatively with others are developed in the early years of schooling. How will you, an early childhood teacher, organize the classroom and other environments to support children's cooperative efforts and interactions?

frequently too competitive and that students who are neither competitive nor high achievers are left behind. Cooperative learning would seem to be one of the better ways to reduce classroom competitiveness and foster "helping" attitudes.

Character Education

Character education is back in many elementary classrooms (and middle and senior high schools as well) across the United States, for several reasons. As a society, we are alarmed by what we see as a decline in moral values and abandonment of ethical values. The character education movement is also a reaction to the "anything goes" 1980s characterized by the savings and loan scandals and the "me first" and "I want everything—now" attitudes. Of course, we are also alarmed by substance abuse, teenage pregnancies, violence, and juvenile delinquency. Character education is seen as a way of reducing, and possibly preventing, these societal problems.

Character education programs seek to teach a set of traditional core values that will result in civic virtue and moral character, including honesty, kindness, respect, responsibility, tolerance for diversity, racial harmony, and good citizenship.

The Naturalness of Literacy Development

Educators today stress the "naturalness" of children's literacy development. The case is made that many children learn to write and read in natural ways, many times on their own and without formal instruction. The example par excellence of this naturalness at work in literacy development is the many kindergarten and first grade children who come to school with rather well-developed writing and reading skills. Of course, Maria Montessori discussed this process as part of her program.

The naturalness with which many children develop an interest in reading and writing and read and write at home and in preschool settings is frequently sharply contrasted with what many critics maintain are less natural approaches to teaching language arts. These "less than natural" approaches include what is frequently referred to as "sit-down instruction," in which teachers teach children how to read and write. Other practices that critics label unnatural include the use of photocopies, worksheets, and mindless, repetitive exercises. For example, story starters, a technique by which teachers give children sentences to begin stories, can discourage writing and creativity if used unimaginatively. If teachers start every story with, "Today is [the day of the school week], and it is cold outside. . .," should it come as a surprise that students soon lose interest in learning to write?

Efforts to promote a "natural" approach to reading and writing are seen in programs aimed at involving parents in reading to their children at home and encouraging children and their families to use public libraries, and have resulted in the growth of children's book clubs. The process of "being read to" at home and in school is gaining in attention and popularity. Children who have been read to

- have developed crucial insights about written language being essential for learning to read and write;
- realize that written language, while related to it, is not the same as spoken language;
- have discovered that both spoken and written language can serve the same function; and
- have learned to follow plot and character development.[9]

Reading, Writing, and Literature

Learning to write and improving students' writing through reading is also receiving renewed emphasis today, which is why so many students are encouraged to read good literature as part of their reading/writing programs. This concept is affecting not only how children are taught (e.g., through literature); it is also influencing publishing companies, which are including more literature in their reading books.

The inclusion of literature in the reading/language arts curriculum is characterized by several important features:

- The inclusion of literature by well-known authors (e.g., Cynthia Rylant, A. A. Milne, Langston Hughes).
- The inclusion of the unabridged works of famous authors. Critics of the status of children's literacy have complained that rather than reading the "real thing," students have been subjected to the watered-down versions of famous authors. They cite this as one more example of the "dumbing-down" of textbooks and the curriculum.
- The use of literature as the context within which to teach reading and language arts skills.

The Whole-Language Curriculum

A whole-language literacy program has a number of important components:[10]

- It uses and incorporates *functional language;* that is, children are offered involvement with written language in and from the environment. Examples of the involvement of children in functional language include making signs and posters, writing letters, and making lists.
- It uses *predictable materials* such as signs, nursery rhymes, and poems, as well as classical and contemporary children's stories. Predictable books are especially important because of their repetitive language, match between text and illustration, and familiar content.

- It incorporates *language experience* stories that evolve from the children's interests and activities.

- It uses *shared reading.* This is essentially a process in which teachers read favorite stories to children. This emphasis on shared reading has led to the development of "big books." These oversized books enable teachers to involve children in a shared reading experience so they can see, participate, and feel that they are part of the process.

- It involves *story reading* in which children are read to one-on-one by older children, and then the younger child reads to the older child. This process can also incorporate adults reading to children and vice versa.

- It uses *sustained silent reading,* which is a process in which a brief period of time is set aside daily so that just about all those in the school—children, teachers, principal, and in some schools custodians and cafeteria workers—read by themselves.

- It encourages children to *control their own learning* by initiating reading and writing activities. For example, they determine what books to read and when to read them.

A Holistic Approach

As discussed in Chapters 9 and 10, more professionals are adapting a balanced approach to promoting children's literacy development. One such approach is holistic literary education, which advocates a complete systematic approach to children's literacy development. The following are characteristic of the holistic approach:

- Teachers integrate the teaching of the language arts into a single period. They recognize the interrelatedness of reading, writing, speaking, and listening. . . . Holistic teachers therefore provide children with opportunities to talk, write, listen, and speak to each other, and to the teacher. . . .

- Teachers use children's oral language as the vehicle for helping them make the transition to the written language. Children are given opportunities to write messages, letters, and stories, using their own words and sentence patterns, even before they can accurately read, write, or spell.

- Teachers encourage students to write as soon as they enter school. Children may dictate experiences or stories for others to write, as is done in the Language Experience Approach to reading instruction; however, holistic teachers emphasize children's doing their own writing, following their belief that children's writing skills develop from scribbling to invented spellings to eventual mature writing.

- In addition to using children's written documents as reading material, holistic teachers frequently use literature books, rejecting vocabulary-controlled, sentence-controlled stories in favor of those containing predictable language patterns. They choose the best children's literature available to read to and with children.

- Holistic teachers organize literacy instruction around themes or units of study relevant to students. Children use all of the language arts (listening, speaking, reading, and writing) as they study a particular theme. Many teachers also integrate the teaching of music, art, social studies, and other subjects into these units of study.

- Holistic teachers believe in intrinsic motivation, and when children enjoy good literature, create stories, write letters, keep personal journals, and share their written documents with others, language learning becomes intrinsically rewarding.

- Holistic teachers believe that literacy development depends on having opportunities to communicate. Since communication is not possible without social interaction, these teachers give children opportunities to read other children's compositions, and to write, listen, and speak to each other.

- Holistic teachers give children opportunities to both teach and learn from each other. They often work collaboratively on a common interest or goal. They react to each other's written products, and they share favorite books with each other.

- Holistic teachers control literacy instruction. It may be student centered, but it is also teacher guided. . . . [H]olistic teachers recognize that some direct instruction, including instruction in phonics, is not incompatible with student empowerment.

- Teachers emphasize holistic reading and writing experiences—children spend most of the classroom time available on meaningful reading and writing experiences. . . .[11]

Authentic Writing

As a result of whole language and holistic literacy education, writing is becoming more authentic; that is, it is more concerned with the real world. Children are writing about real-life topics and issues—the environment, violence, how to help the homeless, and so forth. In today's contemporary classrooms, contrived writing is out the window and the real world is open for discussion and writing.

The Integrated Curriculum

The integrated curriculum is a natural progression from whole language, or whole language may be the result of attempts to integrate the curriculum. The integrated curriculum is an attempt to break down barriers between subject matter areas and help children make connections among all content areas. In integrated learning, for example, children write in their journals about life in the United States or construct bar graphs about the height and weight of their classmates.

Much of literacy development involves engaging children in authentic practices. These include using materials from the environment, such as magazines, menus, posters, advertisements, and so forth, as a means of becoming literate. What are the advantages of using authentic materials to promote children writing?

PROMOTION

Not surprisingly, with the new directions in primary education there is also a new look at grade failure and retention practices. Grade retention as a cure for poor achievement or nonachievement is popular, especially with many professionals and the public. Despite the use of retention as a panacea for poor achievement, "the evidence to date suggests that achievement-based promotion does not deal effectively with the problem of low achievement."[12] Better and more helpful approaches to student achievement include the following strategies:

- Use promotion combined with individualized instruction.
- Promote to a transition class in which students receive help to master skills not previously achieved.
- Use afterschool and summer programs to help students master skills.
- Provide children specific and individualized help in mastery of skills.
- Work with parents to teach them how to help their children work on mastery skills.

- Identify children who may need help before they enter first grade so that developmental services are provided early.

- Use multiage grouping as a means to provide for a broader range of children's abilities and to provide children the benefits that come from multiage grouping.

- Have a professional teach or stay with the same group of children over a period of several years as a means of getting to know children and their families better and, as a result, providing better for children's educational and developmental needs. This approach is also called *sustained instruction.*

- Use a nongraded classroom. The nongraded classroom and nongraded institution go hand in hand. In the nongraded classroom, individual differences are recognized and accounted for. The state of Kentucky mandates that grades 1 through 3 be nongraded. Advocates of nongraded classrooms offer the following advantages:

Opportunities for individualized instruction
An enhanced social atmosphere because older children help younger
    children and there are more opportunities for role modeling
Few, if any, retentions
Students not having to progress through a grade-level curriculum in a
    lockstep approach with their age peers

Any effort to improve student achievement must emphasize helping children rather than using practices that threaten to detract from their self-image and make them solely responsible for their failure.

CHARACTERISTICS OF PRIMARY EDUCATION PROFESSIONALS

When all is said and done, it is the professional who sets the tone and direction for classroom instruction and learning. Without quality professionals, a quality program is impossible. Quality primary education professionals must be humane, loving, and caring people. In addition, they must be capable of interacting with very energetic young children. Unlike upper elementary children, who are more goal oriented and self-directed, primary children need help in developing the skills and personal habits that will enable them to be independent learners. Helping them develop these skills and habits should be the foremost goal of primary education professionals. The following guidelines will help you implement that goal:

- *Plan for instruction.* Planning is the basis for the vision of what professionals want for themselves and for children. Professionals who try to operate without a plan are like builders without a blueprint. Although planning takes time, it saves time in the long run, and it provides direction for instruction.

- *Be the classroom leader.* A quality professional leads the classroom. Some professionals forget this, and although children at all ages are capable of performing leadership responsibilities, it is the professional who sets the guidelines within which effective instruction occurs. Without strong leadership—not overbearing or dictatorial leadership—classrooms do not operate well. Planning for instruction helps a professional lead.

- *Involve children in meaningful learning tasks.* To learn, children need to be active and involved. To learn to read, they must read; to learn to write, they must write. Although these guidelines may seem self-evident, they are not always implemented. To learn, children need to spend time on learning tasks.

- *Provide individualized instruction.* A range of abilities and interests is apparent in any classroom of twenty-five or more children. The early education professional must provide for these differences if children are going to learn to their fullest. There is a difference between individual and individualized instruction; it is impossible to provide individual attention to all children all the time, but providing for children at their individual levels is both possible and necessary. Educators are often accused of teaching to the average, boring the more able, and leaving the less able behind. This criticism can be addressed with individualized instruction. (See Chapter 1 for more information about professionalism and becoming a professional.)

THE FUTURE OF PRIMARY EDUCATION

Although the educational system in general is slow to meet the demands and dictates of society, it is likely the dramatic changes seen in primary education will continue in the next decade. The direction will be determined by continual reassessment of the purpose of education and attempts to match the needs of society to the goals of schools. Drug use, child abuse, the breakup of the family, and illiteracy are some of the societal problems the schools are being asked to address in significant ways.

Increasingly schools are asked to prepare children for their places in the world of tomorrow. All early childhood programs must help children and youth develop the skills necessary for life success. Even with the trend toward having children spend more time in school, we know that learning does not end with school and that children do not learn all they will need to know in an academic setting. It makes sense, therefore, to empower students with skills they can use throughout life in all kinds of interpersonal and organizational settings. Such skills include the following:

- The ability to communicate with others, orally and in writing
- The ability to work well with people of all races, cultures, and personalities
- The ability to be responsible for directing one's behavior
- The desire and ability for success in life—not as measured by earning a lot of money but by becoming a productive member of society
- The desire and ability to continue learning throughout life

ACTIVITIES FOR REFLECTION AND RESEARCH

1. Interview parents and teachers to determine their views pro and con of nonpromotion in the primary grades. Summarize your findings. What are your opinions on retention?

2. List five things primary teachers can do to promote positive assessment in the primary years.

3. In addition to the characteristics of primary teachers listed in this chapter, what others do you think are desirable? Recall your own primary teachers. What characteristics did they have that had the greatest influence on you?

4. You have been asked to submit ten recommendations for changing and improving primary education. Provide a rationale for each of your recommendations.

5. What other issues of primary education would you add to those mentioned in this chapter? How would you suggest dealing with them?

6. Identify five contemporary issues or concerns facing society, and tell how teachers and primary schools could address each of them.

7. Explain how first grade children's cognitive and physical differences make a difference in how they are taught. Give specific examples.

8. Of the three primary grades, decide which you would most like to teach, and explain your reasons.

9. What do you think are the most important subjects of the primary grades? Why? What would you say to a parent who thought any subjects besides reading, writing, and arithmetic were a waste of time?

READINGS FOR FURTHER ENRICHMENT

Kostelnik, M., A. Soderman, and A. Whiren, *Developmentally Appropriate Curriculum: Best Practices in Early Childhood Education* (Upper Saddle River, N.J.: Prentice Hall, 1998).

This comprehensive text brings together the best information currently available for developing an integrated approach to curriculum and instruction in the early years. It is designed for current and future early childhood professionals working in formal group settings with young children ranging in age from three to eight. The text also creates a bridge between the worlds of child care and early education, as well as between preprimary and primary programs.

Wadsworth, Barry J., *Piaget's Theory of Cognitive and Affective Development* (White Plains, NY: Longman, 1996).

Provides a clear and interesting introduction to Piaget's theory and tells how to apply concepts and ideas to primary school practice. Helps teachers develop a better understanding of children and the education process.

Wortham, Sue. *Early Childhood Curriculum: Developmental Bases for Learning and Teaching* (Upper Saddle River, NJ: Merrill Pub, 1998).

This text brings together the issues of child development and curriculum planning to create a cohesive plan for guiding the education of children from infancy to age 8 in child care, preschool, and primary school settings.

RESEARCH ON THE INTERNET

The National Network for Child Care
http://www.nncc.org/

The "Taking Care of Kids" portion of this web site contains several articles with information on the following topic areas: Child Abuse, Child Development, Curriculum, Disability, Diversity, Guidance and Discipline, Health and Safety, Nutrition, Parent Involvement, and School-Age Care. Each category contains detailed information of interest to parents and child care providers and educators.

Funderstanding online

www.funderstanding.com/theories.html

A web site dedicated to keeping you informed about children including learning theories and development.

NOTES

1. S. Tishman, D. Perkins, and E. Jay, *The Thinking Classroom* (Boston: Allyn & Bacon 1995), p. 2.

2. Adapted from "You CAN Teach Thinking Skills," by Scott Willis from *Instructor,* February 1993. Copyright © 1993 by Scholastic, Inc. Reprinted by permission.

3. Hilda Taba, *Teacher's Handbook for Elementary Social Studies* (Reading, MA: Addison-Wesley, 1967), pp. 92–109.

4. P. Kneedler, "California Assesses Critical Thinking," in *Developing Minds: A Resource Book for Teaching Thinking,* ed., A. Costa (Alexandria, VA: Association for Supervision and Curriculum Development, 1985), p. 277.

5. A. Woolfolk, *Educational Psychology* (Boston: Allyn & Bacon, 1995), p. 292.

6. R. E. Slavin, "Cooperative Learning and the Cooperative School," *Educational Leadership,* 45, 1987, pp. 7–13.

7. R. Brandt, "On Cooperation in Schools: A Conversation with David and Roger Johnson," *Educational Leadership,* 45, 1987, pp. 14–19.

8. Slavin, "Cooperative Learning," pp. 8–9.

9. Judith M. Newman, "Using Children's Books to Teach Reading," in *Whole Language: Theory in Use,* ed., Judith M. Newman (Portsmouth, NH: Heinemann Educational Books, 1985), p. 61.

10. Ibid, pp. 62–63.

11. J. Lloyd Eldredge, *Teaching Decoding in Holistic Classrooms,* © 1995, pp. 5–6. Adapted by permission of Prentice Hall, Upper Saddle River, New Jersey.

12. Monica Overman, "Practical Applications of Research: Student Promotion and Retention," *Phi Delta Kappan,* 67, April 1986, p. 612.

CHAPTER

12

Providing Appropriate Education for All

FOCUS QUESTIONS

1. What terminology and legal definitions are related to children with special needs?
2. What language and terminology are associated with multicultural education?
3. What are reasons for contemporary interest in children with diverse needs?
4. What issues relate to teaching children with diverse needs?
5. How do early childhood professionals infuse multicultural content in curriculum, programs, and activities?
6. How would you educate both yourself and young children for living in a diverse society?

Children with diverse needs are in every program, school, and classroom in the United States. As an early childhood professional, you will teach students who have a variety of special needs: These students may come from low-income families or different racial and ethnic groups; they may have exceptional abilities or disabilities. Students with special needs are often discriminated against because of their disability, socioeconomic background, language, culture, or gender. You and your colleagues will be challenged to provide for all students an education that is appropriate to their individual needs in order to help them achieve their best. Your challenge includes learning as much as you can about the diverse needs of children and collaborating with other professionals to identify and develop teaching strategies, programs, and curricula for them. Most of all, you need to be a strong advocate for meeting all children's individual needs.

EVOLVING PRACTICES

Take a few minutes now to review in Chapter 2 the information we discussed on issues relating to teaching children with disabilities. Attitudes toward providing for all children with disabilities have changed and are continuing to change. Today there is recognition that as a society and as an early childhood professional we have to ensure that all the needs of all children are met to the best of our abilities. As the profession has and continues to meet the challenge of providing for all children, a number of significant trends have developed which are and will continue to influence how professionals and programs deliver services. One of these trends is a family-centered approach. (Review this approach again in Chapter 2). Although children come to centers and other programs, they come from homes and families. So, working with parents and other family members is seen as a way of truly meeting children's needs. And, at the same time, you and other professionals can meet family members' needs as well.

A second trend is working with and through community-based programs to provide appropriate services. A community-based approach is based on the ideas that in numbers there is strength and that it is more cost-effective to use existing services to provide for children rather than duplicate them in early childhood programs. When no community-based services are available, then the program has to provide them. When they exist, programs should use them. Part of your role is to identify existing community services.

The community-based approach results in a third trend, the interdisciplinary collaboration between and among professionals. No longer do we view the field of early childhood as sufficient to meet the needs of all children. Rather, it takes the combined efforts of disciplines—child development, psychology, nutrition, social work and others—working together for the good of all children and families. A purpose of such interdisciplinary collaboration is the providing of coordinated and comprehensive services. As an early childhood professional, you will be involved in all of these trends and more.

Legislation and Public Policy

The Individuals with Disabilities Education Act (IDEA) defines *children with disabilities*

> as those children with mental retardation, hearing impairments including deafness, speech or language impairments, blindness, serious emotional disturbance, orthopedic impairments, autism, traumatic brain injury, other health impairments, or specific learning disabilities; and who, by reason thereof, need special education and related services.[1]

Table 12–1 shows the number of persons birth to age twenty-one with disabilities in the various categories. About 10 to 12 percent of the nation's students have disabilities. Please refer to Figure 12–1 (following page) for a glossary of terms related to children with disabilities.

TABLE 12–1
Children Served in Federally Supported Programs by Type of Disability

	Numbers Served	Percent of Total Students Enrollment
All disabilities	5,125,000	12.43
Specific learning disabilities	2,354,000	5.75
Speech or language impairments	996,000	2.28
Mental retardation	519,000	1.27
Serious emotional disturbance	401,000	0.98
Hearing impairments	60,000	0.15
Orthopedic impairments	52,000	0.14
Other health impairments	65,000	0.30
Visual impairments	23,000	0.06
Multiple disabilities	102,000	0.21
Deaf and blind	1,000	0.01
Autism and other	19,000	0.09
Preschool disabled	531,000	1.21

Note: Based on the enrollment in public schools, kindergarten through twelfth grade.
Source: U.S. Department of Education, Office of Special Education and Rehabilitation Services, *Annual Report to Congress on the Implementation of the Individuals with Disabilities Education Act,* various years, and unpublished tabulations; and National Center for Education Statistics, *Common Core of Data Survey.* (Table prepared 1997.)

FIGURE 12–1
Glossary Relating to Children with Disabilities

Adaptive education. An educational approach aimed at providing learning experiences that help each student achieve desired educational goals. The term *adaptive* refers to the modification of school learning environments to respond effectively to student differences and to enhance the individual's ability to succeed in learning in such environments.*

Children with disabilities. Replaces former terms such as *handicapped.* To avoid labeling children, do not use the reversal of these words (i.e., disabled children).

Coteaching. The process by which a regular classroom professional and a special educator or a person trained in exceptional student education team-teach, in the same classroom, a group of regular and mainstreamed children.

Disability. A physical or mental impairment that substantially limits one or more major life activities.

Early education and care settings. Promotes the idea that all children learn and that child care and other programs should be educating children birth to age eight.

Early intervention. Providing services to children and families as early in the child's life as possible in order to prevent or help with a special need or needs.

Exceptional student education. Replaces the term *special education;* refers to the education of children with special needs.

Full inclusion. The mainstreaming or inclusion of all children with disabilities into natural environments such as playgrounds, family day care centers, child care centers, preschool, kindergarten, and primary grades.

Individualized education program (IEP). A written plan for a child stating what will be done, how it will be done, and when it will be done.

Integration. A generic term that refers to educating children with disabilities along with typically developing children. This education can occur in mainstream, reverse mainstream, and full-inclusion programs.

Least restrictive environment (LRE). Children with disabilities are educated with children who are not disabled, and special classes, separate schooling, or other removal of children with disabilities from the regular educational environment occurs only when the nature or severity of the disability is such that education in regular classes with the use of supplementary aids and services cannot be achieved satisfactorily.†

Limited English proficiency (LEP). Describes children who have limited English skills.

Mainstreaming. The social and educational integration of children with special needs into the general instructional process; usually a regular classroom program.

Merged classroom. A classroom that includes—merges—children with special needs and children without special needs and teaches them together in one classroom.

Natural environment. Any environment it is natural for any child to be in, such as home, child care center, preschool, kindergarten, primary grades, playground, and so on.

Normalized setting. A place that is "normal" or best for the child.

Reverse mainstreaming. The process by which typically developing children are placed in programs for children with disabilities. In reverse mainstreaming, children with disabilities are in the majority.

Typically developing children. Children who are developing according to and within the boundaries of normal growth and development.

*Margaret C. Wang, *Adaptive Education Strategies: Building on Diversity* (Baltimore: Brooks, 1992), pp. 3–4.
†Public Law 101-476, 30 October 1990. Stat. 1103.

IDEA's Six Principles

IDEA established the following six principles for professionals to follow as they provide educational and other sources to children with special needs:[2]

1. *Zero reject.* A rule against excluding any student.
2. *Nondiscriminatory evaluation.* Requiring schools to evaluate students fairly to determine if they have a disability and, if so, what kind and how extensive a disability they have.
3. *Appropriate education.* Requiring schools to provide individually tailored education for each student based on the evaluation and augmented by related or supplementary services.
4. *Least restrictive environment.* Requiring schools to educate students with disabilities with nondisabled students to the maximum extent appropriate for the students with disabilities.
5. *Procedural due process.* Providing safeguards for students against schools' actions, including a right to sue in court.
6. *Parental and student participation.* Requiring schools to collaborate with parents and adolescent students in designing and carrying out special education programs.

Guaranteeing a Free and Appropriate Education

IDEA mandates a free and appropriate education (FAPE) for all persons between the ages of three and twenty-one. To guarantee students a free appropriate public education, IDEA provides federal money to state and local educational agencies to help educate students in the following age groups:

1. From birth to age three (early intervention)
2. From age three to age six (early childhood special education)
3. From age six to age eighteen
4. From age eighteen to age twenty-one (transition or aging out of school)

The state and local agencies, however, must agree to comply with the federal law or else they will not receive federal money. Exceptional education and related services specified by IDEA are shown in Figure 12–2.

Creating an Individualized Education Program

Exceptional student education laws currently mandate the creation of an individualized education program (IEP), which requires a plan for the individualization of each student's instruction. This requires creating learning objectives, and basing each student's learning plan on his or her specific

FIGURE 12–2
Services Provided by IDEA

1. "Audiology" includes identification of children with hearing loss; determination of the range, nature, and degree of hearing loss; and creation and administration of programs for [treatment and] prevention of hearing loss.

2. "Counseling services" means services provided by qualified social workers, psychologists, guidance counselors, or other qualified personnel.

3. "Early identification and assessment of disabilities in children" means the implementation of a formal plan for identifying a disability as early as possible in a child's life.

4. "Medical services" means services provided by a licensed physician to determine a child's medically related disability that results in the child's need for special education and related services.

5. "Occupational therapy" includes improving, developing, or restoring functions impaired or lost through illness, injury, or deprivation.

6. "Parent counseling and training" means assisting parents in understanding the special needs of their child and providing parents with information about child development.

7. "Physical therapy" means services provided by a qualified physical therapist.

8. "Psychological services" includes administering psychological and educational tests, and other assessment procedures; interpreting assessment results; obtaining, integrating, and interpreting information about child behavior and conditions relating to learning; consulting with other staff members in planning school programs to meet the special needs of children as indicated by psychological tests, interviews, and behavioral evaluations; and planning and managing a program of psychological services, including psychological counseling for children and parents.

9. "Recreation" includes assessment of leisure function, therapeutic recreation services, recreation programs in schools and community agencies, and leisure education.

10. "Rehabilitative counseling services" means services that focus specifically on career development, employment preparation, achieving independence, and integration in the workplace and community of a student with a disability.

11. "School health services" means services provided by a qualified school nurse or other qualified person.

12. "Social work services in schools" includes preparing a social or developmental history on a child with a disability, group and individual counseling with the child and family, working with those problems in a child's living situation (home, school, and community) that affect the child's adjustment in school, and mobilizing school and community resources to enable the child to learn as effectively as possible in his or her educational program.

13. "Speech pathology" includes identification, diagnosis, and appraisal of specific speech or language impairments, provision of speech and language services, and counseling and guidance of parents, children, and teachers regarding speech and language impairments.

14. "Transportation" includes travel to and from school and between schools, travel in and around school buildings, and specialized equipment (such as special or adapted buses, lifts, and ramps), if required to provide special transportation for a child with a disability.

15. Assistive technology and services are devices and related services that restore lost capacities or that improve capacities.

needs, disabilities, and preferences, as well as on those of the parents. A collaborative team of regular and special educators creates these objectives. The IEP must specify what will be done for the child, how and when it will be done, and by whom; and this information must be in writing. In developing the IEP, a person trained in diagnosing disabling conditions, such as a school psychologist, must be part of the IEP team, as well as the parent and, when appropriate, the child.

Function of the IEP

The IEP has several purposes:

- First, it protects children and parents by ensuring that planning will occur.
- Second, the IEP guarantees that children will have plans tailored to their individual strengths, weaknesses, and learning styles.
- Third, the IEP helps professionals and other instructional and administrative personnel focus their teaching and resources on children's specific needs, promoting the best use of everyone's time, efforts, and talents.
- Fourth, the IEP helps ensure that children with disabilities will receive a range of services from other agencies. The plan must not only include an educational component, but also specify how the child's total needs will be met. If a child can benefit from special services such as physical therapy, for example, it must be written into the IEP. This provision is beneficial not only for children but for classroom professionals as well, because it broadens their perspective of the educational function.
- Fifth, the IEP helps clarify and refine decisions about what is best for children—where they should be placed, how they should be taught and helped. It also ensures that children will not be categorized or labeled without discussion of their unique needs.
- Finally, review of the IEP at least annually encourages professionals to consider how and what children have learned, to determine whether what was prescribed is effective, and to prescribe new or modified strategies.

IDEA for Infants and Toddlers

Under Part H of IDEA, funds are provided for infants and toddlers to receive early intervention services for the following purposes:

- Enhance the child's development and minimize the potential for any developmental delays.
- Reduce the costs of educating the child by minimizing the need for special education when the child reaches school age.
- Minimize the likelihood that the family will institutionalize the child and increase the chances that the child, when an adult, will live independently.
- Enhance the family's capacities to meet the child's special needs.[3]

FIGURE 12–3

Services That Can Be Provided
under Part H

Source: From 34 *Code of Federal
Register* (CFR) §303.12(d).

Assistive Technology Devices and Services
Audiology
Family Training, Counseling, and Home Visits
Health Services
Medical Services for Diagnosis or Evaluation
Nursing Services
Nutrition Services
Occupational Therapy
Physical Therapy
Psychological Services
Service Coordination Services
Social Work Services
Special Instruction
Speech-Language Pathology
Transportation and Related Costs
Vision Services

Services that can be provided under Part H include (but are not limited to) those shown in Figure 12–3.

The Individualized Family Service Plan. As we discussed in Chapter 2, the Individualized Family Service Plan (ISFP) is a written document that documents and details the implementation of early intervention services for infants and toddlers and their families. The process of developing the IFSP consists of several steps. First, an assessment plan is conducted in cooperation with the parent(s). This assessment determines the child's status in the following developmental areas: physical, cognitive, communication/language, social-emotional, and adaptive—meaning how well the child can function in daily life. Second, an assessment is made of the family's resources, needs, and concerns and the child's strengths and needs. Third, in consultation and collaboration with the family, the IFSP is developed. Finally, the IFSP is implemented as soon as possible. This final step also includes monitoring how well the implementation is proceeding and ongoing evaluation of its effectiveness in meeting stated needs and goals. By law, the IFSP has to be reviewed at least every six months.

As an early childhood professional you may be involved in developing and implementing IFSPs. You will also play a key role in helping parents identify, access, and receive the services they and their children need. Also, you will play a major role in helping assure that there is a continuity of services between your program and other programs.

**VIDEO
VIEWPOINT**

TEACHER'S LITTLE HELPER

As more children become more difficult for teachers to teach and control, teachers are increasingly recommending that children be placed on medication such as Ritalin and Prozac to control their behavior. This practice of using drugs to control children's behavior, rather than teaching children to control their own behavior, is a growing concern for many early childhood professionals. Growing numbers of professionals object to Ritalin, Prozac and other drugs being part of the teacher's "bag of tricks."

Reflective Discussion Questions: What are the controversies surrounding the use of Ritalin to control children's behaviors? What are some reasons why teachers would recommend that children should be placed on Ritalin? Would you as an early childhood professional consider Ritalin an appropriate alternative for use with young children? Do you think the use of Ritalin is an epidemic?

Reflective Decision Making: Interview parents whose children are on Ritalin. Why was the child placed on Ritalin? Do the parents believe that Ritalin is helping their child? How? What advice would you give to a parent who asked you if you thought Ritalin is an appropriate response to children's destructive/aggressive/hyperactive behavior? What would be some activities you could recommend for controlling children's behavior without medication? Interview early childhood teachers and ask their opinions regarding the use of Ritalin. Based on your discussions with teachers, do you think they are pressuring parents into having Ritalin prescribed for their children?

What Is Inclusion?

Inclusion is the practice of ensuring that all students with disabilities participate with other students in all aspects of the educational setting of which they are a part, including playgrounds, family day care centers, child care centers, preschools, and general education classrooms. IDEA specifies that

> To the maximum extent appropriate, children with disabilities . . . are educated with children who are not disabled, and that special classes, separate schooling, or other removal of children with disabilities from the regular environment occurs only when the nature or severity of the disability is such that education in regular classes with the use of supplementary aids and services cannot be achieved satisfactorily.[4]

What Are Practices for Inclusion in Preschool Settings?

"Inclusion is . . . the underlying supposition that all children will be based in classrooms they would attend if they did not have a disability."[5] Inclusive practices accommodate the diverse needs of all children by "including" them in physical, social, and academic activities with typically developing children in regular classrooms or physical educational environments—natural environments to the maximum extent possible. Natural environments are identified as any environment in which it would be natural for any young child to be, such as child care centers, family day care centers, preschools, kindergartens, primary grades, and playgrounds. Inclusion of young children with disabilities in natural environments is an example of a *best practice*. Best practices in early childhood programming for children with disabilities have traditionally been based on a special education perspective.[6,7] As early childhood educational practice moves toward a more equitable inclusion of children with disabilities, professionals must integrate early childhood special education (ECSE) practices with early childhood education practices.[8]

PROGRAM IN ACTION

SPECIAL CARE, INC.

Special CARE, Inc. is a private, non-profit, licensed, NAEYC accredited, child-care center. The program serves 150 children with developmental disabilities on a full-time or part-time basis. Two-thirds of the population are children with various developmental and/or physical disabilities, while one-third are non-disabled or "typically" developing children.

Special CARE believes that children with disabilities learn more effectively and develop a positive self image through playing and learning with their developmental peers. In addition, non-disabled children benefit by learning to appreciate individual differences. They are able to understand that children are children first. They recognize very early that having a disability is not the same as "who" you are.

Special CARE recognizes that the number one need identified by parents of children with disabilities is that of child care services. To meet this need, Special CARE's pre-school programs are designed to serve children ages six weeks to six years. Our before/after and summer school programs generally serve children up to age twenty-one. Special CARE is open year round and our hours of operation are 7:00 AM to 6:00 PM Monday to Friday.

The second need identified by parents is for respite services. This is a short term "break" for the parent to have personal time, take care of household responsibilities, have time with their spouse, take time for a sibling, or be able to meet any other family needs. Special CARE also provides a Saturday afternoon Respite Program from 1:00 PM to 5:00 PM bi-monthly, year round as funding permits.

Special CARE provides use of the facility to host parent support group meetings which are coordinated by parents to assist families with emotional needs as well as information. There are several stages of acceptance that parents and other family members experience when a child with a disability joins the family. The support group allows families an opportunity to realize they are not alone and that others can help them.

The concept of Special CARE is that early intervention programs and parent education help to prevent the cumulative effects of disabilities. The earlier the intervention program begins, the greater the benefits to the child, family, and to society. It is also more cost effective for parents and future service providers to begin intervention as early as possible. Research shows that early intervention services help remediate deficits, minimize failures, and increase socialization skills.

ECSE programs are oriented more toward teacher-directed activities, with a focus on behavioral learning, and are designed to meet individualized goals and objectives. Implicit in the ECSE design is the fact that children with disabilities may not get to take advantage of typical environmental experiences and child-initiated activities promoted as more developmentally appropriate practice by professional organizations such as NAEYC. Thus, by its very nature and language, "best practices" generated by the field of special education has inadvertently communicated that what professionals do for children with disabilities must be somehow very different from the goals set for typically developing children by the rest of the early childhood profession.[9] Early childhood professionals increasingly are proposing the creation of one

Classroom environments are designed to meet the individual needs of the children enrolled. We provide a Comprehensive Approach for Rehabilitation and Education. All areas of development are addressed within the daily routines and provided in a positive, nurturing atmosphere. Developmental goals are established through standardized and/or developmental evaluations. Individual Education Plans are developed annually for children with and without disabilities.

In addition to child care services, therapeutic interventions are provided on-site to reduce scheduling conflicts while parents work and/or further their education. By providing Speech, Physical and Occupational therapies on-site, parents have fewer appointment demands, teachers are able to consult with therapists and incorporate goals into the classroom routines, and children are able to receive therapies at times that are suitable for their developmental needs.

A team approach is fundamental to meeting children's needs. Teams include all relevant teaching staff, therapists, the parent(s), the child, administrators, and any other professionals who assist the family/child. Methods for carry over of goals

are discussed with team members to ensure consistency for the child.

The benefits of Special CARE's approach are documented by a study conducted by the Oklahoma Health Sciences Center, Department of Psychiatry and Behavioral Sciences. In this study, students were evaluated over the course of one year.

This study concluded that Special CARE's students with disabilities are in fact progressing at a more rapid rate than would be statistically expected for the disability. Also, and equally significant, the study concluded that non-disabled children were in no way ill affected by being essentially the "minority" within a program for children with disabilities. This conclusion has far reaching implications for mainstreaming and/or inclusion efforts for all levels of education and public opinion.

Special CARE, Inc. also serves as a practicum site for university students in Early Childhood Education, Special Education, Physical, Speech, and Occupational Therapies, Nursing and Medical Residents, and other related fields. The program also involves other groups, such as the Foster Grandparent Program, civic organizations, high school student groups, and individuals.

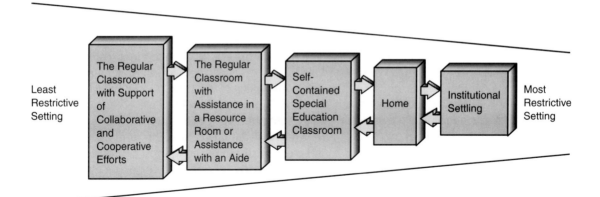

FIGURE 12–4
A Continuum of Services
Source: G. S. Morrison, *Teaching in America* (Needham Heights, MA: Allyn & Bacon, 1997), p. 171. Copyright © 1997 by Allyn & Bacon. Reprinted by permission.

system of early childhood education for all. Essentially this system would frame a plan based on what it takes to allow all young children to succeed. Practices that seem to be working for all children focus on developing language in inclusive, natural settings.

A Continuum of Inclusive Services

The policy of the Council for Exceptional Children (CEC), a professional organization of special educators, is as follows:

> CEC believes that a continuum of services must be available for all children, youth, and young adults. CEC also believes that the concept of inclusion is a meaningful goal to be pursued in our schools and communities. In addition, CEC believes children, youth, and young adults with disabilities should be served whenever possible in general education classrooms in inclusive neighborhood schools and community settings. Such settings should be strengthened and supported by an infusion of especially trained personnel and other appropriate supportive practices according to the individual needs of the child.[10]

A *continuum of services* means that a full range of services is available for individuals from the most restrictive to the least restrictive placements. This continuum implies a graduated range of services, with one level of services leading directly to the next. For example, a continuum of services for students with disabilities would define institutional placement as the most restrictive and a general education classroom as the least restrictive (Figure 12–4).

The web sites shown in Figure 12–5 will help you access information you can use in your work with children and their families.

FIGURE 12–5
Web Sites

http://www.ed.gov/offices/OSERS
http://www.census.gov/
http://www.cfoc.org/
http://nch.ori.net/families.html
http://www.medaccess.com/abuse/abuse_toc.html
http://child.cornell.edu/capn.html
http://www.aed.org:80/nichcy/
http://curry.edschool.virginia.edu/curry/dept/cise/ose

STRATEGIES FOR TEACHING CHILDREN WITH DISABILITIES

In addition to the teaching tips I shared with you in Chapter 2, here are some other ideas for you to consider when teaching children with disabilities.

- Use social interactions as a basis for your teaching. Learning is a social process; that is, social interactions provide both the context and the means for children to learn. So, involve children in interactions with you, their peers, and other adults.

- Provide motivating activities and events. While motivation plays a powerful role in everyone's learning, this is especially true of children with disabilities. Identify those objects, activities, and people for which the child shows high preference and use these as a basis for teaching and learning.

- Help children be independent, successful, and in control of their efforts to interact with the environment and others. Provide for children to initiate activities with objects and people in the world around them. Be sure to tell children how their actions are making a difference in their learning and how they contribute to the learning of others. A personal feeling of control and success is a powerful incentive for learning.

- Communicate, communicate, and communicate. How adults talk to children has a powerful influence on learning. How children talk to each other also influences learning. When communicating with children use the names of things and actions and be specific and concrete about what you are talking about. Make sure children understand what you are talking about. Talk about what children are doing and what they are talking about. Engage children in the communication process.

- Establish routines. Routines provide a psychological zone of comfort and security. Routines bring predictability to the learning process and make it easier for children to learn.

- Use play as a primary basis for teaching and learning. Review our previous discussions about how play supports learning and how to implement play-based programs.

- Arrange the environment to maximize learning. The social environment is an important part of learning. So is the physical. Make adjustments in the environment that are necessary to accommodate children's particular disabilities. Remember that you are trying to provide as natural a learning environment as possible so children feel a part of and involved in all activities.

WHAT IS MULTICULTURALISM?

In its simplest form, multicultural awareness is the appreciation for and understanding of peoples' cultures, socioeconomic status, and gender. It also includes understanding one's own culture. Some early childhood professionals assume they are promoting multicultural awareness when they are actually presenting only a fragment of the concept.

Multicultural awareness in the classroom is not the presentation of other cultures to the exclusion of the cultures represented by children in the class. Rather, multicultural awareness programs and activities focus on other cultures while at the same time making children aware of the content, nature, and richness of their own. The terms and concepts for describing multicultural education and awareness (Figure 12–6) are not as important as the methods, procedures, and activities for developing meaningful early childhood programs. Learning about other cultures concurrently with their own culture enables children to integrate commonalties and appreciate differences without inferring inferiority or superiority of one or the other.

WHO ARE MULTICULTURAL CHILDREN?

The population of young children in the United States reflects the population at large, and represents a number of different cultures and ethnicities. Thus, many cities and school districts have populations that express great ethnic diversity, including Asian Americans, Native Americans, African Americans, and Hispanic Americans. For example, the Dade County, Florida, school district has children from 122 countries of the world, each with its own culture.

The great diversity of young children creates interesting challenges for early childhood educators. Many children speak languages other than English, behave differently reflective of cultural customs and values, and come from many socioeconomic backgrounds. Because of the multicultural composition of society, as an early childhood educator, you will want to promote multicultural awareness in your classroom.

In Chapters 1 and 2 we stressed the diverse nature of U.S. society. We emphasize it again here. The reality today is that the United States is a multicultural country. Early childhood professionals must prepare themselves and their children to live happily and productively in this society.

FIGURE 12–6
Glossary Relating to Multiculturalism

The following terms will assist you as you study this chapter:

Antibias: An active/activist approach to challenging prejudice, stereotyping, bias, and the "isms."

Bias-free: Programs, activities, materials, and behaviors that are free from biased perceptions, language, attitudes, and actions.

Bilingual education: "The use of two languages for the purposes of academic instruction with an organized curriculum that includes, at a minimum, (1) continued primary language (language 1) development, (2) English (language 2) acquisition, and (3) subject matter instruction through (language 1) and (language 2). Bilingual education programs assist limited-English-proficient (LEP) students in developing literacy both in English and the primary language to a level at which they can succeed in an English-only classroom. Programs may also include native speakers of English [these are children whose primary language is English and are learning a second language]."*

Diversity: Describes various cultures, ethnic groups, socioeconomic groups, languages, and gender identities that exist in society at large and early childhood programs in particular. Diversity is seen as a positive rather than negative state. Consequently, diversity is celebrated, studied, and respected. Additionally, early childhood professionals try to ensure that cultural diversity exists in curriculum, teaching, caregiving practices, and activities.

Infusion: A process of integrating multicultural perspectives into the curriculum, as well as promoting content awareness, sensitivity, knowledge, and behaviors. Infusion is used as a means of transforming existing or new curricula so that they are truly multicultural.

Language maintenance: "The preservation of a native language when a second language is learned as opposed to displacement of the native language by the second language."

Limited-English-proficient (LEP) parents: "Parents whose children have been identified as limited-English-proficient and/or who are also limited in their proficiency in English."

Limited-English-proficient (LEP) student: "A student whose primary language is other than English and who does not comprehend, speak, read, or write at a level necessary to receive instruction only in English with native English-speaking peers."

Mainstream: "In the field of bilingual education, this term refers to the monolingual English curriculum or classroom."

Multicultural education: Multicultural education is education that prepares students to live, learn, communicate, and work to achieve common goals in a culturally diverse world by fostering understanding, appreciation, and respect for people of other ethnic, gender, socioeconomic, language, and cultural backgrounds.

Nonsexist: Attitudes and behaviors that convey that the sexes are equal.

*Quoted definitions are from the Division of Human Resource Development, Florida Atlantic University Multifunctional Resource Center. *Empowering ESOL Teachers: An Overview.* vol. 2 (Tallahassee, FL: Florida Department of Education, 1993). Appendix A. Glossary, sections VII-X, pp. i-vi.

Today's society is multiculturally pluralistic. Early childhood professionals must consider the diverse needs of students, including gender, ethnicity, race, and socioeconomic factors, when planning learning opportunities in activities and programs.

Yet how to prepare children of all cultures for productive living is a major challenge for everyone. For instance, how can early childhood professionals use technology to help millions of immigrant children become literate both in their native language and in English? How can professionals help ensure that multicultural children will not become technological illiterates? The answers to these questions are not easy to give or implement.

Promoting multiculturalism in an early childhood program has implications far beyond the program itself. Multiculturalism influences and affects work habits, interpersonal relations, and a person's general outlook on life. Early childhood professionals must take these multicultural influences into consideration when designing curriculum and instructional processes for the impressionable children they will teach. One way to accomplish the primary goal of multicultural education—to positively change the lives of children and their families—is to infuse multiculturalism into early childhood activities and practices.

WHAT IS MULTICULTURAL INFUSION?

Infusion means that multicultural education permeates the curriculum to alter or affect the way young children and teachers look at diversity issues. In a larger perspective, infusion strategies are used to ensure that multiculturalism becomes a part of the entire center, school, and home. Infusion processes used by early childhood programs encompass a range of practices that embody the following precepts:

1. Foster cultural awareness.
2. Teach to children's learning styles.
3. Encourage cooperative learning.
4. Promote and use conflict resolution strategies.
5. Welcome parent and community involvement.

We will discuss each of these practices in detail so you may fully understand how to apply them to your life and program. Keep in mind that as an early childhood professional, you will want to be in a constant process of developing your multicultural awareness, attitude, knowledge, and skills.

Foster Cultural Awareness

Assess Your Attitudes toward Children

- Do you have different expectations of children from different neighborhoods? For example, do you expect a higher level of work from students who live in affluent neighborhoods than from those who live in trailer parks?
- With which children do you feel most comfortable? Are you influenced by what children wear? The positions their parents hold? The color of their skin?
- What do you know about children's communities? In order to provide schooling relevant to students' lives, teachers need a sense of children's worldviews. What is it like living in the community? What roles and relationships are most important?
- Do you expect children to learn through your ways of teaching only, or do you find out in which modes of instruction children learn best? When teaching in a multicultural manner, do not try to mold children to fit your manner of teaching. Instead, learn about them and change your teaching to affirm them.[11]

Guidelines and Processes for Fostering Awareness

As an early childhood professional, you must keep in mind that you are the key to a multicultural classroom. The following guidelines can help you in teaching multiculturalism:

- Recognize that all children are unique. They all have special talents, abilities, and styles of learning and relating to others. Provide opportunities for children to be different and to use their abilities.

Not all children learn in the same way. Some children have individual styles of learning. It is important to assess each child's learning style and teach each child appropriately. What style of learning do you use to learn best?

- Promote uniqueness and diversity as positive.
- Get to know, appreciate, and respect the cultural backgrounds of your children. Visit families and community neighborhoods to learn more about cultures and religions and the ways of life they engender.
- Infuse children's culture (and other cultures as well) in your teaching.
- Use authentic situations to provide for cultural learning and understanding. For example, a field trip to a culturally diverse neighborhood of your city or town provides children an opportunity for understanding firsthand many of the details about how people conduct their daily lives. Such an experience provides wonderful opportunities for involving children in writing, cooking, reading, and dramatic play activities.
- Use authentic assessment activities to assess fully children's learning and growth. Portfolios (see Chapter 7) are ideal for assessing children in non-biased and culturally sensitive ways. The point is that early childhood professionals should use varied ways of assessing children.
- Infuse culture into your lesson planning, teaching, and caregiving. Use all subject areas—math, science, language arts, literacy, music, art, and social studies—to relate culture to all the children and all you do.
- Use children's interests and experiences to form a basis for planning lessons and developing activities. This approach makes students feel good about their backgrounds, cultures, families, and experiences. Also, when children can relate what they are doing in the classroom to the rest of their daily lives, their learning is more meaningful to them.

- Be knowledgeable about, proud of, and secure in your own culture. Children will ask about you, and you should share your background with them.

Select Appropriate Instructional Materials

In addition to assessing your own attitudes and instituting guidelines for infusing personal sensitivity into a multicultural classroom, you need to carefully consider and select appropriate instructional materials to support the infusion of multicultural education.

Avoid Sexism and Sex-Role Stereotyping

Current interest in multiculturalism in general and nondiscrimination in particular have also prompted concern about sexism and sex-role stereotyping. The Civil Rights movement and its emphasis on equality provides the impetus for seeking more equal treatment for women as well as for minority groups. Encouraged by the Civil Rights Act of 1964, which prohibits discrimination on the basis of race or national origin, civil rights and women's groups successfully sought legislation to prohibit discrimination on the basis of sex. Title IX of the Education Amendments Acts of 1972, as amended by Public Law 93-568, prohibits such discrimination in the schools: "No person in the United States shall, on the basis of sex, be excluded from participation in, be denied the benefits of, or be subjected to discrimination under any education program or activity receiving Federal financial assistance."[12]

The *Federal Register* defines sexism as, "the collection of attitudes, beliefs, and behaviors which result from the assumption that one sex is superior. In the context of schools, the term refers to the collection of structures, policies, practices, and activities that overtly or covertly prescribe the development of girls and boys and prepare them for traditional sex roles."[13]

Parents and teachers should provide children with less restrictive options and promote a more open framework in which sex roles can develop. Following are some ways to provide a non-sex-stereotyped environment:

- Provide opportunities for all children to experience the activities, materials, toys, and emotions traditionally associated with both sexes. Give boys as well as girls opportunities to experience tenderness, affection, and the warmth of close parent-child and teacher-pupil relationships. Conversely, girls as well as boys should be able to behave aggressively, get dirty, and participate in what are typically considered male activities, such as woodworking and block building.

- Examine the classroom materials you are using and determine whether they contain obvious instances of sex-role stereotyping. When you find examples, modify the materials or do not use them. Let publishers know your feelings, and tell other faculty members about them.

• Examine your behavior to see whether you are encouraging sex stereotypes. Do you tell girls they cannot empty wastebaskets, but they can water the plants? Do you tell boys they should not play with dolls? Do you tell girls they cannot lift certain things in the classroom because those things are too heavy for them? Do you say that "boys aren't supposed to cry"? Do you reward only females who are always passive, well behaved, and well mannered?

• Determine what physical arrangements in the classroom promote or encourage sex-role stereotyping. Are boys encouraged to use the block area more than girls? Are girls encouraged to use the quiet areas more than boys? Do children hang their wraps separately—a place for boys and a place for girls? All children should have equal access to all learning areas of the classroom; no area should be reserved exclusively for one sex. In addition, examine any activity and practice that promotes segregation of children by sex or culture. Cooperative learning activities and group work offer ways to ensure that children of both sexes work together.

• Counsel with parents to show them ways to promote nonsexist child rearing. If society is to achieve a truly nonsexist environment, parents will be the key factor, for it is in the home that many sex-stereotyping behaviors are initiated and practiced.

• Become conscious of words that promote sexism. For example, in a topic on community helpers, taught in most preschool and kindergarten programs at one time or another, many words carry a sexist connotation. *Fireman, policeman,* and *mailman,* for instance, are all masculine terms; nonsexist terms are *firefighter, police officer,* and *mail carrier.* You should examine all your curricular materials and teaching practices to determine how you can make them free from sexism.

Implement an Antibias Curriculum

The goal of an antibias curriculum is to help children learn to be accepting of others regardless of gender, race, ethnicity, socioeconomic status, or disability. Children participating in an antibias curriculum are comfortable with diversity and learn to stand up for themselves and others in the face of injustice. Additionally, in this supportive, open-minded environment, children learn to construct a knowledgeable, confident self-identity.

Young children are constantly learning about differences and need a sensitive teacher to help them form positive, unbiased perceptions about variations among people. As children color pictures of themselves, for example, you may hear a comment such as, "Your skin is white and my skin is brown." Many teachers are tempted, in the name of equality, to respond, "It doesn't matter what color we are—we are all people." While this remark does not sound harmful, it fails to help children develop positive feelings about themselves. A more appropriate response might be, "Tabitha, your skin is a beautiful dark brown, which is just right for you; Christina, your skin is a beautiful light tan, which is just right for you." A comment such as this positively acknowledges each child's different skin color, which is an important step for developing a positive self-concept.

Through the sensitive guidance of caring teachers, children learn to speak up for themselves and others. By living and learning in an accepting environment, children find that they have the ability to change intolerable situations and can have a positive impact on the future. This is part of what empowerment is all about, and it begins in the home and in early childhood programs. It is important, then, that an antibias curriculum start in early childhood and continue throughout the school years.

Teach to Children's Learning Styles

Different Children, Different Intelligences

Piaget's theory of intelligence (see Chapter 4) is based primarily on one intelligence, logical-mathematical. In his book *Frames of Mind,* Gardner hypothesizes that rather than one overall intelligence, there are at least eight distinct intelligences:[14]

linguistic

logical-mathematical

spatial

musical

bodily kinesthetic

interpersonal

intrapersonal

naturalist

Further, Gardner maintains that all children possess all eight of these intelligences, although some intelligences may be stronger than others. These eight intelligences imply that students have unique learning styles appropriate to the particular intelligences. Consequently, early childhood professionals must consider children's learning styles and make efforts to accommodate their teaching styles, activities, and materials to them. Table 12–2 will help you make the connection using Gardner's theory.

Encourage Cooperative Learning

Cooperative learning is a popular child-centered approach. As a tool to infuse multicultural education, an early childhood educator can form small cooperative groups to engage in discussions about a number of cultural issues including prejudice, stereotyping, discrimination, and segregation. Using role playing or puppets in these groups can promote communication and create a sense of equity. Some discussions may be initiated through the use of good multicultural literature.

TABLE 12–2

Eight Styles of Learning Applied to Technology

	Highly developed in:	Students with a high degree:	May benefit from
Verbal/Linguistic Intelligence			
The capacity to use words effectively—either orally or in writing.	story-tellers, orators, politicians, poets, playwrights, editors, and journalists	think in words; learn by listening, reading, and verbalizing; enjoy writing; like books, records, and tapes; have a good memory for verse, lyrics, or trivia	word processors that allow voice annotations; desktop publishing programs; programs with speech output; programs which encourage them to create poetry, essays, etc.; multimedia authoring; using videodiscs and barcode programs to create presentations; tape recorders; telecommunications/electronic networking
Visual/Spatial Intelligence			
The ability to perceive the world accurately and to perform transformations upon one's perceptions.	guides, interior designers, architects, artists, and inventors	think in images and pictures; like mazes and jigsaw puzzles; like to draw and design things; like films, slides, videos, diagrams, maps, and charts	drawing and painting programs; reading programs that use visual clues such as rebus method or color coding; programs which allow them to see information such as maps, charts, or diagrams, i.e. charting capability of spreadsheet program; multimedia programs; science probeware
Musical Intelligence			
The capacity to perceive, discriminate, transform, and express musical forms.	musical performers, aficionados, and critics	learn through rhythm and melody; play a musical instrument; may need music to study; notice nonverbal sounds in the environment; learn things more easily if sung, tapped out, or whistled	programs that combine stories with songs; reading programs which associate letter/sounds with music; programs which allow them to create their own song; constructing presentations using CD audio discs, videodisc player, and barcode program; sing along videodisc programs that display words "karaoke" style
Logical/Mathematical Intelligence			
The capacity to use numbers effectively and to reason well.	mathematicians, tax accountants, statisticians, scientists, computer programmers, and logicians	reason things out logically and clearly; look for abstract patterns and relationships; like brain teasers, logical puzzles, and strategy games; like to use computers; like to classify and categorize	database and spreadsheet programs; problem solving software; computer programming software; strategy game formats/simulations; calculators; multimedia authoring programs

	Highly developed in:	Students with a high degree:	May benefit from
Bodily-Kinesthetic Intelligence			
Expertise in using one's whole body to express ideas and feelings, and facility in using ones hands to produce or transform things.	actors, mimes, athletes, dancers, sculptors, mechanics, and surgeons	process knowledge through bodily sensations; move, twitch, tap, or fidget while sitting in a chair; learn by touching, manipulating, and moving; like role playing and creative movement	software requiring alternate input such as joystick, mouse, or touch window; keyboarding and word processing programs; animation programs; programs which allow them to move objects around the screen; science probeware
Interpersonal Intelligence			
The ability to perceive and make distinctions in the moods, intentions, motivations, and feelings of other people.	Intelligence can include: sensitivity to facial expressions, voice, and gestures, as well as the ability to respond effectively to such cues.	understand and care about people; like to socialize; learn more easily by relating and cooperating; are good at teaching other students	telecommunications programs; programs which address social issues; programs which include group presentation or decision making; games which require two or more players; tv production-team approach
Intrapersonal Intelligence			
Self-knowledge and the ability to act adaptively on the basis of that knowledge.	Intelligence can include: having an accurate picture of one's strengths and limitations, awareness of one's moods and motivations, and the capacity for self-discipline.	seem to be self-motivating; need their own quiet space; march to the beat of a different drummer; learn more easily with independent study, self-paced instruction, and individualized projects and games	computer assisted instruction/ILS labs; instructional games in which the opponent is the computer; programs which encourage self-awareness or build self-improvement skills; any programs which allow them to work independently; brainstorming or problem solving software
Naturalist Intelligence			
The human ability to discriminate among living things (plants, animals) as well as sensitivity to other features of the natural world (clouds, rock configurations).	botanist, chef, biologist, veterinarian, geologist	observe, understand and organize patterns in the natural environment; show expertise in the recognition and classification of plants and animals	computer and other technology such as games involving birds, butterflies, insects; any software that provides opportunities for classification of plant and animal species, programs which enable students to explore a geographic feature relating to mountains, oceans, and other geologic features; software that provides for study of the planets and exploration of the universe

At the heart of multiple intelligence theory is the concept that children are individuals with individual backgrounds, abilities, and needs. The eight separate intelligences develop in different children, in different times, and different ways. Early childhood professionals are challenged how to provide for children's ongoing and constantly developing intelligences. By integrating technology into the curriculum teachers can provide learning activities which enable all children's intelligence to develop.

Cooperative learning provides an ideal way for children to work together. Additionally, working together helps children learn more about themselves and others. Cooperative learning supports the multicultural goals of today's classrooms. What multicultural understandings can children learn by working together?

Promote and Use Conflict Resolution Strategies

We all live in a world of conflict. Television and other media bombard us with images of violence, crime, and international and personal conflict. Unfortunately, many children live in homes where conflict and disharmony are ways of life rather than exceptions. Increasingly, early childhood professionals are challenged to help children and themselves resolve conflicts in peaceful ways. For this reason, conflict resolution strategies seek to help children learn how to solve problems, disagree in appropriate ways, negotiate, and live in harmony with others. Part of your goal is to have children reach mutually agreeable solutions to problems without the use of power (fighting, hitting, pushing, shoving, etc.). You may wish to adopt the following strategies for helping children resolve conflicts:

Steps in using the "no-lose" method of conflict resolution:

1. Identify and define conflict in nonaccusatory way (e.g., "Vinnie and Rachael, you have a problem. You both want the green paint . . .").

2. Invite children to participate in fixing problem ("Let's think of how to solve the problem").

3. Generate possible solutions with children. Accept a variety of solutions. Avoid evaluating them (". . . Yes, you could both use the same paint cup . . . you could take turns . . .").

4. Examine each idea for merits and drawbacks. With children, decide which to try. Thank children for thinking of solutions (". . . You want to both use the green paint at the same time . . .").

5. Put plan into action ("You might have to take turns dipping your brushes into the paint. . . . Try your idea").

6. Follow up. Evaluate how well the solution worked (Teacher comes back in a few minutes, ". . . looks like your idea of how to solve your green paint problem really worked").[15]

Welcome Parent and Community Involvement

As an early childhood professional, you will work with children and families of diverse cultural backgrounds. As such, you will need to learn about the cultural background of children and families so that you can respond appropriately to their needs. For example, let's take a look at the Hispanic culture and its implications for parent and family involvement (see also Box 12–1).

Throughout Hispanic culture there is a widespread belief in the absolute authority of the school and teachers. In many Latin American countries it is considered rude for a parent to intrude into the life of the school. Parents believe that it is the school's job to educate and the parent's job to nurture and that the two jobs do not mix. A child who is well educated is one who has learned moral and ethical behavior.

Hispanics, as a whole, have strong family ties, believe in family loyalty, have a collective orientation that supports community life, and have been found to be field dependent with a sensitivity to nonverbal indicators of feeling.[16] Culturally this is represented by an emphasis on warm, personalized styles of interaction, a relaxed sense of time, and a need for an informal atmosphere for communication. Given these preferences, a culture clash may result when Hispanic students and parents are confronted with the typical task-oriented style of most American teachers.

While an understanding of the general cultural characteristics of Hispanics is helpful, it is important to not overgeneralize. Each family and child is unique, and care should be taken to not assume values and beliefs just because a family speaks Spanish and is from Latin America. It is important that teachers spend the time to discover the particular values, beliefs, and practices of the families in the community.

Based on this knowledge, you can use the following guidelines to involve Hispanic parents:

- *Use a personal touch.* It is crucial to use face-to-face communication in the Hispanic parents' primary language when first making contact. Written flyers or articles sent home have proved to be ineffective even when written in Spanish. It may also take several personal meetings before the parents gain sufficient trust to actively participate. Home visits are a particularly good way to begin to develop rapport.

- *Use nonjudgmental communication.* In order to gain the trust and confidence of Hispanic parents, teachers must avoid making them feel they are to blame or are doing something wrong. Parents need to be supported for their strengths, not judged for perceived failings.

- *Be persistent in maintaining involvement.* To keep Hispanic parents actively engaged, activities planned by the early childhood program must respond to a real need or concern of the parents. Teachers should have a good idea about what parents will get out of each meeting and how the meeting will help them in their role as parents.

BOX 12–1 IMPLICATIONS OF LATINO CHILD DEVELOPMENT FOR EARLY CHILDHOOD PROFESSIONALS

In order to provide appropriate programs and services to Latino populations (i.e., people whose origins are Mexican, Puerto Rican, Cuban, Central or South American, or some other Spanish origin) residing in the United States, early childhood professionals must begin to understand what aspects of the developmental process are "culturally specific" and what aspects are universal or common to all humans regardless of cultural background. This differentiation is not easily made. One of the primary reasons for our lack of understanding is the absence of systematic research targeting minority children in general. Much of what we know is often based on data that implicitly or explicitly compares low-income minority children against middle-class Anglo populations.

The problem with this approach is that minority children's development tends to be viewed as less optimal when compared to their middle-class counterparts. Rather, an understanding of minority children's development must be based within the contextual parameters of a particular culture. Given this guideline, what, as early childhood professionals, do we know about the Latino child's growth and development that is "culturally specific" and what implications does that knowledge have for how programs and services should be structured?

First, we know that cultural background and socioeconomic background are highly interrelated so that what we think may be "culturally specific" may be more a function of the group's adaptation to their socioeconomic conditions. When social class is similar, differences between middle-income Anglos and middle-income Latinos may decrease. For example, research shows that maternal teaching strategies are different when comparing low-income Latinos and middle-income Anglos. However, differences are less substantial when comparisons are made between middle-income Latinos and middle-income Anglos.

Social class standing is an important indicator of available resources such as the quality of housing, employment opportunities, medical services, and, most importantly, the quality of educational programs. For Latinos residing in the United States, level of acculturation also plays an important role. *Acculturation* refers to the degree to which an individual is able to function effectively in the dominant culture. This quality includes the ability to speak the language and knowledge of the dominant group's values and cultural expressions (e.g., foods, art). These factors play a major role in determining an individual's ability to adapt to the society. The early childhood professional must appreciate the relationship between social class standing and acculturation and those behaviors that stem from living in different socioeconomic situations.

Second, in understanding Latino child development, it is important to cultivate an awareness of Latino parents' orientation to children and examine how this affects the goals of childrearing. Previous research on parental beliefs suggests that cultural background is an important determinant of parental ideas. The type of competence parents expect of young children may vary from culture to culture. For low-income immigrant Latino parents, expectation for their children's skill development may differ from Latinos born in the United States; foreign-born Latinos perceive the behavioral capabilities of young children as developing later than do U.S.-born Latinos. It may be that low-income immigrant Latinos have a more maturational orientation to children's development so that the early emphasis on cognitive stimulation promoted in the United States is somewhat inconsistent with their expectations.

A maturational approach to childrearing may stem from the social and historic backgrounds of Latino groups living in the United States. In cultures in which children are expected to take part in the cultural activities of adults, such as sibling caretaking and economic maintenance of the family, certain parent-child interaction patterns will emerge. Thus, in more rural, traditional culture, parents may socialize their children by stressing observation and immediate assistance in task development rather than explicit instruction, which tends to be valued by middle-class U.S. parents. On the other hand, in U.S. culture children are segregated into age-graded classrooms in which information is given in bits and pieces over an extended period.

Early childhood professionals need to consider how parental orientation may differ from the specific goals and objectives of a particular intervention program. When working with immigrant families it is sometimes appropriate to indicate how the expectations of the school explicitly differ from the group's orientation. For many immigrant families, adaptation and innovation are a way of life, and accepting different ways of doing things is part and parcel of the immigrant experience. However, for second-generation or more acculturated groups reared in the United States, such explicit contrast may not suffice. In these instances, practitioners must become familiar with the degree of acculturation that characterizes the group and adjust their services accordingly.

Third, Latinos hold certain values and beliefs that are important for childhood socialization. The following sections present an overview of important core values and beliefs that will vary in individual families depending on their acculturation level, socioeconomic standing, and ethnic loyalty. It is very important to see these core values as broad generalizations subject to adaptations to local conditions.

Familialism

This value is viewed as one of the most important culture-specific values of Latinos. *Familialism* refers to strong identification and connections to the immediate and extended family. Behaviors associated with familialism include strong feelings of loyalty, reciprocity, and solidarity. Familialism is manifested through the following: (1) feelings of obligation to provide both material and emotional support to the family, (2) dependence on relatives for help and support, and (3) reliance on relatives as behavioral and attitudinal referents.

Respeto

Associated with familialism is the cultural concept of *respeto,* which is an extremely important underlying tenet of interpersonal interaction. Basically, *respeto* (respect) refers to the deference ascribed to various members of the family or society because of their position. Generally speaking, respect is accorded to the position and not necessarily the person. Thus, respect is expected toward elders, parents, older siblings within the family, and teachers, clergy, nurses, and doctors outside the family. With respect comes deference; that is, the person will not question the individual in the authority position; will exhibit very courteous behavior in front of them, and will appear to agree with information presented to them by the authority figure.

Bien Educado

If a person exhibits the characteristics associated with *respeto,* then they are said to be *bien educado.* What is important here is that the term *educado* (education) refers not to formal education but to the acquisition of the appropriate social skills and graces within the Latino cultural context. For traditional Latinos, someone having honors from Harvard University, but who did not conform to this system, would be considered badly educated.

Incorporation of important cultural values and beliefs into the early childhood professional's interpersonal conduct provides families with a semblance of cultural continuity and maintains feelings of self-respect. The professional can accomplish this by demonstrating high degrees of courtesy, by understanding that indirect communication on the part of the child and parent is a reflection of *respeto* to teachers as authority figures, and by viewing the broader family configuration as an important resource for understanding Latino family dynamics. Within this general framework, the professional must accommodate individual differences and local community conditions.

Contributed by Marlene Zepeda. California State University, Los Angeles, California.

- *Provide bilingual support.* All communication with Hispanic parents, written and oral, must be provided in Spanish and English. Many programs report that having bicultural and bilingual staff helps promote trust.[17]

- *Provide strong leadership and administrative support.* Flexible policies, a welcoming environment, and a collegial atmosphere all require administrative leadership and support. As with other educational projects or practices that require innovation and adaptation, the efforts of teachers alone cannot bring success to parent involvement projects. Principals must also be committed to project goals.

- *Provide staff development focused on Hispanic culture.* All staff must understand the key features of Hispanic culture and its impact on their students' behavior and learning styles. It is the educator's obligation to learn as much about the children and their culture and background as possible.

- *Conduct community outreach.* Many Hispanic families could benefit from family literacy programs, vocational training, ESL programs, improved medical and dental services, and other community-based social services. A school or early childhood program can serve as a resource and referral agency to support the overall strength and stability of the families.

BILINGUAL EDUCATION

For most people, bilingual education means that children (or adults, or both) will be taught a second language. Some people interpret this to mean that a child's *native language* (often referred to as the *home language*)—whether English, Spanish, French, Italian, Chinese, Tagalog, or any of the other 125 languages in which bilingual programs are conducted—will tend to be suppressed. For other people, bilingual education means that children will be taught in both the home language and the primary language. The Bilingual Education Act, Title VII of the Elementary Secondary Education Act (ESEA), sets forth the federal government's policy toward bilingual education:

> The Congress declares it to be the policy of the United States, in order to establish equal educational opportunity for all children and to promote educational excellence, (A) to encourage the establishment and operation, where appropriate, of educational programs using bilingual educational practices, techniques, and methods, (B) to encourage the establishment of special alternative instructional programs for students of limited English proficiency in school districts where the establishment of bilingual education programs is not practicable or for other appropriate reasons, and (C) for those purposes, to provide financial assistance to local educational agencies.[18]

Programs for Students with Limited English Proficiency

Early childhood programs and schools can make several responses to language learning for children with limited English proficiency (LEP). First, they can use an immersion program, in which children typically are placed in a program in which English is the exclusive language and all instruction is conducted in English. A teacher may or may not know the child's native language. The goal of an immersion program is to have children learn English as quickly and fluently as possible. Little if any effort is made to maintain or improve the child's native language ability.

Other than immersion, there are three broad categories of programs aimed at LEP students: English as a second language programs, transitional bilingual education programs, and maintenance bilingual education programs. While there are variations within each, the first two place value only on developing English language competency, and the third tries to create bilingual, biliterate students. (Note that bilingual programs may have different names in different states.)

- English as a second language (ESL) programs generally provide a special English class for students learning the language along with sheltered English approaches to other subjects. *Sheltered English* involves a high degree of visualization of subject matter and a vocabulary adapted to the student's level of English proficiency.

- Transitional bilingual programs have an ESL component and use the native language as a medium of instruction in the other subjects. As students learn more English, the native language use is de-emphasized until students fully adapt to a curriculum that uses English only.

- Maintenance bilingual programs, like transitional ones, also teach English while using the native language to teach other subjects. As students learn more English, it is woven into content area instruction. What makes maintenance bilingual programs unique is that native language instruction is continued after students are fully functional in English. The goal of maintenance bilingual programs is to create students who are not only bilingual, but also biliterate.

HEAD START AND MULTICULTURAL PROGRAMMING

Head Start has identified the following principles as a framework for multicultural programming:[19]

- Every individual is rooted in culture.
- The cultural groups represented in the communities and families of each Head Start program are the primary sources for culturally relevant programming.

THE BAY AREA HISPANO INSTITUTE FOR ADVANCEMENT

For over twenty-one years, the Bay Area Hispano Institute for Advancement, Inc. (BAHIA) has provided child care to the Latino community, a service that remains unduplicated and very much in demand in Berkeley, California. BAHIA meets the needs of the Latino community by creating an environment in which working families know their children are cared for in a place of learning that is clean, safe, warm, affordable, and most importantly, bilingual.

Parents of BAHIA children, diverse in their professions, are linked by their desire for their children to be bilingual. Services offered by BAHIA are directly linked to giving children and families different and consistent opportunities to be bilingual.

What Are Highlights of the BAHIA Program?

Bilingual Emphasis   BAHIA's services are enhanced by its resolution to be 100 percent bilingual in every child, parent, and staff activity; written communication, meetings, and the hiring of individuals from youth workers to the Executive Director exemplify the value of bilingualism in the community. BAHIA's philosophy is that success as a bilingual person does not come at the expense of a child's first or second language. Instead, language is used as a gateway to understand and build a broader cultural sensitivity through activities and environment planning that promote diversity, identity, and understanding. Evidence of a successful bilingual program is observed in children learning and playing games in Spanish, practicing their English with friends, or writing or dictating stories in Spanish to share with their parents.

Service to Familias   At BAHIA, familias are looked upon as an integral part of a child's healthy and positive development. Support for familias is therefore a high priority for the BAHIA program. For example, parents are provided a continuum of services for their children from two to ten years of age including referrals to social services as needed. Parents are able to hold down jobs, seek employment, receive training and/or improve their education by attending school. Additionally, BAHIA provides an opportunity for parents to participate in bilingual parenting workshops and parent-teacher conferences scheduled twice a year.

Servicing Two Age Groups   To further help Latino families the BAHIA program provides subsidized and full-cost child care at two sites: Centro VIDA preschool offers full-time care for 64 children ages two to five years; BAHIA School-Age Program serves 65 children ages five to ten years by providing afterschool care during the regular school year and full-time care during holidays and the summer months.

Linking Familias   Latinos have been the majority, culturally and linguistically, in BAHIA's programs. However, a more diverse community of children is now enrolling in BAHIA, so Latino parents and children have a greater exposure to familias that are not Latino. Specifically, in this environment, Latino parents have opportunities to meet, share, and work alongside familias who are African American, Asian, gay, single father, single mother, biracial, Anglo parents with adopted Latino children, and grandparents rearing children. Their link to one another as familias is that they all value Spanish, bilingualism, and the services provided by BAHIA.

How Do You Know Your Program Is Successful?

Success and results are reflected in many forms. It is seen in

- The children who grow up to become successful and proud bilingual individuals as a result of early and positive learning experiences

- Familias connecting with one another and staying connected over the years

- Recognition received from the City of Berkeley for serving the Latino community for the past twenty years

- Annually surpassing the administration and management standards for child development set by the California State Department of Education

- Recognition in 1996 by the National Latino Children's Agenda as an exemplary program serving children

BAHIA also considers itself successful because of the support it receives from parents in all its endeavors to improve its program. Parent collaborators help raise funds to purchase supplies and materials and even help write grants to support new program ideas. Additionally, parent contributions have helped reduce costs to improve and expand services by donating time and labor, including the construction of two new specialized classrooms for math and science and the landscaping and maintenance of a play yard for schoolage children at both sites.

Parents once served by BAHIA (over the past twenty-one years) often return to donate time, money, or labor to continue the tradition of caring that they experienced when BAHIA served them. Parents and children especially like being able to still see themselves in the colorful picture collages that are displayed in the child care centers. Volunteers from the community have provided over 500 hours of time to the children's programs.

What Barriers Has BAHIA Had to Overcome?

In society, bilingual child care continues to be high in demand, yet limited, underfunded, and undervalued. Certain professional requirements for bilingual child care teachers sometimes create a barrier for native speaking, credentialed teachers from Mexico and Latin America. Thus, BAHIA has had some difficulty filling teacher job openings because prospective teachers do not have the units in child development required by the State of California. To overcome this limited supply of teachers, BAHIA provides stipends to teacher assistants each year to help them in their professional development, paying for classes, conferences, books, and supplies. This plan includes young Latino men and women who were not previously interested in college, but who demonstrate leadership, interest, and an understanding of working with children. Providing these stipends for professional development and job training results from the belief that the quality of bilingual learning experiences for children is of the utmost importance to the long-term development of children.

The need to nurture bilingualism is not only particular to Latinos, but also to familias that see the value of two languages in building cross-cultural understanding, and is what prompted the events leading to BAHIA's creation in 1974. Its growth and improvements since that time have been inspired and reinspired by the parents, staff, and a committed Board of Directors to keep BAHIA, and its bilingual children's program, vital and active assets to the community.

Contributed by Beatriz Leyva-Cutler, BAHIA, Inc.

- Culturally relevant and diverse programming requires learning accurate information about the culture of different groups and discarding stereotypes.

- Addressing cultural relevance in making curriculum choices is a necessary, developmentally appropriate practice.

- Every individual has the right to maintain his or her own identity while acquiring the skills required to function in our diverse society.

- Effective programs for children with limited English-speaking ability require continued development of the primary language while the acquisition of English is facilitated.

- Culturally relevant programming requires staff who reflect the community and families served.

- Multicultural programming for children enables children to develop an awareness of, respect for, and appreciation of individual cultural differences. It is beneficial to all children.

- Culturally relevant and diverse programming examines and challenges institutional and personal biases.

- Culturally relevant and diverse programming and practices are incorporated in all components and services.

TRENDS IN MULTICULTURAL EDUCATION

As with most areas of early childhood education, we can identify trends that will affect multicultural curricula, programs, and practices. The following trends, and others to come, will affect how you teach young children:

- Multicultural curricula are becoming more pluralistic and are including knowledge and information about many cultures. Children learn to look at the world through the eyes of other cultures and ethnic groups. As a result, more children will examine a full range of cultures rather than looking at only two or three, as is often the current practice.

- More early childhood teachers are recognizing that just because children are young does not mean that they cannot learn about multicultural perspectives. Consequently, multicultural activities and content are being included in curricula from the time children enter preschool programs. For example, kindergarten children might be encouraged to look at Thanksgiving through the eyes of both Native Americans and Pilgrims instead of being taught only the Pilgrims' point of view.

- Many early childhood professionals are being challenged to preserve children's natural reactions to others' differences before they adopt or are taught adult stereotypical reactions. Young children are, in general, understanding and accepting of differences in others.

PROGRAM IN ACTION

PROMISE, POWER, PROSPERITY

In the Socorro Independent School District, in El Paso, Texas, a two-way dual language/multiage program has begun practicing additive bilingualism for its students. Classroom teachers Antonio A. Fierro and Olga Escobar-Mendoza teach English and Spanish to a classroom of 38 five- and six-year-old students. Using thematic units, they teach concepts in the primary language and reinforce them in the second language through additional teacher-directed instruction, thematic boards, and homogeneous and heterogeneous groupings. (Homogeneous groups have children who speak only one language; heterogeneous groups have a mixture of English speakers and Spanish speakers.)

Separate language groupings introduce the children to a new language, a new instructional program, and new cultures. Research has indicated that the most productive dual language instruction is one that maintains the students together for the majority of the instructional day. Because of this research, students receive same-language instruction depending on the language of the week. Since this program is utilizing a 50/50 language development model, language instruction is given biweekly (two weeks in English followed by two weeks in Spanish). Throughout the learning process, the instructional team will be sensitive to students' native language and scaffolding techniques may be utilized to ensure comprehension. The switch from one language to the other will occur, not for direct interpretation, but to aid children's ability to fully comprehend the content.

Fierro and Mendoza use such holistic strategies as the language experience approach, webbing, wordless books, dramatizations, total physical response, and shared reading. These strategies allow their students to be challenged and to become risk takers. To further complement their instructional design, they have set up fourteen learning centers and workstations in the classroom with activities that target a range of ages and learning possibilities. Most importantly, the classroom environment respects individual language and cultural differences.

Early childhood programs must develop and support programs that value the linguistic diversity of all students. "Promise, Power, Prosperity" does just that.

Contributed by Antonio Fierro, 1996 Texas kindergarten teacher of the year, Socorro Independent School District, El Paso, Texas.

- The amount and kind of multicultural materials will continue to increase so that teachers will have ever-more decisions to make regarding what kind of materials they want and can use. Because not all materials are of equal value or worth, this abundance will mean that professionals will need to be increasingly diligent when selecting appropriate materials for young children.

You have read in this chapter about methods and strategies for teaching multicultural curricula to young children. Early childhood professionals will continue to create classroom environments that accommodate cultural and personal differences among students. These accommodations are taking place and will continue to take place through the use of specific teaching strategies designed to address children's cultural and learning needs, including cooperative team learning, peer and cross-age tutoring, and the involvement of all children in multiage, multigender, and multicultural group learning. While we have a long way to go to ensure that all classrooms and curricula provide for children's multicultural needs, we are making progress. You can be at the forefront of making even greater advances.

ACTIVITIES FOR REFLECTION AND RESEARCH

1. Visit several public schools to see how they provide individualized and appropriate programs for children with disabilities. What efforts are being made to involve parents?

2. Visit an inclusive classroom. What specific skills would you need to become a good professional in such settings?

3. What programs does the federal government support for children with special needs in your area? Give specific information.

4. Choose ten children's books and evaluate them for multicultural content. Decide how you would use these materials to promote awareness and acceptance of diversity.

5. Examine children's readers and supplemental materials to determine instances of sexism. What recommendations would you make to change such practices?

6. Observe children in both school and nonschool settings for examples of how dress reflects sex stereotyping and how parents' behaviors promote sex stereotyping (see Chapter 7 for suggestions of observing).

7. Stories and literature play an important role in transmitting to children information about themselves and what to expect in life. What books and literature played an important role in your growing up? Why? Identify five children's books and state why you think they would be good to use with children.

8. Interview at least three local principals to discover how they are dealing with issues of multiculturalism in their schools. What are they doing to actively promote a truly multicultural setting?

READINGS FOR FURTHER ENRICHMENT

Bennett, C. *Comprehensive Multicultural Education: Theory and Practice,* 4th ed. (Boston: Allyn & Bacon, 1999).

Bennett offers an in-depth research-based treatment of the history of education for diversity in the United States and contemporary theory and methods in multicultural education.

Davis, G. A., and S. B. Rimm. *Education of the Gifted and Talented,* 4th ed. (Boston: Allyn & Bacon, 1998).

Provides an overview of the gifted and talented field, including an introduction to giftedness, characteristics, program types, curriculum, identification, and program evaluation.

Friend, M., and W. Bursuck. *Including Students with Special Needs* (Boston: Allyn & Bacon, 1999, 2e).

A practical guide for classroom teachers on teaching all students in inclusive classrooms. This book explains how to modify curricula, textbooks, classrooms, student groupings, assessments, and instruction to meet all students' learning needs.

Lewis, Rena B., and Donald H. Doorlag. *Teaching Special Students in General Education Classrooms,* 5th ed. (Upper Saddle River, NJ: Merrill/Prentice Hall, 1999).

Presents practical strategies for adapting standard instruction to meet the learning needs of all children in a mainstreamed classroom. Clear and informative account of providing for children with special needs; includes tips and practical advice.

Smith, D. D., and R. Luckasson. *Introduction to Special Education: Teaching in an Age of Challenge,* 3rd ed. (Boston: Allyn & Bacon, 1999).

A well-written and understandable discussion of the field of special education. Provides many useful examples of educational procedures that can be applied to classrooms. Addresses in separate chapters all the special needs of students and their families.

NOTES

1. Public Law 101-476, October 30, 1990, Stat. 1103.

2. A. Turnbull, H. Turnbull III, M. Shank, and D. Leal, *Exceptional Lives* (Upper Saddle River, NJ: Merrill/Prentice Hall, 1995), pp. 64–71.

3. Ibid., p. 84.

4. Public Law 101-476, October 30, 1990, Stat. 1103.

5. Christine L. Salisbury, "Mainstreaming during the Early Childhood Years," *Exceptional Children,* October/November 1991, p. 147.

6. A. McDonnell and M. Hardman, "A Synthesis of 'Best Practice' Guidelines for Early Childhood Services," *Journal of the Division for Early Childhood,* 12(4), 1988.

7. L. H. Meyer, J. Eichinger, and S. Park-Lee, "A Validation of Program Quality Indicators in Educational Services for Students with Severe Disabilities," *Journal of the Association for Persons with Severe Handicaps,* 12(4), 1987.

8. Gerald Mahoney, Cordelia Robinson, and Amy Powell, "Focusing on Parent-Child Interaction: The Bridge to Developmentally Appropriate Practices," *Topics in Early Childhood Special Education,* 12(1), Spring 1992, pp. 105–120.

9. Salisbury, "Mainstreaming during the Early Childhood Years."

10. Council for Exceptional Children, 1996. Internet address http://www.cec.sped.org/

11. Valerie Ooka Pang and Jesus Nieto, "Multicultural Teaching," *Kappa Delta Pi Record,* 29(1), Fall 1992, pp. 25–27.

12. *Federal Register,* June 4, 1975, p. 24128.

13. *Federal Register,* August 11, 1975, p. 33803.

14. Howard Gardner, *Frames of Mind* (New York: Basic Books, 1983).

15. Marian Marion, *Guidance of Young Children,* 4th ed. (Upper Saddle River, NJ: Merrill/Prentice Hall, 1995), pp. 290–291.

16. N. Williams, *The Mexican American Family* (Dix Hills, NY: General Hill, 1990).

17. L. Espinosa, *Hispanic Parent Involvement in Early Childhood Programs* (Washington, DC: Office of Educational Research and Improvement, 1995).

18. Statute 2372, Section 703. Bilingual Education Act, Title VII of the Elementary Secondary Education Act, Statute 2268, Vol. 92, November 1978.

19. U.S. Department of Health and Human Services, Administration for Children, Youth, and Families, Multicultural Principles for Head Start Programs, CYF-IM-91-03 (Washington, DC: U.S. Government Printing Office, March 1991), pp. 5–6.

CHAPTER

13

Cooperation and Collaboration

FOCUS QUESTIONS

1. What changes in contemporary society and families influence children and early childhood programs?
2. Why is parent, family, and community involvement important in early childhood programs?
3. Why is it important to involve all parents and families represented in early childhood programs?
4. How is your personal philosophy of parent involvement important for success as an early childhood professional?
5. How can early childhood professionals and others encourage and support programs for involving families and communities?
6. How can a plan for assessing parent and family needs and involving parents and families in early childhood programs benefit you and others?

One thing we can say with certainty about the educational landscape today is that parents, families, and communities are as much a part of the educational process as are teachers and staff. At no time in U.S. educational history has support for family and community been so high. All concerned view the involvement of families and communities as critical for individual student success as well as for the success of the "American dream" of providing all children with an education that will meet their needs and enable them to be productive members of society. In this chapter, we look at some of the reasons why parent, family, and community involvement in education is so important.

CHANGES IN SCHOOLING

Schooling used to consist mostly of teaching children social and basic academic skills. But as society has changed, so has the content of schooling. Early childhood programs have assumed many parental functions and responsibilities. Part of the broadening of the role and function of early education and schooling includes helping parents and families meet their problems and involving them in decisions regarding the ways programs function.

Goals 2000

As a result of the readiness goal of the Goals 2000: Educate America Act (formerly America 2000; see Chapter 2), early childhood professionals are now trying to help children come to school ready to learn. These efforts also focus attention on parents as the first teachers of their children. One of the first such programs is the state of Missouri's Parents as Teachers (PAT) program, a home-school partnership designed to give children a good start in life by maximizing their overall development during the first three years of life.

PAT is a model for other programs throughout the country. It provides all parents with information about children's development and activities that promote language, intellectual, and social development. Additionally, the partnership goal of Goals 2000 states, "Every school and home will engage in partnerships that will increase parental involvement and participation in promoting the social, emotional, and academic growth of children."[1] As a result, early childhood programs and public schools are mounting an unprecedented effort to truly make parents and community members collaborative partners.

Political and Social Forces

Political and social forces have led to our rediscovery of the need to strengthen the relationship between families and schools. The accountability and reform movements of the last decade have convinced families that they should no longer be kept out of their children's schools. Education professionals and families realize that mutual cooperation is in everyone's best interest. In response to the changing landscape of contemporary society, early childhood professionals are working with parents to develop programs to help them and their children develop to their fullest and lead productive lives. Early childhood professionals are very supportive of such efforts. Indeed, parents and the public at large view parent involvement as an important factor in children's success in school. Ninety-five percent of parents with children in school and 97 percent of people with no children in school think it is important to encourage parents to take a more active part in educating their children.[2]

CHANGING FAMILIES

The family of today is not the family of yesterday. Table 13–1 shows some of the ways families have changed over the years. Several changes stand out. One is that more young mothers are entering the workforce than ever before.

TABLE 13–1
How Families Have Changed

	1993*	1994[†]	1995[‡]	1998
Married couples	53,117	53,171	53,858	54,317
Married couples with children	24,707	24,515	25,241	25,269
Male householder (no spouse) with children	1,324	2,913	3,226	3,911
Female householder (no spouse) with children	7,226	12,406	12,220	12,652
Average number of children per family	1.84	1.84	1.84	1.9

Note: All figures are in thousands.
Source: *U.S. Department of Commerce, Bureau of the Census, *Current Population Reports,* Series P-20, No. 477, Household and Family Characteristics (1993).
[†]U.S. Department of Commerce, Bureau of the Census, *Current Population Reports,* Series P-20, No. 483, Household and Family Characteristics (1994).
[†]*Digest of Education Statistics* (Washington, DC: U.S. Department of Education, 1997).

Families continue to change and, as they do, early childhood professionals must adapt and adopt new ways of involving family members and providing for their needs. For example, growing numbers of fathers have sole responsibility for rearing their children. What can professionals do to ensure the involvement of single fathers in their programs?

This means that at an early age, often beginning at six weeks, children are spending eight hours a day or more in the care of others. Thus, working parents are both turning their young children over to others for care and also spending less time with their children. Parents need more help with rearing their children at earlier ages. As a result, opportunities have blossomed for child-serving agencies, such as child care centers and preschools, to assist and support parents in their child-rearing efforts.

EDUCATION AS A FAMILY AFFAIR

Education starts in the home, and what happens there profoundly affects the trajectory of development and learning. According to the U.S. Department of Education (DOE), education is a family affair because the greater the family's involvement in children's learning the more likely it is that students will receive a high-quality education. The DOE identifies three main reasons that families play a critical role in education:[3]

- Three factors over which families have control—student absenteeism, variety of reading material in the home, and amount of television watching—explain differences in students' mathematics achievement. School attendance rates, exposure to print in the home, and restricted television time all correlate with higher achievement as measured by the National Assessment of Educational Progress.

- While math and science achievement is based on learning activities in the home, literacy is even more dependent on home life. The single most important activity for building the knowledge required for eventual success is reading aloud to children.

- What the family does with and for its children is more important to student success than family income or education. This is true whether the family is rich or poor, whether the parents finished high school or not, or whether the child is in preschool or in the upper grades.

The central role families play in children's education is a reality that teachers and schools must address as they make plans for how to reform schools and increase student achievement. Partnering with parents is a process whose time has come, and the benefits far outweigh any inconveniences or barriers that may stand in the way of bringing schools and parents together.

Family-Centered Teaching

Family-centered teaching focuses on meeting the needs of students through the family unit, whatever that unit may be. Education professionals recognize that to most effectively meet the needs of students, they must also meet the needs of family members and the family unit. Family-centered teaching makes sense for a number of reasons.

- First, the family unit has the major responsibility for meeting children's needs. Children's development begins in the family system, and this system is a powerful determiner of developmental processes, both for better and for worse. Therefore, helping parents and other family members meet their children's needs in appropriate ways means that everyone stands to benefit. Helping individuals in the family unit become better parents and family members benefits children and consequently promotes their success in school.

- Second, it is frequently the case that to help children effectively, family issues and problems must be addressed first. For instance, helping parents gain access to adequate and affordable health care increases the chances that the whole family, including children, will be healthy.

- Third, teachers can do many things concurrently with children and their families that will benefit both. Literacy is a good example. Adopting a family approach to literacy means that helping parents learn to read, build literacy, and read aloud to their children helps ensure children's literacy development as well. Figure 13–1 summarizes the concept of family-centered teaching.

An example of family-centered teaching is Even Start, a federally funded family literacy program that combines adult literacy and parenting training

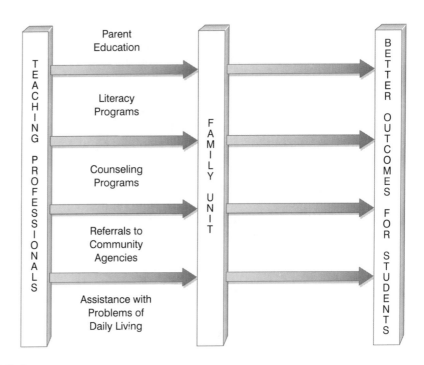

FIGURE 13–1
Family-Centered Teaching
Source: G. S. Morrison, *Teaching in America* (Needham Heights, MA: Allyn & Bacon, 1997),
p. 208. Copyright © 1997 by Allyn & Bacon. Reprinted by permission.

with early childhood education to break cycles of illiteracy that are often passed on from one generation to another. Even Start is funded under Title I of the Improving America's Schools Education Act and is operated through the public school system. In particular, Even Start helps parents become full partners in the education of their children, assists children in reaching their full potential, and provides literacy training for parents. Even Start projects are designed to work cooperatively with existing community resources to provide a full range of services and to integrate early childhood education and adult education.

Family-Centered Curriculum and Instruction

Family-centered curriculum and instruction exists at three levels. First, it consists of programs and materials designed to help parents be better parents and teachers of their children. To support parents in these roles, schools and teachers provide materials on parenting, conduct parenting classes, and furnish ideas about teaching their children reading and math skills through daily living activities. At a second level, instruction focuses on helping parents with everyday problems and issues of family living. For example, classes and information on tenant rights, nutritional meals, the importance of immunizations, and access to health services would be in keeping with the ideas of addressing families' daily living needs. At a third level, family-centered curriculum and instruction attempts to integrate students' classroom learning with learning in the home. For example, providing parents with books to read to their children at home would support efforts to link in-school learning with learning in the home.

Two-Generation and Intergenerational Programs

Two-generation programs involve parents and their children and are designed to help both generations and at the same time to strengthen the family unit. Intergenerational programs involve grandparents and others, as well. Two-generation delivery of services can and should begin before children's birth because many problems relating to child health can be prevented by good prenatal care. The preventive approach to maternal and prenatal health is reflected in the growing numbers of schools that have on-site health clinics. Services often include both health and education in which students and parents receive medical care and information that will support their efforts to lead healthy lives.

For example, Avance is a center-based parent support and education program serving low-income Hispanic families at centers in Dallas, San Antonio, Houston, and the Rio Grande Valley in Texas. Parents and their children up to three years of age are enrolled through an aggressive door-to-door recruitment of families into the program. The heart of Avance is a nine-month parent education program in which parents are taught how they can be their children's first teachers and how to facilitate their children's development. To support parents in this effort, Avance provides transportation to the center, home visits, literacy development, employment training, family planning information, education in the use of community resources, and referrals and advocacy for other social service needs.

Mercedes Perez de Colon, director of the National Family Resource Center for Avance, states the following:

> Our main goal has always been to help parents prepare their children for school success by focusing on the first three years of a child's life. We help parents understand how children grow and learn and what they can do to maximize opportunities for their children. We provide a comprehensive array of services and opportunities to enable parents to become their children's first teachers. We try to help parents use resources available in the community and understand that helping their children to be prepared for school does not require money, it requires time and effort on the part of parents. We show parents how to help their children learn through language and through their five senses and through play.

Two areas of great need in our society are young children and the elderly. Many programs are looking for ways that they can effectively integrate the care of both of these groups into their programs. What are some advantages of providing for the education and care of young children and the elderly in the same program?

We also stress healthy lifestyles for parents and children, so we focus on immunizations, nutrition, safety, and understanding the importance of healthy and preventive lifestyles. We have been very successful. Parents who attend our program increase their understanding of child growth and development, have a positive change in attitudes toward child rearing, and have better home environments for their children. We know that their children are meeting with success in school.

Intergenerational programs are those that promote cooperation, interaction, and exchange between two or more generations. Intergenerational programming is becoming a popular way of bringing younger and older generations together. There are a number of reasons for efforts to join generations. First, Americans tend to become segregated by age and life stages. The young are in child care and schools, adults are in workplaces, and the elderly are in age-segregated housing and nursing homes. Second, with cutbacks in federal support for health and social programs, the young and old especially are in competition for funds and services. One way to reduce this competition and to use existing funds effectively is to provide intergenerational programs for the mutual benefit of all. Most often, intergenerational programming focuses on young people below the age of twenty-five and adults over the age of sixty.[4]

Intergenerational programming also includes programs in which young people provide services to older persons, in which older persons provide services to youth, and in which two generations work cooperatively on a project.

IMPLICATIONS OF FAMILY PATTERNS FOR EARLY CHILDHOOD PROFESSIONALS

Given the changes in families today, there are a number of things you can do as an early childhood professional to help parents, including the following:

• *Provide support services.* Support can extend from being a "listening ear" to organizing support groups and seminars on single parenting. Professionals can help families link up with other agencies and groups, such as Big Brothers and Big Sisters and Families without Partners. Through newsletters and fliers, professionals can offer families specific advice on how to help children become independent and how to meet the demands of living in single-parent families, step families, and other family configurations.

• *Avoid criticism.* Professionals should be careful not to criticize families for the jobs they are doing. They may not have extra time to spend with their children or know how to discipline them. Regardless of their circumstances, families need help, not criticism.

• *Avoid being judgmental.* Similarly, professionals should examine and clarify their attitudes and values toward family patterns and remember that there is no "right" family pattern from which all children should come.

• *Arrange educational experiences.* Professionals need to address the issue of changing family patterns in the educational experiences they arrange. They must offer experiences children might not otherwise have because of their family organization. For example, outdoor activities such as fishing trips and sports events can be interesting and enriching learning experiences for children who may not have such opportunities.

• *Adjust programs.* Professionals need to adjust classroom or center activities to account for how particular children cope with their home situations. Children's needs for different kinds of activities depend on their experiences at home. For example, opportunities abound for role playing, and such activities help bring into the open situations that children need to talk about. Use program opportunities to discuss families and the roles they play. Make it a point in the classroom to model, encourage, and teach effective interpersonal skills.

• *Be sensitive.* There are specific ways to sensitively approach today's changing family patterns. For example, avoid having children make presents for both parents when it is inappropriate to do so and awarding prizes for bringing both parents to meetings. Replace such terms as *broken home* with *single-parent family.* Be sensitive to the demands of school in relation to children's home lives. For instance, when a professional sent a field-trip permission form home with children and told them to have their mothers or fathers sign it, one child said, "I don't have a father. If my mother can't sign it, can the man who sleeps with her sign it?" Seek guidance and clarification from families about how they would like specific situations handled; for example, ask whether they want you to send notices of school events to both parents.

 • *Seek training.* Request in-service training to help you work with families. In-service programs can provide information about referral agencies, guidance techniques, ways to help families deal with their problems, and child abuse identification and prevention. Professionals need to be alert to the signs of all kinds of child abuse, including mental, physical, and sexual abuse.

 • *Increase parent contacts.* Finally, professionals should encourage greater and different kinds of parent involvement through visiting homes; talking to families about children's needs; providing information and opportunities to parents, grandparents, and other family members; gathering information from families (such as through interest inventories); and keeping in touch with parents. Make parent contacts positive.

Parent and family involvement is a process of helping families use their abilities to benefit themselves, their children, and the early childhood program. Families, children, and the program are all part of the process; consequently, all three parties should benefit from a well-planned program of family involvement. Nonetheless, the focus in parent/child/family interactions is the family, and you must work with and through families if you want to be successful.

GUIDELINES FOR INVOLVING PARENTS AND FAMILIES

As an early childhood professional, you can use the following tips to develop programs of parent and family involvement.

 • Get to know your children's parents and families. One good way to do this is through home visits. This approach works better in early childhood programs where the number of students is limited. However, teachers who have large numbers of students find that visiting a few homes based on special circumstances can be helpful and informative.

 • Ask parents what goals they have for their children. Use these goals to help you in your planning. Encourage parents to have realistically high expectations for their children.

 • Build relationships with parents so you may communicate better with them.

 • Learn how to best communicate with parents based on their cultural communications preferences. Take into account cultural features that can inhibit collaboration.

- Learn how families rear children and organize themselves. Political, social, and moral values of families all have implications for parent participation and how to teach children.

- Support parents in their roles as first teachers of their children. Support can include information, materials, and help with parenting problems.

- Provide frequent, open communication and feedback on student progress, including good news.

- Train parents as mentors, classroom aides, tutors, and homework helpers. For example, communicate guidelines for helping students study for tests.

- Support fathers in their roles as parents. By supporting and encouraging fathers, you support the whole family.

- On the basis of parents' needs, identify resources they can use to help solve family and personal problems.

- Work with and through families. Ask parents to help you in working with and involving other parents. Parents respond positively to other parents, so it makes sense to have parents helping families.

Four Approaches to Parent and Family Involvement

In looking at and designing programs of parent and family involvement, early childhood professionals may proceed in several different ways.

Task Approach

The most common and traditional way to approach parent and family involvement is through a task orientation. This method seeks to involve parents in order to get assistance completing specific tasks that support the school or classroom program. In this orientation, faculty, staff, and administration work to involve parents and other family members as tutors, aides, attendance monitors, fund-raisers, field-trip monitors, and clerical helpers. This is the type of parent and family involvement many professionals are comfortable with and the sort that usually comes to mind when planning for some kind of parent or family involvement. However, while this type of parent involvement has many benefits, by itself it does not represent a sufficient program of family involvement.

Process Approach

In this approach, families are encouraged to participate in certain activities that are important to the educational process, such as curriculum planning, textbook review and selection, membership on task forces and committees, professional review and selection, and setting of behavior standards. This approach is becoming popular because professionals realize the importance of sharing these processes and decisions with parents, family members, and members of the community. Parents and others need preparation and support for this kind of involvement. Some professionals may think parents lack the necessary skills to help in certain areas, but with some assistance and an opportunity to participate, many family members are extremely effective.

Developmental Approach

This orientation seeks to help parents and families develop skills that benefit themselves, children, schools, professionals, and families and, at the same time, enhance family growth and development. This humanistic orientation is exemplified in such programs as cooperative preschools, community schools, and Head Start.

Comprehensive Approach

A comprehensive approach to parent and family involvement includes elements of all the preceding approaches, especially the developmental approach (see Figure 13–2). It goes beyond the other three approaches, however, in that it makes the family the center or focus of activities. This method does not seek involvement from parent or family members for the sake of involvement or the benefit of a particular agency. Rather, it works with, in, and through the family system to empower, assist, and strengthen the family. As a result, all family members are helped, including children.

The comprehensive approach seeks to involve parents, families, and members of the community in school processes and activities, including decisions about the school. It also provides parents choices about which school or program their children will attend. Over the past decade, school choice, permitting parents to select the school their children will attend, has gained popularity. Some states and many school districts allow parents to

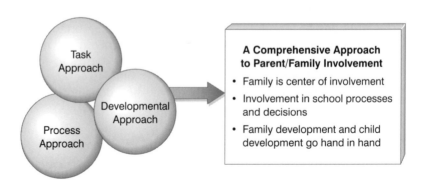

FIGURE 13–2
A Comprehensive Approach to Family Involvement

enroll their children in the schools of their choice. While most parents of preschool children have had this choice based on the fact that they pay for their children's education, many public school parents have not. Now many do, which has helped change the public's attitude toward school choice.

A comprehensive program also provides involvement through family development and support programs. Many programs not only are encouraging involvement in family-centered programs, but are providing them. These family support programs include parenting programs, home visitations, substance abuse education and treatment programs, discussion and support groups, job training and referral programs, basic skills training programs, and programs that link parents to existing community resource programs.

Activities for Involving Families

Unlimited possibilities exist for family involvement, but a coordinated effort is required to build an effective, meaningful program that can bring about a change in education and benefit all concerned: families, children, professionals, and communities. Families can make a significant difference in their children's education, and with early childhood professionals' assistance, they will be able to join teachers and schools in a productive partnership. The following are examples of activities that allow for significant family involvement.

Schoolwide Activities

- *Workshops.* To introduce families to the school's policies, procedures, and programs. Most families want to know what is going on in the school and would do a better job of parenting and educating if they knew how.
- *Family nights, cultural dinners, carnivals, and potluck dinners.* To bring families and the community to the school in nonthreatening, social ways.
- *Adult education classes.* To provide the community with opportunities to learn about a range of subjects.
- *Training programs.* To give parents, family members, and others skills as classroom aides, club and activity sponsors, curriculum planners, and policy decision makers. When parents, family members, and community persons are viewed as experts, empowerment results.
- *Support services such as carpools and baby-sitting.* To make attendance and involvement possible.
- *Fairs and bazaars.* To involve families in fund-raising.
- *Performances and plays.* To bring families to school. These are especially successful in accomplishing the goal of bringing parents to school when their children have a part in the performance or play; however, the purpose of children's performances should not be solely to get families involved.

PROGRAM IN ACTION

INVOLVING PARENTS THROUGH TECHNOLOGY—
THE TRANSPARENT SCHOOL MODEL

The Transparent School Model is an original plan for using electronic telecommunications technology to expand and improve parent involvement. The model provides voice-based information exchange between teachers and parents.

How It Works

The system consists of two primary functions. First, parents can call and listen to a teacher's daily message. At the end of each school day, teachers write a brief script describing (1) what students learned and how they learned it; (2) specific home learning assignments; and (3) parent education suggestions with other school information. Each teacher records his or her message in a voice mailbox from any touch-tone phone, and parents can call to hear the message at any time from any phone. Other message boxes at the school may include the daily lunch menu, principal's message, information from the parent/teacher group, and so on. The voice mailbox function allows every parent to receive the information needed to support the student's learning at home every day, with only a one- to two-minute phone call.

Second, the system can place automated calls to parents with information they need, including routine reminders ("The museum field trip is on Tuesday"), sending good news home, and emergency notification. Strategic outcalling is also used to encourage more parents to call for teacher messages, and to make specific contact with certain parents. Schools often use outcalling for attendance notification, community outreach, and dozens of other applications. The messages can be delivered in any language.

The best way for a school to implement the Transparent School Model is to acquire a special voice-messaging computer that is designed to manage all the parent involvement and other school communications. The equipment supplier also should provide help with planning, installation, and staff development.

Preschool Readiness

The technology can also be used for preschool readiness. The outcall function can

Communication Activities

- *Telephone hotlines.* Hotlines staffed by families can help allay fears and provide information relating to child abuse, communicable diseases, and special events.

- *Newsletters.* Newsletters planned with parents' help are an excellent way to keep families informed about program events, activities, and curriculum information. Newsletters in parents' native languages help keep language-minority families informed.

- *Home learning materials and activities.* A monthly calendar of activities is one good way to keep families involved in their children's learning.

call parents weekly with parenting suggestions from birth until the child enters the child care, preschool, or kindergarten setting.

Effects

More than 1,000 schools (preschool through high school) use the Transparent School Model. In most schools, the results have been astonishing. At least half of the parents call every day to hear teacher messages. Parent involvement rates have risen 500 to 800 percent. Students' learning performance goes up and success improves. In two matched-demographic trials, significant improvement in achievement test scores were found.

Parent attitudes become much more positive as they have more information about the school program. There has also been independent confirmation of dramatic improvement in student grade point averages at the secondary level after schools began using the model. The easy and open exchange of information between school and home allows for new levels of partnership and cooperation with an influence on achievement, student success, attendance, parent attitudes, and community interest.

Implementation

Quality implementation of the Transparent School Model depends on the following:

- Cooperative planning from the beginning
- Baseline and ongoing evaluation
- Full school commitment
- Effective parent orientation
- Teacher staff development
- High-quality messages

It rarely takes a teacher more than a few extra minutes per day to meet all the expectations of the model, and these minutes are multiplied many times by the technology. Teachers say it is extremely easy to use, and parents wonder how they ever got along without it. Communities find that the greatly expanded communication opens new avenues for partnerships.

Contributed by Jerold P. Bauch, director, the Betty Phillips Center for Parenthood Education, Peabody College, Nashville, Tennessee.

Educational Activities

- *Participation in classroom and center activities.* While not all families can be directly involved in classroom activities, encourage those who can. Those who are involved must have guidance, direction, and training. Involving parents and others as paid aides is an excellent way also to provide employment and training. Many programs, such as Head Start, actively support such a policy.

- Involvement of families in writing individualized education programs (IEPs) for special needs children. Involvement in writing an IEP is not only a legal requirement but also an excellent learning experience (see Chapter 12).

Service Activities

- *Resource libraries and materials centers.* Families benefit from books and other articles relating to parenting. Some programs furnish resource areas with comfortable chairs to encourage families to use these materials.

- *Child care.* Families may not be able to attend programs and become involved if they do not have child care for their children. Child care makes their participation possible and more enjoyable (see Chapter 6).

- *Respite care.* Some early childhood programs provide respite care for parents and other family members, which enables them to have periodic relief from the responsibilities of parenting a chronically ill child or a child with disabilities.

- *Service exchanges.* Service exchanges operated by early childhood programs and other agencies help families in their needs for services. For example, one parent provided child care in her home in exchange for having her washing machine repaired. The possibilities for such exchanges are endless.

- *Parent support groups.* Parents need support in their roles. Support groups can provide parenting information, community agency information, and speakers.

- *Welcoming committees.* A good way to involve families in any program is to have other families contact them when their children first join a program.

Decision Activities

- *Hiring and policy making.* Parents and community members can and should serve on committees that set policy and hire staff.

- *Curriculum development and review.* Parents' involvement in curriculum planning helps them learn about and understand what constitutes a quality program and what is involved in a developmentally appropriate curriculum. When families know about the curriculum, they are more supportive of it.

Conducting Parent-Professional Conferences

Significant parent involvement can occur through well-planned and -conducted parent–early childhood professional conferences (informally referred to as *parent-teacher conferences*). Such conferences are often the first contact many families have with school. Conferences are critical both from a public relations point of view and as a vehicle for helping families and professionals accomplish their goals. The following guidelines will help you as an early childhood professional prepare for and conduct successful conferences:

- *Plan ahead.* Be sure of the reason for the conference. What are your objectives? What do you want to accomplish? List the points you want to cover, and think about what you are going to say.

- *Get to know the parents.* This is not wasted time; the more effectively you establish rapport with a parent, the more you will accomplish in the long run.

- *Avoid an authoritative atmosphere.* Do not sit behind your desk while the parent sits in a child's chair. Treat parents and others like the adults they are.

- *Communicate at the parent's level.* Do not condescend or patronize. Instead, use words, phrases, and explanations the parent understands and is familiar with. Do not use jargon or complicated explanations, and speak in your natural style.

- *Accentuate the positive.* Make every effort to show and tell the parent what the child is doing well. When you deal with problems, put them in the proper perspective: what the child is able to do, what the goals and purposes of the learning program are, what specific skill or concept you are trying to get the child to learn, and what problems the child is having in achieving. Most important, explain what you plan to do to help the child achieve and what specific role the parent can have in meeting the achievement goals.

- *Give families a chance to talk.* You will not learn much about them if you do all the talking, nor are you likely to achieve your goals. Professionals are often accustomed to dominating a conversation, and many parents will not be as verbal as you, so you will have to encourage families to talk.

- *Learn to listen.* An active listener holds eye contact, uses body language such as head nodding and hand gestures, does not interrupt, avoids arguing, paraphrases as a way of clarifying ideas, and keeps the conversation on track.

- *Follow up.* Ask the parent for a definite time for the next conference as you are concluding the current one. Another conference is the best method of solidifying gains and extending support, but other acceptable means of follow-up are telephone calls, written reports, notes sent with children, or brief visits to the home. While these types of contacts may appear casual, they should be planned for and conducted as seriously as any regular parent-professional conference. No matter which approach you choose, advantages of a parent-professional conference follow-up are these:

Families see that you genuinely care about their children.

Everyone can clarify problems, issues, advice, and directions.

Parents, family members, and children are encouraged to continue to do their best.

It offers further opportunities to extend classroom learning to the home.

You can extend programs initiated for helping families and formulate new plans.

- *Develop an action plan.* Never leave the parent with a sense of frustration, not knowing what you are doing or what the parent is to do. Every communication with families should end on a positive note, so that everyone knows what can be done and how to do it.

Children and Conferences

A question frequently asked is, "Should children be present at parent-teacher conferences?" The answer is, "Yes, of course." The only caveat to the yes response is, "If it is appropriate for them to be present." In most instances it is appropriate, and offers a number of benefits:

- Children have much to contribute. They can talk about their progress and behavior, offer suggestions for improvement and enrichment, and discuss their interests.
- The locus of control is centered in the child. Children learn they have a voice and opinions and that others think this is important and are listening.
- Children's self-esteem is enhanced because they are viewed as an important part of the conference and because a major purpose of the conference is to help them and their families.
- Children become more involved in their classroom and their education. As Richard Stiggins, an authority on the child-centered classroom, notes: "Students take pride not only in their own accomplishments and their ability to share them, but also in the opportunity to help each other prepare for and succeed at their conferences. A team spirit—a sense of community—can emerge and this can benefit the motivation and achievement of all."[5]
- Children learn that education is a cooperative process between home and school.

Involving Single-Parent Families

Sometimes, family involvement activities are conducted without much regard for single-parent families. Professionals sometimes think of single-parent families as problems to deal with rather than as people to work with. Involving single-parent families need not present a problem if you remember some basic points.

First, many adults in one-parent families are employed during school hours and may not be available for conferences or other activities during that time. Professionals must be willing to accommodate family schedules by arranging conferences at other times, perhaps early morning (breakfast), midmorning, noon (lunch), early afternoon, late afternoon, or early evening. Some employers, sensitive to the needs of their single-parent employees, give release time to participate in school functions, but others do not. Profes-

Many early childhood professionals conduct home visits as a means of assessing the home environment for learning and to help parents learn how to support their children's learning at home. Additionally, parents can provide professionals with much useful information about children's learning, experiences, and growth and development. Do you plan to make home visits a part of your early childhood program? Why? Why not?

sionals and principals need to think seriously about going to families rather than having families always come to them. Some schools have set up parent conferences to accommodate families' work schedules, while some professionals find that home visits work best.

Second, you need to remember that such families have a limited amount of time to spend on involvement with their children's school and their children at home. When you confer with single-parent families, make sure that (1) the meeting starts on time, (2) you have a list of items (skills, behaviors, achievements) to discuss, (3) you have sample materials available to illustrate all points, (4) you make specific suggestions relative to one-parent environments, and (5) the meeting ends on time. One-parent families are more likely to need child care assistance to attend meetings, so child care should be planned for every parent meeting or activity.

Third, illustrate for single-parent families how they can make their time with their children more meaningful. If a child has trouble following directions, show families how to use home situations to help in this area. Children can learn to follow directions while helping families run errands, get a meal, or do housework tasks.

Fourth, get to know families' lifestyles and living conditions. An early childhood professional can easily say that every child should have a quiet place to study, but this may be an impossible demand for some households. You need to visit some of the homes in your community before you set meeting times, choose what family involvement activities to implement, or decide what you will ask of families during the year. All professionals, particularly early childhood professionals, need to keep in mind the condition of the home environment when they request that children bring certain items to school or carry out certain tasks at home. When asking for parents' help, you must be sensitive to parents' talents and time constraints.

Fifth, help develop support groups for one-parent families within the school, such as discussion groups and classes on parenting for singles. You must include the needs and abilities of one-parent families in your family involvement activities and programs. After all, single-parent families may be the majority of families represented in the program.

Involving Language-Minority Parents and Families

The developmental concept of family involvement is particularly important when working with language-minority families. Language-minority parents are individuals whose English proficiency is minimal and who lack a comprehensive knowledge of the norms and social systems in the United States. Language-minority families often face language and cultural barriers that greatly hamper their ability to become actively involved, although many have a great desire and willingness to participate in their children's education.

Because the culture of language-minority families often differs from that of the majority in a community, those who seek a truly collaborative community, home, and school involvement must take into account the cultural features that can inhibit collaboration. Traditional styles of child rearing and family organization, attitudes toward schooling, organizations around which families center their lives, life goals and values, political influences, and methods of communication within the cultural group all have implications for parent participation.

Language-minority families often lack information about the U.S. educational system, including basic school philosophy, practice, and structure, which can result in misconceptions, fear, and a general reluctance to respond to invitations for involvement. Furthermore, this educational system may be quite different from what these families are used to. They may have been taught to avoid active involvement in the educational process, with the result that they prefer to leave all decisions concerning their children's education to professionals and administrators.

The U.S. ideal of a community-controlled and community-supported educational system must be explained to families from cultures in which this concept is not as highly valued. Traditional roles of children, professionals, and administrators also have to be explained. Many families, especially language-minority families, are quite willing to relinquish to professionals any rights and responsibilities they have for their children's education, and need to be taught to assume their roles and obligations toward schooling.

Culturally Sensitive Family Involvement

The following suggestions are provided by Janet Gonzalez-Mena for working with families:

*   *Know what each parent in your program wants for his or her child.* Find out families' goals. What are their caregiving practices? What concerns do they have about their child? Encourage them to talk about all of this. Encourage them to ask questions. Encourage the conflicts to surface—to come out in the open.

*   *Become clear about your own values and goals.* Know what you believe in. Have a bottom line, but leave space above it to be flexible. When you are clear, you are less likely to present a defensive stance in the face of conflict. When you are ambiguous, you come on the strongest.

*   *Become sensitive to your own discomfort.* Tune in on those times when something bothers you instead of just ignoring it and hoping it will go away. Work to identify what specific behaviors of others make you uncomfortable. Try to discover exactly what in yourself creates this discomfort. A conflict may be brewing.

*   *Build relationships.* When you do this, you enhance your chances for conflict management or resolution. Be patient. Building relationships takes time, but it enhances communications and understandings. You'll communicate better if you have a relationship, and you'll have a relationship if you learn to communicate.

*   *Become effective cross-cultural communicators.* It is possible to learn these communication skills. Learn about communication styles that are different from your own. Teach your own communication styles. What you think a person means may not be what he or she really means. Do not make assumptions. Listen carefully. Ask for clarification. Find ways to test for understanding.

*   *Learn how to create dialogues—how to open communication instead of shutting it down.* Often, if you accept and acknowledge the other person's feelings, you encourage him or her to open up. Learn ways to let others know that you are aware of and sensitive to their feelings.

*   *Use a problem-solving rather than a power approach to conflicts.* Be flexible—negotiate when possible. Look at your willingness to share power. Is it a control issue you are dealing with?

*   *Commit yourself to education—both your own and that of the families.* Sometimes lack of information or understanding of each other's perspective is what keeps the conflict going.[6]

Involving Fathers

More fathers are involved in parenting responsibilities than ever before. Over one-fifth of preschool children are cared for by their fathers while their mothers work outside the home.[7] The implication is clear: Early childhood professionals must make special efforts to involve all fathers in their programs.

More professionals recognize that fathering and mothering are complementary processes. Definitions of nurturing are changing to include the legitimate and positive involvement of fathers in children's lives. Many fathers are competent caregivers, directly supervising children, helping set the tone for family life, providing stability to a relationship, supporting the mother's parenting role and her career goals, and personifying a masculine role model for the children. More fathers, as they discover or rediscover these parenting roles, turn to professionals for support and advice.

There are many styles of fathering. Some fathers are at home while their wives work; some have custody of their children; some are single; some dominate home life and control everything; some are passive and exert little influence in the home; some are frequently absent because their work requires travel; some take little interest in their homes and families; some are surrogates. Regardless of the roles fathers play in their children's lives, as an early childhood professional, you must make special efforts to involve them, using the methods discussed in this chapter.

COMMUNITY INVOLVEMENT AND MORE

A comprehensive program of family involvement has, in addition to families, professionals, and schools, a fourth important component: the community. More early childhood professionals realize that neither they alone nor the limited resources of their programs are sufficient to meet the needs of many children and families. Consequently, early education professionals are seeking ways to link families to community services and resources. For example, if a child needs clothing, a professional who is aware of community resources might contact the local Salvation Army for assistance.

Using the Community to Teach

The community offers a vital and rich array of resources for helping you teach better and for helping you meet the needs of parents and their children. Schools and teachers cannot address the many issues facing children and youth without the partnership and collaboration of powerful sectors of society, including community agencies, businesses, and industry. Following are suggested actions you can take to learn to use your community in your teaching:

- *Know your students and their needs.* By knowing your students through observations, conferences with parents, and discussions with students, you can identify any barriers to their learning and learn what kind of help to seek.

- *Know your community.* Walk or drive around the community. Ask a parent to give you a tour to help familiarize you with agencies and individuals. Read the local newspaper and attend community events and activities.

- *Ask for help and support from parents and the community.* Keep in mind that many parents will not be involved unless you personally ask them. The only encouragement many individuals and local businesses will need is your invitation.

- *Develop a directory of community agencies.* Consult the business pages of local phone books, contact local chambers of commerce, and ask parents what agencies are helpful to them.

- *Compile a list of people who are willing to come to your classroom to speak to or work with your students.* You can start by asking parents to volunteer and also to suggest and recommend others.

Only by helping families meet their needs and those of their children will you create opportunities for these children to reach their full potential. For this reason alone, regardless of all the other benefits, family involvement programs and activities must be an essential part of every early childhood program. Families should expect nothing less from the profession, and we, in turn, must do our very best for them.

National Organizations

National programs dedicated to family involvement are a rich resource for information and support. Some of these are listed here:

- Institute for Responsive Education (IRE), 50 Nightingale Hall, Northeastern University, Boston, MA 02115; 617-373-2595; fax (617) 373-8924.

- Center on Families, Communities, Schools and Children's Learning, 605 Commonwealth Avenue, Boston University, Boston, MA 02215; 617-353-4233.

- Families United for Better Schools, 31 Maple Wood Mall, Philadelphia, PA 19144; 215-829-0442. This is an organization of families working to help other families work for better schools.

- The Home and School Institute, 1201 16th Street, NW, Washington, DC 20036; 202-466-3633.

- National Committee for Citizens in Education (NCCE), 900 Second Street, NE, Suite 8, Washington, DC 20002-3557; 800-638-9675. This organization seeks to inform families of their rights and to get them involved in the public schools.

- National Congress of Parents and Teachers (the National PTA), 330 N. Wabash Avenue, Suite 2100, Chicago, IL 60611; 312-670-6782.

ACTIVITIES FOR REFLECTION AND RESEARCH

1. Arrange with a local school district to be present during a parent-teacher conference. Discuss with the teacher, prior to the visit, his or her objectives and procedures. After the conference, assess its success with the teacher.

2. List the various ways early childhood professionals communicate pupils' progress to families. Which methods do you think are the most and least effective? What specific methods do you plan to use?

3. Describe the methods and techniques you would use to publicize a parent meeting about how your school plans to involve families in their children's education.

4. List six reasons why early childhood professionals might resist involving families. For each reason, give two strategies you could use for overcoming the resistance.

5. You have just been appointed the program director for a family involvement program in first grade. Write objectives for the program. Develop specific activities for involving families and for providing services to them.

6. Visit social service agencies in your area, and list the services they offer. Describe how early childhood professionals can work with these agencies to meet the needs of children and families. Invite agency directors to meet with your class to discuss how they and early childhood professionals can work cooperatively to help families and children.

7. Reflect on your own school experiences. How did community resources contribute to your learning? Could you use these same resources to help those children (and their families) that you will teach? How?

8. As families change, so too do the services they need. Interview families in as many settings as possible (e.g., urban,

suburban, rural), from as many socioeconomic backgrounds as possible, and from as many kinds of families as possible. Determine what services they believe can help them most, and then tell how you as a professional could help provide those services.

9. Develop specific guidelines that a child care center could use to facilitate the involvement of fathers, language-minority families, and families of children with disabilities.

READINGS FOR FURTHER ENRICHMENT

Springate, K. W., and D. A. Stegelin. *Building School and Community Partnerships through Parent Involvement.* (Upper Saddle River, NJ: Prentice Hall, 1999).

> This text focuses on the family as the "first teacher" of the child and provides the most effective strategies for involving parents in school settings. The authors examine the diversity of families in regard to culture, lifestyle, and specific issues, such as children with disabilities.

Fuller, M. L., and G. Olsen. *Home-School Relations: Working Successfully with Parents and Families* (Boston, MA: Allyn and Bacon, 1998).

> This book examines the nature of the contemporary family and its relationship to the school. It provides practical advice for developing strong home-school relationships.

ERIC Clearinghouse on Urban Education for the U.S. Department of Education and the National Parent Information Network. (1999). Based on *Strong Families, Strong Schools,* written by Jennifer Ballen and Oliver Moles, (Washington, DC: U.S. Department of Education, 1994).

Available online at: *http://eric-web.tc.columbia.edu/families/strong*

> This book describes successful school efforts to involve families and communities.

INTERNET RESOURCES

NPIN Homepage

http://www.npin.org

> Identifies specific Internet resources for parents and for those who work with parents.

The Family Education Network

http://www.familyeducation.com

> The Family Education network is committed to strengthening and empowering families by providing communities with the counseling, education, resources, information, and training needed to promote a positive and nurturing environment in which to raise children.

Parent Soup

http://www.parentsoup.com

> Offers resources and features on a wide array of educational topics.

> You may find other sites by entering the following keywords into one of the Internet's many available search engines:

parent involvement

community involvement

school partnerships

school-business relationships

school-community collaboration

NOTES

1. U.S. Department of Education, *Goals 2000* (Washington, DC: Author, 1994), n.p.

2. Stanley M. Elam, Lowel C. Rose, and Alec M. Gallup, "The 25th Annual Phi Delta Kappa/Gallup Poll," *Phi Delta Kappan,* October 1993, p. 149.

3. U.S. Department of Education, *Strong Families, Strong Schools: Building Community Partnerships for Learning* (Washington, DC: Author, 1994).

4. Generations United, *Linking Youth and Old through Intergenerational Programs* (Washington, DC: Author, n.d.), n.p.

5. Richard J. Stiggins, *Student-Centered Classroom Assessment,* 2nd ed. (Upper Saddle River, NJ: Merrill/Prentice Hall, 1997), p. 499.

6. J. Gonzalez-Mena, "Taking a Culturally Sensitive Approach in Infant-Toddler Programs," *Young Children,* 1, 1992, pp. 8–9. Used with permission of the author.

7. J. S. Cohen, *Parental Involvement in Education,* ED 1.2:P75/6 (Washington DC: U.S. Government Printing Office, 1991), p. 7.

APPENDIX

The National Association for the Education of Young Children Code of Ethical Conduct

PREAMBLE

NAEYC recognizes that many daily decisions required of those who work with young children are of a moral and ethical nature. The NAEYC Code of Ethical Conduct offers guidelines for responsible behavior and sets forth a common basis for resolving the principal ethical dilemmas encountered in early childhood education. The primary focus is on daily practice with children and their families in programs for children from birth to eight years of age: preschools, child care centers, family day care homes, kindergartens, and primary classrooms. Many of the provisions also apply to specialists who do not work directly with children, including program administrators, parent educators, college professors, and child care licensing specialists.

Standards of ethical behavior in early childhood education are based on commitment to core values that are deeply rooted in the history of our field. We have committed ourselves to:

Appreciating childhood as a unique and valuable stage of the human life cycle

Basing our work with children on knowledge of child development

Source: This Code of Ethical Conduct and Statement of Commitment was prepared under the auspices of the Ethics Commission of the National Association for the Education of Young Children. The commission members were Stephanie Feeney (chairperson), Bettye Caldwell, Sally Cartwright, Carrie Cheek, Josué Cruz, Jr., Anne G. Dorsey, Dorothy M. Hill, Lilian G. Katz, Pamm Mattick, Shirley A. Norris, and Sue Spayth Riley. Copyright © 1992 by the National Association for the Education of Young Children. Reprinted by permission.

Appreciating and supporting the close ties between the child and family

Recognizing that children are best understood in the context of family, culture, and society

Respecting the dignity, worth, and uniqueness of each individual (child, family member, and colleague)

Helping children and adults achieve their full potential in the context of relationships that are based on trust, respect, and positive regard

The Code sets forth a conception of our professional responsibilities in four sections, each addressing an arena of professional relationships: (1) children, (2) families, (3) colleagues, and (4) community and society. Each section includes an introduction to the primary responsibilities of the early childhood practitioner in that arena, a set of ideals pointing in the direction of exemplary professional practice, and a set of principles defining practices that are required, prohibited, and permitted.

The ideals reflect the aspirations of practitioners. The principles are intended to guide conduct and assist practitioners in resolving ethical dilemmas encountered in the field. There is not necessarily a corresponding principle for each ideal. Both ideals and principles are intended to direct practitioners to those questions which, when responsibly answered, will provide the basis for conscientious decision making. While the Code provides specific direction for addressing some ethical dilemmas, many others will require the practitioner to combine the guidance of the Code with sound professional judgment.

The ideals and principles in this Code present a shared conception of professional responsibility that affirms our commitment to the core values of our field. The Code publicly acknowledges the responsibilities that we in the field have assumed and in so doing supports ethical behavior in our work. Practitioners who face ethical dilemmas are urged to seek guidance in the applicable parts of this Code and in the spirit that informs the whole.

SECTION I: ETHICAL RESPONSIBILITIES TO CHILDREN

Childhood is a unique and valuable stage in the life cycle. Our paramount responsibility is to provide safe, healthy, nurturing, and responsive settings for children. We are committed to supporting children's development by cherishing individual differences, by helping them learn to live and work cooperatively, and by promoting their self-esteem.

IDEALS

I-1.1   To be familiar with the knowledge base of early childhood education and to keep current through continuing education and in-service training.

I-1.2   To base program practices upon current knowledge in the field of child development and related disciplines and upon particular knowledge of each child.

I-1.3   To recognize and respect the uniqueness and the potential of each child.

I-1.4   To appreciate the special vulnerability of children.

I-1.5   To create and maintain safe and healthy settings that foster children's social, emotional, intellectual, and physical development and that respect their dignity and their contributions.

I-1.6   To support the right of children with special needs to participate, consistent with their ability, in regular childhood programs.

PRINCIPLES

P-1.1   Above all, we shall not harm children. We shall not participate in practices that are disrespectful, degrading, dangerous, exploitative, intimidating, psychologically damaging, or physically harmful to children. *This principle has precedence over all others in this Code.*

P-1.2   We shall not participate in practices that discriminate against children by denying benefits, giving special advantages, or excluding them from programs or activities on the basis of their race, religion, sex, national origin, or the status, behavior, or beliefs of their parents. (This principle does not apply to programs that have a lawful mandate to provide services to a particular population of children.)

P-1.3   We shall involve all of those with relevant knowledge (including staff and parents) in decisions concerning a child.

P-1.4   When, after appropriate efforts have been made with a child and the family, the child still does not appear to be benefitting from a program, we shall communicate our concern to the family in a positive way and offer them assistance in finding a more suitable setting.

P-1.5   We shall be familiar with the symptoms of child abuse and neglect and know and follow community procedures and state laws that protect children against abuse and neglect.

P-1.6   When we have evidence of child abuse or neglect, we shall report the evidence to the appropriate community agency and follow up to ensure that appropriate action has been taken. When possible, parents will be informed that the referral has been made.

P-1.7   When another person tells us of their suspicion that a child is being abused or neglected but we lack evidence, we shall assist that person in taking appropriate action to protect the child.

P-1.8   When a child protective agency fails to provide adequate protection for abused or neglected children, we acknowledge a collective ethical responsibility to work toward improvement of these services.

P-1.9   When we become aware of a practice or situation that endangers the health or safety of children, but has not been previously known to do so, we have an ethical responsibility to inform those who can remedy the situation and who can keep other children from being similarly endangered.

SECTION II: ETHICAL RESPONSIBILITIES TO FAMILIES

Families are of primary importance in children's development. (The term *family* may include others, besides parents, who are responsibly involved with the child.) Because the family and the early childhood educator have a common interest in the child's welfare, we acknowledge a primary responsibility to bring about collaboration between the home and school in ways that enhance the child's development.

IDEALS

I-2.1   To develop relationships of mutual trust with the families we serve.

I-2.2   To acknowledge and build upon strengths and competencies as we support families in their task of nurturing children.

I-2.3   To respect the dignity of each family and its culture, customs, and beliefs.

I-2.4   To respect families' childrearing values and their right to make decisions for their children.

I-2.5   To interpret each child's progress to parents within the framework of a developmental perspective and to help families understand and appreciate the value of developmentally appropriate early childhood programs.

I-2.6   To help family members improve their understanding of their children and to enhance their skills as parents.

I-2.7   To participate in building support networks for families by providing them with opportunities to interact with program staff and families.

PRINCIPLES

P-2.1   We shall not deny family members access to their child's classroom or program setting.

P-2.2   We shall inform families of program philosophy, policies, and personnel qualifications, and explain why we teach as we do.

P-2.3   We shall inform families of and, when appropriate, involve them in policy decisions.

P-2.4   We shall inform families of and, when appropriate, involve them in significant decisions affecting their child.

P-2.5   We shall inform the family of accidents involving their child, of risks such as exposures to contagious disease that may result in infection, and of events that might result in psychological damage.

P-2.6   We shall not permit or participate in research that could in any way hinder the education or development of the children in our programs. Families shall be fully informed of any proposed research projects involving their children and shall have the opportunity to give or withhold consent.

P-2.7   We shall not engage in or support exploitation of families. We shall not use our relationship with a family for private advantage or personal gain, or enter into relationships with family members that might impair our effectiveness in working with children.

P-2.8   We shall develop written policies for the protection of confidentiality and the disclosure of children's records. The policy documents shall be made available to all program personnel and families. Disclosure of children's records beyond family members, program personnel, and consultants having an obligation of confidentiality shall require familial consent (except in cases of abuse or neglect).

P-2.9   We shall maintain confidentiality and shall respect the family's right to privacy, refraining from disclosure of confidential information and intrusion into family life. However, when we are concerned about a child's welfare, it is permissible to reveal confidential information to agencies and individuals who may be able to act in the child's interest.

P-2.10   In cases where family members are in conflict we shall work openly, sharing our observations of the child, to help all parties involved make informed decisions. We shall refrain from becoming an advocate for one party.

P-2.11   We shall be familiar with and appropriately use community resources and professional services that support families. After a referral has been made, we shall follow up to ensure that services have been adequately provided.

SECTION III: ETHICAL RESPONSIBILITIES TO COLLEAGUES

In a caring, cooperative work place human dignity is respected, professional satisfaction is promoted, and positive relationships are modeled. Our primary responsibility in this arena is to establish and maintain settings and relationships that support productive work and meet professional needs.

A—RESPONSIBILITIES TO CO-WORKERS: IDEALS

I-3A.1   To establish and maintain relationships of trust and cooperation with co-workers.

I-3A.2   To share resources and information with co-workers.

I-3A.3   To support co-workers in meeting their professional needs and in their professional development.

I-3A.4   To accord co-workers due recognition of professional achievement.

PRINCIPLES

P-3A.1   When we have concern about the professional behavior of a co-worker, we shall first let that person know of our concern and attempt to resolve the matter collegially.

P-3A.2   We shall exercise care in expressing views regarding the personal attributes or professional conduct of co-workers. Statements should be based on firsthand knowledge and relevant to the interests of children and programs.

B—RESPONSIBILITIES TO EMPLOYERS: IDEALS

I-3B.1   To assist the program in providing the highest quality of service.

I-3B.2   To maintain loyalty to the program and uphold its reputation.

PRINCIPLES

P-3B.1   When we do not agree with program policies, we shall first attempt to affect change through constructive action within the organization.

P-3B.2   We shall speak or act on behalf of an organization only when authorized. We shall take care to note when we are speaking for the organization and when we are expressing a personal judgment.

C—RESPONSIBILITIES TO EMPLOYEES: IDEALS

I-3C.1   To promote policies and working conditions that foster competence, well-being, and self-esteem in staff members.

I-3C.2   To create a climate of trust and candor that will enable staff to speak and act in the best interests of children, families, and the field of early childhood education.

I-3C.3   To strive to secure an adequate livelihood for those who work with or on behalf of young children.

PRINCIPLES

P-3C.1   In decisions concerning children and programs, we shall appropriately utilize the training, experience, and expertise of staff members.

P-3C.2   We shall provide staff members with working conditions that permit them to carry out their responsibilities, timely and non-threatening evaluation procedures, written grievance procedures, constructive feedback, and opportunities for continuing professional development and advancement.

P-3C.3   We shall develop and maintain comprehensive written personnel policies that define program standards and, when applicable, that specify the extent to which employees are accountable for their conduct outside the work place. These policies shall be given to new staff members and shall be available for review by all staff members.

P-3C.4 Employees who do not meet program standards shall be informed of areas of concern and, when possible, assisted in improving their performance.

P-3C.5 Employees who are dismissed shall be informed of the reasons for the termination. When a dismissal is for cause, justification must be based on evidence of inadequate or inappropriate behavior that is accurately documented, current, and available for the employee to review.

P-3C.6 In making evaluations and recommendations, judgments shall be based on fact and relevant to the interests of children and programs.

P-3C.7 Hiring and promotion shall be based solely on a person's record of accomplishment and ability to carry out the responsibilities of the position.

P-3C.8 In hiring, promotion, and provision of training, we shall not participate in any form of discrimination based on race, religion, sex, national origin, handicap, age, or sexual preference. We shall be familiar with laws and regulations that pertain to employment discrimination.

SECTION IV: ETHICAL RESPONSIBILITIES TO COMMUNITY AND SOCIETY

Early childhood programs operate within a context of an immediate community made up of families and other institutions concerned with children's welfare. Our responsibilities to the community are to provide programs that meet its needs and to cooperate with agencies and professions that share responsibility for children. Because the larger society has a measure of responsibility for the welfare and protection of children, and because of our specialized expertise in child development, we acknowledge an obligation to serve as a voice for children everywhere.

IDEALS

I-4.1 To provide the community with high-quality, culturally sensitive programs and services.

I-4.2 To promote cooperation among agencies and professions concerned with the welfare of young children, their families, and their teachers.

I-4.3 To work, through education, research, and advocacy, toward an environmentally safe world in which all children are adequately fed, sheltered, and nurtured.

I-4.4 To work, through education, research, and advocacy, toward a society in which all young children have access to quality programs.

I-4.5 To promote knowledge and understanding of young children and their needs. To work toward greater social acknowledgement of children's rights and greater social acceptance of responsibility for their well-being.

I-4.6 To support policies and laws that promote the well-being of children and families. To oppose those that impair their well-being. To cooperate with other individuals and groups in these efforts.

I-4.7 To further the professional development of the field of early childhood education and to strengthen its commitment to realizing its core values as reflected in this Code.

PRINCIPLES

P-4.1 We shall communicate openly and truthfully about the nature and extent of services that we provide.

P-4.2 We shall not accept or continue to work in positions for which we are personally unsuited or professionally unqualified. We shall not offer services that we do not have the competence, qualifications, or resources to provide.

P-4.3 We shall be objective and accurate in reporting the knowledge upon which we base our program practices.

P-4.4 We shall cooperate with other professionals who work with children and their families.

P-4.5 We shall not hire or recommend for employment any person who is unsuited for a position with respect to competence, qualifications, or character.

P-4.6 We shall report the unethical or incompetent behavior of a colleague to a supervisor when informal resolution is not effective.

P-4.7 We shall be familiar with laws and regulations that serve to protect the children in our programs.

P-4.8 We shall not participate in practices which are in violation of laws and regulations that protect the children in our programs.

P-4.9 When we have evidence that an early childhood program is violating laws or regulations protecting children, we shall report it to persons responsible for the program. If compliance is not accomplished within a reasonable time, we will report the violation to appropriate authorities who can be expected to remedy the situation.

P-4.10 When we have evidence that an agency or a professional charged with providing services to children, families, or teachers is failing to meet its obligations, we acknowledge a collective ethical responsibility to report the problem to appropriate authorities or to the public.

P-4.11 When a program violates or requires its employees to violate this Code, it is permissible, after fair assessment of the evidence, to disclose the identity of that program.

APPENDIX

CDA Competency Goals and Functional Areas

COMPETENCY GOALS	FUNCTIONAL AREAS

COMPETENCY GOALS

FUNCTIONAL AREAS

I. To establish and maintain a safe, healthy learning environment

1. Safe: Candidate provides a safe environment to prevent and reduce injuries.

2. Healthy: Candidate promotes good health and nutrition and provides an environment that contributes to the prevention of illness.

3. Learning Environment: Candidate uses space, relationships, materials, and routines as resources for constructing an interesting, secure, and enjoyable environment that encourages play, exploration, and learning.

II. To advance physical and intellectual competence

4. Physical: Candidate provides a variety of equipment, activities, and opportunities to promote the physical development of children.

5. Cognitive: Candidate provides activities and opportunities that encourage curiosity, exploration, and problem solving appropriate to the developmental levels and learning styles of children.

Source: United Nations, *Convention on the Rights of the Child* (New York: United Nations Department of Public Information, 1993), pp. 4–8. Reprint 24717-May 1993-20M; Publication Source DPI/1101, United Nations. Used by permission.

COMPETENCY GOALS

FUNCTIONAL AREAS

6. Communication: Candidate actively communicates with children and provides opportunities for support for children to acquire, and use, verbal and nonverbal means of communicating thoughts and feelings.

7. Creative: Candidate provides opportunities that stimulate children to play with sound, rhythm, language, materials, space, and ideas in individual ways and to express their creative abilities.

III. To support social and emotional development and provide positive guidance

8. Self: Candidate provides physical and emotional development and emotional security for each child and helps each child to know, accept, and take pride in himself or herself and to develop a sense of independence.

9. Social: Candidate helps each child feel accepted in the group, helps children learn to communicate and get along with others, and encourages feelings of empathy and mutual respect among children and adults.

10. Guidance: Candidate provides a supportive environment in which children can begin to learn and practice appropriate and acceptable behaviors as individuals and as a group.

IV. To establish positive and productive relationships with families

11. Families: Candidate maintains an open, friendly, and cooperative relationship with each child's family, encourages their involvement in the program, and supports the child's relationship with his or her family.

V. To ensure a well-run, purposeful program responsive to participant needs

12. Program Management: Candidate is a manager who uses all available resources to ensure an effective operation. The Candidate is a competent organizer, planner, record keeper, communicator, and a cooperative co-worker.

VI. To maintain a commitment to professionalism

13. Professionalism: Candidate makes decisions based on knowledge of early childhood theories and practices, promotes quality in child care services, and takes advantage of opportunities to improve competence, both for personal and professional growth and for the benefit of children and families.

INDEX